GETTING INTO VSAM

GETTING INTO VSAM

AN INTRODUCTION AND TECHNICAL REFERENCE

Michael P. Bouros

A WILEY-INTERSCIENCE PUBLICATION
JOHN WILEY & SONS
New York • Chichester • Brisbane • Toronto • Singapore

Library of Congress Cataloging in Publication Data:

Bouros, Michael P.
Getting into VSAM.

"A Wiley-Interscience publication."
Includes index.
1. Virtual computer systems. I. Title. II. Title:
Getting into V.S.A.M.

QA76.9.V5B68 1985 001.64′42 84-19610
ISBN 0-471-81237-4

Printed in the United States of America

10 9 8 7 6 5 4 3 2

To
my wife, Mary,
for her constant love
and encouragement

FOREWORD

When VSAM was first introduced it was both hailed and cursed, often by the same person. Why? It was hailed for its philosophical approach to data management. In comparison to predecessor data management methodologies, it promised the magic and majesties of the fabled golden domes of Kublai Khan; but it soon became apparent that the journey to these lofty heights was long and arduous.

The trouble with VSAM is that although it is a tool with many facilities, options, and features, most users misunderstand it. This book will take the reader along the smoothest, easiest route to the pinnacle of VSAM mastery.

Mike Bouros addresses the task of educating the reader in the same fashion he has addressed any task I have ever seen him undertake during the ten years that our professional careers have intersected: start at the beginning, take it one step at a time, and tell it straight. As a matter of fact, watching Mike tackle a complex data-processing problem has always reminded me of watching Gary Cooper in a western movie. The book reflects the style of the man, and its readers will profit from both.

First, Chapters 1 and 2 will show you the lay of the land, the physical structure of disks, and how earlier access methods tried to exploit their potential—where they were successful and where they failed. For most of today's programmers this is extremely important background material for understanding VSAM. This material is important because all of the trends in programming over the last ten to fifteen years have constantly distanced the application programmer and systems designer from the physical realities of what was really happening in the machine. All of these improvements in programming languages, I/O control systems, and the like, have greatly increased programming productivity while increasing the viable life of application programming systems. However, this allows system designers to put together systems that have severe performance problems.

Nowhere are these performance degradations more apparent than in systems using VSAM. First of all, the information in the VSAM catalog maintains a host of performance statistics for VSAM data sets. The only problem is that most people do not understand what this information means, nor do they know how to use it. Most people, in my experience, don't even know how to read a LISTCAT.

One of the main strengths of this book is that it draws upon Mike Bouros's considerable experience at places like Merrill Lynch, Avis, and Grumman. From the earliest phases of his career Bouros has had to deal with the impact of massive volume upon computer performance. The book is peppered with all kinds of tips and explanations about how various options can degrade or enhance VSAM performance. A mistake in setting up a VSAM file with 10,000 records that causes severe degradation will probably go unnoticed. Make that same mistake with a 1,000,000-record file and you will be forced to take notice. For this reason, I would strongly suggest that "old VSAM hands" add this book to their library of working tools. They will be glad they did.

GENE MCMAHON
New York Post

PREFACE

The data processing world today seems to be moving in two different directions. From the viewpoint of the programmer responsible for the development of business applications, programming is becoming simpler all the time. On the other hand, the growing mountain of software that makes everything work is becoming increasingly more complex for the systems programmer who must install, maintain, and fine-tune it.

As application programmers continue to utilize more of the development tools available to them, data processing management is finding that as software is added to the system to simplify the task of the applications programmer, the systems programmer's job is becoming increasingly complex. For the level of simplicity certain software packages lend toward application development, difficulties are added to the systems programmer's lot in direct proportion. There is an ever-widening gulf emerging between the two areas. As with many other types of software, VSAM seems to fall under this category.

The typical application programmer need not know very much about VSAM in order to write an application program. That is, he or she need not necessarily know anything more than that which is required to write an ISAM, BDAM, or sequential access program.

VSAM can be extremely complex both for the individual who has responsibility over the data inventory and for the operating system specialists, who, between them, must decide about things such as optimal space utilization, VSAM data structures, buffering, strings, global/local shared resources, and multicomputer considerations. This book is an attempt to deal with both categories—to provide the application programmer with a vehicle through which he or she can attain a greater understanding of VSAM and, at the same time, to fill in some knowledge gaps which the systems programmer might have, resulting from nonexposure to certain little-used facilities.

MICHAEL P. BOUROS

Farmingville, New York
September 1984

ACKNOWLEDGMENTS

I'd like to thank the following individuals for the assistance lent me during the preparation of this book: Alvin Dean, consultant, EJR Assoc.; Joseph Hartman, consultant, Teltech; David Hershkowitz, Systems Programming Department, Federal Home Loan Bank; Paul Lemberg, Vice President of Strategic Systems, Hogan Services; Ward Lyke Jr., Vice President, J. W. Mays Inc.; Anthony Mea, Systems Programming, Pfizer; Vito Miloscia, Manager of Operational Development, SIAC; and Karol Winograd, Data Processing Manager, J. W. Mays Inc.

Special thanks to the following individuals: Alida Jatich, author of *CICS Command Level Programming*, for all of her valuable advice and suggestions; Roger Williams, super Systems Programmer, perhaps the sharpest and most knowledgeable I've ever known; and Edward Jensen Sr., Systems Analyst, who helped me in the beginning.

M. P. B.

CONTENTS

CHAPTER 4—THE THREE FACES OF VSAM 32

CHAPTER 5—FILE PROCESSING USING VSAM 50

CHAPTER 14—VSAM—ADVANCED PROCESSING OPTIONS 277

chapter 1

OVERVIEW OF DIRECT ACCESS DEVICES

The main purpose of this chapter is to provide the reader with an overview of IBM Direct Access Storage Devices. Readers already well acquainted with this subject should feel free to skip ahead to Chapter 2.

1.1 IN THE BEGINNING . . .

The early '70s was a time of great change in the data processing industry: within the space of a few years a succession of technological advances would completely revolutionize many basic philosophies pertaining to the processing of data.

Heading the list of important events was the announcement by IBM of a series of new computers collectively entitled **System/370**, which introduced a new concept, **Dynamic Address Translation**. This recent innovation would support another new concept called **virtual storage**.[1]

Heretofore, the amount of processing performed in a multiprogramming environment was restricted by two major physical limitations,[2] the availability of peripheral equipment (tape, disks, etc.) and memory (storage) capacity. The concept of virtual storage dealt directly with the problem of memory limitation in two ways:

By extending memory onto a high-speed direct-access device such as disk or drum.

By optimizing main storage through a sharing of real memory among programs operating in **virtual** mode.

It is in this setting that IBM was to announce a new access method, the **Virtual Storage Access Method** (VSAM), as *the* access method of the future.

1.2 ACCESS METHODS

The term **Access Method** is used to describe the software designed to access records stored on a peripheral device such as a disk or drum.[3] Since VSAM is only concerned with the manipulation of data on direct-access devices, our discussion of access methods is restricted to these.

1.3 DIRECT ACCESS DEVICES

Records on a magnetic tape device can only be processed sequentially. In order to retrieve a record located near the end of a reel, all previous records must be first read. Direct access devices allow direct retrieval of a record by simply supplying the access method with an **address** or **key** that is translated to an exact location on disk.

Figure 1.1 shows the physical layout of a disk device. As can be seen in the illustration, a disk (or disc) unit is usually made up of a series of disk-like platters connected together at the center. This device is also referred to as a disk pack, volume, module, or spindle.

The surface of each individual platter or disk is made up of tracks in which data is recorded. This is somewhat similar to the way in which recordings are made on phonograph records. The major differences between the two are that recordings made on disk can be rerecorded or changed over and over again, whereas a phonograph record contains a permanent recording. The other major difference is that although a phonograph needle will follow a spiral groove to the center of the

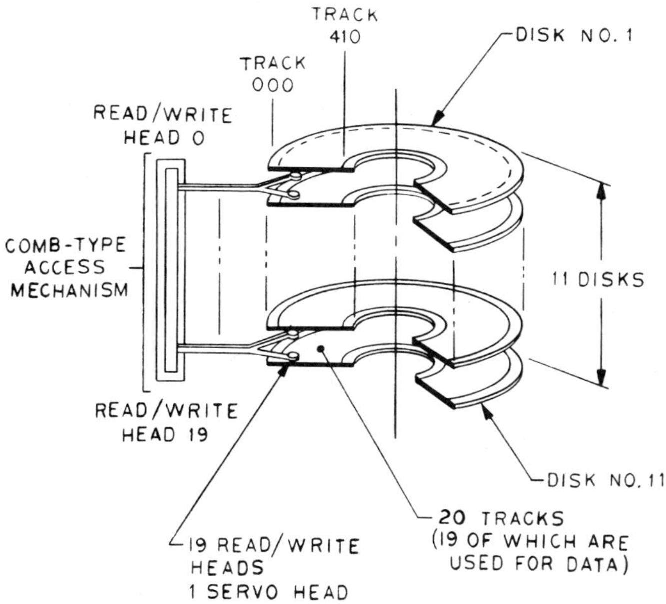

Figure 1.1 The physical layout of a disk.

record, a disk device is made up of concentric circles of tracks (see Figure 1.2).

Refer back to Figure 1.1. Notice that each disk is addressed separately. For instance, the disk at the top of the pack contains disk surface 0 which is accessed by read/write head 0 (normally, the top and bottom platters have only one read/write surface, whereas the rest have two). Disk surface 1 is accessed by disk head 1, and so on. Typically, these read/write heads do not move separately; rather, the entire comb-assembly of read/write heads will move simultaneously.

1.4 THE CONCEPT OF THE CYLINDER

Although it might seem wasteful to us at first that the entire assembly must move in order to access a record on a single track, one must understand the method in which data is recorded initially on disk in order to understand the reasoning behind this.

In Figure 1.3 (at the top) we see an imaginary line (dotted line) drawn from the top to the bottom intersecting the disk volume on track 60 of each surface. If one were to drill a hole through all surfaces along the

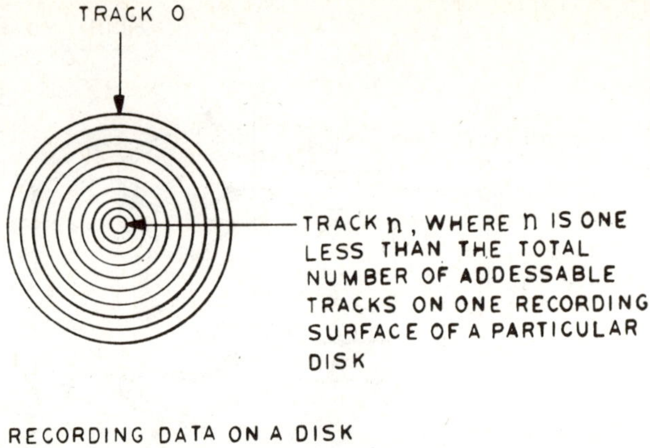

Figure 1.2 The surface of a disk.

dotted line, pass a rod through the holes, and spin the disk at high speed, it would almost appear as though a **cylindrical** object were located between disk platters (see Figure 1.3 bottom).

Since the entire comb-assembly moves in unison, all heads therefore are positioned along different tracks of the same **cylinder**. If the read/write mechanism is positioned at track 60, for instance, it is positioned at track 60 on *all* platters. This position, along all surfaces, would then be referred to as cylinder 60. If a disk spindle contains 30 read/write surfaces as in the case of an IBM 3350 disk unit, a cylinder for that device then contains 30 tracks.

Normally, when data is recorded on a disk, it is recorded on a cylinder basis in order to minimize movement of the read/write assembly; this saves read/write time. The data is written from head 0 through head 29 of a specific cylinder before the read/write mechanism moves on to the next cylinder.

Figure 1.4 gives a table of the most commonly used IBM disk devices and their various capacities.

1.5 DRUM DEVICES

Now look at Figure 1.5. One notices some significant differences between disk and drum devices. First, the drum has no movable read/write assembly; the heads are positioned permanently over each drum track. The second thing to be noticed is that unlike disk spindles, there is only one drum surface.

When considering which device best suits a purpose, certain things must be considered:

1. Because of its fixed heads, the retrieval of data from a drum device is usually faster than disk.
2. Because of the larger surface area of a disk pack, disk devices have a much greater capacity.

It is worth noting at this point that in the near future another option will be available from which to choose: high-speed semiconductor storage. Actually, this is not a new concept; it was used way back in the 1960s to support online systems used by some of the airlines. It was called LCS or Large Capacity Storage. This form of memory was much slower than main storage, too slow, in fact, to execute instructions, but great for storing data. This idea has been revitalized in recent years and is now being offered by several vendors. This option will become increasingly popular as the cost of memory continues to plummet.

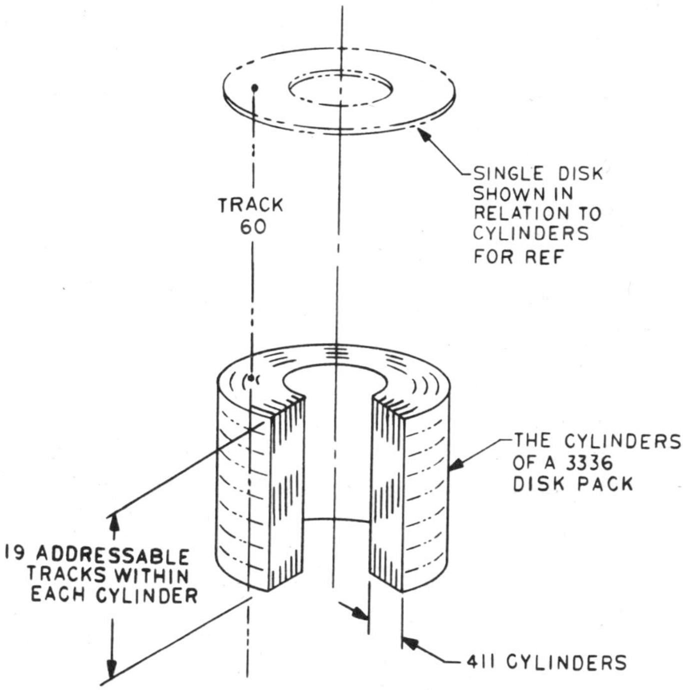

Figure 1.3 The concept of a cylinder.

DASD CAPACITY BY DEVICE
CKD DEVICES

MODEL	TYPE	TRACKS/ SURFACE	BANDS SURFACE	TRACKS/ BAND	BYTES/ TRACK	TRACKS/ CYLINDER
3330-1	DISK	404			13030	19
3330-11	DISK	808			13030	19
2305	DRUM	64			14660	
3340-35	DISK		2	348	8368	12
3340-70	DISK		2	696	8368	12
3350	DISK		2	555	19069	30
3375	DISK	959*			35616	12
3380	DISK	885*			47476	15

* Denotes tracks per actuator (read/write assembly), 2 actuators per drive.

DASD CAPACITY BY DEVICE
FBA DEVICES

MODEL	TYPE	TRACKS/ SURFACE	BANDS SURFACE	BYTES/ BLOCK	BLOCKS/ TRACK	TRACKS/ CYLINDER
3310	DISK	358		512	32	11
3370	DISK	750#	2	512	62	12

# Denotes tracks per band

Figure 1.4 Track and sector capacities.

To complicate matters more, some disk devices have both fixed and movable heads. Because of its faster access time, the fixed area is often used for something called the **page data set** (see Chapter 9).

1.6 HOW DATA IS RECORDED

Data is recorded on a disk or drum device using two distinct methods:

CKD—Count/Key/Data
FBA—Fixed Block Architecture

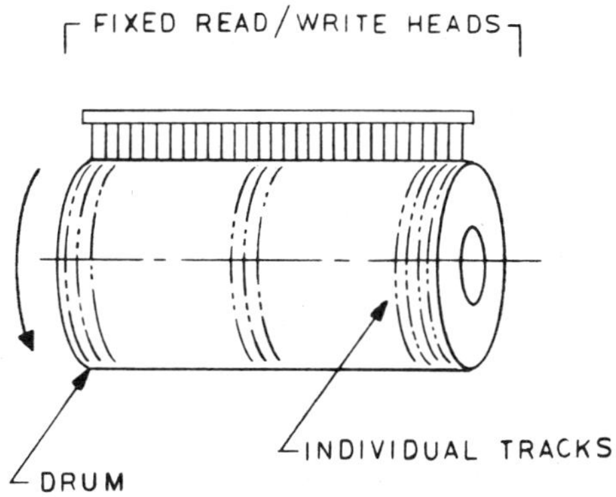

Figure 1.5 The structure of a drum.

1.7 CKD-TYPE DEVICES

Looking at Figure 1.6 we see the following items for each data record written:

1. The **count** field which contains the address of the data record, its length, and the length of its key portion; the address is made up of the cylinder, head, and the record location.

INDEX POINT: ON EACH TRACK OF THE RECORDING SURFACE THERE IS ONE INDEX POINT. IT INDICATES THE PHYSICAL BEGINNING OF THE TRACK.

HOME ADDRESS: ON EACH TRACK, THERE IS ONE HOME ADDRESS IT DEFINES THE PHYSICAL LOCATION OF THE TRACK.

FLAG: THIS IS A 1-BYTE FIELD INDICATING THE CONDITION OF THE TRACK (OPERATIVE OR DEFECTIVE) AND THE USE OF THE TRACK (PRIMARY OR ALTERNATE).

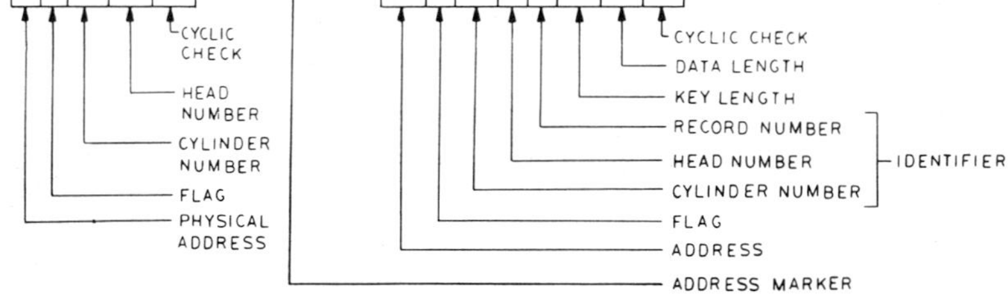

Figure 1.6 Records using CKD/FBA.

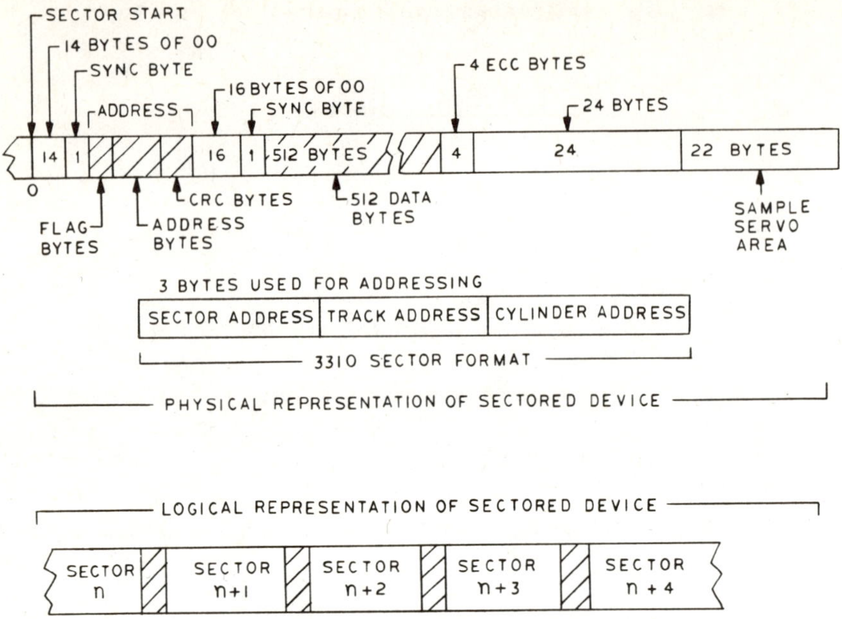

Figure 1.7 Fixed Block Architecture.

2. The **key** field is optional and, if present, provides a unique identifier for the data record following: for instance, an employee or social security number.
3. The **data** portion is the actual data record itself.

The spaces between these items are called inter-record gaps (**IRG**); these gaps are also found between sectors on FBA-type devices.

1.8 FBA-TYPE DEVICES

The second method of recording data is called **Fixed Block Architecture** (**FBA**). In this method all records are composed of data items called sectors which are of a fixed length throughout the volume. Unlike CKD devices, there is no count or key component. See Figure 1.7. (This has nothing to do with whether data can be accessed by key.)

Individual records are addressed by their **sector** or block address. The first sector is sector 0, the second is sector 1, and so on. See Figure 1.4 for sector capacities.

In the next chapter we discuss the access methods available prior to the introduction of VSAM, their methods of operation, and their various deficiencies. They are then compared, on a one-for-one basis, with VSAM.

NOTES

1. The use of virtual storage, although relatively unknown, was used in a specialized way on the System 360/44. The concept was brought to fruition on the System/370.
2. Some other considerations are speed, sharing of channels, direct access devices, and communications overhead.
3. Discussion of direct access storage devices (DASD) in this book centers primarily around disk. The author is aware, however, that VSAM was designed to work with other devices such as drum and the Mass Storage System (MSS). VSAM, however, does not support Data Cell.

TEST YOUR UNDERSTANDING

1. What is the difference between disk and drum devices?

2. Explain how CKD and FBA devices differ.

3. Is a cylinder the same as a drum? Explain.

4. What is an access method?

5. Explain the benefits of using a disk versus drum and vice versa.

6. How is data recorded on a disk? On a drum?

chapter **2**

ACCESS METHODS

2.1 PURPOSE

The purpose of this chapter is to acquaint the reader with the workings of both the **Indexed Sequential** (**ISAM**) and **Direct Access Methods** (**DAM**). This discussion should help the reader to understand the differences between **ISAM**, **BDAM**, and **VSAM**. Once a working knowledge of these access methods has been attained, a comparison of the functional differences between them can be made and the reasons behind the development and introduction of VSAM can be better understood.

Those individuals already thoroughly familiar with these access methods and the difficulties they present should feel free to skip to the next chapter.

2.2 ISAM

Even when first introduced with the advent of the IBM System/360 when little else was available, **ISAM** (**Indexed Sequential Access Method**) was viewed by many as both a blessing and a curse. Up until that time, the only random file access method supported by IBM was the **direct-**

access method (**BDAM**). BDAM uses direct addressing; that is, records are read or written to a direct-access device either by specifying cylinder/track (CKD) address, or addressing by sector number.[1]

The ability that ISAM provided to store and retrieve records based upon a key was badly needed and was welcomed with open arms. Although access to file records by means of a **key** such as employee number, part number, and so on, was accomplished through the efforts of individual inventive programmers at various locations, no generalized industry-wide method was available to *all* users in the IBM world prior to ISAM.[2]

2.2.1 THE STRUCTURE OF ISAM

ISAM files are composed of three elements: **Index**, **Prime Data**, and **Overflow Areas** (see Figure 2.1).

2.2.2 THE INDEX

The index, which is functionally similar to the VSAM index, contains **keys** that uniquely identify each record in the data areas. In addition to this there is a **pointer** associated with each key which contains the actual direct-access record address.

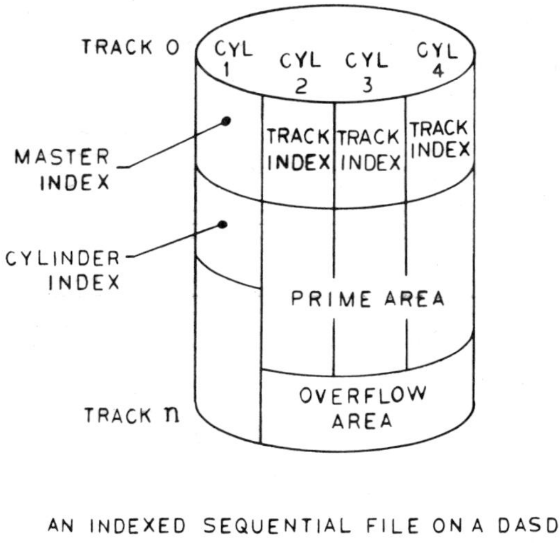

Figure 2.1 Structure of ISAM files.

The index in an ISAM file is, in fact, made up of three different types of indices: the **Master Index**, the **Cylinder Index**, and the **Track Index**. Each of these is discussed shortly.

2.2.3 THE PRIME DATA AREA

There are actually two data areas in an ISAM file: the prime data and the overflow area. The bulk of the data records are found in the prime data area, which is where *all* records are placed in sequential order during initial file creation (load). Records in the prime data area may be blocked or unblocked depending on program requirements.

2.2.4 THE OVERFLOW AREAS

The overflow areas are used to hold records displaced during the record addition process. Additions cause the **last record of a Prime Data track** to be bumped into this area (rather than the addition itself as is commonly supposed).

There are actually two overflow areas:

Cylinder Overflow
Independent Overflow

Both overflow areas are optional. If no additions are ever to be made to the file after its initial creation, overflow area(s) need not be allocated.

The Cylinder Overflow (**CO**) Area and the Prime Data area occupy the same cylinder. The cylinder overflow area occupies one or more of the last tracks of a given cylinder and is adjacent to the prime data area (see Figure 2.2). This area is reserved for record additions made within that particular cylinder. The CO is optional (the decision made at file creation time). If not used, this part of the cylinder reverts to prime data area space.

The independent overflow area is a catch-all. It is used in the same manner as is the cylinder overflow: for record additions. When the cylinder overflow area of a particular cylinder becomes full, the independent overflow area is then used. If no cylinder overflow area exists, *all* records are directed to the independent overflow area.

2.2.5 ISAM RANDOM RECORD RETRIEVAL

When an application program wishes to retrieve a record from an ISAM file, a **key** is passed to ISAM. ISAM then examines the indices looking

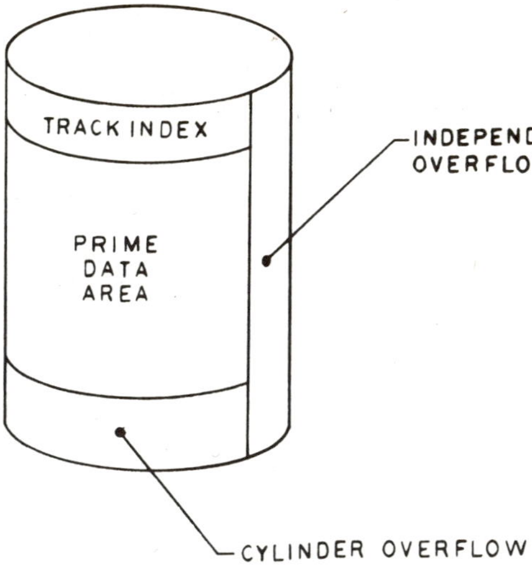

Figure 2.2 ISAM overflow areas.

for a match on that key. When a match is found, the actual data record is retrieved using the address pointer associated with the key and the data is passed back to the application program.

2.2.6 THE ISAM INDEX

The index structure of an ISAM file is composed of the following (see Figure 2.3):

The Master Index
The Cylinder Index
The Track Index

The actual methodology to retrieve a record is as follows:

1. A search is made for the location of the key in the master index (if one exists). This then points ISAM to an area of the cylinder index containing the keypointer.
2. The cylinder index is searched for the keypointer to the particular cylinder containing the track index which, in turn, contains the keypointer to the actual track in which the record should be found.
3. The track index is then searched to determine if the record sought (if it exists) is contained within one of the prime data tracks of *that* cylinder or in some overflow area (cylinder or independent).

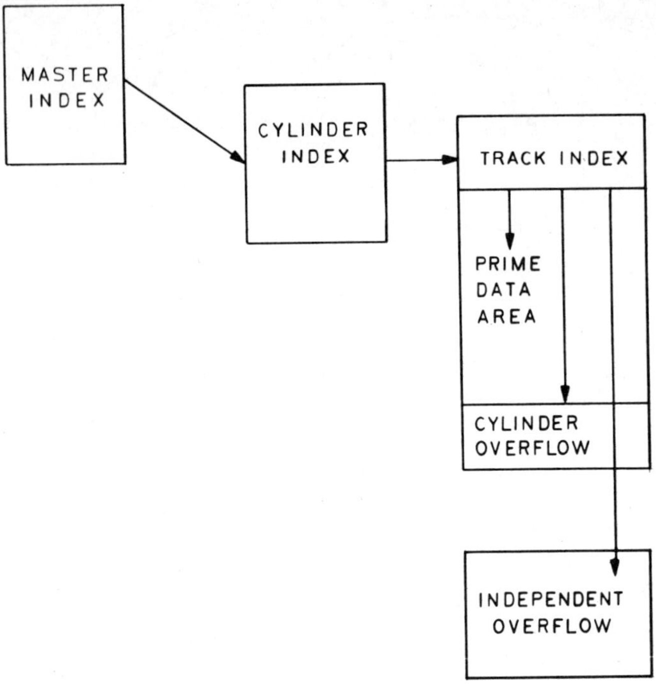

Figure 2.3 ISAM index structure.

4. ISAM then searches the actual **track** for that record. If the record exists, it is passed back to the program; if it does not exist, an indication to that effect is passed back to the program instead.

Of the three index types, only the master index is optional. It is, however, rarely used, its primary function being to speed up record retrieval when accessing very large files.

2.2.7 ISAM RECORD ADDITION

The steps involved in adding a record to an ISAM data set are as follows:

1. All indices are searched as described under **Random Record Retrieval** to obtain the proper location at which an addition should take place.
2. When an area is located by means of the track index in which to add a record (in its proper sequential order according to key), ISAM then checks to determine if a record with that key already exists. If so,

the record is not added and a **duplicate** condition is sent back to the program.

3. Assuming a record with that key does not already exist, ISAM will place the record in its proper location on the track according to key sequence. In order to do this, however, all records from that location to the end of the track are shifted right one position, the last record being **bumped** off the end of the track and placed into the next available slot in the overflow area (see Figure 2.4). The track index is then updated to reflect this.

2.2.8 THE GROWING OVERFLOW AREA

Figure 2.5 shows an example of records residing in an overflow area. As indicated in the illustration, each record contains a **pointer** called a **Sequence Link Indicator (SLI)**. The purpose of the SLI is to point to the actual physical location of the next record in sequence, according to the value of the key.

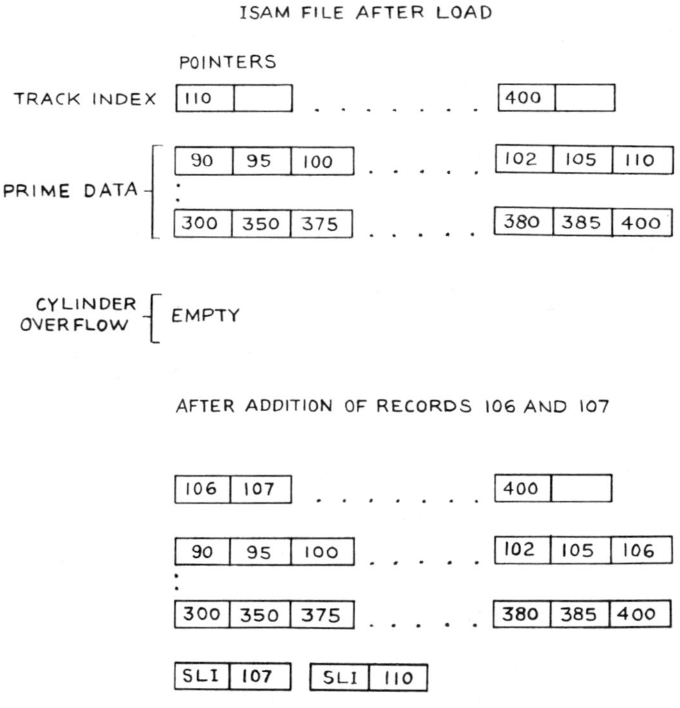

Figure 2.4 ISAM record additions.

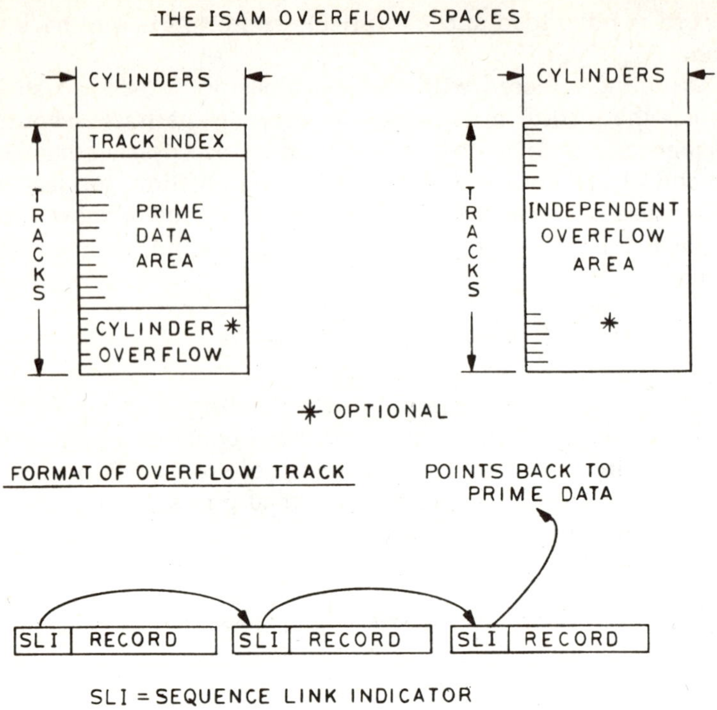

Figure 2.5 ISAM overflow areas with pointers.

When record additions to an ISAM file are light and evenly distributed, most SLI pointers will point back to the prime data area (the location of the next sequential record).

2.2.9 ISAM'S DOWNFALL

As long as record additions continue in this manner ISAM works very well. The difficulty with ISAM and its downfall becomes apparent when *many* records with closely related keys are all added into the same area of the file.

As was stated earlier, when records are placed into the overflow area the SLI field points to the location of the next sequential record. When massive insertions take place within a specific area of the file, many records will be pushed into the overflow area.

The overflow pointer, instead of pointing back toward the **Prime Data Area** for the location of the next record, begins to point to other overflow records. As more and more additions are made into this same area, the **chain** of overflow records pointing to each other becomes greater with each additional record. Furthermore, for each new record that is added, the time required to make each new addition increases because all the records in the chain have first to be searched in order to find its proper location and to update the various pointers. The same problem occurs when simply trying to retrieve a record that happens to be contained within a long chain.

The other major downfall of ISAM is that space used by deleted records (OS only) cannot be recovered.

The only solution for both of these problems, although temporary, is to reorganize the file. Reorganization involves copying the file to another disk or tape, and then re-creating (loading) the file. This then restructures all the indices and places *all* the data into the prime data area.

2.3 THE DIRECT ACCESS METHOD (DAM)

Now that we have discussed the single greatest weakness of ISAM let us proceed to review the only generalized alternative available prior to the introduction of VSAM, the **Direct Access Method** (**DAM**). It is also known as BDAM (The Basic Direct Access Method).

With the introduction of ISAM the popularity of the Direct Access Method waned considerably. In most instances ISAM greatly simplified the work involved in designing new file applications. Whenever records were to be added to a file, ISAM would now perform the task of finding a place to store the new record and also handle the mechanics involved in retrieving it afterward.

The DAM method, in contrast, often required a great deal of thought when used as the file access method. Although DAM allowed the programmer, through one of its addressing schemes, to place a record anywhere within the extent defined for the file, it did not provide any methodology that would assist in this function. This would be left entirely to the programmer to figure out.

2.3.1 THE DAM METHODS OF RECORD ADDRESSING

The DAM provides three methods of addressing:

Absolute addressing
Relative addressing
Sector addressing

2.3.2 ABSOLUTE ADDRESSING

The **absolute addressing method** allows one to point to a record at a specific location on a direct access device by providing its true absolute address. On a CKD device (Chapter 1) the address of a record is provided by the programmer by specifying its **absolute** cylinder, head, and record (**CHR**) location.

Some readers might already be wondering about what happens when it becomes necessary to place that same file on another location of the disk. Without doubt, for many applications it could literally mean back to the drawing board. For this very reason the individual responsible for file design would more likely use the relative method of DAM addressing.

2.3.3 RELATIVE ADDRESSING

The **relative addressing** method provides greater flexibility when allocating space for a file. This is of even greater importance under those operating systems in which space is dynamically assigned.

When using the relative addressing method, the programmer is no longer concerned with the absolute location of records. Record positions are specified as a function of their location relative to the beginning of the file.

A typical relative address might take the form of **TTTR** where T = track and R = record. If the DASD device being used is a 3330 (19 tracks per cylinder), in order to specify the relative location of a record, for instance, the fifth record on the twentieth track from the beginning of the file, an address of **0135** (TTTR-hexadecimal) would be provided, the TTTR being relative to zero. If it becomes necessary to relocate a file, it can now be done with ease.

2.3.4 SECTOR ADDRESSING

The third method of DAM addressing involves addressing by sector address (see Figure 2.6).

For DASD devices that use **sector addressing**, the address in which the record is located is provided by a sector number. On sector-type devices every track contains a specific number of logical (*usually*) blocks (sectors). I say usually because there are some devices that use what are called hard sectors. Such devices have a built-in facility (timing marks) that signal when the next sector is rotating past the head. This

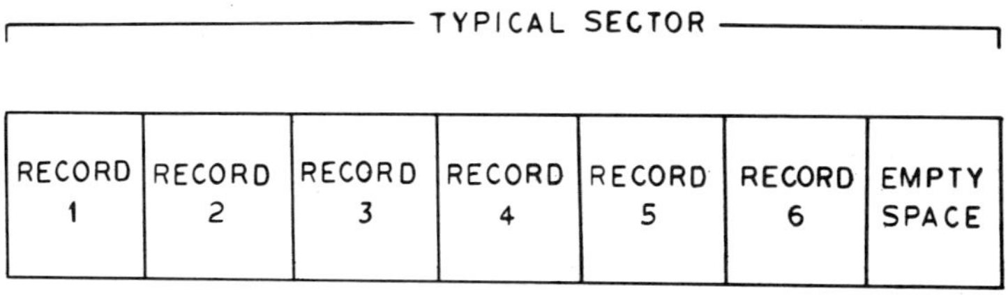

Figure 2.6 The DAM using sectors.

book is confined to standard IBM-type equipment that uses a logical sector only.

A sector may contain one or more records. When a programmer wishes to retrieve a record from a sector-type device, he or she merely provides the number of the sector in which the record is contained. Since the application programmer, however, accesses data through some access method, sector addressing is almost never used directly.

2.3.5 DAM FILE CREATION

Regardless of the addressing method used to add or retrieve records on disk, there are basically two methods of **loading** (creating) a DAM file:

Sequential loading
Randomized loading

2.3.6 SEQUENTIAL LOADING

In the sequential loading method all records are written sequentially one after another, regardless of the record key (i.e., employee number). With this loading method two ways of later retrieving those records can be used:

Loading Report
Index Creation

2.3.7 THE LOADING REPORT

By simply printing a report showing the record address and its associated key, a user could later refer to a specific record by providing, from the report, a record address. This method was used often in the early days of DASD when the only method of addressing was by sector.

2.3.8 INDEX CREATION

The second method is more complex, involving the creation of an index. This index would be composed of two items: the key of each record and its associated address. These records might be sorted by key and written out to a separate file. Later, this index would be accessed for each record retrieved by simply matching the key and then extracting the record address.

A performance improvement to this involves copying the entire index into main storage, which greatly reduces record retrieval time.

2.3.9 RANDOMIZING

The second method of loading a DAM file is the Randomizing method; this is usually a two-step process:

File Formatting
File Loading

For the most part before a file can be loaded using this method it must first be formatted.

This involves preformatting a record with some predetermined character and writing these records out for the entire extent of the file. This accomplishes two things: for a CKD device it establishes a specific record length, and for both FBA and CKD, it formats each record with a specific character that indicates to this program that this **slot** is empty.

The second step, the load, is then ready to deposit records in these various preformatted record locations. This process incorporates a technique entitled **randomizing**. Randomizing is a process involving the calculation of a specific DASD address through some operation on the record key. An algorithm designed for the specific file to be created is invoked, and the digits that make up the key are manipulated in such a way that the result can be used as an address on a DASD device.

One drawback to this method is that data in which the key values are not close render large gaps in the file area between records, causing much DASD space to be wasted.

2.3.10 THE BIGGEST PROBLEM

For the computer installation in which DASD space is not a consideration, there still remains one area of operation which causes great difficulty: record additions. Whether the DAM involves a sequential or randomizing technique, the programmer will spend a tremendous amount of time developing a record addition scheme.

When the method involves a *sequential* mode of the DAM, the program must be able to keep track of the next available space on the DASD device in order to be able to add records to it. This involves keeping file pointers somewhere that must be updated after each write or series of writes (additions). Following this, it may be necessary to update an index as well as optionally sort and reload the file at the end of the add operation. This could create other problems, especially for online systems, since this added data may not be accessible until the file is reorganized.

The second method, **randomized** DAM, presents an entirely different set of problems. Sometimes the randomizing algorithm attempts to pack the records so closely together that two or more record keys will compute to the same identical DASD address. These records are called **synonyms**. Various schemes are used in an attempt to deal with synonyms, one of which might involve writing all these records into a sequential **overflow** area. Another might simply involve adding **1** to the track number up to a specific number of times in an attempt to find an empty slot.

Whatever method is used, one can easily see the difficulties involved with either a sequential or randomized approach. As in the case of ISAM, the greatest problem encountered with this method occurs when record additions are to be made.

2.4 ENTER VSAM

We have discussed in general the ISAM and DAM methods, their good points, and their weaknesses. We have determined that the single greatest difficulty lies in the area of record additions. Efficient processing of record additions is most probably the single biggest reason for the development of VSAM and, because of this, one of its greatest strengths.

Add to this the ability of VSAM to reuse deleted record space, create and maintain alternate indices, dynamically allocate space when needed, VSAM freespace, and many other facilities, makes VSAM number one among the access methods.

NOTES

1. The discussion in this chapter on sector-type devices pertains to the IBM 3340 and 3370 class of FBA devices. There are some variations to this in

such devices as the IBM 1411, floppy disk, and non-IBM devices that use hard sectors (physical versus logical).

2. A possible exception to this would be DBOMP, which not only provides access by key but is considered by many to be the first DBMS system used in the IBM world. It was not, however, widely used.

TEST YOUR UNDERSTANDING

1. What are the two methods of *physically* recording data on a DASD device?
2. How does the relative addressing method of the DAM work?
3. Explain the ISAM file structure.
4. Name a major advantage that ISAM has over BDAM.
5. What are some of the difficulties involved in adding records using BDAM? Using ISAM?

chapter 3

VSAM—AN OVERVIEW

3.1 PURPOSE

In order to compete with and ultimately replace other access methods, **VSAM** had to offer enough new capabilities and options to make one want to convert to it. In addition to this, VSAM had to address those deficiencies found in the other access methods. Among those problems are: insertion of records, recovery/restart, and overall performance.

With this chapter we begin our examination of the Virtual Storage Access Method: what it does, and how it works. This chapter gives the reader a brief overview of some of the main features of VSAM. A more detailed description of its facilities is given in Chapters 4, 5, and 6.

3.2 THE THREE FACES OF VSAM

Although packaged as a single **access method**, VSAM actually can operate in either of three distinct **file access modes**:

KSDS
ESDS
RRDS

Each of these **access modes** can be thought of as competing directly with other non-VSAM access methods, for instance: **KSDS**, or the **Keyed Sequence Data Set** method, closely resembles ISAM in operation and can be directly compared to it. Like ISAM, file access is accomplished by means of a **key**. **ESDS**, the **Entry Sequence Data Set** method, operates very similarly to the Sequential Access Method (SAM) in which records are physically written one after the other and subsequently retrieved in the same manner. **RRDS**, the **Relative Record Data Set** method, is a latecomer to VSAM; not having been present in the original introduction, it was added by IBM as a third option two years later. This method competes directly with BDAM (DAM). Like BDAM, the RRDS has no **index**. Records are retrieved directly by using a **Relative Record Number** (**RRN**).

3.3 SIMILARITIES WITH OTHER ACCESS METHODS

Regardless of the VSAM mode selected, similarities exist in the basic *structure* of files used for each method. All three methods contain a **data** area in which data records are placed. In the case of the Keyed Sequential Data Set (KSDS), VSAM, in addition to the data area, also creates and maintains an **index** area.

3.4 THE CONTROL INTERVAL

Regardless of the VSAM method used, the basic building block of each VSAM file type is the **control interval** (**CI**). The control interval is somewhat, although not entirely, analogous to the concept of blocking used in non-VSAM methods (see Figure 3.1). In these methods, especially the SAM and ISAM methods, logical records are packed (blocked) together to form larger physical records. This greatly reduces the I/O time required when reading or writing records sequentially because a greater number of records can be transferred with one I/O operation. This also means that other considerations such as **rotational delay** and **arm movement** are reduced proportionately to the number of logical records contained in a block.

Whereas the physical size of a block is equal to the sum of its logical records, a control interval is always of a fixed length (selected at file creation time), regardless of the size of the logical records contained within it (Figure 3.1).

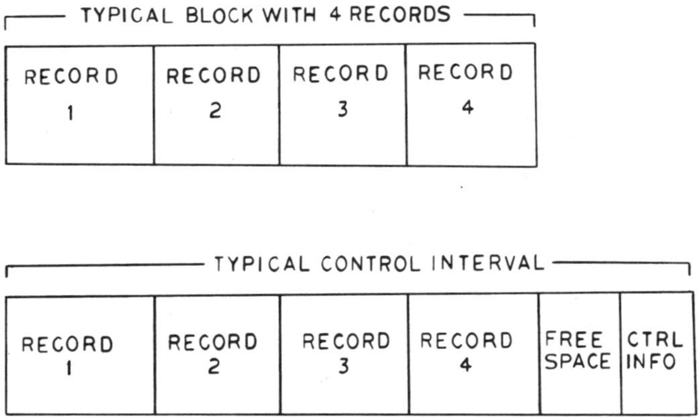

Figure 3.1 The block versus the control interval.

The size of the control interval is chosen and specified when the data set is **defined** to VSAM through Access Method Services (more about this later). A **data** CI can occur in the following sizes: ($n \times 512$) or ($n \times 2048$), where n = multiplier. The data CI can be up to 32k in length. The size of the **Index** CI must be 512, 1024, 2048, or 4096 in length. Figure 3.2 illustrates the structure of a VSAM control interval. As can be seen there are three different elements contained within the CI: the data records themselves, plus the **CIDF** and **RDF** fields (see Figure 3.3).

3.5 CIDF

The **CIDF (Control Interval Descriptor Field)** contains information about available space within that CI. For example, in the case of a KSDS when

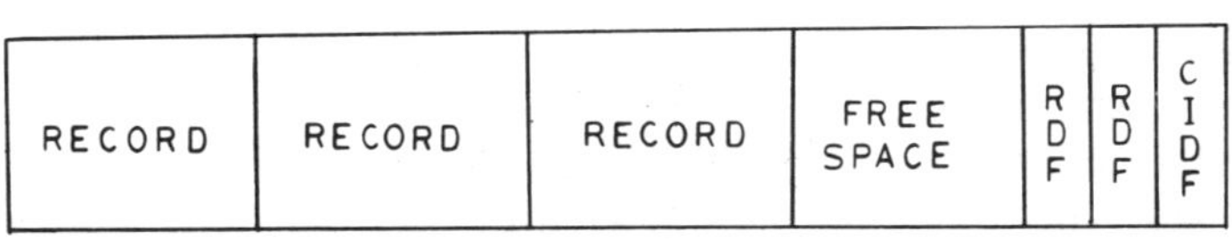

RDF: RECORD DESCRIPTOR FIELD

CIDF: CONTROL INTERVAL DESCRIPTOR FIELD

Figure 3.2 The format of a control interval.

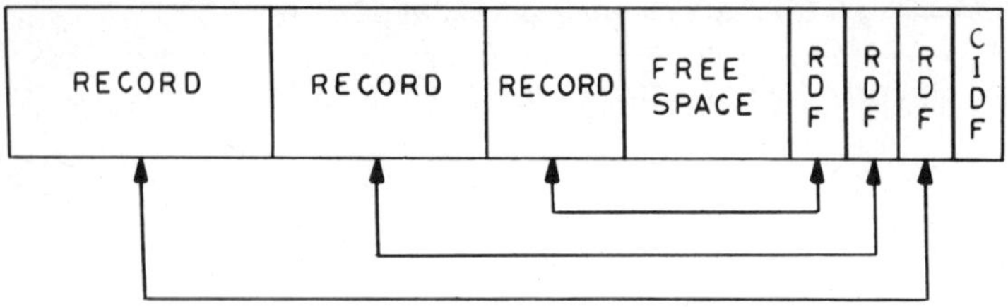

Figure 3.3 The CIDF and RDF fields.

a record addition is to be made, VSAM will first determine the CI to which the record logically belongs. It will then check the CIDF to determine if the number of bytes available is great enough to contain the addition of this record.

3.6 RDF

The purpose of the **RDF** (**Record Descriptor Field**) is to store pointers to each logical record in the control interval. This pointer actually contains the length of each record in addition to other information. The format of the RDF and CIDF areas is found in Appendix B.

In the case of a **variable length** record file (Figure 3.3), the CI will contain a pointer for each record, rendering one RDF for each logical record. As records are added to the CI, they are placed in the control interval beginning from the left-most section of the CI. Corresponding RDFs will be added at the right-most area of the CI and to the left of any existing RDFs, with any remaining freespace lying between the data records and the RDF and CIDF fields.

In the case of a **fixed** length file, since all records are of the same length a separate RDF for each record is not required. In this case (fixed length records) VSAM always uses *two* RDFs per control interval (Figure 3.3).

A third type of record exists called **spanned**. With this method a record may span across several control intervals because it is too large to fit in one. This method is handled in the same manner as the fixed length record. Any freespace left in the last CI of a spanned record cannot be used, however.

3.7 CI SIZE

The individual responsible for the design of the file also specifies the size of the CI. What was not mentioned was that this pertains to the size of the CI only, but not for the physical record used to house the CI.

VSAM does not give you absolute control over the *physical* size of the slot, or slots, used to hold a CI. Although the designer is given a large number of options from which to tailor a file, important items such as physical record size and the size of a **control area** (more about this later) are not fully under the control of the file designer. Perhaps some future release of VSAM will correct this. The file designer must then be aware of both the CI size and the physical records used to contain them.

The size of the CI is chosen usually to optimize some resource(s) such as DASD or main storage. The maximum size of the physical record VSAM uses for CIs is 4096.

Assume that the file designer, wanting to optimize a certain type of DASD, selects a CI size of 6144. Although VSAM will accept this as CI size, more likely than not, VSAM will force the *physical* record size to 4096, thereby nullifying in some cases the effect that the designer had intended.

In this particular case the CI would actually span two physical records. The subject of CI size selection is discussed more fully in later chapters.

As stated previously, all these methods—KSDS, ESDS, and RRDS—utilize a **data area** in which the control intervals within are used to store data. Besides this, an **index** area is always present in the case of a KSDS file and can be optionally defined in the case of the ESDS file. An RRDS cannot have an index.

In addition to a base (primary) index a data set may also have **alternate** indices (more about this later).

3.8 CLUSTERS

All VSAM data sets are identified by a single unique name which is referred to as its **cluster** name. The original purpose of this was to allow a single name to be used to address the **collective** components of a file, that is, the data area and the base index (see Figure 3.4). As stated earlier, when VSAM was first announced it contained only the KSDS and ESDS methods, and both of these (index and data area) could be present in these methods. It was necessary then to have a means by which to address a file by a single name regardless of the number of components contained therein, hence the **cluster** name.

Under the RRDS method, even though only a **data** area can exist, the file is given a cluster name just as in the KSDS and ESDS methods.

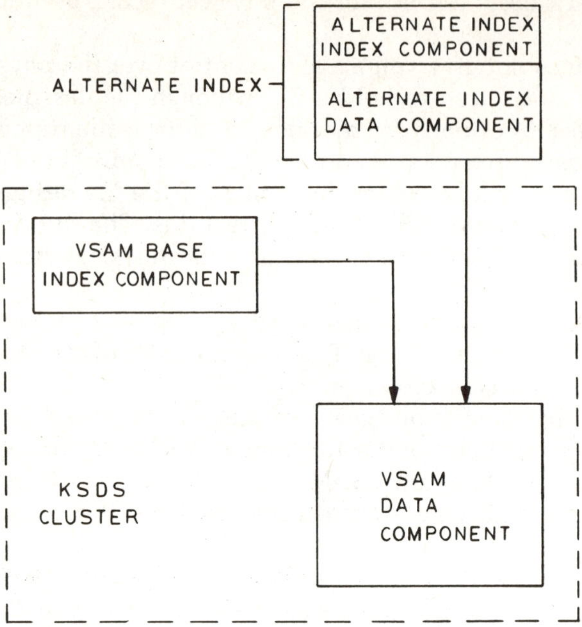

Figure 3.4 The components of a cluster.

In every case then, regardless of method and regardless of the number of components, any VSAM file may be referred to by a single cluster name.

3.9 THE INDEX

The **Index** component of a KSDS is separate from the data component. The structure of an index on its most basic level is identical to that of the data area; that is, control intervals are used to contain the **data records** for the index component. The **data** contained in these control intervals is actually comprised of pointers to the application data records.

The size of the CI in the index component can be different from that specified for the data component. It is chosen when the file is defined (with the DEFINE command) at creation time.

As VSAM adds records to the data area, pointers in the index area are updated. If a file has multiple indices, which occurs when alternate indices exist, all the indices can be updated at this time. In the case of alternate indices, the file designer also can choose *not* to update these indices during an update operation for performance reasons. This is a file design consideration.

3.10 VSAM SPACES

Before any clusters can be created, the Database or DASD Administrator must first allocate **space** on a DASD device for VSAM to use.

The two most common objects found in a VSAM space are clusters and catalogs (more about this later). There are also two variations of VSAM space (Figure 3.5):

Unique
Suballocation

When a cluster is defined in a **Unique** space, nothing else may reside within the space except that cluster. In the case of **Suballocation**, a larger VSAM space is defined in which many clusters may reside. Extra space can be left in this VSAM space for future addition of clusters. In addition to this, extra space should be left for dynamic file expansion when the addition of data records to a specific cluster requires more space than was initially assigned when the file was created.

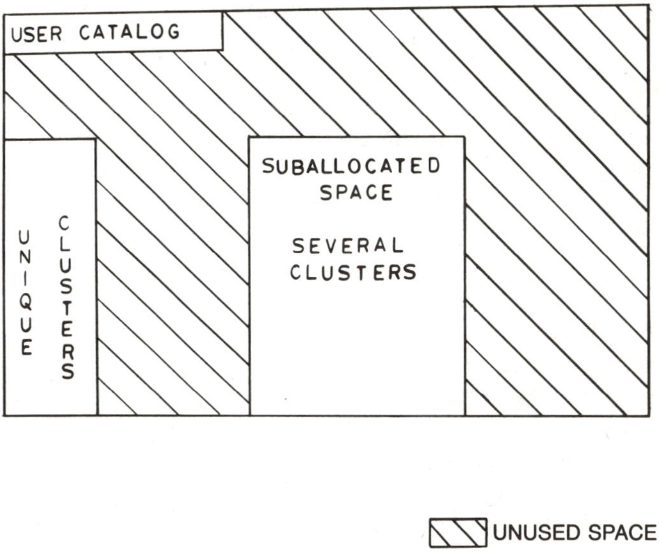

Figure 3.5 Unique versus suballocated VSAM spaces.

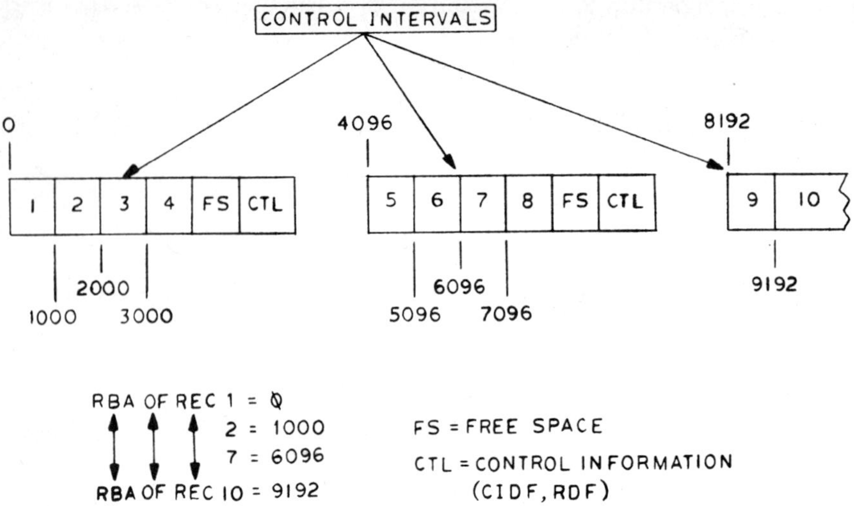

Figure 3.6 The relative byte address.

Clusters contained within suballocated VSAM spaces need not be contiguous. In other words, a particular VSAM data set need not be entirely contained within one extent within the suballocated space. A cluster may be comprised of several extents, some of which were added dynamically as the file was extended through record additions, **or** more than one extent allocation may have taken place during file creation.

Regardless of whether the cluster is contained within one extent or several, VSAM views the file **logically** as one continuous extent of control intervals placed side by side.

3.11 RELATIVE BYTE ADDRESS

Since VSAM views the data set in this manner, it is actually possible to address individual records by specifying their displacement, in bytes, from the beginning of the file. This is called its **Relative Byte Address (RBA)**, shown in Figure 3.6. VSAM maintains RBA information in its catalog, for example, a field called **High-Allocated-RBA** is used to indicate the highest byte (end of extent) that can be used. Another field called **High-Used-RBA** points to the actual end of the data (logical end-of-file).

3.12 THE VSAM CATALOG

VSAM contains a special **directory** in which it maintains control over its spaces. This directory is called a **catalog**. In addition to keeping track of VSAM spaces, the catalog also contains information about the locations of all data, index, and alternate index areas both by their individual names and also by their cluster names.

There are two kinds of catalogs; the **master catalog** (of which there is only one), and the **user catalog**. The master catalog is the controlling catalog for *all* VSAM files and, in addition to containing pointers to all the areas described, will also contain pointers to any user catalog which may exist. The subject of catalogs is discussed more thoroughly in Chapter 6.

TEST YOUR UNDERSTANDING

1. Name the VSAM types. What are some of their differences?
2. What is a cluster?
3. What is a CIDF? An RDF?
4. Name the two most common types of VSAM space usage.
5. What physical considerations must be made when choosing the CI size?
6. What is meant by Relative Byte Address?
7. What is a VSAM catalog?

chapter 4

THE THREE FACES OF VSAM

4.1 VSAM'S THREE METHODS OF PROCESSING

As mentioned in Chapter 3, VSAM operates in three different **modes**:

KSDS—Key Sequenced Data Set method
ESDS—Entry Sequenced Data Set method
RRDS—Relative Record Data Set method

KSDS. The Keyed Sequential Data Set method is used in applications where it is important to be able to directly access any record in the data set with a key, and optionally, access records sequentially either in prime key sequence or through an **alternate** key sequence.
ESDS. The Entry Sequenced Data Set method is used in a manner somewhat similar to a typical sequential file in which records are added one after the other and usually retrieved in the same manner.
RRDS. The Relative Record Data Set method is similar to the Direct Access Method (DAM) where records are accessed by their relative record address. If the record number is available, this method provides

the *fastest* record retrieval. This could be a critical factor in either online or large volume batch processing systems where speed is essential.

4.2 THE KSDS METHOD

Of the three, the most important **method** by far is the Keyed Sequential Data Set method (**KSDS**), because of the dynamic flexibility it affords. VSAM allows access to a Keyed Sequential Data Set in one of the following ways:

1. **Randomly by a key.**
2. **Randomly by the records' RBA.**
3. **Sequentially/skip sequentially in order by the base file key.**
4. **Sequentially/skip sequentially in order by an alternate key.**

4.2.1 KSDS RANDOM RETRIEVAL

VSAM/KSDS allows two methods of random file access: through a record key or by the records' RBA.

In almost all cases, KSDS access will be through a key such as a part-number, account code, or employee number. Because of the nature of the KSDS structure, the RBA of any given record will not necessarily be the same after record additions have been made to the data set. VSAM will sometimes have to shuffle existing records around during an **insert** operation, in order to place a record into its proper position. This subject is discussed in greater detail in Chapter 5.

4.2.2 KSDS SEQUENTIAL RETRIEVAL

After a KSDS file has been **loaded**, the records in the data component will be in physical sequence by key. The **key** order of records in the CI is always maintained. The physical order of records on a control interval basis will not be maintained, however, after record additions cause CI splits (Chapter 5). These records, although no longer in physical sequence, can still be retrieved in sequence **logically** by key. This is accomplished through VSAM's use of the index component.

VSAM allows for the sequential retrieval of records in one of two ways: either fully **sequential** or **skip-sequential**. With the sequential method, records are retrieved one after the other without any breaks in between. In the skip-sequential method a new key (higher) can be presented to VSAM during processing. At that point, VSAM can **skip** over whole range of records in the file so as to allow the sequential retrieval of only those records necessary to that specific application. With either method, the user can start the retrieval operation at any location in the file. Whether it be a **load** or **add** operation, VSAM keeps track of the actual location of records by updating the index, when necessary, for each record added. It is not necessary, however, to update the index for *every* record added. This is discussed more fully in Chapter 5 in Section 5.4.1.

4.2.3 THE CONCEPT OF KSDS FREESPACE

There are several features that make KSDS unique, one of which is the concept of **freespace**. There are two types of freespace: **control interval freespace** and **control area freespace**. Since we are already familiar with the concept of control intervals, let us discuss this first.

When a VSAM/KSDS file is created, VSAM can be instructed to allocate a certain percentage of each control interval as freespace. For instance, if we asked VSAM to set aside 30% of each control interval as freespace, records placed in this CI load time will not occupy more than 70% of each CI. Although this may seem wasteful at first, it can greatly improve processing time later when adding records. The purpose of reserving space in a CI is to allow the later addition of records without the typical system overhead that occurs when no space is immediately available in a CI. As long as the key range of a record allows its addition to a particular CI, and as long as space is available, VSAM will continue to place records in that CI. When the situation arises in which VSAM attempts to add a record to a CI but no more available space exists, VSAM will perform what is called a **control interval split**. CI splits are discussed in Chapter 5.

4.2.4 THE CONTROL AREA

A feature also found only in VSAM/KSDS is the concept of **control areas**. A **control area (CA)** is the name given to a logical group of control intervals. The size of a control area is variable depending on the device type and other factors, it **never** exceeds a cylinder, however. It is not a physical entity as are control intervals (Figure 4.1). Control areas are used as allocation units for freespace, the main purpose of which is to support record insertions. During file creation and sequential mass-insert operation, space within a VSAM space is acquired one control area at a time. Control areas cannot be fractional; the last CA within an extent must be a whole CA.

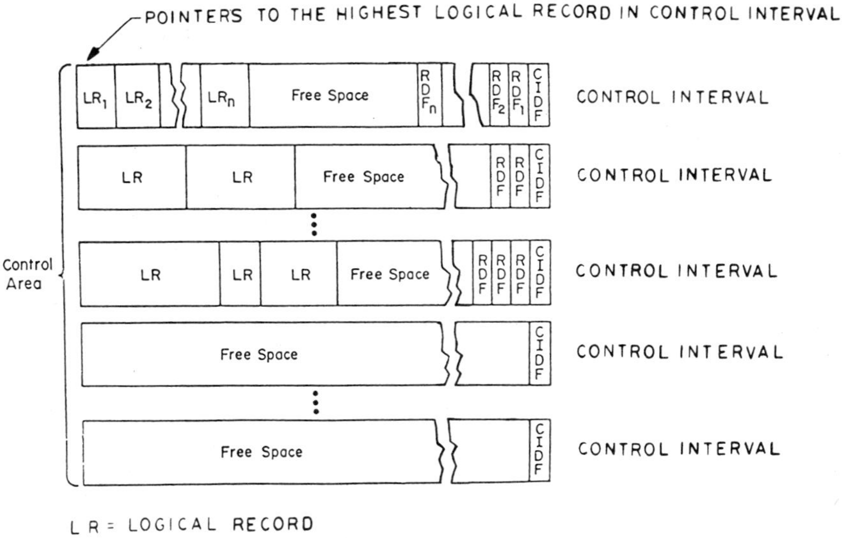

Figure 4.1 The concept of control area.

4.2.5 CONTROL AREA FREESPACE

As we are about to see, VSAM makes use of CAs in several ways. In our discussion of freespace we mentioned that VSAM/KSDS can allocate a percentage of freespace at file creation time. Just as we are able to specify the amount of freespace desired in each CI, we may specify the amount of freespace desired in each CA as well.

Looking at Figure 4.1 we can see how a typical VSAM/KSDS cylinder would look (assuming a CA of one cylinder) after a load operation. Again, the question might come to mind about the value and purpose of assigning freespace. There is no doubt that the decision regarding the allocation of freespace is one that must not be considered lightly. In many installations DASD space is at a premium. Often an individual is required to keep track of its use and allocate new file space when required.

4.2.6 THE ALLOCATION OF FREESPACE

The allocation of freespace, then, is not something arbitrarily assigned. It is the result of considerations such as the following.

Addition of Records. If you expect **several small group insertions** of records into existing CIs in which keys are tightly packed together, it is usually best to allow for a large CI freespace percentage. This leaves plenty of room in the control interval at load time in which to place these consecutive insertions later.

If **frequent massive record additions** are to be made in key ranges that do not currently exist, and that will not affect the current CIs, then it is probably best to allow for a small percentage of CI freespace and a much larger amount of CA freespace. This will allow VSAM to place these new records into the empty CIs located at the end of the control area.

If there are to be **evenly dispersed** additions throughout the file, then it would probably be best to request VSAM to allocate a modest percentage, say, 20%, for CI freespace and little or no CA freespace.

Another possibility might be the **addition of records with keys higher** than any that currently exist. An example of this might be an application that requires access to data by date, and date is in the high-order part of the key. Records with key ranges outside a given CA will never be placed in that CA, even if freespace is available. Since in these cases records will be added at the end of the file, little or no CI or CA freespace would be required when initially loading the file. The thing to watch for in this case would be the occurrence of new CA allocation which could cause excessive system overhead. Although this may be acceptable in a batch system, it would not be as acceptable in an online application. In this type of application one might consider using the ESDS method instead with the addition of an alternate index.

No Record Additions. In those cases where records will never be added to a data set once it is loaded, both CI and CA freespace can be set to zero. There is no reason to allocate space if you are certain that no records will ever be added to this data set.

4.2.7 Alteration of Freespace Specifications

A trick that can be used at times is to **partially** load a file with a certain key range using a certain CI/CA freespace percentage, then **altering** the CI/CA specifications for the next key range, continuing this until the file is completely loaded. This can be accomplished by using the Access Method Services (AMS) utility. AMS is discussed in later chapters. Of course, the purpose of this would be to optimize the file space along with the desired performance characteristics. Obviously, this would require some study involving the measurement of file key allocations as well as daily and seasonal file usages. Another VSAM/KSDS function that must be considered along with freespace is the *method* of record insertions.

4.2.8 THE TWO METHODS OF RECORD INSERTIONS

There are two methods of record insertions (additions): **direct** and **sequential**. When using the sequential insertion technique, VSAM will accumulate records that are in sequential order during an add operation in a buffer, formatted like control intervals. The insertion of records in the sequential insertion mode operates identically to a load operation; that is, along with the formatting of control intervals, freespace is also maintained. When adding many adjacent records, this method of operation is call **sequential mass-insertion** or just plain mass-insertion. It is important to remember when planning the processing of data and the VSAM data set structure that this only applies to the VSAM sequential insertion method and not to the direct insertion method. This subject is discussed further in Section 5.4.1 of Chapter 5.

As you can see, the selection of VSAM options regarding freespace and record additions is something that requires a great deal of consideration. One can readily see that the optimal allocation of freespace is something that is totally dependent on the actual usage of the data set. The best that a book of this nature can accomplish is to discuss the topic in such a manner as to provide you, the reader, with a working knowledge of the options open to you.

4.2.9 THE KSDS INDEX

A KSDS cluster is made up of two parts: **index** and **data** components. The data records themselves are contained in the data component. Although there are data entries contained in the index component, they are actually used as pointers to the data records. Perhaps more than any other single item, the index is what makes the VSAM/KSDS what it is.

Although both the KSDS and ESDS methods can use an index, it is rarely found in the ESDS method and *always* found in the KSDS method. In actuality the indices used by these two methods are different. The index used in the ESDS method is really an alternate rather than a base index as is used in the case of the VSAM/KSDS.

Figure 4.2 illustrates the structure of a typical KSDS cluster containing both the index and data components. The index itself is multitiered. The lowest level of index record is called the **sequence set**. The highest level is comprised of a single record.

When attempting to retrieve records *directly*, the index is used somewhat similarly to the manner in which the ISAM index is used (Master/Cylinder/Track index). As with ISAM, the search begins at the highest

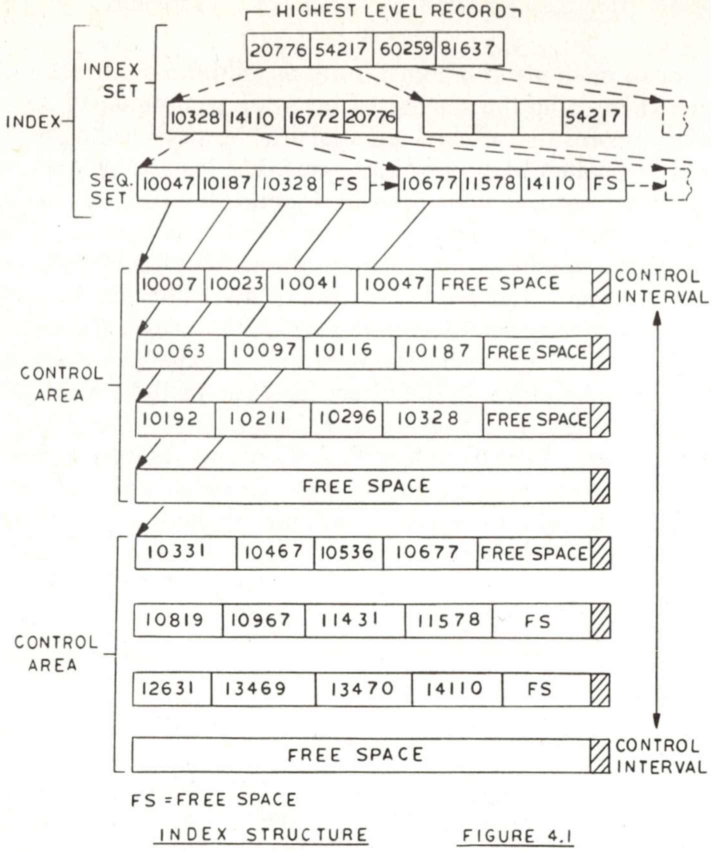

Figure 4.2 The KSDS cluster.

level index and progresses downward toward the actual record location. This is somewhat analogous to the search operation one goes through when looking up a word in a dictionary. Let us say we wanted to look up the word '**DATA**'. The first thing we would do is open the dictionary to the letter '**D**' (first level). Starting at the beginning, we would then flip through the pages examining the words that appear in the upper corner of each page (second level) until we came to a high condition. We would finally scan the words (keys—third level) until finding a match, at which point we would extract the word description (the data). Although the analogy may not be perfect, the principle on which the VSAM index structure works is very similar to this.

The one area in which the analogy breaks down, however, is when you retrieve records sequentially. In the case of the dictionary each entry is stored in perfect sequence. In the case of a VSAM/KSDS data set the physical sequence of the records contained in the data CIs will only be in perfect physical order, from CI to CI, after the initial load operation as stated previously. In order to retrieve the records in their proper sequence VSAM utilizes the sequence set entries. It is here that the proper **logical** sequence of the records is always maintained.

Whenever examining reference material that illustrates the VSAM index, one might notice that the index is almost always shown with three or four levels. Although VSAM is capable of supporting additional levels, most clusters will rarely contain more than four levels. An additional level can be opened, however, when VSAM is required to dynamically **allocate** additional space in which to store additional data records when they cannot be placed within existing control areas, and the initial space allocated at load time is exhausted. This is because the index structure is computed and set up based upon the space allocated for a cluster when the data set is defined initially to VSAM.

When records are inserted into a data set, existing index control intervals may not be able to hold all of the pointer information. When this occurs new index CI's are created as well as higher level index CI's. These can be up to 255 index levels.

4.3 THE STRUCTURE OF THE INDEX RECORD

The index records themselves are actually comprised of control intervals containing records that are used as pointers. The index is logically divided into two classes depending on index level. The lowest level of index, the **sequence set**, contains an entry for each control interval in the data component. The record pointer, as is shown in Figure 4.2, is actually the **highest key** contained in the data control interval, one pointer for each control interval. **Each control interval within the sequence set contains all the entries necessary for one control area in the data portion of the file**. The remaining higher levels of index are referred to as the **index set**.

If the data set was created with CA freespace, there will also be pointers in the sequence set to those control intervals containing freespace. In other words, there will be two types of pointers: one that points to existing records and one that points to the freespace within a control area.

The requirement to contain all the entries necessary for each control area will sometimes interfere with your efforts to optimize the space used for the index component, the size of which can be specified at **DEFINE** time. If the size specified cannot hold the entries required, VSAM will override the entry with an entry of its own. You should watch for this. Make sure you run a **LISTCAT** after data set definition and examine the information that the LISTCAT provides you. (LISTCAT is discussed in Chapter 8.)

The next higher level of index (level 2) contains pointer records in its control interval to each control interval in the sequence set. Another way to look at it is to think of it as containing a pointer record for each control area. As stated previously, the highest level of index consists of a single record, the entries of which contain pointers to the highest entry in each lower level (second level in this case).

4.3.1 THE HORIZONTAL INDEX POINTER

Along with the vertical pointers found in the index control intervals, there are also **horizontal pointers**. Horizontal pointers are used primarily during sequential record retrieval operations. The data control intervals do not contain pointers of any kind. Random or sequential access to the data contained in data control intervals is entirely dependent on the pointer structure found in the index.

Figure 4.3 contains a more detailed view of the VSAM **index** control interval. As shown in the illustration, the index record is comprised of the following entries:

- **The header field**
- **A single record containing pointers to:**
  - **Free data control intervals**
  - **Space between entry types**
  - **Pointers to occupied data CIs**
- **A single RDF (all entries are contained in a single variable length record)**
- **The CIDF**

Although the illustration in Figure 4.3 pertains to a sequence set index record, the structure for a higher level index record is the same. A field in the header identifies the level of the index record.

The following lists some of the information provided in the header field:

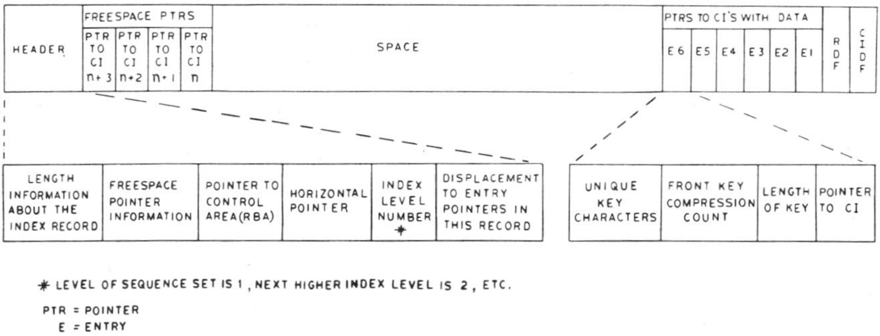

Figure 4.3 The structure of the index CI.

Length in bytes of the index record
Length of the free data CI pointers
Horizontal pointer
Index level number
Information about the entries used as pointers

The **free data CI pointers** exist only in the sequence set level index records and are used to calculate the RBAs of available data CIs.

The entry pointers contained in the sequence set index record are the actual pointers that VSAM/KSDS uses to locate control intervals in the data area. The key values found in these entries will contain the value of the *highest* key found in a data CI. Some of the information maintained by VSAM for each entry is as follows:

Actual key characters that make this key unique
Compression character count
Length of the key field less the compression character count
Pointer to the data or index control interval (this field actually is a pointer to the CI within a CA)

4.3.2 THE CONCEPT OF KEY COMPRESSION

In order to minimize the space used for index record entries VSAM uses a technique called **key compression**. VSAM will eliminate from both the front and back of a key those bytes which are redundant when compared with the record key before and after the current entry. In other words, those characters that are not needed to distinguish a particular entry from the adjacent key will be stripped off. To give an example, suppose records with the following keys were added to the file: 10120, 10130, 10140, 10150. Which characters actually make the keys unique? The fact is the keys are identical except for the 2, 3, 4, and 5 located in the center of the key. In this particular case the keys *could* be reduced to this. Unfortunately, in the real world keys will not compress as well as this. If, however, key compression is performed only some of the time, it is still advantageous. By the way, key compression is not optional; that is, it is not user selected. This function is performed by VSAM automatically whenever it can be used.

4.3.3 IMBEDDING AND REPLICATION

There are two index-related functions (see Figure 4.4) that the user can utilize in order to speed up functions requiring access to the VSAM index:

Imbedded index records
Replication of index records

When you define a VSAM/KSDS file you can specify that the lowest level index (the sequence set) be placed on the first track of each control area for which it exists. This function is called **imbedding**. The purpose of this is to improve processing performance by minimizing arm movement. This is especially helpful when records are retrieved sequentially, in which case VSAM utilizes the sequence set to determine the logical sequence of the file. When this option is selected, the sequence set records will automatically be replicated as many times as they will fit on the first track of a CA. This causes a reduction of **rotational delay** time. Rotational delay is the time required for a given record to move from where it is to the read/write head. Naturally, the more often a record is reproduced on a given track, the less time is required for it to be in position for a read or write operation.

Another option which is user selected is **replication**. This technique allows the KSDS index CIs to be repeated as many times as will fit on a track. This option operates in the same manner as was discussed for the sequence set imbed option; however, the records will not be placed in the data control area as is the case in the imbed option. Both options may be selected for use with the same data set. The tradeoffs are speed versus space. Sometimes you will encounter situations in which all of the available space within a control area is required for data. In this case you would not specify imbed.

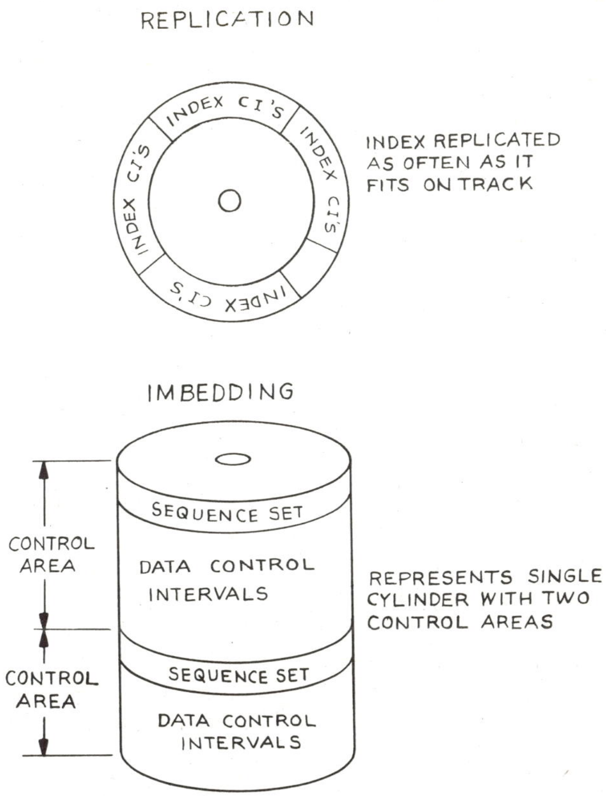

Figure 4.4 Imbedding and replication.

4.4 I/O BUFFERING CONSIDERATIONS

Since we are discussing certain performance options involving the VSAM index, it is a good time to discuss I/O buffering.

The user can specify the amount of memory that VSAM must set aside for the processing of records. The processing of a KSDS involves the use of buffer space for both the index and data CI components of a cluster. The amount of space allocated for I/O buffering can be specified in one of three ways:

Through JCL (OS)
Through the Access Methods DEFINE command
Through parameters specified in the Access Method Control Block (ACB)

If you do not specify any buffer space, VSAM dynamically assigns a space large enough to contain two data CIs and one index CI (if the file is indexed). Any buffer space you allocate beyond this will be utilized for index control intervals. If enough space is made available, the entire index set could be brought into main storage, thereby minimizing access to disk which, in turn, improves record retrieval time. You must decide which of the two is more important to you: memory or DASD space.

4.5 THE ALTERNATE INDEX

Up to this point the discussion on the VSAM index has been centering on the KSDS **base** (prime) index. Although only a KSDS file can contain a base index, both KSDS and ESDS can have an **alternate index**. An RRDS cannot have an index of any kind.

The main function of an alternate index is to allow the accessing of records contained in a particular data component (Figure 4.5) through a key which can be based on *any* field in the record. Multiple indices to the same data component can be defined and maintained by VSAM.

An alternate index (**AIX**) is actually a KSDS cluster containing both index and data components. Prime indices do not contain a data component. The data component of the alternate index contains pointers to the base data component of the KSDS cluster. The pointers used by the AIX data cluster come in two formats: for a KSDS data set the pointers contained therein are actual prime index keys, whereas the pointers used for an ESDS cluster are RBAs. Another feature that makes the AIX different from the prime KSDS index is that keys in an AIX can *optionally* be duplicated or **NONUNIQUE**, while in the prime index they cannot.

4.6 THE CONCEPT OF PATH

Since an AIX is essentially a KSDS, it can be accessed directly as if it were a standard KSDS cluster. When used in this manner the data component of the AIX can be accessed like the data component of any cluster. In order to indicate to VSAM that we wish to access records in alternate key sequence rather than the AIX itself, we must use Access Method Services to DEFINE a **PATH** through the AIX to the base cluster. By using a defined PATH, an application program can access a file through an AIX in a *natural* manner such as is the case when access to a KSDS is done through the prime index.

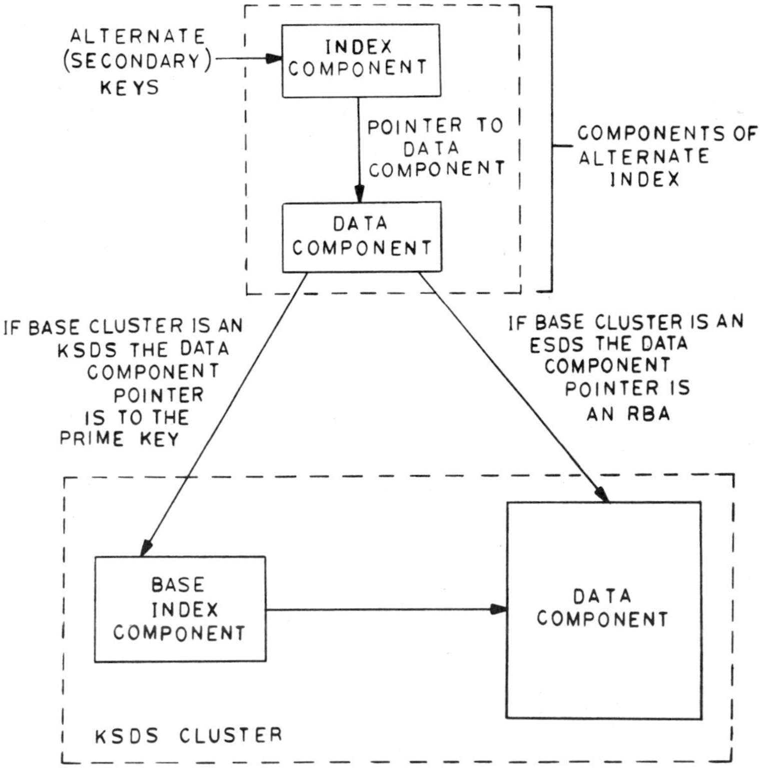

Figure 4.5 The alternate index.

4.7 ACCESSING AN ESDS FILE

Although an ESDS can optionally utilize an AIX, it is not commonly done. The normal use of an ESDS is the storing and subsequent retrieval of sequentially written records. The ESDS cluster, although called a cluster, consists of only a data component. Along with adding to and retrieving from an ESDS data set, records can also be updated **in place**. The ability to physically delete records, although available in both the KSDS and RRDS methods, is *not* available with an ESDS data set. If you wish to delete an ESDS record, it must be done logically. This could be accomplished by reserving a **status byte** somewhere in the record. If you wanted to delete this record, you could do so logically by placing a '**D**', for instance, in the status byte, or by some other similar method. This is the way it is often handled in other access methods.

One aspect of ESDS that *could* be viewed as an asset is the fact that as long as the data set is not reorganized, the RBA for each record remains static. This could be used to access the ESDS data set through some random access scheme. If you were to retrieve a record by its RBA, it would be handled similarly to the method used when accessing by key except that the key in this instance would be a four-byte field containing the RBA as a binary value. When computing an RBA, be sure you keep in mind that the entire control interval must be taken into account and not just the size of the data records.

4.8 RECORD RETRIEVAL UNDER RRDS

The retrieval of records in an RRDS is similar to that of an ESDS when using an RBA. In this case the argument field is also a four-byte field; however, instead of using the RBA which is *not* an available option in the RRDS method, the argument value is the **relative record number** (**RRN**), also specified as a binary value. The first record in a file is designated as being RRN 1, the second is RRN 2, the third RRN 3, and so on. Like a KSDS, records can be deleted, updated, or added.

4.9 SUMMARY OF VSAM ACCESS METHODS

Let us now summarize the three options of file access available through VSAM and the advantages each affords.

4.9.1 SUMMARY OF KSDS FUNCTIONS

Of the three methods available, KSDS (The Key Sequenced Data Set Method) option is by far the most important. Indeed, almost all the resources of VSAM are utilized in supporting this option. To state it plainly, without the KSDS method there would be no VSAM. The following summarize most of the options found in **KSDS/VSAM**:

Access can be both random and sequential
Variable length records are permitted
Access to the data by a base index
Access to the data by alternate indices
Record deletions permitted and space regained
Allocation of freespace

Access by a logical key (e.g., part number)
Access by RBA permitted
Access by relative record number not allowed
Spanned records allowed
Record RBA can change with file activity

4.9.2 SUMMARY OF ESDS FUNCTIONS

The records found in an ESDS (Entry Sequenced Data Set Method) are stored in the same physical sequence in which they were first written. This method operates very much like the non-VSAM Sequential Access Method (SAM). Records cannot be deleted and, for that reason, neither can space be reused as is the case with the other VSAM methods. New records cannot be inserted within the body of the data set itself; they can only be added at the end. Records are added in chronological order.

The entry sequenced method cannot have a base index, but can utilize an alternate index as in the case of the KSDS method. Data records can **span** control intervals (discussed in Chapter 5).

When adding records to the ESDS data set, VSAM returns the records' RBA to you. You can later use this RBA to access the data set randomly. ESDS can be useful in those applications where the order of records is not important, but data collection is.

The following summarizes certain VSAM functions and how they apply to **ESDS**:

Access primarily sequential; random access permitted only by the record RBA
Variable length records are permitted
Cannot have a base index
Optional alternate indices can be built
Physical record deletion is not available
CI/CA freespace cannot be allocated
Access by RBA permitted
No access by relative record number
Spanned records allowed
Record RBA remains static

4.9.3 SUMMARY OF RRDS FUNCTIONS

RRDS (Relative Record Data Set Method), the latest addition to the VSAM method family, was added to allow greater flexibility in random record processing. Accessing a record by a record key under KSDS involves index searches. The only alternative available is record access by RBA which could be complicated. This factor can sometimes make the RRDS method an attractive alternative.

RRDS allows very fast access to data through the use of a relative record number (RRN). The RRDS is basically a file comprised of control intervals that contain **slots** in which records can be placed. Each slot has a unique number (RRN) that identifies that particular slot number.

A slot may be empty or occupied by a record. The actual number of records contained within a CI is a function of the CI size and the record slot size. The user can choose the size of the slots that will contain the records.

Records in a RRDS can be deleted, and the space reused. An RRDS cannot have an alternate index nor can it contain spanned records since all the slots in the CI are of a fixed size. The only random access available is by the RRN. Sequential access is permitted; in this mode unoccupied slots are skipped over during sequential retrieval operations.

The following summarizes certain VSAM options and how they apply to the **RRDS** method:

Access primarily random; sequential access also permitted
Fixed length records only
Cannot have a base index
Cannot have an alternate index
Record deletions permitted and space regained
CI/CA freespace cannot be allocated
No data access by logical key, as in KSDS
Access by RBA not permitted
Access by relative record number is the only random access method available
Spanned records not permitted
No RBA processing of any kind permitted

TEST YOUR UNDERSTANDING

1. What is KSDS freespace? What are the two kinds of freespace?
2. Name the two types of VSAM index. How are they physically different?

3. What is the minimum number of levels for an index?
4. What is a sequence set? How is it used by VSAM?
5. Explain what is meant by key compression.
6. How are imbedding and replication used?
7. What is a PATH?
8. What method of random retrieval is available for RRDS?
9. How can ESDS records be deleted?
10. Can *all* VSAM file types be accessed by RBA?

chapter **5**

FILE PROCESSING USING VSAM

5.1 PROCESSING TECHNIQUES FOR VSAM DATA SETS

There are three distinct **modes** in which VSAM can operate. The individual responsible for writing the programs that use VSAM data sets must be fully aware of the particular method being used before coding a program. The programming techniques used to update one VSAM type is usually not valid for another type. The term **update** is used here to mean any processing in which records are added, deleted, or changed in a VSAM file. On the following pages each of the VSAM methods is discussed, as well as the unique processing characteristics of each.

5.2 ESDS PROGRAMMING CONSIDERATIONS

If you are considering the **ESDS** method, be sure you keep in mind the following:

1. When making file additions, any records **added** will be placed at the end of the data sheet.

2. Records cannot be physically deleted. The structure of the data set remains static throughout its life. If records are to be **deleted**, they must be deleted **logically**. This can be done by placing some indicator in the record that signals to the program that, although present physically, the record should be treated as though it does not exist.

3. Records can be **updated** in place. This can be done either sequentially, as records are being read, or randomly, by accessing the record through its RBA. In either case after **reading** the record it is rewritten to the file.

4. If an alternate index exists, records can be retrieved by a **key** such as a part-number and subsequently updated. The processing in this case is identical to that in which the record is accessed by its RBA. Records added using an AIX will cause VSAM to place an **entry** for that record in its alternate index.

5. If you run out of DASD space when adding records, VSAM will attempt to allocate additional space, providing the option was planned for when the data set was initially defined.

6. Records in an ESDS file can be **spanned**; that is, they can actually be broken up in such a way that the first part of a record will be located in a control interval which is different from the last.

5.3 RRDS PROGRAMMING CONSIDERATIONS

The **RRDS** method presents an entirely different set of rules that require consideration by the programmer:

1. Programs randomly adding records to a data set must supply VSAM with a Relative Record Number (RRN). The RRN is used to point VSAM to a **slot** in which the record is to be added. If VSAM finds the slot vacant, the record is placed in that slot. If the slot is already occupied, VSAM will present a status condition to the program that indicates that the add operation was unsuccessful.

2. Programs may add records *sequentially* to an RRDS file. In this case, as records are added they are placed in the vacant slot adjacent to and higher than the previously used slot. In other words, they are added sequentially into these slots.

3. Records can be physically deleted. When this occurs the space used in that slot now becomes available again. Control information contained in the CIDF and RDF indicates to VSAM that the slot is either free or occupied.

4. Records are **changed** in an RRDS by first supplying VSAM with a RRN. After processing the record, the program then rewrites it. The record formerly in that slot is now replaced. The RRN is a four-byte binary value.

5. RRDS records cannot be **spanned**. This is because each slot in an RRDS is of a fixed length for each RRN. For any given RRDS, VSAM knows the length of the control interval and the size of a physical record. A simple mathematical calculation is all that is needed for VSAM to compute the location of any record. This capability could not exist if records were spanned.

6. No indexing capability of any kind is available for RRDS files.

7. If the program presents VSAM with an RRN that is outside the boundary of the initial **extent** allocation, VSAM will attempt to acquire additional space at the end of the data set. This is dependent upon whether the data set was defined to VSAM with this option.

5.4 KSDS PROGRAMMING CONSIDERATIONS

Without a doubt, the choice for most VSAM applications will be the **KSDS** method.

1. Records can be added to a KSDS file by presenting VSAM the record key. Records can also be added to reserved and unused spaces.

2. Records added to a file can be subsequently retrieved either by key or RBA.

3. When inserting, VSAM will attempt to place added records next to sequentially adjacent records in an existing CI. If no room is available in that CI, a **control interval split** will take place in order to satisfy the need to store the new record (more about this later).

4. Records can be physically deleted. When this occurs, the space occupied previously by these records is made available for future additions.

5. To update a records contents, you can identify the record to VSAM by specifying either its key or its RBA.

6. A base index is always present and maintained by VSAM for a KSDS file.

7. Alternate indices can also be utilized. As an option, they may be updated whenever new records are added to the data set. This is an option you can request VSAM to perform at DEFINE time.

8. Records in a KSDS file can be spanned.

As far as the ESDS and RRDS methods are concerned, not much else can be said about them. If you have any prior data processing experience at all, you will no doubt find many similarities between ESDS and SAM (The Sequential Access Method), and RRDS and DAM (The Direct Access Method). Both of these, ESDS and RRDS, are fairly straightforward and simple to comprehend. It is the KSDS method that is the most complex. Since, however, it is also the VSAM method used in the majority of cases, every effort must be made to understand it in its entirety.

The one item that most clearly separates KSDS from the others is the way in which VSAM adds records to a KSDS file. In the case of an ESDS or RRDS file, VSAM will add a new record at the end of the data set (ESDS) or into an existing slot (RRDS), respectively. KSDS uses neither of these methods.

In the last chapter we discussed how the KSDS method allows us to reserve some **freespace** during the file load, or later, using sequential mass-insertion. This freespace can be in the CI, the CA, or both. You will find that even though freespace is optional, most KSDS files will have been defined with some. In the examples being discussed we assume that some space is present.

5.4.1 ADDING RECORDS TO A KSDS DATA SET

Figure 5.1 illustrates a typical KSDS file. For the purpose of clarity we show only one control area with its index pointers.

When adding records to a file, VSAM/KSDS will first search the index for the control interval in which the record should be placed. The search for this begins at the highest level index and proceeds downward until reaching the proper sequence set entry.

If you recall, each of the entries in the sequence set CI contains one entry per CI in the data control area. The entries in the second level index each point to a data control area. In the highest level index record, the entries point to the index CIs for the level below it. There is one entry for each CI being pointed to.

The pointers contained in these entries are based upon keys found in the data component. Each sequence set entry contains the value of the highest key found in the CI to which it points. The next higher level index entry contains the value of the highest key found in the control area.

When VSAM is requested to add a record to a KSDS file it begins its search at the top of the index. The key of the record to be added is matched against the keys found in each index level entry. When a high condition occurs, VSAM will then descend to the next lower level to

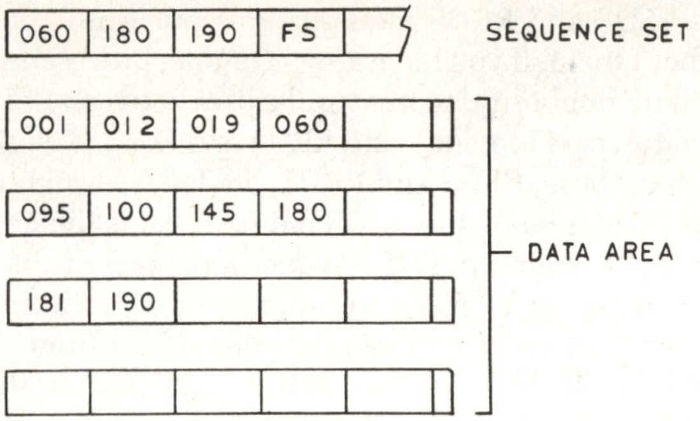

(a)

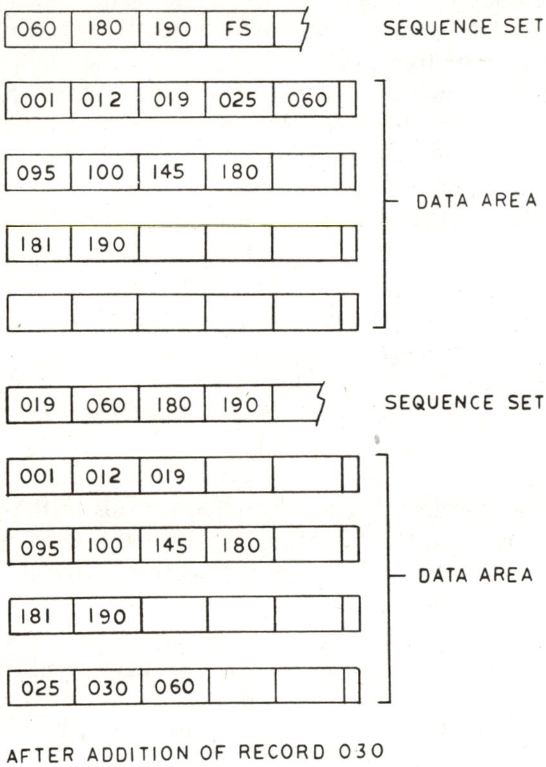

(b)

Figure 5.1 (*a*) Typical KSDS data set before record additions. (*b*) Cluster after addition of record 025 and 030. (*c*) After addition of record 110. (*d*) Control area split after addition of 111.

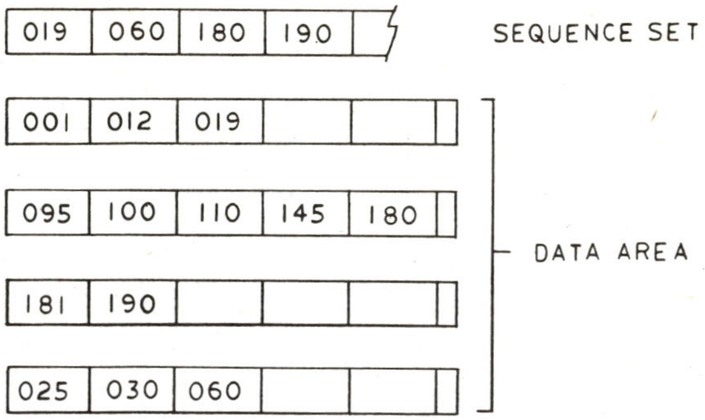
019 060 180 190
SEQUENCE SET
001 012 019
095 100 110 145 180
181 190
025 030 060
DATA AREA

(c)

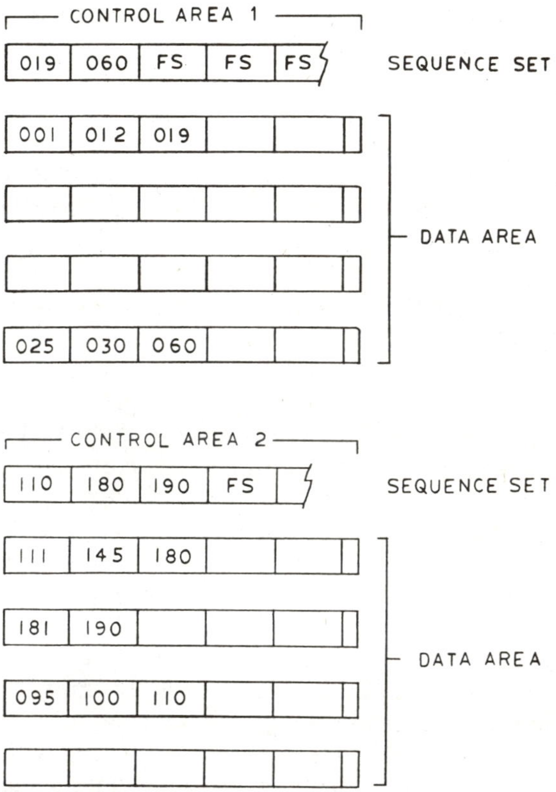
CONTROL AREA 1
019 060 FS FS FS
SEQUENCE SET
001 012 019
025 030 060
DATA AREA
CONTROL AREA 2
110 180 190 FS
SEQUENCE SET
111 145 180
181 190
095 100 110
DATA AREA

(d)

continue the search. VSAM will continue to descend whenever it encounters a **high** condition.

In this manner the proper data control interval is found in which the record should be placed. It is not until VSAM actually examines the CIDF field that it will know for sure whether space is really available in this CI. As long as room exists in the control interval, VSAM will insert a record into its proper position within the CI according to key sequence. Records will be shifted to the right into the freespace area in order to make room for it. This shifting operation will change the RBAs of the records shifted.

What happens if VSAM finds that there is no room in a CI to add a new record? If this occurs, VSAM initiates what is called a **control interval split**. This does not mean that VSAM divides a CI into two parts. Rather, what VSAM does is to move some of the records in the control interval into an empty control interval.

5.4.2 THE DIRECT AND SEQUENTIAL MODES OF INSERT

The exact manner in which a CI split is performed is dependent upon the **insert mode** in which VSAM was running. There are two insert modes: **direct** and **sequential**.

5.4.3 THE CONTROL INTERVAL SPLIT—DIRECT INSERT

In the **direct insert mode** VSAM will move approximately half the records in the CI to another empty CI. The rightmost records will be moved into the new CI. The record is then added into the CI in which it belongs, in its proper sequential order. The corresponding sequence set entries are then adjusted to reflect the changed CIs. If the record addition does not result in a CI split, no sequence set adjustment need be made.

An example of direct insert is shown beginning in Figure 5.1*a*. The illustration shows a control area containing control intervals with freespace. There is enough freespace to contain at least one additional record (the first two CIs) and a CI that is totally empty.

Let us examine what would happen if we were to add three records to this file with keys of 025, 030, and 110. Beginning with the addition of record 025, VSAM searches the index down to the sequence set until it finds a **high** key. This happens immediately since 060 is greater than 025. This causes VSAM to look in the control interval in the data area that contains the 060 record in order to determine if there is any freespace. Since in this case freespace already exists in the CI, all VSAM has to do is shift record 060 to the right and insert record 025. The CIDF will be updated to show that the CI freespace has been reduced by the size of the record. In our example there remains no additional freespace in this CI for record additions (see Figure 5.1*b*). The sequence set entry need not be updated since the highest key in the CI (060) has not changed. The **RBA** for record 060 *has* changed, however.

Let us now add record 030. VSAM once again searches for the CI in which the addition should take place. VSAM once again arrives at the same CI. This time, however, there is no freespace in the CI. This causes VSAM to search the sequence set to determine if an **empty** CI exists in the same control area. VSAM now discovers that the last CI in our example is completely empty. VSAM now performs what is called a **control interval split**.

Look at Figure 5.1*c*. Because the insertion mode is direct, VSAM removes approximately half the right-most records to the empty CI. The record being added (030) is now placed in its proper position within the previously empty CI. The sequence set entries must be updated to reflect the changes that took place in the control area. Although there is still an entry for record 060, it now points to a new CI. A new entry is added to the sequence set to point to the control interval ending with record 019.

VSAM now adds record 110 to the data set. Because CI freespace already exists, VSAM handles the update in the same manner in which it was handled for record 025 (Figure 5.1*d*).

Now let us *really* cause some trouble! Let us add record 111 to the file. VSAM now finds that it cannot add this record to the control interval in which it belongs. It now attempts to locate an **empty** CI within that control area. Because we used the last entry when adding record 030, VSAM cannot find an empty CI in which to perform a control interval split. What happens now?

All hope is not lost. Enter the **control area split**!

5.4.4 THE CONTROL AREA SPLIT—DIRECT INSERT

Another of the VSAM functions that make KSDS unique is the **control area split**. A CA split functions very much like the CI split that occurred during our sample record insertion.

When a direct insertion mode CA split must be performed, VSAM moves the data from approximately half the control intervals in the control area to a new control area located at the end of the data set (see Figure 5.1*d*). In most cases the space allocated during initial file creation is greater than that needed to hold all the data. This unused space can be later drawn upon to place new control areas that might be created by file updates. If no unused space exists, VSAM can dynamically allocate space if it was chosen as an option when the data set was defined.

5.4.5 THE SEQUENTIAL INSERTION MODE

Up until this point we have been discussing the concept of CI and CA splits using **direct insertion**. Let us now review how CI/CA splits work when operating in **sequential insertion mode**.

One major difference between the direct and sequential insert modes has to do with freespace. When we add records to a KSDS file using sequential insertion mode, **VSAM will maintain the freespace requirements we requested when the cluster was defined**. In order to simplify matters, in the example that follows we do not concern ourselves with maintaining freespace; we assume a freespace requirement of (0,0), in other words, no freespace.

5.4.6 CONTROL INTERVAL SPLITS—SEQUENTIAL INSERTION MODE

Let us observe what happens to our file in Figure 5.2*a* when we add records 23 and 110. As you can see, since space was available in the CI in both cases, the records were merely integrated into the proper CIs, in their correct sequential order. No CI splits take place, nor does the sequence set need updating. Figure 5.2*b* shows the results of the insert.

We now add records 13, 14, and 15 (one at a time, of course). After locating the proper CI in which to place these records, VSAM discovers that there is not enough space in the CI to contain even one of them. A CI split must therefore take place.

CI splits work a little differently in the sequential insertion mode than in the direct mode. When a CI split takes place in this mode, instead of VSAM automatically moving records from the halfway point of the current CI into a new CI, VSAM will move the records into a new control interval *from the point of insertion*. Since records 13, 14, and 15 fit between record 1 and 18 (Figure 5.2*c*), records 18 through 60 which make up the remainder of the CI are moved into a new CI. The idea behind this is the assumption that further sequential additions are likely to be made in this same area when in sequential insert mode.

This method therefore provides freespace in the place where it is most likely to be required. Another difference using this mode is that VSAM determines whether the record being inserted is at the end of the CI. If it is, this record and records following sequentially will go into a new CI.

5.4.7 CONTROL AREA SPLITS—THE SEQUENTIAL INSERTION MODE

A CA split under the sequential insertion mode operates exactly like its CI split counterpart. If the insert is not in the last CI of a control area, all CIs after the split are moved to a new CA (see Figure 5.2*d*). If the insert is to take place at the end of the last CI in a CA, the inserted record is placed into the new CA. This is essentially how a load or mass-insert operation works.

5.4.8 MORE ON CI/CA SPLITS

Up until this point, the discussion has revolved around record insertions. This helped to simplify the discussion. Under the KSDS method records can be variable in length. The size of a record can be modified during normal processing. If the rewritten record is larger than what was retrieved, there may not be enough freespace within the CI to contain it. This condition can also cause a CI split. Along with everything else, be sure to take this into consideration when planning a KSDS data set.

One more item needs to be stressed in our discussion of CI/CA splits. Excessive CI splits can dramatically slow down the processing time required to run a job. If this occurs during the operation of an online system, it could be very irritating to your users. If CA splits occur as well, the system may turn out to be unacceptable to the operations department as well as to the users.

Beginning in Chapter 7, a VSAM utility called **Access Methods Services** (**AMS**) is discussed. One of the functions provided by AMS is the **LISTCAT** facility. This facility can provide you with some very useful statistics about the well-being of your data set. Be sure to check this report periodically; it contains a gold mine of information. One of the most important things to check is whether any CA or CI splits have occurred, and if so, how many. Since every application is different, you will have to be the judge as to what levels of performance are tolerable.

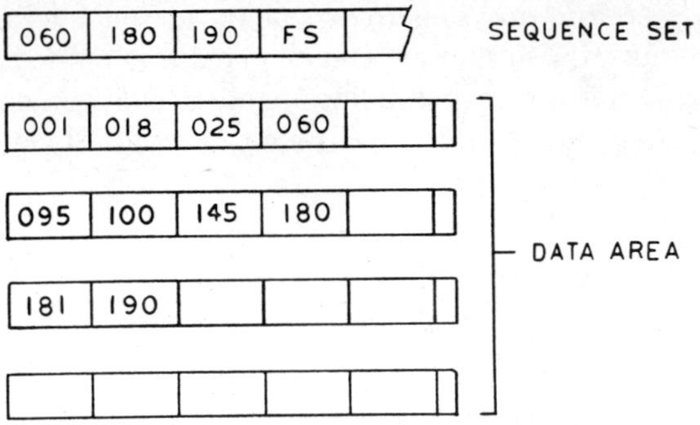

(a)

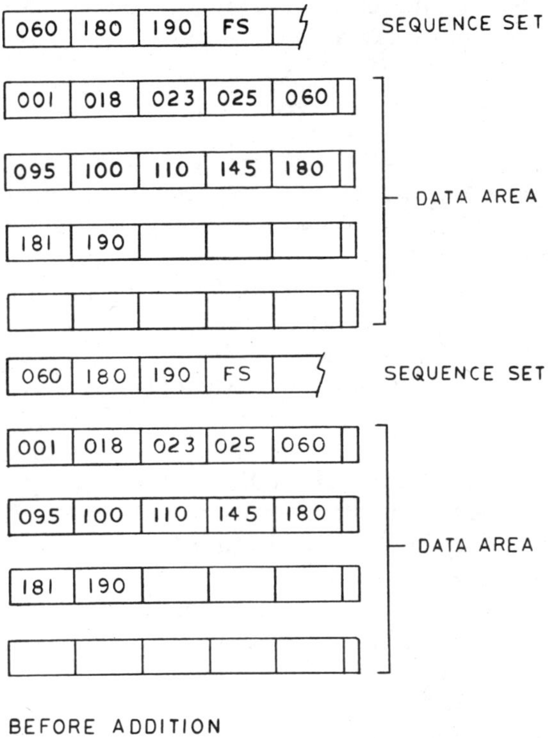

(b)

Figure 5.2 (*a*) Cluster before addition of records 23 and 110. (*b*) Results of insertion of records 23 and 110. (*c*) Insertion of records 13–15. (*d*) CA split after addition of record 111.

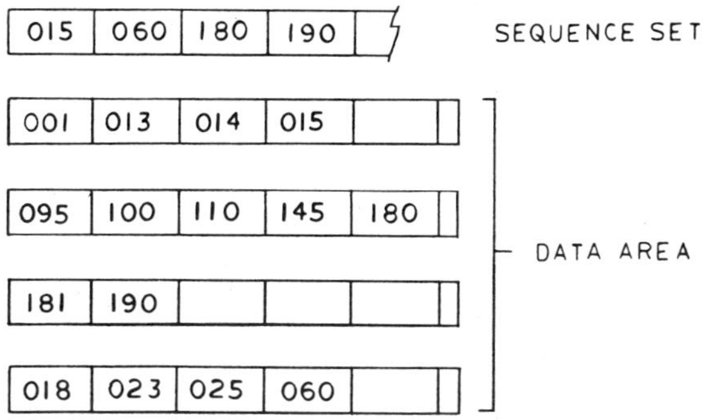
015 060 180 190
SEQUENCE SET
001 013 014 015
095 100 110 145 180
181 190
018 023 025 060
DATA AREA

(c)

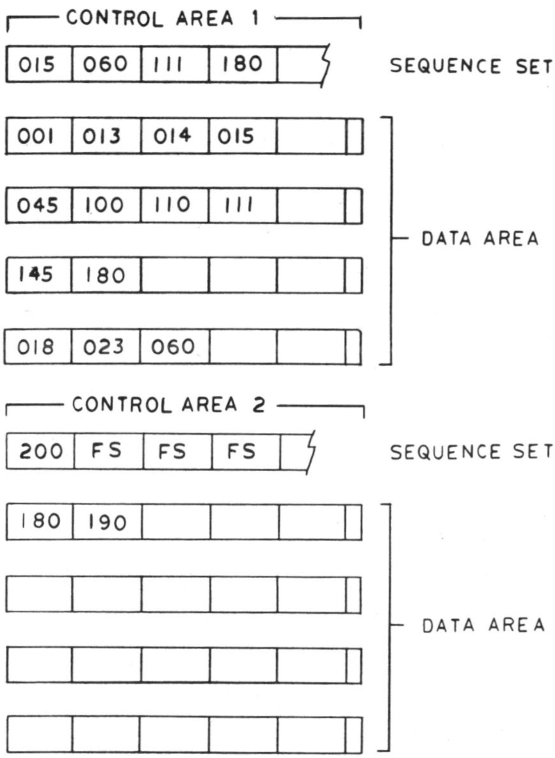
CONTROL AREA 1
015 060 111 180
SEQUENCE SET
001 013 014 015
045 100 110 111
145 180
018 023 060
DATA AREA
CONTROL AREA 2
200 FS FS FS
SEQUENCE SET
180 190
DATA AREA

(d)

TEST YOUR UNDERSTANDING

1. What are some things that distinguish the KSDS method from others?
2. What is a control interval split?
3. What is the difference between the direct and sequential insertion methods?
4. How is the index searched during an addition or retrieval operation?
5. Can anything besides a record addition cause a control interval split? Why?
6. Explain the control area split.
7. What are the similarities between CI and CA splits?

chapter 6

The VSAM Catalog and Data Spaces

6.1 THE CONCEPT OF THE CATALOG

The concept of the **catalog** has been around for a long time. Even before the introduction of VSAM, the use of a catalog was well established at OS installations. The catalog capability of VSAM offers major advantages for DOS VSAM users who heretofore had *no* similar capabilities whatsoever. The VSAM catalog is a special-purpose file residing on DASD. Its main function is to serve as a central repository for information about all the data sets and data spaces under its control.

6.1.1 WHAT THE CATALOG CONTROLS

Information maintained about data sets includes the following.

1. Name and physical location of data sets.
2. Security password information required for access to protected data sets.

3. Statistics about the data set: for example, the number of records read, added, deleted, and other information such as the number of records in the file, the number of CI/CA splits, and so forth. The information you view when you run an Access Methods Services LISTCAT comes from the catalog.
4. Information about the data records themselves: the record sizes, key length, and location, the type of data set (KSDS/ESDS/RRDS), and other information.
5. The physical **extents** of data sets.
6. Location of the **Catalog Recovery Area** (CRA), if present.

Information is also provided in the catalog about data spaces. This includes information such as device characteristics, and the type and physical location of data space.

Entries can be **defined** and information kept in the catalog for each of the following:

Aliases*
Alternate indices
Catalog Recovery Areas
Clusters (including data and index areas)
CVOLS*
Generation Data Groups*
Non-VSAM data sets
Pagespace*
Paths
Space
User catalogs

Some of the more specialized entries are discussed in Chapters 9 and 10.

6.1.2 THE MASTER CATALOG

There are two kinds of catalogs: the **master** catalog and the **user** catalog. Every VSAM installation requires a master catalog. Only **one** master catalog can be connected to the system. The master catalog may point

* This function is not available under VSE.

to individual data sets and spaces; it can also point to **user** catalogs (see Figure 6.1).

In an OS/MVS installation the VSAM master catalog also doubles as the **System** catalog (see Figure 6.1). It can also contain pointers to non-VSAM catalogs called CVOLs (Control Volumes).

In OS/VS1 the System catalog cannot be the same as the VSAM master catalog. Under this operating system the System catalog **points** to the VSAM master catalog.

Under DOS/VS or VSE there is no such thing as a System catalog. The VSAM catalog is the *only* catalog that exists under DOS.

6.1.3 USER CATALOGS

There can be any number of user catalogs. User catalogs can contain the same type of information that a master catalog can contain with

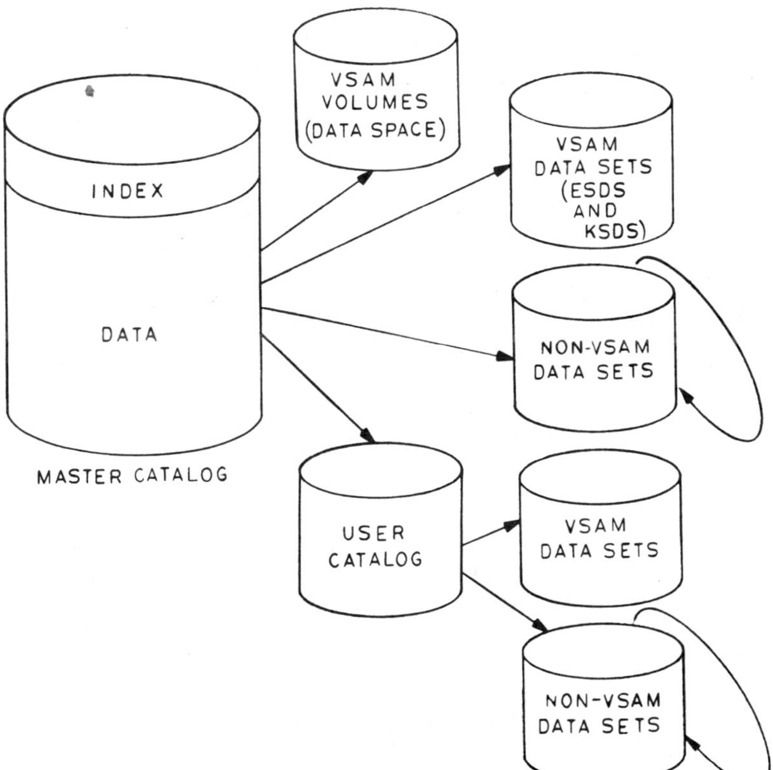

Figure 6.1 Master and user catalog.

the exception that it cannot utilize entries pointing to another catalog. The format of a master and a user catalog is identical. *They are both KSDS data sets* and as such contain both index and data components.

6.1.4 THE CATALOG STRUCTURE

The index component of a catalog has entries containing pointer information for data sets and data spaces under its control. These pointers point to entries in the data component. The keys themselves are either the 44-byte (maximum) names of components (i.e., clusters) or a volume serial number key. The volume serial key is used to point to owned volumes. This is especially important when a CRA is used. Control intervals in the catalog are always 512 bytes. Furthermore, the concept of a control area is not used in the catalog.

The data component of the catalog consists of entries describing the data sets and volumes. This information is made up of physical data set and data space information such as the physical location of data sets and the location of available freespace.

Access to data sets and data spaces can only be made through a master or user catalog.

6.1.5 THE ADVANTAGES OF THE USER CATALOG

Entries describing data sets can be made in *either* the master catalog or in a user catalog. If, however, all the entries for data sets and data spaces are made in the master catalog, two problems can present themselves, one minor and the other major.

The minor problem presents itself at file allocation time. If all the entries for the installation are in the master catalog, additional system overhead will be incurred as partitions or regions contend for access to the master catalog for data set or data space information. Every time a data set is opened, closed, or dynamically expanded, the master catalog must be accessed. This multiplied by the number of partitions or regions requiring one of these operations could, of course, degrade the overall performance of the system.

The major problem might occur when a master catalog becomes damaged. This could occur if there were a physical failure on a DASD device such as a head crash. In most cases it is caused by a hardware failure (such as a machine-check), a software failure, or an operator **IPL** that occurred while the catalog was being updated.

A damaged master catalog at an installation that only uses a master catalog is an extremely serious problem. Remember that access to VSAM data sets is *only* through a VSAM catalog. This might very well mean the loss of all of the installation's VSAM data sets if there has been little or no prior **disaster** planning. Even under the best of circumstances it might take days to totally re-create all the VSAM objects involved, even if backup were available.

To minimize the likelihood of problems such as this occurring, the user catalog is used extensively at most installations. In most instances each volume containing VSAM data sets or spaces will contain a user catalog. In other words, one volume, one catalog. Only one user catalog may reside on a volume (1). The user catalog, however, *could* control any number of volumes besides the one on which it resides. If a user catalog is damaged, only those volumes controlled by that particular catalog are affected. If the data sets on those volumes have been backed up, only a few steps need to be taken to rebuild the volume.

In Chapter 11 on **disaster recovery** we discuss the specifics involved in recovering from failures such as those described. We also discuss the advance planning that must take place in order to recover successfully from such failures.

6.2 UNIQUE AND SUBALLOCATED DATA SPACES

All VSAM objects require space, including catalogs. There are two kinds of VSAM data spaces. Data spaces can be defined as either **Unique** or **Suballocated**. When a data set is defined as **Unique** to VSAM, **only** the cluster being defined can occupy that space. **Nothing else can reside there** (see Figure 6.2). Data spaces defined as **SUBALLOCATED** can contain **any number of data sets**. These data sets may not even be related. Typically, whole volumes are allocated for VSAM use. If the space defined for such volumes is non-Unique, it is treated as a sort of **pool** in which portions could be suballocated as needed. If, for instance, a space has been defined and allocated for 300 cylinders, a later request to suballocate 45 cylinders for a data set will still leave 255 cylinders in the pool which can be used to define other data sets or VSAM objects.

As data sets are added, space is *suballocated* from the initial allocation as needed. It is for this reason that non-Unique space is also referred

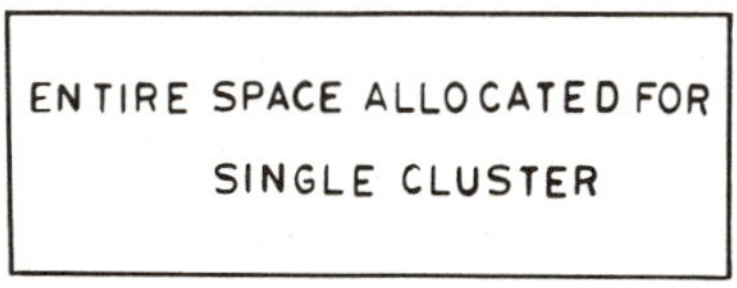

Figure 6.2 The unique data space.

to as **Suballocated**. A VSAM space is then understood to be either UNIQUE or SUBALLOCATED.

When space is allocated for a VSAM catalog, it need not occupy a space by itself. The catalog can be contained within a SUBALLOCATED data space. The rest of the space in the data space could then be used for data sets. If you choose to define a catalog in this manner, it must be defined on a volume at the same time that the first space allocation is made, otherwise the allocation will not work. This is done by using an Access Method Services DEFINE USERCATALOG command. This command causes VSAM to dynamically allocate space on that volume even though space was never before defined.

6.2.1 A SECOND TYPE OF SUBALLOCATION

There is another use for the term **suballocate**. VSAM will dynamically acquire additional space when needed. This can occur at any level. For instance, if a program is in the process of adding records to a file and it runs out of space, VSAM can dynamically acquire more space for it. If the data set exists within a VSAM non-UNIQUE space, VSAM will suballocate additional space from the pool and assign it to that data set. If there is no space to be found, VSAM can acquire additional space on that volume dynamically and assign it to that non-UNIQUE space. If the data set is UNIQUE, additional space can be dynamically acquired from the volume itself as it does in the case of the non-UNIQUE data space (see Figure 6.3).

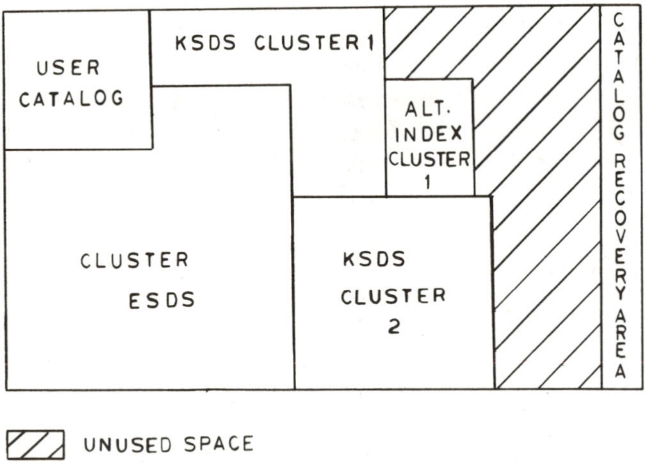

Figure 6.3 The suballocated data space.

The decision as to whether to suballocate additional space dynamically is determined by suballocation parameters given to VSAM when the data sets and data spaces are defined to VSAM through Access Methods Services (AMS).

Regardless of whether a data space is Unique or Suballocated, the volume on which the data space exists is **owned** by a single catalog. When additional space *is* acquired by VSAM the proper entries are made in the catalog to reflect this.

6.3 THE CONCEPT OF VOLUME OWNERSHIP

The very first time that space is defined for a particular volume, it is necessary to specify the catalog with which the space is to be associated. In what might be termed **basic** VSAM, if the object being defined is on a volume that is owned by a user catalog, the object must belong to that user catalog. It is referred to here as **basic** VSAM because this is the version most installations are still using. With VSE/VSAM version 3 and the DF/EF function available under the MVS operating system, objects can be defined on the same volume but belong to different catalogs. This subject is discussed more fully in Chapter 14. The remainder of this discussion is based upon the basic version of VSAM. For each space that has been defined and allocated, VSAM places a corresponding entry in the appropriate catalog. Whenever you try to assign space to a volume VSAM checks to see if the volume is already owned. It will then check the AMS statements you use to define the space to see if the catalog specified in the CATALOG parameter for this space is indeed the catalog that owns this volume.

When a catalog is said to own a volume, all *VSAM* data sets found on that particular volume belong to *that* catalog. There can be no VSAM data sets on a volume that belongs to another catalog.[1] This rule does *not*, however, pertain to non-VSAM data sets. Both VSAM and non-VSAM can occupy the same DASD volume (non-VSAM files cannot be defined within a VSAM space).

How does VSAM know that a volume is owned? It might seem at first that VSAM may determine this by checking the master catalog. However, this information is not in the master catalog. It **is** in one of the user catalogs, however (assuming user catalogs are used). The information indicating to VSAM which catalog is associated with which volume is in that catalog alone. There is no indication on the volume itself exactly as to which catalog owns it. How then does VSAM **know** that a volume is owned if it does not know which catalog owns the volume? It knows this by checking a **bit** field which is located in the **Volume Table of Contents (VTOC) located on the DASD volume.**

6.4 VSAM USE OF THE VOLUME TABLE OF CONTENTS (VTOC)

The VTOC is a non-VSAM file found on *every* DASD volume. Its purpose is to serve as a director with which the operating system can locate both available space and non-VSAM data sets. It is also used to hold entries for VSAM spaces. This allows both VSAM and non-VSAM data management routines to determine how much space is available on a volume and where it is located (see Figure 6.4).

There are several different types of records found in the VTOC. They are called Format-1, Format-2, Format-3, and so on, records. The **format** or type of record in the VTOC is dependent on its function.

The VTOC control record itself is called the Format-4 record. There is only one of these. In this record there are several fields that are used

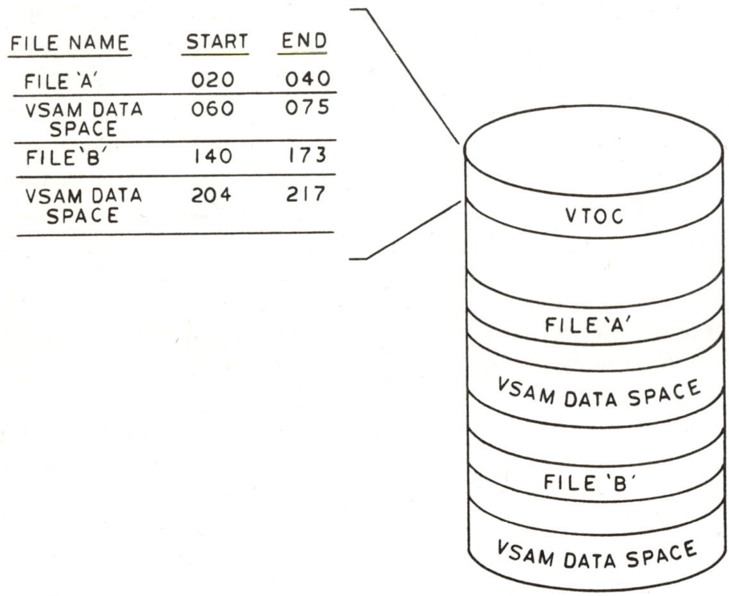

THE VOLUME TABLE OF CONTENTS (VTOC)

Figure 6.4 The volume table of contents.

by VSAM. One of the fields contains a bit called the **ownership bit**. If this bit is set to 1 (on) it means that some catalog owns this volume. There is no indication, however, *which* catalog owns the volume.

The ownership bit is set on in one of two cases: when VSAM space is defined on a particular volume for the first time, or when a volume is defined through Access Method Services as a **CANDIDATE**. When a volume is defined as a **CANDIDATE** it then **belongs** to a particular catalog even though no space may as yet have been assigned. The CANDIDATE function is merely a way in which to earmark a volume as being owned by a particular catalog.

6.4.1 HOW VTOC ENTRIES ARE USED BY VSAM

There is a Format-1 record in the VTOC for each VSAM data space on the volume. This happens to be the same format used for SAM files. An entry will be made for each VSAM space whether it be Unique or Suballocated. In the case of the Suballocated space, although any number of VSAM data sets might reside therein, only a single entry will be made in the VTOC for the entire space. If VSAM later dynamically acquires additional space on this volume, or if space is allocated through Access Methods Services, another VTOC entry for each data space will be added. By the way, if you ever decide to relinquish the space used on a particular volume, you must first delete all the entries for objects on that volume before attempting to delete the space. (VSAM objects are data sets, catalogs, alternate indices, and so forth.)

If the volume contains Unique data sets, an entry will be made for each Unique space as well. In the case of the user-named Unique KSDS data set two entries will be made: one for the index and one for the data component. User-named Unique data sets are those in which the data and index components have been given names in the DEFINE command.

Chances are that if you looked at a listing showing the entries in the VTOC, you would notice some pretty unusual names listed wherever VSAM spaces are located. This is because with the exception of Unique data sets, VSAM dynamically assigns the names it uses for its objects.

6.5 NAMING THE COMPONENTS

VSAM always assigns names to its components. In addition to these names, you may give the components any name you choose when you define a data set through AMS. You may later refer back to these names through AMS or with JCL. These names are recorded in the catalog. These names, however, will not appear in a VTOC unless they happen to be the components of a Unique data set. In this case you will see the exact name you specified for the data component and the index component, when one exists. You will not, however, see the name of the **cluster** you specified to AMS. This entry is kept in the catalog alone. If you have a UNIQUE data set but do not specify names for the index and data components, VSAM will assign a name for each and make the corresponding Format-1 entry for it.

If you ever need to **relate** the name you used to the name VSAM uses, you can do this by looking at an **AMS LISTCAT** report.

VSAM assigns names in order to ensure the integrity of the data. Whenever a data space is defined, an entry is made in both the Format-4 VTOC record for that volume and the catalog controlling that volume. The entries of both are date and time-stamped. Whenever you try to access a VSAM data set, VSAM first checks to see if these entries **match** (are in synch). If the volume's time-stamp is earlier than the catalogs, the volume is considered **down-level**. VSAM will not open a **down-level** data set.

How can a volume be down-level when both the VTOC and the catalog are time-stamped at the same time? The most common reason for this is that a non-VSAM utility program was used to restore the entire contents of a volume, and the data restored was actually an old backup copy. When this happens, the catalog and space date/time stamps no longer match. This renders the combination unusable, since VSAM cannot trust that which took place outside its control.

What does a VSAM-generated name look like? The names generated by VSAM have the following format:

For a data space that contains **Suballocated** objects the format is as follows:

Z999999n.VSAMDSPC.Taaaaaaa.Tbbbbbbb

where:

n = 2 If no catalog resides in this data space.

n = 4 If a user catalog resides in this space.

n = 6 If a master catalog resides in the space.

aaaaaaabbbbbbb is the time-stamp value.

For **Unique** data spaces a VSAM-generated name would look like this:

VSAMDSET.DFDyyddd.Taaaaaaa.Tbbbbbbb

where:

yyddd is the Julian date.
aaaaaaabbbbbbb is the time-stamp value.

Once again this format is used only when the components for a UNIQUE data set are not user-named. In the case of user-named components the index and data components will both appear in a VTOC display with the name given.

While we are discussing bits and bytes you might be interested in the actual location within the VTOC Format-4 record of some of the fields used by VSAM:

Offset	Length	Description
77	8	VSAM timestamp value
85	3	VSAM indicators: *Byte 1* Bit 0 = 1 Volume owned *Byte 2–3* Location of Catalog Recovery area if present
88	8	VSAM time-stamp 2 used by OS only

6.6 THE CATALOG RECOVERY AREA (CRA)

Earlier in this chapter we discussed the problems that might arise if a catalog has been damaged. We did not discuss, however, an option that VSAM makes available to us if we choose to use it, that is, the **Catalog Recovery Area** (**CRA**).

The CRA is essentially a duplicate of the catalog with which it is associated. As entries are made and updated in the catalog, they are also maintained in the CRA. The space used by the CRA is acquired whenever a catalog is defined with that attribute. When you define a catalog with the CRA attribute, remember to allocate enough space for both the catalog and the CRA. If you do not, the DEFINE command will fail.

When space associated with this catalog is later acquired on a new volume, VSAM will also acquire additional space for the CRA. The

CRA, then, is located on all volumes owned by a catalog. The CRA on each volume pertains only to the objects on *that* particular volume.

For the initial allocation of a CRA space, VSAM will assign the equivalent of one cylinder. If space is defined for a Suballocated data space (including a catalog) with the CRA attribute, the space required for the CRA is taken from this allocation. If space is allocated for a Unique data set, the extra area required for the CRA is *added* to the initial allocation made through the DEFINE control statement.

6.6.1 UTILITY FUNCTIONS AVAILABLE WHEN USING THE CRA

If you ever suspect that you might be having catalog problems, you can run the Access Method Services **LISTCRA** report. One of the options of this report is to **COMPARE** the entries of the catalog with those of the CRA. Differences will be highlighted.

If you do find that there are differences between the two, you might want to **reset** the catalog entries to those of the CRA. This can be done with an Access Method Services **RESETCAT** command. The RESETCAT command forces the catalog entries to agree with the information in the CRA. You should also run this if your catalog is inaccessible; it just might save the day! See Chapters 10 and 11 for more information on the RESETCAT command.

Another option available to you if you use a CRA is the AMS **EXPORTRA**. This function allows you to copy (**EXPORT**) the data set to a tape or disk volume. Without this backup, you might not be able to get to your data if the catalog becomes inaccessible. The copy can later be restored by means of the AMS **IMPORTRA** command.

You should now be able to see clearly the value in having a Catalog Recovery Area. Just why one would define catalogs without this option is hard to understand. As far as I am concerned, the CRA should *not* be optional under VSAM.

Up until this point we have been making references to the VSAM utility known as Access Method Services, and certain of the commands. In the next chapter we begin discussing these functions in detail.

NOTES

1. For plain vanilla VSAM there can only be one catalog per volume and only one catalog can own space on that volume. This is now changing in VSE/VSAM and the ICF Facility. These facilities are discussed in Chapter 14.

TEST YOUR UNDERSTANDING

1. What is the purpose of a catalog?
2. What are some of the benefits of using user catalogs?
3. Explain the difference between UNIQUE and SUBALLOCATED.
4. How does VSAM make use of the VTOC?
5. What is volume ownership?
6. What is the value in having a Catalog Recovery Area?

chapter 7

ACCESS METHOD SERVICES—BASIC FUNCTIONS

7.1 ACCESS METHOD SERVICES

Access Method Services (**AMS**) is the name collectively given to those utility functions that support VSAM. Using these functions, data sets and data spaces are **DEFINED**, **ALTERED**, and **DELETED**. Data sets can be **REPRO**duced, **ALTERNATE INDEX**es built and objects can be **LIST**ed.

All of these functions and many more are actually performed by the Access Method Services program called **IDCAMS**. **IDCAMS** is the name you place in the EXEC JCL card whenever you wish to invoke **AMS**.

In this chapter we begin to study the basic AMS functions that must be used by anyone responsible for the definition and maintenance of VSAM objects. The functions presented in this chapter and the next are introduced in the order in which they are likely to be used rather than alphabetically as is done in technical reference manuals on the subject. In order to accomplish this, an imaginary environment is introduced in which we have been given responsibility for the installation of an inventory system using VSAM data sets.

7.2 THE SCENARIO

We begin with the following assumptions:

1. Our installation is not currently using VSAM.
2. We will be using VSAM data sets for an inventory system.
3. We will be using user catalogs.
4. We must provide **backup** JCL.
5. A **LISTCAT** will be necessary for weekly review.
6. Reorganization will be required periodically.

In addition to this it will be necessary at times to **PRINT** some records in our VSAM data sets especially during the test phase. We may also find it necessary to **ALTER** some of the options we have selected after **DEFIN**ing them to VSAM.

Occasionally, an application program which is in the process of updating a VSAM data set will abend. When this occurs the VSAM file will not be closed. VSAM will not permit a program to subsequently access that data set while it is in a **not closed** state.[1] In order to continue processing this file, the IDCAMS command **VERIFY** will adjust the catalog entry to adjust various pointers and indicate the data set has been closed. Our JCL must handle this situation when it occurs.

Finally, commands that we can use to modify the execution of an IDCAMS command stream are reviewed. These commands are sometimes referred to as **modal** commands because they change the **mode** or direction of execution. The following represent only some of the modal commands available: **IF**, **THEN**, **ELSE**, **DO**, and **SET**.

7.3 THE LOGICAL STEPS FOR DEFINITION (FIGURE 7.1)

In our example the following standards are followed:

1. Most clusters will use SUBALLOCATED space.
2. Each volume will have its own USERCATALOG.

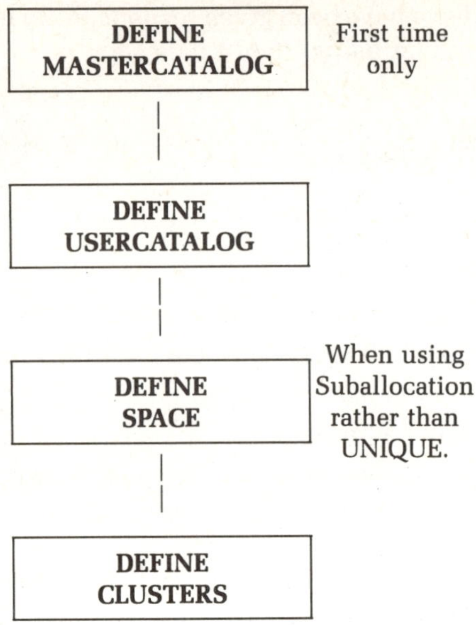

File Creation can now begin.

Figure 7.1 Logical steps to data set definition.

The following COMMANDS or TOPICS are covered in this Chapter and in Chapter 8:

DEFINE MASTERCATALOG
DEFINE USERCATALOG
DEFINE SPACE
DEFINE CLUSTER/INDEX/DATA
REPRO
IMPORT/EXPORT
LISTCAT
DELETE
VERIFY
PRINT
ALTER
MODELS
Modal commands

Beginning here, the commands utilized by Access Method Services to accomplish our task are presented. Each command is shown followed by its parameters. An explanation of each parameter then follows.

7.4 DEFINING THE CATALOG

Because the commands to DEFINE both user and master catalogs are virtually identical, they are both defined here.

COMMAND	PARAMETERS	NOTES
	The following parameters apply to both the index and data components of the catalog.	
DEFINE	**MASTERCATALOG** | **USERCATALOG**	REQ'D
	(	REQ'D
	NAME(catname)	REQ'D
	DEDICATE |	DOS
	CYLINDERS(prime [sec]) |	
	BLOCKS(prime [sec]) |	
	TRACKS(prime [sec])	
	RECORDS(prime [sec])	
	[FILE(jcl-dname)]	R-DOS
	VOLUME(volser no.)	REQ'D
	[ATTEMPTS(number)]	
	[AUTHORIZATION(entrypoint [string])]	
	[BUFFERSPACE(size)]	
	[CLASS(value)]	DOS
	[CODE(code)]	
	[CONTROLPW(password)]	
	[DESTAGEWAIT | NODESTAGEWAIT]	OS
	[EXCEPTIONEXIT (modname)]	
	[FOR(days) | TO(date)]	
	[IMBED | NOIMBED]	
	[MASTERPW(password)]	
	[MODEL(ename [/pass] [cname[/pass]])]	OS
	[ORIGIN(track | block)]	DOS
	[OWNER(owner id)]	
	[READPW(password)]	
	[RECOVERABLE | NOTRECOVERABLE]	
	[UPDATEPW(password)]	
	[WRITECHECK | NOWRITECHECK]	
	)	REQ'D

(Continued on p. 80)

```
COMMAND          PARAMETERS                                        NOTES
------------------------------------------------------------------------
                 The following parameters pertain to the
                 optional DEFINITION of the DATA
                 component.
[DATA
                 (
                 [BUFFERSPACE( size ) ]
                 [CYLINDERS( prime [ sec ] ) ]
                    [BLOCKS( prime [ sec ] ) ]
                    [TRACKS( prime [ sec ] ) ]
                    RECORDS( prime [ sec ] ) ]
                 [DESTAGEWAIT | NODESTAGEWAIT ]                    OS
                 [RECOVERABLE | NOTRECOVERABLE ]
                 [WRITECHECK | NOWRITECHECK ]
                 ) ]

                 The following parameters pertain to the
                 optional DEFINITION of the INDEX
                 component.
[INDEX

                 [BUFFERSPACE( size ) ]
                 [CYLINDERS( prime [ sec ] ) ]
                    [BLOCKS ( prime [ sec ] ) ]
                    [TRACKS( prime [ sec ] ) ]
                    [RECORDS( prime [ sec ] ) ]
                 [DESTAGEWAIT | NODESTAGEWAIT ]                    OS
                 [IMBED | NOIMBED ]
                 [WRITECHECK | NOWRITECHECK ]
                 ) ]
                 CATALOG( catname [/ password][ dname])
```

7.4.1 EXPLANATION OF SYMBOLS

Before continuing, it is necessary to discuss the usage of symbols in the preceding illustration. This will help you to understand the way in which you must code the control statements.

The bracket (**[** and **]**) symbols always appear in sets and are used to denote those parameters/subparameters which are optional. There are some cases, however, where it is necessary to code one of these parameters. This will occur in those cases in which another optional parameter is used which requires this parameter to accompany it.

The | symbol has become a standard data processing symbol to emphasize when a choice must be made between certain items. It is for this reason sometimes referred to as the **OR** symbol.

The parentheses are used to contain the *value* of a given parameter.

Parameters that are underlined are AMS **defaults**. In other words, if not specified, they will be *assumed* by IDCAMS. A "—" (not shown in previous example) at the end of a command or parameter statement denotes continuation of the definition.

REQ'D:

Represents those parameters that must be coded. They are *required*.

R-DOS:

Specifies an item that is used only by the Disk Operating System (DOS/VS or DOS/VSE) and is required by that operating system.

R-OS:

Specifies an item that is used only by the Full Operating System (VS1 or MVS) and is required by that operating system.

DOS:

Specifies an item that is used only by the Disk Operating System (DOS/VS or DOS/VSE) and is optional.

OS:

Specifies an item that is used only by the Full Operating System (VS1 or MVS) and is optional.

EXPLANATION OF PARAMETERS

DEFINE MASTERCATALOG/USERCATALOG:

This AMS command specifies that you wish to **DEFINE** to VSAM the characteristics of either a VSAM MASTER or USER catalog. The term MASTERCATALOG can be abbreviated to **MCAT**; the term USERCATALOG can be abbreviated to **UCAT**. DEFINE can be abbreviated **DEF**.

NAME(catname):

This entry allows you to give a name to the catalog being defined. The name can be up to 44 characters in length and can be any combination of alphabetical characters, numbers, or the special symbols @, #, and $. The name must begin with an alpha character and if longer than eight digits, must be broken into segments of one to eight digits separated by periods. For example:

DEFINE MCAT(MASTER.CATALOG.SYSTEM.A)

DEDICATE: (DOS ONLY)

This parameter specifies that all the unused disk space on the device pointed to with the VOLUME parameter (up to 16 extents) is to be allocated to this catalog. This parameter cannot be specified with the space allocation parameters that follow; they are mutually exclusive. The abbreviation is **DED**.

CYLINDERS/TRACKS/RECORDS/BLOCKS(prime/sec):

This parameter cannot be used in conjunction with the DEDICATE parameter (DOS only) previously described. The purpose of this parameter is twofold: to allocate the primary (prime) space for the catalog and to specify the dynamic secondary (sec) allocation to be made in the event that the primary space allocation becomes exhausted. The space allocation can be specified in either CYLINDERS, TRACKS, RECORDS, or BLOCKS. The first three entries are used for CKD devices. The first two entries are the ones most commonly used, especially CYLINDERS. If you wish to specify the catalog entries in RECORDS, the record size for the catalog entries will be 512 bytes. For FBA devices the allocation must be specified in BLOCKS. The abbreviation for CYLINDERS is **CYL**, TRACKS is **TRK**, RECORDS is **REC**, and BLOCKS is **BLK**.

FILE(jcl-dname):

This parameter is required by DOS only and is used to point to the // DLBL JCL card. The name specified here must match the name specified by the DLBL card. This is used by DOS to establish the beginning and ending extents of the space being DEFINED for the catalog. If more space is defined than is used for the catalog, this space can be used either for catalog expansion or for suballocated data clusters. Be sure you specify at least one cylinder of space for the CRA if it is used. The following illustrates the relationship between the JCL and the FILE (jcl-name):

// DLBL **CATDEF**,'USER.CATALOG.SPACE',,VSAM

FILE(**CATDEF**)

This parameter can also be used in OS environments.

EXCEPTIONEXIT(modname):

This parameter specifies the name of an exit routine written by the user to which control is given whenever an unusual error condition takes place. This is usually an I/O error. This exit routine is Link Edited to your Load (OS) or Core-Image (DOS) library. To find out more about providing this EXIT routine see Chapter 12. This parameter can be abbreviated **EEXT**.

VOLUME(volser no.):

This designates the Volume upon which the catalog is to be placed; **volser no.** is the serial number with which the disk volume was initialized. This parameter is required. It can be abbrevaited **VOL**.

ATTEMPTS(number):

This parameter is used only in those cases where the catalog is password protected. The number of attempts the operator can make before IDCAMS aborts is specified here. If ATTEMPTS(0) is specified, the operator is not allowed to enter a password from a system console. Password protection is discussed in Chapter 12. This parameter can be abbreviated **ATT**.

AUTHORIZATION(entrypoint/string):

This parameter specifies the name of a routine (entrypoint) to which control is passed every time this catalog is accessed. This routine is called a **user exit**. It is usually written by the systems programmer at the installation in which the catalog will be used. For additional information on this subject see Chapter 12. In addition to passing control to the user exit, a character **string** of up to 256 characters in length can also be passed to the routine. The characters passed can be specified as either character or hexadecimal values. See Chapter 12 for more information on this subject. This parameter can be abbreviated **AUTH**. Example:

AUTHORIZATION(CHECKRTN authdata) or
AUTHORIZATION(CHECKRTN X'C1E4E3C8C4C1E3C1')

BUFFERSPACE(size):

This specifies the space to be provided for buffers when the catalog is being used. The amounts that can be specified are 3072, 4096, 5120, 6144, 7168, or 8192. The default is 3072. This parameter can be abbreviated **BUFSP** or **BUFSPC**.

CLASS(value): (DOS ONLY)

This parameter allows you to categorize the VSAM data space according to **class** (0–7). This applies to VSAM space DEFINED either as MCAT, UCAT, or SPACE. The purpose of this function is to allow some control over where data can be placed on a DASD volume, for instance. For those DASD devices that contain both fixed head and movable head capability, VSAM space of class type **1** is usually used for the fixed head area. The common usages are:

CLASS(0)—Common usage area
CLASS(1)—Spaces DEFINED in fixed head area
CLASS(2–7)—User designated

CODE(code):

This parameter is used for those catalogs that are password protected. The designated **code** is used in lieu of the catalog name when prompting the operator for the password. In those instances in which it is not desirable for the operator to know *which* catalog the password is for, specify this parameter. Conceivably, every catalog could have a different password but the same code. See Chapter 12 for more information on this subject.

CONTROLPW(password):

A password can be specified when trying to access the catalog itself as a data cluster using control interval access (remember that the catalog is a KSDS data set). The catalog need not be password protected at all. However, if desired, there are several levels of passwords that can be assigned. The entire subject of passwords is covered in Chapter 12. A discussion on accessing the catalog such as a KSDS is covered in Chapter 14. This parameter can be abbreviated **CTLPW**.

DESTAGEWAIT | NODESTAGEWAIT:

This parameter pertains only to the OS operating system using the **Mass Storage System** (**MSS**). A VSAM object stored on an MSS must be first **staged**, that is, copied to a 3330/3350-type volume before it can be used. When the object is no longer needed (the application program closes the file), the volume can then be **DESTAGED**. This parameter allows you to specify whether the application program should wait for the conclusion of the destaging (DESTAGEWAIT) operation or whether it can be done asynchronously (NODESTAGEWAIT). NODESTAGEWAIT is the default. This parameter can be abbreviated **DSTGW** or **NDSTGW**, respectively.

FOR(days) TO (date):

With this parameter you can specify the retention period for this catalog. It can be specified either in days or by date. If the specification is made in days, you must use the **FOR** parameter. The days may be specified as any value between 0 and 1830. Any value higher than this will force a retention through the year 1999. In order to specify a specific date use the **TO** parameter. A specific date is specified in the form yyddd, where yy = year and ddd is the Julian day of the year (001–366). Example 87365 is interpreted as being the 365th day of 1987. If no value is specified with either the FOR or TO parameter, the catalog can be deleted any time it contains *no* entries.

IMBED | NOIMBED:

This option allows you to decide where you would like the sequence set to be placed. The sequence set, you recall, is the lowest level of the VSAM KSDS index structure. If you specify the IMBED option, VSAM will place the sequence set on the first track of the control area to which it belongs. This means that the sequence set will be located physically adjacent to the data to which it pertains. This is usually beneficial if the data will primarily be accessed sequentially. With this option the sequence set is replicated as many times as it will fit on the first track of the control area. If NOIMBED is specified, the sequence set remains physically with the rest of the index. This parameter can be abbreviated IMBD or NIMBD, respectively.

MASTERPW:

This parameter specifies a password that is to be used for the catalog being defined. Unless this parameter is specified, the associate parameters CODE,

ATTEMPTS, and AUTHORIZATION are of no significance. The password must be one to eight characters in length, and can contain alpha, numeric, or special characters. When using special characters the entire password should be contained within apostrophes. The password can also be specified in hexadecimal. The subject of passwords is covered more thoroughly in Chapter 12. Examples:

MASTERPW(MIKEB)
MASTERPW('MIKEB')
MASTERPW(X'D4C9D2C5C2')

The abbreviation is **MRPW**.

MODEL(ename / password cname / password):

This parameter allows you to point VSAM to some other catalog that you have already defined in order to obtain and fill in parameters that you optionally omit. In our current example we are referring specifically to the catalog. This parameter, however, can be used in defining *any* VSAM object. The **ename** parameter refers to the master or user catalog being used for the model. The **cname** parameter is used when the catalog being used as the model is neither the master catalog nor any catalog referred to by a JOBCAT or STEPCAT JCL card.

ORIGIN(track | block): (DOS only)

This parameter allows you to specify the starting block or track of the catalog. VSAM will round this off to a control area boundry.

OWNER(owner id):

This parameter is used for documentation purposes only. It specifies the name of the **OWNER** of the catalog. The owner id, if used, must be one to eight characters in length and follow the same rules described under MASTERPW.

READPW(password):

This specifies the password to be used whenever the catalog is accessed for **read** purposes. This parameter, once specified, must be used even to list the entries within the catalog (LISTCAT). This parameter can be abbreviated **RDPW**.

RECOVERABLE | NOTRECOVERABLE:

This parameter allows you to determine whether a **CRA** (**Catalog Recovery Area**) is to be provided for the catalog being defined (RECOVERABLE). If RECOVERABLE is specified, space for a CRA will be obtained from the space being defined for this catalog. Furthermore, any volumes owned by this catalog will also contain CRA space taken from the first space defined for that volume. If NOTRECOVERABLE is specified, no CRA is created. This parameter can be abbreviated **RVBL** or **NRVBL**, respectively.

UPDATEPW(password):

This specifies the password to be used any time this catalog is **updated**, that is, entries added, deleted, or changed. See the rules described under MASTERPW for a description of the password format. This parameter can be abbreviated UPDPW.

WRITECHECK | NOWRITECHECK:

If WRITECHECK is specified, a special verification function is performed on the data just written to **verify** that it was written correctly. A special I/O operation called a **soft-read** is performed to accomplish this. When WRITECHECK is specified VSAM constructs a special channel program for the I/O operation that, when chained to a WRITE operation, allows the soft-read operation. When using a soft-read, the data, although read, is not actually transferred back to the CPU. Unless a high volume of data makes this prohibitive, WRITECHECK should be specified. Although more time is required to write with verification than is required merely to write, the time involved is less than the time it would take to write and read using a normal read operation. The abbreviation for this is **WCK** or **NWCK**, respectively.

7.4.2 THE FLEXIBILITY OF THE DEFINE COMMAND

It has been stated several times that a catalog is basically a KSDS; as such it is composed of both an INDEX and a DATA component. Some of the parameters previously described can be specified differently for the DATA and INDEX components as opposed to the CLUSTER level of the catalog. Among the parameters that can be specified separately are these:

```
BUFFERSPACE
CYLINDERS      |
   BLOCKS      |
   TRACKS      |
   RECORDS
DESTAGEWAIT      |    NODESTAGEWAIT
RECOVERABLE      |    NORECOVERABLE
WRITECHECK       |    NOWRITECHECK
```

These parameters are all described in the preceding pages.

For the sample inventory system with which we will be working, we now **DEFINE** a master and user catalog. The catalogs themselves we DEFINE as **RECOVERABLE** and **NOIMBED**ing.

7.4.3 DEFINING THE MASTER CATALOG

For the master catalog definition:

```
DEFINE    MASTERCATALOG                      —
          NAME(MCATLG.A)                     —
```

```
CYL(15 2)             —
VOL(VSAM01)           —
TO(99366)             —
NOIMBED               —
OWNER(SYSTEMA)        —
RECOVERABLE           —
WRITECHECK
```

In the previous example we specified that the name of the master catalog is **MCATLG**. Its initial space allocation will be 15 cylinders with secondary allocations (if needed in the future) of 2 cylinders at a time. The space not actually occupied by the catalog itself will be used for the CRA and can also be used for other VSAM objects such as data clusters. Very often the volume containing the master catalog will contain only a small VSAM space, enough for the catalog alone with ample space for catalog expansion. It is also usually placed on what is considered one of the **systems** packs.

7.4.4 DEFINING THE USER CATALOG

The following control statements will be used to create a second VSAM volume, and will contain a user catalog:

```
DEFINE   USERCATALOG          —
         (                    —
         NAME(UCATLG01)       —
         FILE(USRCAT)         —    R-DOS
         CYL (40 3)           —
         VOL(VSAM02)          —
         TO(99366)            —
         NOIMBED              —
         OWNER(SYSTEMA)       —
         RECOVERABLE          —
         WRITECHECK           —
         )                    —
         CATALOG(MCATLG.A)    —
```

7.4.4.1 The JCL Requirements for DOS

The JCL required for the preceding user catalog would look something like this:

For a DOS/VSE system:

```
// JOB UCATCRET ACCT-DATA[2]
// DLBL USRCAT, 'UCATLG01',,VSAM
```

```
// EXTENT SYS006,VSAM02,,,30,3000³
// EXEC IDCAMS,SIZE=AUTO

   CONTROL CARDS GO HERE

/*
```

Putting it together, the entire DOS jobstream looks like this:

```
// JOB UCATCRET ACCT-DATA
// DLBL USRCAT,'UCATLG01',,VSAM
// EXTENT SYS006,VSAM02,,,30,3000
// ASSGN SYS006,DISK,VOL=VSAM02,SHR
// EXEC IDCAMS,SIZE=AUTO
              DEFINE         USERCATALOG              -
                             (                        -
                             NAME(UCATLG01)           -
                             FILE(USRCAT)             -
                             CYL(40 3)                -
                             VOL(VSAM02)              -
                             TO(99366)                -
                             NOIMBED                  -
                             OWNER(SYSTEMA)           -
                             RECOVERABLE              -
                             WRITECHECK               -
                             )                        -
                             CATALOG(MCATLG.A)
/*
```

7.4.4.2 The JCL Required for OS

For an OS system:

```
//UCATCRET     JOB     ACCTDATA,'MIKE BOUROS',CLASS=R
//AMS          EXEC    PGM=IDCAMS
//USRCAT       DD      DSN=UCATLG01,DISP=NEW, UNIT=3350,
//                     SPACE=(CYL,3000),
//                     VOL=SER=VSAM02
//SYSPRINT     DD      SYSOUT=A
//SYSIN        DD      *
                  CONTROL CARDS GO HERE
/*
```

In the preceding example the DD card could have been omitted if the FILE parameter were left out.

Putting it all together, the OS jobstream looks like this:

```
//UCATCRET     JOB     ACCTDATA,'MIKE BOUROS',CLASS=R
//AMS          EXEC    PGM=IDCAMS
//USRCAT       DD      DSN=UCATLG01,DISP=NEW,
//                     UNIT=3350,SPACE=(CYL,3000),
//                     VOL=SER=VSAM02
//SYSPRINT     DD      SYSOUT=A
//SYSIN        DD      *

DEFINE    USERCATALOG              -
          (                        -
          NAME(UCATLG01)           -
          CYL(40 3)                -
          VOL(VSAM02)              -
          FILE(USRCAT)             -       (Optional)
          TO(99366)                -
          NOIMBED                  -
          OWNER(SYSTEMA)           -
          RECOVERABLE              -
          WRITECHECK               -
          )                        -
          CATALOG(MCATLG.A)
/*
```

7.4.4.3 The Effects of the Catalog Definitions

After running AMS for both catalogs as described, our two VSAM volumes now look like this:

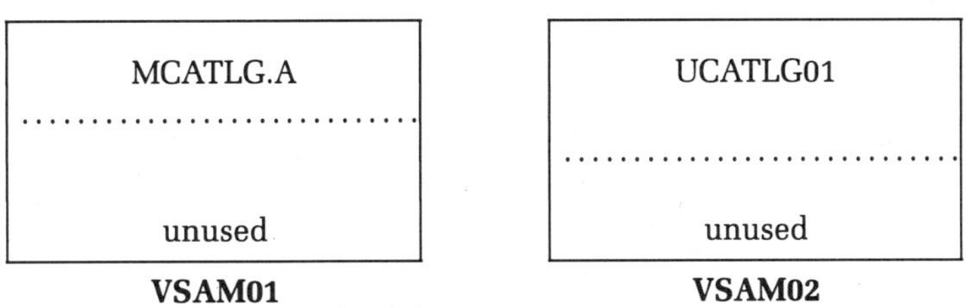

7.4.5 DEFINING A VSAM SPACE

In the illustration there might already be enough room to suballocate some cluster space from the VSAM space defined on VSAM02. However, in order to demonstrate how we would go about acquiring additional space on this volume, we now discuss the DEFINE SPACE command.

COMMAND	PARAMETERS	NOTES
DEFINE SPACE		REQ'D
	(	REQ'D
	CANDIDATE |	
	DEDICATE |	DOS
	CYLINDERS(prime [sec]) |	
	BLOCKS(prime [sec]) |	
	TRACKS(prime [sec]) |	
	RECORDS(prime [sec])	
	[RECORDSIZE(avg. max.)]	
	[FILE(jcl-dname)]	R-DOS
	VOLUME(volser no.)	REQ'D
	[CLASS(value)]	DOS
	[ORIGIN(track | block)]	DOS
	)	REQ'D
	CATALOG(catname [/ password][dname])	

Definitions for most of the preceding parameters are found under the DEFINE command for the MASTER/USER catalogs. The only parameter that is new is RECORDSIZE.

RECORDSIZE(avg. max.):

This parameter is used only in combination with the RECORDS parameter. This is so VSAM can calculate the space requirements. The **avg.** subparameter represents the average record size expected to occupy most of the space being defined. The **max.** subparameter specifies the maximum record size expected to be placed in this space.

The following control statements will be used to create a second space on volume **VSAM02**:

```
DEFINE    SPACE              —
          (                  —
          FILE(VSPACE)       —     R-DOS
          CYL(40 3)          —
          VOL(VSAM02)        —
          )                  —
          CATALOG(UCATLG01)
```

7.4.5.1 The JCL Requirements

The following is the DOS JCL required for the preceding IDCAMS control statements:

```
// JOB VSAMSPCE ACCTDATA CREATE VSAM SPACE
// ASSGN SYS006,DISK,VOL=VSAM02,SHR
```

```
// DLBL VSPACE,,,VSAM
// EXTENT SYS006,VSAM02,,,3030,1200
// EXEC IDCAMS,SIZE=AUTO

                    CONTROL CARDS GO HERE

/*
```

Putting it all together, the DOS jobstream looks like this:

```
// JOB VSAMSPCE ACCTDATA CREATE VSAM SPACE
// ASSGN SYS006,DISK,VOL=VSAM02,SHR
// DLBL VSPACE,,,VSAM
// EXTENT SYS006,VSAM02,,,3030,1200
// EXEC IDCAMS,SIZE=AUTO
   DEFINE    SPACE                    —
             (                        —
             FILE(VSPACE)             —
             CYL(40 3)                —
             VOL(VSAM02)              —
             )                        —
             CATALOG(UCATLG01)
/*
```

For an OS installation the JCL would look something like this:

```
//VSAMSPCE    JOB     ACCTDATA,'MIKE BOUROS',CLASS=R
//DEF         EXEC    PGM=IDCAMS
//SYSPRINT    DD      SYSOUT=A
//SYSIN       DD      *

                    CONTROL CARDS GO HERE

/*
```

The entire OS jobstream would then look like this:

```
//VSAMSPCE    JOB     ACCTDATA,'MIKE BOUROS',CLASS=R
//DEF         EXEC    PGM=IDCAMS
//SYSPRINT    DD      SYSOUT=A
//SYSIN       DD      *
   DEFINE    SPACE                    —
             (                        —
             CYL(40 3)                —
             VOL(VSAM02)              —
```

```
                    )                        —
                    CATALOG(UCATLG01)
    /*
```

As in the case of the user catalog definition, the FILE parameter, which is required by DOS, is not needed for OS.

Our two VSAM volumes now look something like the following:

7.4.5.2 Volume Status After Space Allocation

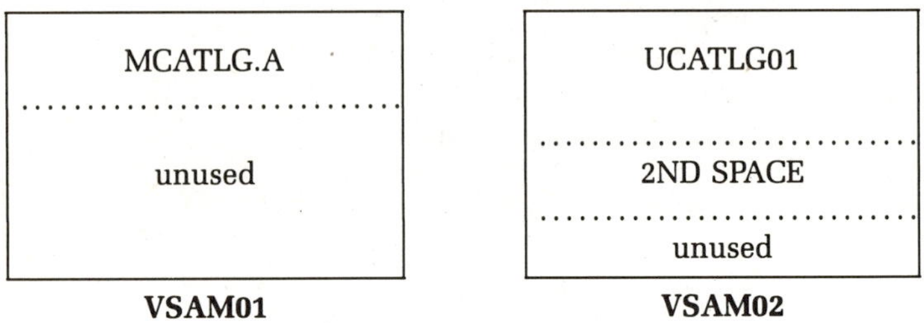

7.4.6 DEFINING THE CLUSTER

Now that we have our two volumes set up to receive data, we can now begin the definition of the data sets (clusters) needed for our inventory application. Let us now take a look at the coding statements available to DEFINE a cluster.

COMMAND	PARAMETERS	NOTES
	The following parameters apply to both the index and data components.	
DEFINE CLUSTER		REQ'D
	(	REQ'D
	NAME(clname)	
	CYLINDERS(prime [sec]) |	
	BLOCKS(prime [sec]) |	
	TRACKS(prime [sec]) |	
	RECORDS(prime [sec])	
	[ERASE | <u>NOERASE</u>]	
	[EXCEPTIONEXIT(modname)]	
	[FILE(jcl-dname)]	R-DOS
	[ATTEMPTS(number)]	
	[AUTHORIZATION(entrypoint [string])]	
	[BUFFERSPACE(size)]	
	[CODE(code)]	

COMMAND	PARAMETERS	NOTES
	[CONTROLINTERVALSIZE(size)]	
	[CONTROLPW(password)]	
	[DESTAGEWAIT | NODESTAGEWAIT]	OS
	[FOR(days) | TO(date)]	
	[FREESPACE(cipct capct)]	
	[IMBED | NOIMBED]	
	[INDEXED | NONINDEXED | NUMBERED]	
	[KEYRANGES(lkey hkey) (lkey hkey).....]	
	[KEYS(len offset)]	
	[MASTERPW(password)]	
	[MODEL(ename [/pass] [cname[/pass]])]	
	[ORDERED | UNORDERED]	
	[OWNER(owner id)]	
	[READPW(password)]	
	[RECORDFORMAT(format)]	
	[RECORDSIZE(avg. max.)]	
	[RECOVERY | SPEED]	
	[REPLICATE | NOREPLICATE]	
	[REUSE | NOREUSE]	
	[SHAREOPTIONS(opt1 opt2)]	
	[SPANNED | NONSPANNED]	
	[STAGE | BIND | CYLINDERFAULT]	OS
	[UNIQUE | SUBALLOCATION | NOALLOCATION]	
	[UPDATEPW(password)]	
	[USECLASS(prim sec)]	
	[VOLUMES(vol1 vol2...) | DEFAULTVOLUMES]	
	[WRITECHECK | NOWRITECHECK]	
	)	REQ'D
	The following parameters pertain to the optional DEFINITION of the DATA component.	
[DATA		
	NAME(dname)	R-DOS
	CYLINDERS(prime [sec]) |	
	BLOCKS(prime [sec]) |	
	TRACKS(prime [sec]) |	
	RECORDS(prime [sec])	
	[ERASE | NOERASE]	

(Continued on p. 94)

COMMAND	PARAMETERS	NOTES
	[EXCEPTIONEXIT(modname)]	
	[FILE(jcl-dname)]	
	[ATTEMPTS(number)	OS
	[AUTHORIZATION(entrypoint [string])]	
	[BUFFERSPACE(size)]	
	[CODE(code)]	
	[CONTROLINVERVALSIZE(size)]	
	[CONTROLPW(password)]	
	[DESTAGEWAIT | NODESTAGEWAIT]	
	[FREESPACE(cipct capct)]	OS
	[KEYRANGES(lkey hkey) (lkey hkey).....]	
	[KEYS(len offset)]	
	[MASTERPW(password)]	
	[MODEL(ename [/pass] [cname[/pass]])]	
	[ORDERED | UNORDERED]	
	[OWNER(owner id)]	
	[READPW(password)]	
	[RECORDSIZE(avg. max.)]	
	[RECOVERY | SPEED]	
	[REUSE | NOREUSE]	
	[SHAREOPTIONS(opt1 opt2)	
	[SPANNED | NONSPANNED]	
	[STAGE | BIND | CYLINDERFAULT]	
	[UNIQUE | SUBALLOCATION |	
	NOALLOCATION]	DOS
	[UPDATEPW(password)]	
	[USECLASS(prim sec)]	
	[VOLUMES(vol1 vol2...) |	
	DEFAULTVOLUMES]	
	[WRITECHECK | NOWRITECHECK]	
	)]	
	The following parameters pertain to the optional DEFINITION of the INDEX component.	
[INDEX		
	NAME(iname)	R-DOS
	CYLINDERS(prime [sec]) |	
	BLOCKS(prime [sec]) |	
	TRACKS(prime [sec]) |	
	RECORDS(prime [sec])	
	[EXCEPTIONEXIT(modname)]	

```
[FILE(jcl-dname)]
[ATTEMPTS( number )]                                OS
[AUTHORIZATION(entrypoint [string]) ]
[CODE( code ) ]
[CONTROLINTERVALSIZE( size )]
[CONTROLPW( password) ]
[DESTAGEWAIT | NODESTAGEWAIT ]
[IMBED | NOIMBED ]
[INDEXED | NONINDEXED | NUMBERED]
[MASTERPW( password ) ]                             OS
[MODEL(ename [/pass] [ cname[/pass]] ) ]
[ORDERED | UNORDERED]
[OWNER( owner id ) ]
[READPW( password ) ]
[REPLICATE | NOREPLICATE]
[REUSE | NOREUSE]
[SHAREOPTIONS( opt1 opt2)
[STAGE | BIND | CYLINDERFAULT]
[UNIQUE | SUBALLOCATION |
   NOALLOCATION]
[UPDATEPW( password ) ]
[VOLUMES( vol1 vol2...) |
   DEFAULTVOLUMES ]
[WRITECHECK | NOWRITECHECK ]
) ]
CATALOG( catname [/ password][ dname])
```

EXPLANATION OF PARAMETERS

DEFINE CLUSTER

This AMS command specifies that you wish to DEFINE to VSAM the characteristics of a VSAM CLUSTER. This command can be abbreviated **DEF CL**.

NAME(catname):

This entry allows you to give a name to the cluster being defined. The name can be up to 44 characters long and can be any combination of letters, numbers, or the special symbols @, #, and $. The name must begin with a letter and, if greater than eight digits, must be broken into segments of one to eight digits separated by periods, for example:

```
DEFINE CLUSTER(INVENT.ITEMS.SYS.A)
```

CYLINDERS/TRACKS/RECORDS/BLOCKS(prime sec):

The purpose of this parameter is twofold: to allocate the initial (prime) space for the cluster and to specify the dynamic secondary (sec) allocation to be made if the primary space allocation becomes exhausted. The space allocation can be specified in either CYLINDERS, TRACKS, RECORDS, or BLOCKS. The first three entries are used for CKD devices. The first two entries are the ones most commonly used, especially CYLINDERS. For FBA devices the allocation must be specified in BLOCKS. The abbreviation for CYLINDERS is **CYL**, TRACKS is **TRK**, RECORDS is **REC**, and BLOCKS is **BLK**.

[ERASE | NOERASE]:

For sensitive data the specification of ERASE will cause VSAM to erase the entire area occupied by the cluster when the entry is deleted from the catalog. The extent formerly occupied by this cluster will be overwritten with binary zeros (low-value). The abbreviation for this parameter is **ERAS** (ERASE) or **NERAS** (NOERASE).

EXCEPTIONEXIT(modname):

This parameter specifies the name of an exit routine written by the user to which control is given whenever an unusual error condition takes place. This is usually an I/O error. This exit routine is Link Edited to the Load (OS) or Core-Image (DOS) library. To find out more about preparing EXIT routines see Chapter 12 and the *IBM VSAM Programmer's Guide*.

FOR(days) TO (date):

With this parameter you can specify the retention period for this cluster. It can be specified either in days or by date. If the specification is made in days, you must use the FOR parameter. The days may be specified as any value between 0 and 1830. Any value higher than this will force a retention through the year 1999. In order to specify a specific date use the TO parameter. A specific date is specified in the form yyddd, where yy = year and ddd is the Julian day of the year (001–365). Example 84365 is interpreted the 365th day of 1984.

FILE(jcl-dname):

This parameter is required by DOS, but can also be used in OS. It is used to point to the DLBL JCL card (DOS) or a DD JCL card (OS). The name specified here must match the name specified by the DLBL or DD card. The following illustrates the association between the JCL and the FILE (jcl-name):

```
// DLBL CLDEF .........        DOS
//CLDEF DD .............       OS
     FILE(CLDEF)
```

ATTEMPTS(number):

This parameter is used only in those cases where the cluster is password protected. The number of attempts the operator can make before VSAM aborts is specified here. If ATTEMPTS (0) is specified, the operator is not allowed to enter the password from a system console. Password protection is discussed in Chapter 12. This parameter can be abbreviated **ATT**.

AUTHORIZATION(entrypoint/string):

This parameter specifies the name of a routine (entrypoint) to which control is passed every time this cluster is accessed. This routine is called a **user exit**. It is usually written by the systems programmer at the installation in which the cluster will be used. For the specifics in writing a user exit routine, see Chapter 12. In addition to passing control to the user exit, a character string up to 256 characters in length can also be passed to the routine. The characters passed can be specified as either character or hexadecimal values. See Chapter 12 for more information on this subject. This parameter can be abbreviated **AUTH**. Example:

```
AUTHORIZATION(CHECKRTN authdata) or
AUTHORIZATION(CHECKRTN X'C1E4E3C8C4C1E3C1')
```

BUFFERSPACE(size):

This specifies the space to be provided for buffers when the cluster is in use. The space defined should be large enough to contain at least two data control intervals and one index control interval if this is a KSDS file. If enough BUFFERSPACE is allocated for this cluster, the entire index could be brought into main storage (KSDS). If this parameter is left out, VSAM will compute the BUFFERSPACE required. This parameter can be abbreviated **BUFSP** or **BUFSPC**, respectively.

CODE(code):

This parameter is used for those clusters that are password protected. The designated **code** is used in lieu of the cluster name when prompting the operator for the password. See Chapter 12 for more information on this subject.

CONTROLINTERVALSIZE(cisize):

With this parameter, you can set the size (cisize) of the control interval. The CI size for the index and data components can be specified separately. For the index the allowable CI sizes are 512, 1024, 2048, or 4096. The CI size for the data component must be a multiple of 512 or 2048 and can be any size between 512 and 32768. There are several factors that must be taken into account when calculating the CI size for the data component. The most obvious of these is the size of the data record itself. Besides this you must also take into consideration the following:

The CIDF and RDF fields of the CI
Whether the cluster contains fixed or variable length records

The physical size of the records that VSAM will use to store these CIs
BUFFERSPACE

These issues are discussed more thoroughly in Chapter 17.

For the size of the index CI it is usually best to let VSAM calculate this for you. If you decide to calculate this for yourself, however, see the discussion on this in Chapter 13. This parameter can be abbreviated **CISZ** or **CNVSZ**.

CONTROLPW(password):

A special method of file access called Control Interval Access enables a program to read or write entire CIs at a time rather than individual records. With this parameter you can control the access to the cluster by specifying a password. The entire subject of passwords is covered in Chapter 12. This parameter can be abbreviated **CTLPW**.

DESTAGEWAIT | NODESTAGEWAIT (OS ONLY)

This parameter pertains only to the OS operating system using the Mass Storage System (MSS). A VSAM object stored on an MSS must be first **staged**, that is, copied to a 3330/3350-type volume before it can be used. When the object is no longer needed (i.e., the application program closes the file) the volume can then be **DESTAGED**. This parameter allows you to specify whether the application should wait for the conclusion of the destaging (DESTAGEWAIT) operation or whether it can be done asynchronously (NODESTAGEWAIT). NODESTAGEWAIT is the default. This parameter can be abbreviated **DSTGW** or **NDSTGW**, respectively.

FREESPACE(cipct capct):

This parameter pertains only to KSDS clusters. It specifies the amount of FREESPACE to be left in a control interval or control area. When a cluster is initially loaded, or when record insertions are made in **sequential insert mode**, VSAM will maintain the FREESPACE specified with this parameter. Both **cipct** (CI%) and **capct** (CA%) are specified as percentages of space to be *left* in the CI/CA. Specification of (0 0) allows no FREESPACE to be reserved in the CI/CA. There is one exception to the way that this parameter is handled by VSAM—when a specification of (100 100) is made. When this option is used, VSAM allows only one record per CI and only one CI per CA will contain data. This parameter can be abbreviated **FSPC**.

IMBED | NOIMBED:

This option allows you to decide where you would like the sequence set placed. The sequence set is the lowest level of the VSAM index structure. If you specify the IMBED option, VSAM will place the sequence set on the first track of the control area to which it belongs. This means that the sequence set will be located physically adjacent to the data to which it pertains. This is usually beneficial if the data access will primarily be sequential. With this option the sequence set is replicated as many times as it will fit on the first track of the control area. If NOIMBED is specified, the sequence set remains with the rest of the index. This parameter can be abbreviated **IMBD** (IMBED) or **NIMBD** (NOIMBED).

INDEXED | NONINDEXED | NUMBERED:

With this parameter you specify the VSAM mode that this cluster will use. INDEXED must be specified for a KSDS file, NONINDEXED for an ESDS file, and NUMBERED for an RRDS file. These parameters can be abbreviated **IXD**, **NIXD**, or **NUMD**, respectively.

KEYRANGES(Lkey1 Hkey1 Lkey2 Hkey2....):

This option allows you to place different ranges of records on different volumes. This parameter is used in conjunction with the VOLUMES parameter. Each KEYRANGE previously specified corresponds to the respective volume serial number coded in the VOLUMES parameter. Up to 123 KEYRANGES can be specified. **Lkey** pertains to the low key of a given range and **Hkey** pertains to the high key of the same range. You might be wondering at this time about what happens if you cannot contain *all* the records of a given KEYRANGE on a particular volume. If the number of VOLUMES exceeds the KEYRANGES, the excess data records will overflow onto the extra VOLUMES without any consideration given to the keys. If the number of VOLUMES is less than the KEYRANGES specified, the excess records will be placed on the last VOLUME specified. See also the ORDERED parameter. This parameter can be abbreviated **KRNG**.

KEYS(len offset):

This parameter pertains to KSDS clusters only. It specifies the length (len) and location (offset) of the key within a data record. The maximum length of a key is 64 bytes. The key is made up of contiguous character positions or fields; it cannot be comprised of separate, multiple fields. The offset is specified as relative to zero. For example, a cluster containing records with a key length of 16 and beginning in the first byte of the record would be specified as:

MASTERPW:

This parameter specifies a password that is used for the cluster being defined. Unless this parameter is specified, the associate parameters CODE, ATTEMPTS, and AUTHORIZATION are of no significance. The password must be one to eight characters in length, and can contain alpha, numeric, or special characters. When using special characters the entire password should be contained within apostrophes. The password can also be specified in hexadecimal. Examples:

```
MASTERPW(MIKEB)
MASTERPW('MIKEB')
MASTERPW(X'D4C9D2C5C2')
```

Passwords are discussed more thoroughly in Chapter 12. The abbreviation for this is **MRPW**.

MODEL(ename / password cname / password):

This parameter allows you to point VSAM to some other cluster that you have already defined to obtain and fill in parameters that you optionally omit. In this example we are referring specifically to clusters. This parameter, however, can be used to refer to *any* VSAM object. The ename parameter refers to the cluster being used for the model. The cname parameter is used to name the catalog in which the cluster being referenced is defined.

ORDERED | UNORDERED:

This parameter is used in conjunction with the VOLUMES parameter. It specifies whether the volumes are to be used in the ORDER specified. When KEYRANGES is also specified the first range of keys is placed on the first volume, the second range on the second volume, and so on. This differs slightly from the use of KEYRANGES without the ORDERED parameter in that VSAM has more flexibility in placing the data records when UNORDERED is specified. UNORDERED is the default. These parameters can be abbreviated **ORD** and **UNORD**, respectively.

OWNER(owner id):

This parameter is used for documentation purposes only. It specifies the name of the **owner** of the cluster. The owner id must be specified as one to eight characters and follows the same rules described under MASTERPW.

READPW(password):

This specifies the password to be used whenever the cluster is accessed for **read** purposes. This parameter can be abbreviated **RDPW**.

RECORDFORMAT (DOS ONLY):

This parameter pertains only to DOS. A special DOS feature called the **Space Management** feature, is used by VSAM to control SAM data sets. This is a special feature and is not typically found even in DOS installations. For more information on this subject see Chapter 14.

RECORDSIZE(avg. max.):

This parameter specifies in bytes the average (avg.) and maximum (max.) size of records in the data component. If **avg.** and **max.** are equal, VSAM understands this to be a file of fixed length records. When avg. and max. are different, VSAM understands this cluster to be a file of variable length records. If the size specified is larger that what has been specified for the CI size, you must specify SPANNED records. This parameter can be abbreviated **RECSZ**.

RECOVERY | SPEED:

This parameter gives you control over the method used during the initial **loading** of a VSAM data set. When RECOVERY is specified, each control area is preformatted before data records are written into it. In addition, VSAM also writes end-of-file indicators in the control area during the load operation. For each data record written an EOF marker record is written immediately after it which tells VSAM that the record before it is the last record written. If the load operation then fails, you can simply continue the load operation beginning with the next record to be loaded; an application program is usually written to support this, however. This option is very useful when the load operation involves a very large number of records. Since most systems are not designed for RECOVERY, the SPEED option is the one most used. With SPEED no preformatting is performed during the load operation. If the load program fails for any reason, the load process must be started over from the beginning. The abbreviation for RECOVERY is **RCVY**; no abbreviation for SPEED.

REPLICATE | NOREPLICATE:

With this option you can tell VSAM to REPLICATE the index entries (KSDS only) as many times as they will fit on one track. This, of course, reduces the rotational delay because a shorter time is required for the correct index record to be in position to pass under the Read/Write head. The tradeoff is that there are more index entries to update when index entry update is required. This parameter can be abbreviated **REPL** or **NREPL**, respectively.

REUSE | NOREUSE:

This option is often selected when a cluster is used as a work file or temporary data set. When this cluster is opened as an output file with DISP=NEW (as opposed to input or I/O), the HIGH-USED RBA (end-of-file pointer) is reset to zero as if *no* records exist on this file. For all practical purposes, once the HIGH-USED RBA pointer is reset to zero, records on this file are no longer accessible. The alternative to this would be to DELETE and reDEFINE the cluster each time it is to be used. There are some restrictions to the use of reusable data sets such as:

No Alternate indexes permitted

KEYRANGES cannot be used

The typical installation will *not* specify normal production data sets as REUSable. NONREUSABLE data sets are safer to use since a NONREUSable cluster must be specifically DELETED in order to be erased. A JCL statement or OPEN command/macro erroneously coded could wipe out a REUSable data set, whereas this type of error would leave a NONREUSable data set relatively unaffected. This parameter is abbreviated **RUS** or **NRUS**, respectively.

SHAREOPTIONS(opt1 opt2):

This parameter specifies how a cluster is to be SHAREd between partitions or regions (opt1). For OS installations only the second option (opt2) specifies how this cluster is to be shared across systems, that is, in multi-CPU environments. For **opt1** you must code one of the following:

Cross-Partition/Region Options:

'1' This specifies that the data set can be shared between any number of users for **read** purposes *or* only one user for read and write processing.

'2' This code allows any number of users to be reading the data set and one user to write to the data set at any given time.

'3' With this option a cluster can be shared by any number of users for both read and write purposes. Neither VSAM nor the operating system does anything in order to ensure the integrity of the data set. If two users are writing to this cluster at the same time, there is a good chance that the cluster will be destroyed. When using this option it is up to the user to ensure that this does not happen. This could possibly be accomplished through proper scheduling and through the use of ENQ and DEQ (enqueue and dequeue) macros. This is discussed more fully in Chapter 14.

'4' With this option VSAM can offer *some* protection and assistance when a data set is to be shared for both read and write purposes by multiple partitions or regions. When using this option VSAM will retrieve a fresh copy of the control interval containing the desired record (random read) even if a copy of the record is presently in the CPU. This helps ensure read integrity. When records are written to the data set the first partition/region to issue the write will get exclusive control over the data set until the write operation is completed.

Cross-system (OS Only):

'1' Not currently used.

'2' Not currently used.

'3' This function is to cross-system what **3** is to cross-partition/region. VSAM will allow you to perform any kind of operation but delegates all responsibility to you. Improper use of this option can result in destroyed data sets and program check interruptions within VSAM.

'4' With this cross-system option VSAM expects you to use OS RESERVE and DEQ macros in order to hardware RESERVE (plus software enqueue) and hardware release (plus software dequeue) a data set. A hardware reserve is actually a special channel command that causes a CPU to **seize** a particular DASD device causing a second CPU to be locked out in a true hardware sense. In order to accomplish this a RESERVE macro is issued. A DEQ macro is required to return the DASD device to an **available to anyone** state. This is performed with a DEQ macro which, in turn, issues a hardware command (CCW) called RELEASE. Some other things to know about the use of these macros are covered in Chapter 14. Another service that VSAM performs under this option is to prevent the occurrence of a CA or CI split that results in a

CA split. When a CA split takes place, a new CA is acquired from the end of the data set. This cannot be allowed to take place because it would then change the HIGH-USED RBA, in other words, the indicator that marks the end of the data set. If this happened on one system, there is currently no way for the other system to find out about it. This topic is discussed further in Chapter 14. The abbreviation for this option is **SHR**.

SPANNED | NONSPANNED:

This option is used to specify that data records larger than a control interval will be allowed to overflow (SPAN) over into one or more additional control intervals. Unused space in the last CI cannot be used to place another record. In other words, only the last **part** of the data record can occupy the last CI used for a single spanned record. Freespace remaining in that CI cannot be utilized. The abbreviation for this option is **SPND** and **NSPND**, respectively.

STAGE | BIND | CYLINDERFAULT (OS ONLY):

This option pertains only to users of MSS (Mass Storage Systems). When STAGE is specified, the cluster is to be staged to a DASD device when the data set is opened. If the cluster cannot be STAGEd at that time because of heavy staging activity, the *data* is staged as the program needs it. The BIND parameter is similar to STAGE; it ensures, however, that the data, once staged, is **bound** to the DASD device to which it was staged until the cluster is closed. If CYLINDERFAULT is specified, the cluster is not staged when the data set is opened. Rather, the data is staged as it is required. The entire operation of these options very closely resembles the paging operation that takes place in virtual memory.

UNIQUE | SUBALLOCATION | NOALLOCATION:

This parameter identifies the type of space that this cluster is to occupy. If UNIQUE is specified, the cluster will be the only object contained within the space that is acquired for it. When UNIQUE is specified, the space that contains the cluster is created at the same time the cluster is defined. If SUBALLOCATION is specified, the space used to contain the cluster is obtained from space already in existence on the volume or volumes pointed to by the VOLUMES parameter. If NOALLOCATION is specified, no allocation is made for the cluster but the cluster name is added to the catalog. This capability could be useful for defining MODELs. UNIQUE can be abbreviated **UNQ**. SUBALLOCATED can be abbreviated **SUBAL**. There is no abbreviation for NOALLOCATION.

UPDATEPW(password):

This specifies the password to be used any time this cluster is **updated**, that is, records added, deleted, or changed. See the rules described under MASTERPW for a description of the password format. This parameter can be abbreviated **UPDPW**.

VOLUMES(vol1 vol2 ....) | DEFAULTVOLUMES:

This designates the VOLUMES upon which this cluster is to be placed; vol1 and vol2... are the serial numbers with which the DASD volumes were initialized. The data and index components can be located on separate VOLUMES, if desired (see Chapter 17). DEFAULTVOLUMES is used in conjunction with the MODEL parameter. It specifies to VSAM that the information pertaining to VOLUMES should be obtained from the MODEL. This parameter can be abbreviated **VOL**.

WRITECHECK | NOWRITECHECK:

If WRITECHECK is specified, a special verification function is performed on the data just written to verify that it was written correctly. A special I/O operation called a **soft-read** is performed to accomplish this. When WRITECHECK is specified, VSAM constructs a special channel program for the I/O operation which, when chained to a WRITE operation, allows the soft-read operation. When using a soft-read, the data, although read, is not actually transferred back to the CPU. Unless high volume data makes this prohibitive, WRITECHECK should be specified. Although more time is required to perform this than is required to merely write, the time involved is less than the time it would take to write and read using a normal read operation. This option can be abbreviated **WCK** or **NWCK**, respectively.

7.4.6.1 Defining the Clusters

Now that we have reviewed the parameters required by AMS we are ready to begin DEFINing the clusters we will be needing for our inventory application. For now we will be working with the following data sets:

Inventory Master	**—KSDS, NONREUSABLE, SUBALLOCATED**
Sales File	**—KSDS, UNIQUE**
Purchases File	**—ESDS, REUSABLE, SUBALLOCATED**
Receiving File	**—RRDS, SUBALLOCATED**

7.4.6.2 Defining the Inventory File Cluster

The cluster we DEFINE for the inventory file contains fixed length records of 200 bytes. The record key begins in the first byte of the file and is 12 bytes in length. Because 200 goes *almost* evenly into 4096, this size was chosen for the size of the CI. We shall assume that we are using a device in which the physical capacity of the track fits the control intervals well (e.g., 3350s). Enough additions occur to warrant 25% FREESPACE in the CI. Most of the records added contain keys similar to what already exists in the data set. The cluster is placed on the VSAM02 volume.

DEFINE CLUSTER

```
(                                 —
NAME(INVENTRY.CLUSTER)            —
VOL(VSAM02)                       —
CYL(60 5)                         —
CISZ(4096)                        —
FILE(INVCLUS)                     —    R-DOS
INDEXED                           —
KEYS(12 0)                        —
FREESPACE(25 10)                  —
RECSZ(200 200)                    —
SHR(2 3)                          —
)                                 —
CATALOG(UCATLG01)                 —
```

7.4.6.3 The Job Control Requirements

The Job Control for the preceding would look something like this:

For DOS:

```
// JOB INVLOAD ACCTDATA
// DLBL INVCLUS,'INVENTRY.CLUSTER',,VSAM
// EXEC IDCAMS,SIZE=AUTO

                    CONTROL CARDS GO HERE

/*
```

For OS the JCL might look like this:

```
//INVLOAD     JOB     ACCTDATA,'MIKE BOUROS',CLASS=R
//INVAMS      EXEC    PGM=IDCAMS
//STEPCAT     DD      DSN=UCATLG01,DISP=SHR (OPTIONAL)
//SYSPRINT    DD      SYSOUT=A
//SYSIN       DD      *

                    CONTROL CARDS GO HERE

/*
```

Now putting it all together:

For DOS:

```
// JOB INVLOAD ACCTDATA
// DLBL INVCLUS,'INVENTRY.CLUSTER',,VSAM
// EXEC IDCAMS,SIZE=AUTO
   DEFINE CLUSTER                       -
              (                         -
              NAME(INVENTRY.CLUSTER)    -
              VOL(VSAM02)               -
              CYL(60 5)                 -
              CISZ(4096)                -
              FILE(INVCLUS)             -
              INDEXED                   -
              KEYS(12 0)                -
              FREESPACE(25 10)          -
              RECSZ(200 200)            -
              SHR(2 3)                  -
              )                         -
              CATALOG(UCATLG01)         -
/*
```

For OS:

```
//INVLOAD     JOB     ACCTDATA,'MIKE BOUROS',CLASS=R
//INVAMS      EXEC    PGM=IDCAMS
//STEPCAT     DD      DSN=UCATLG01,DISP=SHR (OPTIONAL)
//SYSPRINT    DD      SYSOUT=A
//SYSIN       DD      *
   DEFINE CLUSTER                       -
              (                         -
              NAME(INVENTRY.CLUSTER)    -
              VOL(VSAM02)               -
              CYL(60 5)                 -
              CISZ(4096)                -
              INDEXED                   -
              KEYS(12 0)                -
              FREESPACE(25 10)          -
              RECSZ(200 200)            -
              SHR(2 3)                  -
              )                         -
              CATALOG(UCATLG01)
/*
```

7.4.6.4 Defining the Sales File Cluster

The cluster defined for the Sales file contains variable length records of from 35 to 74 bytes in length. The record key begins in the first byte of the file and is 12 bytes in length. There will be *no* additions to this file once it is built. This cluster is located on the VSAM02 volume.

```
DEFINE CLUSTER                          -
               (                        -
               NAME(SALES.CLUSTER)      -
               VOL(VSAM02)              -
               INDEXED                  -
               UNIQUE                   -
               SHR(2 3)                 -
               )                        -
          DATA                          -
               (                        -
               NAME(SALES.DATA)         -
               CISZ(4096)               -
               CYL(40 2)                -
               KEYS(12 0)               -
               FILE(SALDATA)            -    R-DOS
               FREESPACE(0 0)           -
               RECSZ( 35 74 )           -
               )                        -
          INDEX                         -
               (                        -
               NAME(SALES.INDEX)        -
               CISZ(512)                -
               CYL( 2 1 )               -
               FILE(SALINDX)            -    R-DOS
               )                        -
               CATALOG(UCATLG01)
```

7.4.6.5 The Job Control Requirements

The Job Control for the preceding would look something like this:

For DOS:

```
// JOB SALELOAD ACCTDATA
// DLBL SALDATA,'SALES.DATA',,VSAM
// EXTENT ..............................
// DLBL SALINDX,'SALES.INDEX',,VSAM
// EXTENT ..............................
// EXEC IDCAMS,SIZE=AUTO

                    CONTROL CARDS GO HERE

/*
```

For OS the JCL might look like this:

```
//SALELOAD    JOB ACCTDATA,'MIKE BOUROS',CLASS=R
//SALAMS      EXEC PGM=IDCAMS
//STEPCAT     DD     DSN=UCATLG01,DISP=SHR (OPTIONAL)
//SALDATA     DD     DSN=SALES.DATA,DISP=NEW,
//            VOL=SER=VSAM02,UNIT=3350,
//            SPACE=(CYL(40))
//SALINDX     DD     DSN=SALES.INDEX,DISP=NEW,
//                   VOL=SER=VSAM02,UNIT=3350,
//                   SPACE=(CYL(2))
//SYSPRINT    DD SYSOUT=A
//SYSIN       DD *

                 CONTROL CARDS GO HERE

/*
```

Now putting it all together:

For DOS:

```
// JOB SALELOAD ACCTDATA
// DLBL SALDATA,'SALES.DATA',,VSAM
// EXTENT ..............................
// DLBL SALINDX,'SALES.INDEX',,VSAM
// EXTENT ..............................
// EXEC IDCAMS,SIZE=AUTO
  DEFINE CLUSTER                  —
       (                          —
       NAME(SALES.CLUSTER)        —
       VOL(VSAM02)                —
       INDEXED                    —
       UNIQUE                     —
  SHR(2 3)                        —
       )                          —

  DATA                            —
       (                          —
       NAME(SALES.DATA)           —
       CISZ(4096)                 —
       CYL(40 2)                  —
       KEYS(12 0)                 —
       FILE(SALDATA)              —
       FREESPACE(0 0)             —
       RECSZ( 35 74 )             —
```

```
        )                          —
    INDEX                          —
        (                          —
        NAME(SALES.INDEX)          —
        CISZ(512)                  —
        CYL( 2 1 )                 —
        FILE(SALINDX)              —
        )                          —
        CATALOG(UCATLG01)
/*
```

For OS:

```
//SALELOAD    JOB     ACCTDATA,'MIKE BOUROS',CLASS=R
//SALAMS      EXEC    PGM=IDCAMS
//STEPCAT     DD      DSN=UCATLG01,DISP=SHR (OPTIONAL)
//SALDATA     DD      DSN=SALES.DATA,DISP=NEW,
//                    VOL=SER=VSAM02,UNIT=3350,
//                    SPACE=(CYL(40))
//SALINDX     DD      DSN=SALES.INDEX,DISP=NEW,
//                    VOL=SER=VSAM02,UNIT=3350,
//                    SPACE=(CYL(2))
//SYSPRINT    DD      SYSOUT=A
//SYSIN       DD      *
   DEFINE CLUSTER          —
       (                   —
   NAME(SALES.CLUSTER)     —
   VOL(VSAM02)             —
   INDEXED                 —
   UNIQUE                  —
   SHR(2 3)                —
   )                       —
   DATA                    —
       (                   —
       NAME(SALES.DATA)    —
       CISZ(4096)          —
       CYL(40 2)           —
       KEYS(12 0)          —
       FILE(SALDATA)       —
       FREESPACE(0 0)      —
       RECSZ( 35 74 )      —
       )                   —

   INDEX                   —
       (                   —
       NAME(SALES.INDEX)   —
```

```
CISZ(512)              -
CYL( 2 1 )             -
FILE(SALINDX)          -
)                      -
CATALOG(UCATLG01)
```

7.4.6.6 Defining the Purchases File Cluster

The cluster defined for the Purchases file contains fixed length records 120 bytes long. The record key begins in the first byte of the file and is 16 bytes in length. This cluster is an ESDS data set, and is REUSABLE. This cluster is located on the VSAM02 volume.

```
DEFINE CLUSTER                                 -
                 (                             -
                 NAME(PURCH.CLUSTER)           -
                 VOL(VSAM02)                   -
                 NONINDEXED                    -
                 SHR(2 3)                      -
                 CYL(10 2)                     -
                 KEYS(16 0)                    -
                 FILE(PURCLUS)                 -   R-DOS
                 RECSZ(120 120)                -
                 REUSABLE                      -
                 )                             -
                 CATALOG(UCATLG01)
```

7.4.6.7 The Job Control Requirements

The Job Control for the preceding would look something like this:

For DOS:

```
// JOB PURLOAD ACCTDATA
// DLBL PURCLUS,'PURCH.CLUSTER',,VSAM
// EXEC IDCAMS,SIZE=AUTO

              CONTROL CARDS GO HERE

/*
```

For OS the JCL might look like this:

```
//PURLOAD    JOB     ACCTDATA,'MIKE BOUROS',CLASS=R
//PURAMS     EXEC    PGM=IDCAMS
```

```
//STEPCAT     DD     DSN=UCATLG01,DISP=SHR (OPTIONAL)
//SYSPRINT    DD     SYSOUT=A
//SYSIN       DD     *

                   CONTROL CARDS GO HERE

/*
```

Now putting it all together:

For DOS:

```
// JOB PURLOAD ACCTDATA
// DLBL PURCLUS,'PURCH.CLUSTER',,VSAM
// EXEC IDCAMS,SIZE=AUTO
   DEFINE CLUSTER              —
      (                        —
      NAME(PURCH.CLUSTER)      —
      VOL(VSAM02)              —
      NONINDEXED               —
      SHR(2 3)                 —
      CYL(10 2)                —
      KEYS(16 0)               —
      FILE(PURCLUS)            —
      RECSZ(120 120)           —
      REUSABLE                 —
      )                        —
      CATALOG(UCATLG01)
/*
```

For OS:

```
//PURLOAD     JOB    ACCTDATA,'MIKE BOUROS',CLASS=R
//PURAMS      EXEC   PGM=IDCAMS
//STEPCAT     DD     DSN=UCATLG01,DISP=SHR (OPTIONAL)
//SYSPRINT    DD     SYSOUT=A
//SYSIN       DD     *
    DEFINE CLUSTER             —
     (                         —
     NAME(PURCH.CLUSTER)       —
     VOL(VSAM02)               —
     NONINDEXED                —
     SHR(2 3)                  —
     CYL(10 2)                 —
```

```
          KEYS(16 0)                    —
          RECSZ(120 120)                —
          REUSABLE                      —
          )                             —
          CATALOG(UCATLG01)
/*
```

7.4.6.8 Defining the Receiving File Cluster

The cluster defined for the Receiving file contains fixed length records 80 bytes in length. The record key begins in the first byte of the record and is 8 bytes in length. This cluster is an RRDS data set. Receiving numbers are generated dynamically by the program and are sequential. The first receiving number for the day is 000001; the second is 000002, and so on. This cluster is located on the VSAM02 volume.

```
DEFINE CLUSTER                              —
              (                             —
              NAME(RECEIVE.CLUSTER)         —
              VOL(VSAM02)                   —
              NUMBERED                      —
              SHR(2 3)                      —
              CYL(10 2)                     —
              KEYS(8 0)                     —
              FILE(RECEIVE)                 —       R-DOS
              RECSZ(80 80)                  —
              )                             —
              CATALOG(UCATLG01)
```

7.4.6.9 The Job Control Requirements

The Job Control for the preceding would look something like this:

For DOS:

```
// JOB RECVLOAD ACCTDATA
// DLBL RECEIVE,'RECEIVE.CLUSTER',,VSAM
// EXEC IDCAMS,SIZE=AUTO

                  CONTROL CARDS GO HERE

/*
```

For OS the JCL might look like this:

```
//RECVLOAD     JOB      ACCTDATA,'MIKE BOUROS',CLASS=R
//RECAMS       EXEC     PGM=IDCAMS
```

```
//STEPCAT      DD      DSN=UCATLG01,DISP=SHR (OPTIONAL)
//SYSPRINT     DD      SYSOUT=A
//SYSIN        DD      *

               CONTROL CARDS GO HERE

/*
```

Now putting it all together:

For DOS:

```
// JOB RECVLOAD ACCTDATA
// DLBL RECEIVE,'RECEIVE.CLUSTER',,VSAM
// EXEC IDCAMS,SIZE=AUTO
   DEFINE CLUSTER              —
       (                       —
       NAME(RECEIVE,CLUSTER)   —
       VOL(VSAM02)             —
       NUMBERED                —
       SHR(2 3)                —
       CYL(10 2)               —
       KEYS(8 0)               —
       FILE(RECEIVE)           —
       RECSZ(80 80)            —
       )                       —
       CATALOG(UCATLG01)
/*
```

For OS:

```
//RECVLOAD     JOB     ACCTDATA,'MIKE BOUROS',CLASS=R
//RECAMS       EXEC    PGM=IDCAMS
//STEPCAT      DD      DSN=UCATLG01,DISP=SHR (OPTIONAL)
//SYSPRINT     DD      SYSOUT=A
//SYSIN        DD      *
  DEFINE CLUSTER               —
       (                       —
       NAME(RECEIVE.CLUSTER)   —
       VOL(VSAM02)             —
       NUMBERED                —
       SHR(2 3)                —
       CYL(10 2)               —
       KEYS(8 0)               —
       RECSZ(80 80)            —
```

```
        )                              —
        CATALOG(UCATLG01)
/*
```

7.5 MODAL COMMANDS

An AMS comamnd stream can contain more than one command. There is no limitation to the number of commands that can be executed. Furthermore, different types of commands can be submitted for the same IDCAMS run. For example, a command stream can contain several DEFINEs, one or more REPROs, a LISTCAT, and other commands.

Sometimes, when submitted several commands, it may not be desirable to continue to the end of the command stream if a difficulty is encountered with one of the commands. By using modal commands error conditions can be tested and a different course of action can be taken.

7.5.1 CONDITION CODES

After execution of every AMS command, a **condition code (CC)** is returned. This condition code indicates how successful the command execution was. The following is a list of possible condition codes and their meaning:

CODE	MEANING
0	Indicates that the command was executed and was successful. Execution continues with the next command.
4	Indicates that some problem occurred during execution of the command but of a minor nature. Execution continues with the next command.
8	Indicates that some major specifications were bypassed during execution of this command. Some aspects of the command may have been executed, however. Execution continues with the next command.
12	Indicates that the command could not be executed at all. This is usually caused by major errors in the command specification. Parameters may be missing or in conflict. Other conditions could cause this condition as well. Execution continues with the next command.
16	The code is caused by error conditions in which AMS cannot continue. When this type of error occurs, the rest of the command stream is flushed.

7.5.2 CONTROLLING COMMAND EXECUTION

The following commands can be used to control AMS command execution:

IF
THEN
ELSE
DO
END
SET

IF, THEN, ELSE, DO, and END are used together. The format for use of this command group is as follows:

```
IF      LASTCC | MAXCC (comparand) (condition code)
        THEN [ command ] |
        THEN DO
                .
                .
                .
                (command group)
                .
                .
                END
        ELSE [ command ] |
        ELSE DO
                .
                .
                .
                (command group)
                .
                .
                END
```

Where:

LASTCC:
Allows for the testing of the **last** condition code returned by AMS.

MAXCC:
Allows for the testing of the **highest** condition code returned thus far by AMS.

comparand:

The following operators can be used for compare purposes: = or EQ, NE, > or GT, < or LT, >= or GE, <= or LE.

command:

Represents a single AMS command.

command group:

Represents more than one AMS command. An example follows:

```
DEFINE .........
IF      LASTCC = 0
THEN    DO
        REPRO ......
        LISTCAT ....
        END
ELSE
        LISTCAT ....
```

In this example a condition code of zero is tested after a DEFINE command has been executed. If the condition code is equal to zero, a REPRO will be performed followed by a LISTCAT. If a nonzero condition code is set, only a LISTCAT will be performed.

In addition to testing for condition codes, you can also set a condition code in the command stream. This is performed using the **SET** command. The format for the SET command is as follows:

SET MAXCC | LASTCC = (number)

An example follows:

```
DEFINE .........
IF      LASTCC = 0
THEN    DO
        REPRO ......
        LISTCAT ....
        END
ELSE
        LISTCAT ....
        SET MAXCC = 8
IF      MAXCC = 0
        THEN DO
        DEFINE ......
```

In this example the maximum condition code will be set, or reset, to the value 8. The DEFINE following the SET command will not be executed **if** the SET command was executed.

NOTES

1. This is being changed with the release of the latest versions of VSAM. A VERIFY operation will now be performed dynamically, if needed, after a cluster has been opened.
2. The DLBL and EXTENT cards are required only if they are not present in the Standard Label Cylinder. In that case, a DLBL card will also be required for IJSYSUC.
3. The number of tracks allocated to the VSAM space in this example exceeds the space requested in the CYL parameter. Space not used for the catalog itself can be used for other objects such as clusters.

TEST YOUR UNDERSTANDING

1. What logical steps are required to DEFINE VSAM objects to AMS in order to process data?
2. What is the function of a REUSABLE data set? What are the restrictions on its use?
3. What is the difference between SPEED and RECOVERY? When would you use one over the other?
4. What is meant by SHAREOPTIONS?
5. What is the function of KEYRANGES? Of what benefit is this parameter?
6. What is meant by the term MODAL? How can you make use of these commands?

chapter **8**

ACCESS METHOD SERVICES—COMMONLY USED FUNCTIONS

In this chapter we continue studying some of the basic AMS commands used to support VSAM files.

8.1 SOME MORE AMS COMMANDS

The following COMMANDS and/or TOPICS are covered in this chapter:

REPRO
IMPORT/EXPORT
LISTCAT
DELETE

VERIFY
PRINT
ALTER
MODELS

8.2 THE REPRO COMMAND

REPRO:

This AMS command can be used to perform any of the following functions:

Copy a VSAM cluster to a sequential data set
Copy a VSAM cluster to another VSAM cluster
Load a VSAM cluster from a non-VSAM file
Merge two VSAM files
Copy a sequential data set to another sequential data set
Reorganize a VSAM data set
Copy an alternate index as if it were a KSDS cluster
Copy a catalog

8.2.1 USING THE REPRO COMMAND

REPRO is short for **reproduce**. It is one of two ways provided by Access Method Services in which to make a copy of a data set. The nice thing about REPRO is that, unlike the EXPORT command, the output of REPRO can be read by an application program. REPRO is commonly used for file conversion. It is very convenient to use this facility to convert a file from ISAM to VSAM. The format for the REPRO command is the same as that used in the AMS DEFINE commands discussed in the previous chapter. The syntax used is identical.

COMMAND	PARAMETERS	NOTES
	For OS Installations:	
REPRO		REQ'D
	INFILE	
	(	
	jcl-dname [/password]	
	[ENVIRONMENT(DUMMY)] |	

```
COMMAND              PARAMETERS                                   NOTES
---------------------------------------------------------------------------
                     )
                     INDATASET
                     (
                     ename/ [password]
                         [ ENVIRONMENT(DUMMY) ]
                     )
                     OUTFILE
                     (
                     jcl-dname [/password]
                       [ ENVIRONMENT(DUMMY) ] |
                     )
                     OUTDATASET
                     (
                     ename/ [password]
                         [ ENVIRONMENT(DUMMY) ]
                     )
                     [REPLACE | NOREPLACE ]
                     [REUSE | NOREUSE ]
                     [FROMKEY ( fkey ) |
                     [FROMADDRESS( fadress)] |
                     [FROMNUMBER( fnumber) ]
                     [SKIP( number )]
                     [COUNT ( number ) ]
                     [TOKEY ( tkey ) |
                     [TOADDRESS( tadress)] |
                     [TONUMBER( tnumber) ]
```

```
COMMAND              PARAMETERS                                   NOTES
---------------------------------------------------------------------------
                     For DOS Installations:
REPRO                                                             REQ'D
                     INFILE                                       REQ'D
                     (                                            REQ'D
                     jcl-dname [/password]                        REQ'D
                       [ENVIRONMENT
                       (
                       BLOCKSIZE( bsize)                          REQ'D
                       [HINDEXDEVICE ( dtype ) ]
                       [NOLABEL | STDLABEL ]
                       [NOREWIND | REWIND | UNLOAD ]
                       [PRIMEDATADEVICE( pdev ) ]
```

COMMAND	PARAMETERS	NOTES
	RECORDFORMAT(format)	REQ'D
	[RECORDSIZE(rsize)]	REQ'D
	)]	
	)	REQ'D
	OUTFILE	REQ'D
	(	REQ'D
	jcl-dname [/password]	REQ'D
	[ENVIRONMENT	
	(	
	BLOCKSIZE(bsize)	REQ'D
	[NOLABEL | STDLABEL]	
	[NOREWIND | REWIND | UNLOAD]	
	[PRIMEDATADEVICE(pdev)]	
	RECORDFORMAT(format)	REQ'D
	[RECORDSIZE(rsize)]	
	)]	
	)	REQ'D
	REPLACE | NOREPLACE]	
	[REUSE | NOREUSE]	
	[FROMKEY (fkey) |	
	[FROMADDRESS(fadress)] |	
	[FROMNUMBER(fnumber)]	
	[SKIP(number)]	
	[COUNT (number)]	
	[TOKEY (tkey) |	
	[TOADDRESS(tadress)] |	
	[TONUMBER(tnumber)]	

8.2.2 EXPLANATION OF SYMBOLS

If you have read Chapter 7 you may skip this discussion of symbols and syntax. If not, it is necessary to discuss the usage of symbols in the illustrations used in this book in order to understand the way in which you would code the control statements.

The bracket ("[" and "]") symbols always appear in sets and are used to denote those parameters or subparameters that are optional. There will be some cases, however, in which it will be necessary to code one of these parameters, especially when another optional parameter is used and the specification of the other becomes a requirement because of it.

The "|" symbol has become a standard data processing symbol when a choice must be made between certain items. It is for this reason sometimes referred to as the **OR** symbol.

The parentheses are used to contain the *value* of a given parameter.

Parameters that are underlined are AMS **defaults**, in other words if not specified they will be *assumed* by IDCAMS. A "—" (not shown in the preceding example) at the end of a command or parameter statement denotes continuation of the definition.

REQ'D:

Represents those parameters that must be coded. They are *required*.

R-DOS:

Specifies an item that is used only by the Disk Operating System (DOS/VS or DOS/VSE) *and* is required by that operating system.

R-OS:

Specifies an item that is used only by the Full Operating System (VS1 or MVS) *and* is required by that operating system.

DOS:

Specifies an item that is used only by the Disk Operating System (DOS/VS or DOS/VSE) *and* is optional.

OS:

Specifies an item that is used only by the Full Operating System (VS1 or MVS) *and* is optional.

8.2.3 THE REPRO PARAMETERS

EXPLANATION OF PARAMETERS

REPRO:

This command indicates to Access Method Services that you wish to perform some form of file copy operation.

INDATASET(ename [/password]): (OS ONLY)

This parameter can be used at OS installations only. It allows you to specify to AMS the name of the date set (ename) to be used as input to this function. This parameter can be abbreviated **IDS**.

INFILE(jcl-dname [/password]):

This entry allows you to specify to AMS the name of the DD (OS) or DLBL (DOS) JCL card that points to the INPUT file. This parameter is optional for OS but required for DOS. It can be abbreviated **IFILE**. Example:

```
                        REPRO INFILE(IFILE)
  // DLBL IFILE,'INPUT.FILE'      DOS
  //IFILE     DD     DSN=INPUT.FILE,DISP=SHR      OS
```

ENVIRONMENT(subparameters):

This parameter comes in two distinct types depending on the operating system. For OS only one parameter is available: **DUMMY**, which allows you to include dummy ISAM records found on the input file in the output data set. In OS systems ISAM records may be logically deleted by placing an X'ff' (HIGH VALUE) in the first byte of the record. If this parameter is omitted, logically deleted records are dropped. For DOS, ENVIRONMENT identifies the file characteristics that cannot be defined through JCL. This parameter can be abbreviated **ENV**.

BLOCKSIZE(bsize): (DOS ONLY)

This parameter is valid for DOS systems only. It is a subparameter of the ENVIRONMENT parameter and is required if ENV is used. With this parameter the size (bsize) of the block is specified for either input or output data sets. It can be abbreviated **BLKSZ**.

HINDEXDEVICE(dtype): (DOS ONLY)

This parameter is valid for DOS systems only. It is an optional subparameter of the ENVIRONMENT command. This parameter is specified only for ISAM files and describes the device type (dtype) on which the highest level index is found (e.g., 2314, 3330, 3340). This parameter can be abbreviated **HDEV**.

NOLABEL | STDLABEL: (DOS ONLY)

This parameter is valid for DOS systems only. It is an optional subparameter of the ENVIRONMENT command. This parameter indicates to AMS whether an input or output file contains standard labels. Default is STDLABEL. This parameter can be abbreviated **NLBL** or **SLBL**, respectively.

NOREWIND | REWIND | UNLOAD: (DOS ONLY)

This parameter is valid for DOS systems only. It is an optional subparameter of the ENVIRONMENT command. This parameter indicates to AMS input or output **tape** control options. Default is NOREWIND. This parameter can be abbreviated **NREW**, **REW**, or **UNLD**, respectively.

PRIMEDATADEVICE(pdev): (DOS ONLY)

This parameter is valid for DOS systems only. It is an optional subparameter of the ENVIRONMENT command. This parameter indicates to AMS the input or output device type (pdev). It is required for ISAM and tape files only. A device type of 2400 must be used for tape files and an ASSGN card using SYS004 as the programmer-logical unit if the data set is input, SYS005 if output. This parameter can be abbreviated **PDEV**.

RECORDFORMAT(format): (DOS ONLY)

This parameter is valid for DOS systems only. It is a required subparameter of the ENVIRONMENT command. This parameter indicates to AMS the type of non-VSAM record being used. The valid record formats are as follows:

FIXUNB	or	F	Fixed unblocked
FIXBLK	or	FB	Fixed blocked
SPNUNB	or	S	Spanned unblocked
SPNBLK	or	SB	Spanned blocked
VARUNB	or	V	Variable unblocked
VARBLK	or	VB	Variable blocked
UNDEF	or	U	Undefined

VB should be used for catalogs.
This parameter can be abbreviated **RECFM**.

RECORDSIZE(rsize): (DOS ONLY)

This parameter is valid for DOS systems only. It is an optional subparameter of the ENVIRONMENT command. This parameter indicates to AMS the size of the logical record for FIXUNB and FIXBLK non-VSAM files. This parameter specifies the maximum record size for SPNBLK, SPNUNB, and UNDEF files. This parameter is not required for VARUNB or VARBLK files. When reloading a back-up copy of a catalog use 516 as the record size. This parameter can be abbreviated **RECSZ**.

OUTDATASET(ename [/password]): (OS ONLY)

This parameter can be used at OS installations only. It allows you to specify to AMS the name of the data set (ename) to be created using to this function.

OUTFILE(jcl-dname [/password]):

This entry allows you to specify to AMS the name of the DD (OS) or DLBL (DOS) JCL card that points to the output file. This parameter is optional for OS but required for DOS. See also the INFILE parameter. This parameter can be abbreviated **OFILE**.

FROMADDRESS(faddress): |
FROMKEY(fkey): |
FROMNUMBER(fnumber):

With this parameter you can specify to Access Method Services the point within an input file at which you would like to begin your copy operation. The specification can be made as either a key (KEY), relative byte address-RBA (ADDRESS), or relative record number-RRN (NUMBER). If an RBA is specified, it must be a valid address (i.e., beginning of a record) or the address will be rejected. If this parameter (FROM...) is omitted, a copy operation will always begin at the first record. The abbreviations are **FADDR**, **FKEY**, and **FNUM**, respectively.

SKIP(number):

This parameter allows you to specify the number of records that AMS is to SKIP over before beginning a copy operation.

COUNT(number):

This parameter allows you to specify the number of records that AMS is to copy to the output data set before ending the copy operation.

TOADDRESS(taddress): |
TOKEY(tkey): |
TONUMBER(tnumber):

With this parameter you can specify to Access Method Services the point within an input file at which you would like to end your copy operation. The specification can be made as either a key (KEY), relative byte address-RBA (ADDRESS), or as a relative record number-RRN (NUMBER). If this parameter is omitted, a copy operation will always end at the last record. The abbreviations are **TADDR** and **TNUM**, respectively.

REPLACE | NOREPLACE:

This parameter is valid for KSDS and RRDS data sets only. With this parameter you can indicate to AMS that in the event an input record should be found equal in key (KSDS) or RRN (RRDS) in the output file, that it should be replaced (REPLACE) or not replaced (NOREPLACE). In effect, this option allows REPRO to be used as a limited file update utility. The default is NOREPLACE. Abbreviations which can be used are **REP** and **NREP**, respectively.

REUSE | NOREUSE:

This parameter allows you to specify whether the VSAM output data set will be opened as a REUSABLE data set. The output file can be declared REUSABLE even if it was originally defined as not REUSABLE providing that the output data set does not already exist and contain data records. The default is NOREUSE. This parameter can be abbreviated **RUS** or **NRUS**, respectively.

In the previous chapter we established that in our inventory system example we would be required to prepare the control cards necessary to back up our data sets. To accomplish this both the REPRO and IMPORT facilities of IDCAMS are used.

8.2.4 SOME EXAMPLES OF REPRO

The following is an example of the IDCAMS control statements necessary to perform the REPRO operation:

For DOS:

```
REPRO                       -
      INFILE(INVFIL)        -
      OUTFILE(INVTAPE)      -
      ENV                   -
        (                   -
        BLKSZ(4000)         -
        SLBL                -
        UNLD                -
        PDEV(2400)          -
        RECFM(FB)           -
        RECSZ(200)          -
        )                   -
```

The preceding INFILE and OUTFILE parameters could have been coded using this format:

```
INFILE     -
(          -
INVFIL     -
)          -
OUTFILE    -
(          -
INVTAPE    -
)          -
```

Now the rest of the REPROs:

```
REPRO                       -
      INFILE(SALFIL)        -
      OUTFILE(SALTAPE)      -
      ENV                   -
        (                   -
        BLKSZ(800)          -
        SLBL                -
        UNLD                -
        PDEV(2400)          -
        RECFM(VB)           -
        RECSZ(074)          -
        )                   -

REPRO                       -
      INFILE(PURFIL)        -
      OUTFILE(PURTAPE)      -
```

```
         ENV                               —
            (                              —
            BLKSZ(3600)                    —
            SLBL                           —
            UNLD                           —
            PDEV(2400)                     —
            RECFM(FB)                      —
            RECSZ(120)                     —
            )                              —

    REPRO                                  —
         INFILE(RECFIL)                    —
         OUTFILE(RECTAPE)                  —
         ENV                               —
            (                              —
            BLKSZ(4000)                    —
            SLBL                           —
            UNLD                           —
            PDEV(2400)                     —
            RECFM(FB)                      —
            RECSZ(080)                     —
            )                              —
```

For OS:

```
    REPRO                                  —
         INFILE(INVFIL)                    —
         OUTFILE(INVTAPE)

    REPRO                                  —
         INFILE(PURFIL)                    —
         OUTFILE(PURTAPE)

    REPRO                                  —
         INFILE(SALFIL)                    —
         OUTFILE(SALTAPE)

    REPRO                                  —
         INFILE(RECFIL)                    —
         OUTFILE(RECTAPE)
```

or:

```
    REPRO                                  —
         INDATASET(INVENTRY,CLUSTER)       —
         OUTFILE(INVTAPE)
```

```
REPRO                                        —
        INDATASET(PURCH.CLUSTER)             —
        OUTFILE(PURTAPE)

REPRO                                        —
        INDATASET(SALES.CLUSTER)             —
        OUTFILE(SALTAPE)

REPRO                                        —
        INDATASET(RECEIVE,CLUSTER)           —
        OUTFILE(INVTAPE)
```

8.2.5 SAMPLE REPRO WITH JCL

The JCL required for the preceding would look like this:

```
// JOB BACKUP ACCTDATA
// DLBL IJSYSUC,'UCATLG01',,VSAM
// DLBL INVFIL,'INVENTRY.CLUSTER',,VSAM
// DLBL SALFIL,'SALES.CLUSTER',,VSAM
// DLBL PURFIL,'PURCH.CLUSTER',,VSAM
// DLBL RECFIL,'RECEIVE.CLUSTER',,VSAM
// TLBL INVTAPE,'INVENTRY.CLUSTER.BACKUP
// TLBL SALTAPE,'SALES.CLUSTER.BACKUP'
// TLBL PURTAPE,'PURCH.CLUSTER.BACKUP'
// TLBL RECTAPE,'RECEIVE.CLUSTER.BACKUP'
// ASSGN SYS005,TAPE
// EXEC IDCAMS,SIZE=AUTO

                    CONTROL CARDS GO HERE

/*
```

Putting it all together:

```
// JOB INVBACK ACCTDATA
// DLBL IJSYSUC,'UCATLG01',,VSAM
// DLBL INVFIL,'INVENTRY.CLUSTER',,VSAM
// DLBL SALFIL,'SALES.CLUSTER',,VSAM
// DLBL PURFIL,'PURCH.CLUSTER',,VSAM
// DLBL RECFIL,'RECEIVE.CLUSTER',,VSAM
// TLBL INVTAPE,'INVENTRY.CLUSTER.BACKUP'
// TLBL SALTAPE,'SALES.CLUSTER.BACKUP'
// TLBL PURTAPE,'PURCH.CLUSTER.BACKUP'
// TLBL RECTAPE,'RECEIVE.CLUSTER.BACKUP'
```

```
// ASSGN SYS005,TAPE
// EXEC IDCAMS,SIZE=AUTO

        REPRO                          —
                INFILE(INVFIL)         —
                OUTFILE(INVTAPE)       —
                ENV                    —
                  (                    —
                  BLKSZ(4000)          —
                  SLBL                 —
                  UNLD                 —
                  PDEV(2400)           —
                  RECFM(FB)            —
                  RECSZ(200)           —
                  )                    —
        REPRO                          —
                INFILE(SALFIL)         —
                OUTFILE(SALTAPE)       —
                ENV                    —
                  (                    —
                  BLKSZ(800)           —
                  SLBL                 —
                  UNLD                 —
                  PDEV(2400)           —
                  RECFM(VB)            —
                  RECSZ(074)           —
                  )                    —
        REPRO                          —
                INFILE(PURFIL)         —
                OUTFILE(PURTAPE)       —
                ENV                    —
                  (                    —
                  BLKSZ(3600)          —
                  SLBL                 —
                  UNLD                 —
                  PDEV(2400)           —
                  RECFM(FB)            —
                  RECSZ(120)           —
                  )                    —
        REPRO                          —
                INFILE(RECFIL)         —
                OUTFILE(RECTAPE)       —
                ENV                    —
```

```
                    (                 —
                    BLKSZ(4000)       —
                    SLBL              —
                    UNLD              —
                    PDEV(2400)        —
                    RECFM(FB)         —
                    RECSZ(080)        —
                    )                 —
/*
```

For OS:

```
//INVBACK    JOB    ACCTDATA,'MIKE BOUROS',CLASS=R
//INVAMS     EXEC   PGM=IDCAMS
//STEPCAT    DD     DSN=UCATLG01,DISP=SHR
//INVFIL     DD     DSN=INVENTRY.CLUSTER,DISP=SHR
//PURFIL     DD     DSN=PURCH.CLUSTER,DISP=SHR
//SALFIL     DD     DSN=SALES.CLUSTER,DISP=SHR
//RECFIL     DD     DSN=RECEIVE.CLUSTER,DISP=SHR
//INVTAPE    DD     DSN=INVENTRY.CLUSTER.BACKUP,DISP=NEW,
//                  VOL=SER=111111,UNIT=TAPE,LABEL=(,SL),
//                  DCB=(LRECL=200,BLKSIZE=4000,RECFM=FB)
//PURTAPE    DD     DSN=PURCH.CLUSTER.BACKUP,DISP=NEW,
//                  VOL=SER=222222,UNIT=TAPE,LABEL=(,SL),
//                  DCB=(LRECL=120,BLKSIZE=3600,RECFM=FB)
//SALTAPE    DD     DSN=SALES,CLUSTER,BACKUP,DISP=NEW,
//                  VOL=SER=333333,UNIT=TAPE,LABEL=(,SL),
//                  DCB=(LRECL=74,BLKSIZE=800,RECFM=VB)
//RECTAPE    DD     DSN=RECEIVE.CLUSTER.BACKUP,DISP=NEW,
//                  VOL=SER=444444,UNIT=TAPE,LABEL=(,SL),
//                  DCB=(LRECL=80,BLKSIZE=4000,RECFM=FB)
//SYSPRINT   DD     SYSOUT=A
//SYSIN      DD     *

                   CONTROL CARDS GO HERE

/*
```

Putting it all together:

```
//INVBACK    JOB    ACCTDATA,'MIKE BOUROS',CLASS=R
//INVAMS     EXEC   PGM=IDCAMS
//STEPCAT    DD     DSN=UCATLG01,DISP=SHR
//INVFIL     DD     DSN=INVENTRY.CLUSTER,DISP=SHR
//PURFIL     DD     DSN=PURCH.CLUSTER,DISP=SHR
```

```
//SALFIL     DD    DSN=SALES.CLUSTER,DISP=SHR
//RECFIL     DD    DSN=RECEIVE.CLUSTER,DISP=SHR
//INVTAPE    DD    DSN=INVENTRY.CLUSTER.BACKUP,DISP=NEW,
//                 VOL=SER=111111,UNIT=TAPE,LABEL=(,SL),
//                 DCB=(LRECL=200,BLKSIZE=4000,RECFM=FB)
//PURTAPE    DD    DSN=PURCH.CLUSTER.BACKUP,DISP=NEW,
//                 VOL=SER=222222,UNIT=TAPE,LABEL=(,SL),
//                 DCB=(LRECL=120,BLKSIZE=3600,RECFM=FB)
//SALTAPE    DD    DSN=SALES.CLUSTER.BACKUP,DISP=NEW,
//                 VOL=SER=333333,UNIT=TAPE,LABEL=(,SL),
//                 DCB=(LRECL=74,BLKSIZE=800,RECFM=VB)
//RECTAPE    DD    DSN=RECEIVE.CLUSTER.BACKUP,DISP=NEW,
//                 VOL=SER=444444,UNIT=TAPE,LABEL=(,SL),
//                 DCB=(LRECL=80,BLKSIZE=4000,RECFM=FB)
//SYSPRINT   DD    SYSOUT=A
//SYSIN      DD    *
               REPRO                                 -
                     INFILE(INVFIL)                  -
                     OUTFILE(INVTAPE)
               REPRO                                 -
                     INDATASET(PURCH.CLUSTER)        -
                     OUTFILE(PURTAPE)
               REPRO                                 -
                     INDATASET(SALES.CLUSTER)        -
                     OUTFILE(SALTAPE)
               REPRO                                 -
                     INDATASET(RECEIVE.CLUSTER)      -
                     OUTFILE(INVTAPE)
/*
```

Or:

```
//INVBACK    JOB   ACCTDATA,'MIKE BOUROS',CLASS=R
//INVAMS     EXEC  PGM=IDCAMS
//STEPCAT    DD    DSN=UCATLG01,DISP=SHR
//INVTAPE    DD    DSN=INVENTRY.CLUSTER.BACKUP,DISP=NEW,
//                 VOL=SER=123456,UNIT=TAPE,LABEL=(,SL),
//                 DCB=(LRECL=200,BLKSIZE=4000,RECFM=FB)
//PURTAPE    DD    DSN=PURCH.CLUSTER.BACKUP,DISP=NEW,
//                 VOL=SER=222222,UNIT=TAPE,LABEL=(,SL),
//                 DCB=(LRECL=120,BLKSIZE=3600,RECFM=FB)
//SALTAPE    DD    DSN=SALES.CLUSTER.BACKUP,DISP=NEW,
//                 VOL=SER=333333,UNIT=TAPE,LABEL=(,SL),
//                 DCB=(LRECL=74,BLKSIZE=800,RECFM=VB)
//RECTAPE    DD    DSN=RECEIVE.CLUSTER.BACKUP,DISP=NEW,
```

```
//              VOL=SER=444444,UNIT=TAPE,LABEL=(,SL),
//              DCB=(LRECL=80,BLKSIZE=4000,RECFM=FB)
//SYSPRINT DD   SYSOUT=A
//SYSIN    DD   *
               REPRO                                       —
                      INDATASET(INVENTRY.CLUSTER)          —
                      OUTFILE(INVTAPE)
               REPRO                                       —
                      INDATASET(PURCH.CLUSTER)             —
                      OUTFILE(PURTAPE)
               REPRO                                       —
                      INDATASET(SALES.CLUSTER)             —
                      OUTFILE(SALTAPE)
               REPRO                                       —
                      INDATASET(RECEIVE.CLUSTER)           —
                      OUTFILE(INVTAPE)
  /*
```

8.3 THE AMS EXPORT/IMPORT COMMANDS

After running the preceding job you will have backed up all of your data clusters onto tape. These can now be sent to a vault or to a sister installation for further processing.

For emergency back-up a job stream to EXPORT the data sets will also be set up and a corresponding job stream to IMPORT them back if necessary. Furthermore a job stream to reorganize our KSDS clusters using a DELETE and DEFINE sequence will be set up.

EXPORT/IMPORT

These AMS commands work together to provide the user with a certain amount of backup security. The IMPORT function provides a backup function somewhat similar to that provided by REPRO. However, the output produced is not in a format that can be read and processed by an application program. The EXPORT/IMPORT facility is commonly used to transport objects between systems.

EXPORT provides a faster method of backup than REPRO. Unlike REPRO, however, IMPORT does not require an IDCAMS DEFINE when restoring a cluster or other object.

EXPORT/IMPORT facilities include the following functions:

Back up a cluster to tape/DASD
Back up an alternate index
Disconnect a user catalog from a master catalog
Restore a cluster
Restore an alternate index
Reconnect a user catalog to a master catalog

8.3.1 USING THE EXPORT/IMPORT COMMAND

The format for this command is the same as that used in the AMS DEFINE commands discussed in the previous chapter. The syntax used is identical. Depending on purpose, there are two formats for the EXPORT/IMPORT commands.

```
COMMAND            PARAMETERS                                    NOTES
-----------------------------------------------------------------------
                   Format type 1.
EXPORT                                                           REQ'D
                   ucat [/password ]                             REQ'D
                   DISCONNECT

                   Format type 2.
EXPORT                                                           REQ'D
                   ename [ password ]                            REQ'D
                   INFILE( dname )                               REQ'D
                   OUTDATASET( dname )                           O-OS
                   OUTFILE
                   (
                   jcl-dname [/password]
                     [ENVIRONMENT                                R-DOS
                      (                                          DOS
                      BLOCKSIZE( bsize )                         R-DOS
                      [NOLABEL | STDLABEL ]                      DOS
                      [ NOREWIND | REWIND | UNLOAD ]             DOS
                      [PRIMEDATADEVICE( pdev ) ]                 DOS
                      )                           ]
                   )
                   [RECORDMODE | CIMODE ]
                   [ERASE | NOERASE ]
                   [INHIBITSOURCE | NOINHIBITSOURCE ]
                   [INHIBITTARGET | NOINHIBITTARGET ]
                   [PURGE | NOPURGE ]
                   [TEMPORARY | PERMANENT ]
```

COMMAND	PARAMETERS	NOTES
	Format type 1.	
IMPORT		REQ'D
	ename [password]	REQ'D
	CONNECT	
	OBJECTS	
	(	
	(ename	
	DEVICETYPE(dtype)	
	VOLUMES(volser volser...)	
	)	
	)	
	[CATALOG(cname [/password])]	
	Format type 2.	
IMPORT		REQ'D
	INFILE	
	(	
	jcl-dname	
	[ENVIRONMENT	R-DOS
	(	DOS
	BLOCKSIZE(bsize)	R-DOS
	[NOLABEL | STDLABEL]	DOS
	[NOREWIND | REWIND | UNLOAD]	DOS
	[PRIMEDATADEVICE(pdev)]	DOS
	)]	
	)	
	OUTFILE(dname [/password])	REQ'D
	[ERASE | NOERASE]	
	[OBJECTS	
	(	
	(ename	
	[FILE(dname)]	
	[KEYRANGES((Lkey Hkey)...(Lkey Hkey)]	
	[NEWNAME(newname)]	
	[ORDERED | UNORDERED]	
	[USECLASS(prim [sec])]	
	[VOLUMES(vol1 [vol2...])] | DEFAULTVOLUMES	
	[OUTPW(password)]	
	[PURGE | NOPURGE]	
	[SAVRAC | NOSAVRAC]	
	[CATALOG(cname [/password])	

8.3.2 THE IMPORT/EXPORT PARAMETERS

EXPLANATION OF EXPORT PARAMETERS

EXPORT:

This command indicates to Access Method Services that you wish to make a back-up copy of a cluster or alternate index. It can also be used to copy-disconnect a user catalog from a master catalog, usually for the purpose of moving it to another system. This parameter can be abbreviated **EXP**.

ucat [/password]):

This parameter is used only with format 1 of the EXPORT command. It specifies the name of the user catalog to be DISCONNECTED. The catalog password must be specified if one exists.

DISCONNECT:

This parameter is used only with format 1 of the EXPORT command. It is used to disassociate a user catalog from a master catalog. Its abbreviation can be **DCON**.

ename [/password]:

This specifies the name of the cluster or alternate index to be exported. Index or data components cannot be exported separately.

INFILE(dname):

This specifies the name (dname) of the DLBL or DD statement that identifies the object to be exported. This parameter can be abbreviated **IFILE**.

OUTFILE(dname):

This parameter specifies the name of the DLBL or DD card used to describe the data set that will receive the exported object. Its abbreviation can be **OFILE**.

OUTDATASET(ename): (OS ONLY)

This specifies the name of the data set that is to receive the exported object. This parameter can be used in lieu of OUTFILE. Its abbreviation can be **ODS**.

ENVIRONMENT(subparameters): (DOS ONLY)

This parameter is used by DOS only. It describes the characteristics of the data set that will receive the exported object. This parameter can be abbreviated **ENV**.

BLOCKSIZE(bsize): (DOS ONLY)

This parameter is valid for DOS systems only. It is a subparameter of the ENVIRONMENT command and is required when using ENV. With this parameter the size (bsize) of the block is specified for the output data set. It can be abbreviated **BLKSZ**.

NOLABEL | STDLABEL: (DOS ONLY)

This parameter is valid for DOS systems only. It is an optional subparameter of the ENVIRONMENT command. This parameter indicates to AMS whether the output file contains standard labels. Default is STDLABEL. This parameter can be abbreviated **NLBL** or **SLBL**, respectively.

NOREWIND | REWIND | UNLOAD: (DOS ONLY)

This parameter is valid for DOS systems only. It is an optional subparameter of the ENVIRONMENT command. This parameter indicates to AMS output tape control options. Default is NOREWIND. This parameter can be abbreviated **NREW**, **REW**, or **UNLD**, respectively.

PRIMEDATADEVICE(pdev): (DOS ONLY)

This parameter is valid for DOS systems only. It is an optional subparameter of the ENVIRONMENT command. This parameter indicates to AMS the output device type (pdev). This parameter is required for ISAM and tape files only. A device type of 2400 must be used for tape files and an ASSGN card using SYS005 as the programmer-logical unit. This parameter can be abbreviated **PDEV**.

CIMODE | RECORDMODE: (DOS ONLY)

This defines to AMS the copy mode to be used to back up a file. CIMODE allows VSAM to copy the object by control interval rather than by logical record (RECORDMODE). For objects copied to OS systems, or for use with systems under Release 34 or earlier of DOS/VS specify RECORDMODE. Default is CIMODE. It can be abbreviated: **CIM** or **RECM**, respectively.

ERASE | NOERASE:

This parameter allows you to request AMS to ERASE the area in which an EXPORTed object existed after backing it up. This is useful in those situations in which an object containing sensitive information is being exported. The area formerly occupied by this object is overwritten with binary zeros (LOW-VALUE). This parameter will override the parameter used when the object was defined. This parameter can be abbreviated **ERAS** or **NERAS**, respectively.

INHIBITSOURCE | NONINHIBITSOURCE:

This specifies the access attributes of the *input* object after the export operation completes. By specifying INHIBITSOURCE the input object can be made read-only. This parameter has no effect on the output copy of the object. This feature can come in handy when a data set, for example, is to be processed at another site and then later restored. The default is NONINHIBITSOURCE. The abbreviations can be **INHS** or **NINHS**, respectively.

INHIBITTARGET | NONINHIBITTARGET:

This specifies the access attributes of the *output* object after the export operation completes. By specifying INHIBITTARGET the output object can be made read-only. This parameter has no effect on the input copy of the object. The default is NOINHIBITTARGET. The abbreviations can be **INHT** or **NINHT**, respectively.

PURGE | NOPURGE:

This specifies whether an object to be permanently exported is to be deleted from the source system regardless of expiration date. If NOPURGE is specified, the object is not deleted if the retention period has not expired. The default is NOPURGE. This parameter can be abbreviated **PRG** or **NPRG**.

TEMPORARY | PERMANENT:

This specifies whether the object being exported is to be deleted from the source catalog. This parameter is used in conjunction with the PURGE/NOPURGE parameter. If PERMANENT is specified, the object will be deleted. Default is PERMANENT. The abbreviation is **TEMP** or **PERM**, respectively.

EXPLANATION OF IMPORT PARAMETERS

IMPORT:

This command indicates to Access Method Services that you wish to restore a back-up copy of a cluster or alternate index. It can also be used to copy-connect a user catalog to a master catalog. This parameter can be abbreviated **IMP**.

ucat [/password]):

This parameter is used only with format 1 of the IMPORT command. It specifies the name of the user catalog to be CONNECTED.

CONNECT:

This parameter is used only with format 1 of the IMPORT command. It is used to associate a user catalog with a master catalog. It can be abbreviated **CON**.

OBJECTS:

This parameter is used to specify changes to be made to the VSAM object when being restored. It can be abbreviated **OBJ**.

DEVICETYPE:

This specifies the type of device that contains the user catalog to be CONNECTED. It can be abbreviated **DEVT**.

VOLUMES(volser volser...:

This parameter specifies the volume serial number of the device that will contain the OBJECT. If this device is the same as the original, this parameter can be omitted. It can be abbreviated **VOL**.

ENVIRONMENT(subparameters): (DOS ONLY)

For DOS, this parameter identifies the file characteristics that cannot be defined through JCL. This parameter can be abbreviated **ENV**.

BLOCKSIZE(bsize): (DOS ONLY)

This parameter is valid for DOS systems only. It is a subparameter of the ENVIRONMENT command and is required if ENV is used. With this parameter the size (bsize) of the block is specified for either input or output data sets. It can be abbreviated **BLKSZ**.

NOLABEL | STDLABEL: (DOS ONLY)

This parameter is valid for DOS systems only. It is an optional subparameter of the ENVIRONMENT command. This parameter indicates to AMS whether an input or output file contains standard labels. Default is STDLABEL. This parameter can be abbreviated **NLBL** or **SLBL**, respectively.

NOREWIND | REWIND | UNLOAD: (DOS ONLY)

This parameter is valid for DOS systems only. It is an optional subparameter of the ENVIRONMENT parameter. This parameter indicates to AMS input or output tape control options. Default is NOREWIND. This parameter can be abbreviated **NREW**, **REW**, or **UNLD**, respectively.

PRIMEDATADEVICE(pdev): (DOS ONLY)

This parameter is valid for DOS systems only. It is an optional subparameter of the ENVIRONMENT command. This parameter indicates to AMS the input or output device type (pdev). It is required for ISAM and tape files only. A device type of 2400 must be used for tape files and an ASSGN card using SYS004 as the programmer-logical. This parameter can be abbreviated **PDEV**.

OUTDATASET(ename [/password]): (OS ONLY)

This parameter can be used at OS installations only. It allows you to specify to AMS the name of the data set (ename) to be created using this function.

OUTFILE(jcl-dname [/password]):

This entry allows you to specify to AMS the name of the DD (OS) or DLBL (DOS) JCL card that points to the output file. This parameter is optional for OS but required for DOS. See also the INFILE parameter. This parameter can be abbreviated **OFILE**.

ERASE | NOERASE:

This parameter allows you to specify if the data component of the cluster or Alternate Index being imported is to be flagged for erasure. The next time this component is deleted or exported the area in which the cluster formerly existed will be overwritten with binary zeros (low-value). Its abbreviations can be **ERAS** or **NERAS**, respectively.

INTOEMPTY: (OS ONLY)

This parameter specifies that you are importing into an empty data set. AMS will not let you import a data set if an entry with that name already exists. There are two exceptions to this, however: if the data set was exported using the TEMPORARY parameter, or if the cluster in the existing catalog is empty. Importing into the empty data set allows the characteristics and profiles of the back-up data set to be maintained if this parameter is used; otherwise, the cluster will take on the characteristics of the empty cluster. Its abbreviation is **IEMPTY**.

OBJECTS(name):

This parameter allows specification of new or changed attributes to be made to the object being imported. The abbreviation is **OBJ**.

FILE(dname):

This specifies the name of the DLBL (DOS) or DD (OS) statement that identifies the volume being imported. This parameter is required when the object is defined with the UNIQUE attribute. Two FILE parameters will be required to define the Index and Data components.

KEYRANGES((Lkey Hkey) [(Lkey Hkey)]):

This parameter works in conjunction with the VOLUMES parameter to allow distribution of data to different volumes according to KEYRANGE. See the DEFINE command for more information on this. Its abbreviation is **KRNG**.

NEWNAME(new name):

This allows you to rename the object being restored. This does not apply to a user catalog. This new name will replace the entry name (ename) specified in the OBJECT parameter. Its abbreviation is **NEWNM**.

ORDERED | UNORDERED:

This parameter works in conjunction with the KEYRANGES and VOLUMES parameters. With this parameter you can specify whether the volumes are to be allocated in the ORDER in which they are coded in the VOLUMES parameter. This parameter will also allow you to change the selection sequence that was specified when the object was originally created (before being exported). If this is not specified, the object will be restored in the same ORDER in which is was exported. For additional information see this parameter in the DEFINE command. Its abbreviation is **ORD** or **UNORD**.

VOLUMES(volser1 [volser2]....):

This specifies the VOLUMES that are to receive the object. This parameter works in conjunction with the KEYRANGES and ORDERED parameter. Its abbreviation is **VOL**.

PURGE | NOPURGE:

This specifies whether the original cluster or alternate index is to be replaced even though the retention period may not as yet have expired. The default is NOPURGE. Its abbreviations are **PRG** or **NPRG**.

SAVRAC | NOSAVRAC: (OS ONLY)

This parameter pertains to those objects protected by the RACF (Resource Access Control Facility) feature. RACF is not part of VSAM. It is used for security purposes and works *with* VSAM. Specification of SAVRAC allows retention of existing RACF profiles. Default is NOSAVRAC. There is no abbreviation for this.

USECLASS (prim [sec]: (DOS ONLY)

This parameter allows the modification of the USECLASS for the object being imported. For a more thorough discussion of this subject, see the DEFINE command. Its abbreviation is **USCL**.

OUTPW (password):

This specifies the password of the data set to receive the object. Its abbreviation is **OPW**.

8.3.3 EXAMPLE IMPORT/EXPORT COMMANDS

Although we have already prepared the JCL and AMS control cards to make copies of our clusters on tape, our battle plan called for us to set up some JCL for EXPORT/IMPORT as well.

The following is an example of the IDCAMS control statements necessary to perform the EXPORT operation:

For DOS:

```
EXPORT                        —
        INVENTRY.CLUSTER      —
        INFILE(INVFIL)        —
        OUTFILE(INVTAPE       —
        ENV                   —
            (                 —
            SLBL              —
            UNLD              —
            PDEV(2400)        —
            )                 —
        )                     —
        RECORDMODE            —
        TEMP
```

Now the rest of the EXPORTS:

```
EXPORT                      -
        PURCH.CLUSTER       -
        INFILE(PURFIL)      -
        OUTFILE(PURTAPE     -
        ENV                 -
           (                -
           SLBL             -
           UNLD             -
           PDEV(2400)       -
           )                -
        )                   -
        RECORDMODE          -
        TEMP

EXPORT                      -
        SALES.CLUSTER       -
        INFILE(SALFIL)      -
        OUTFILE(SALTAPE     -
        ENV                 -
           (                -
           SLBL             -
           UNLD             -
           PDEV(2400)       -
           )                -
        )                   -
        RECORDMODE          -
        TEMP

EXPORT                      -
        RECEIVE.CLUSTER     -
        INFILE(RECFIL)      -
        OUTFILE(RECTAPE     -
        ENV                 -
           (                -
           SLBL             -
           UNLD             -
           PDEV(2400)       -
           )                -
        )                   -
        RECORDMODE          -
        TEMP
```

For OS:

```
EXPORT                          -
        INVENTRY.CLUSTER        -
        OUTFILE(INVTAPE)        -
        TEMPORARY               -

EXPORT                          -
        PURCH.CLUSTER           -
        OUTFILE(PURTAPE)        -
        TEMPORARY               -

EXPORT                          -
        SALES.CLUSTER           -
        OUTFILE(SALTAPE)        -
        TEMPORARY               -

EXPORT                          -
        RECEIVE.CLUSTER         -
        OUTFILE(RECTAPE)        -
        TEMPORARY
```

8.3.4 EXPORT WITH SAMPLE JCL

The JCL required for the preceding would look like this:

For DOS:

```
// JOB EXPORT ACCTDATA
// DLBL IJSYSUC,'UCATLG01',,VSAM
// DLBL INVFIL,'INVENTRY.CLUSTER',,VSAM
// DLBL SALFIL,'SALES.CLUSTER',,VSAM
// DLBL PURFIL,'PURCH.CLUSTER',,VSAM
// DLBL RECFIL,'RECEIVE.CLUSTER',,VSAM
// TLBL INVTAPE,'INVENTRY.CLUSTER.EXPORT'
// TLBL SALTAPE,'SALES.CLUSTER.EXPORT'
// TLBL PURTAPE,'PURCH.CLUSTER.EXPORT'
// TLBL RECTAPE,'RECEIVE.CLUSTER.EXPORT'
// ASSGN SYS005,TAPE
// EXEC IDCAMS,SIZE=AUTO

                    CONTROL CARDS GO HERE

/*
```

For OS:

```
//EXPORT    JOB   ACCTDATA,'MIKE BOUROS',CLASS=R
//INVAMS    EXEC  PGM=IDCAMS
//STEPCAT   DD    DSN=UCATLG01,DISP=SHR
//INVFIL    DD    DSN=INVENTRY.CLUSTER,DISP=SHR
//PURFIL    DD    DSN=PURCH.CLUSTER,DISP=SHR
//SALFIL    DD    DSN=SALES.CLUSTER,DISP=SHR
//RECFIL    DD    DSN=RECEIVE.CLUSTER,DISP=SHR
//INVTAPE   DD    DSN=INVENTRY.CLUSTER.EXPORT,DISP=NEW,
//                VOL=SER=111111,UNIT=TAPE,LABEL=(,SL),
//                DCB=(LRECL=200,BLKSIZE=4000,RECFM=FB)
//PURTAPE   DD    DSN=PURCH.CLUSTER.EXPORT,DISP=NEW,
//                VOL=SER=222222,UNIT=TAPE,LABEL=(,SL),
//                DCB=(LRECL=120,BLKSIZE=3600,RECFM=FB)
//SALTAPE   DD    DSN=SALES.CLUSTER.EXPORT,DISP=NEW,
//                VOL=SER=333333,UNIT=TAPE,LABEL=(,SL),
//                DCB=(LRECL=74,BLKSIZE=800,RECFM=VB)
//RECTAPE   DD    DSN=RECEIVE.CLUSTER.EXPORT,DISP=NEW,
//                VOL=SER=444444,UNIT=TAPE,LABEL=(,SL),
//                DCB=(LRECL=80,BLKSIZE=400,RECFM=FB)
//SYSPRINT  DD    SYSOUT=A
//SYSIN     DD    *

                  CONTROL CARDS GO HERE

/*
```

Putting it all together:

For DOS:

```
// JOB EXPORT ACCTDATA
// DLBL IJSYSUC,'UCATLG01',,VSAM
// DLBL INVFIL,'INVENTRY.CLUSTER',,VSAM
// DLBL SALFIL,'SALES.CLUSTER',,VSAM
// DLBL PURFIL,'PURCH.CLUSTER',,VSAM
// DLBL RECFIL,'RECEIVE.CLUSTER',,VSAM
// TLBL INVTAPE,'INVENTRY.CLUSTER.EXPORT'
// TLBL SALTAPE,'SALES.CLUSTER.EXPORT'
// TLBL PURTAPE,'PURCH.CLUSTER.EXPORT'
// TLBL RECTAPE,'RECEIVE.CLUSTER.EXPORT'
// ASSGN SYS005,TAPE
// EXEC IDCAMS,SIZE=AUTO
                  EXPORT                  -
                        INVENTRY.CLUSTER  -
```

```
          INFILE(INVFIL)        —
          OUTFILE(INVTAPE       —
          ENV                   —
             (                  —
             SLBL               —
             UNLD               —
             PDEV(2400)         —
             )                  —
          )                     —
          RECORDMODE            —
          TEMP
EXPORT                          —
          PURCH.CLUSTER         —
          INFILE(PURFIL)        —
          OUTFILE(PURTAPE       —
          ENV                   —
             (                  —
             SLBL               —
             UNLD               —
             PDEV(2400)         —
             )                  —
          )                     —
          RECORDMODE            —
          TEMP
EXPORT                          —
          SALES.CLUSTER         —
          INFILE(SALFIL)        —
          OUTFILE(SALTAPE       —
          ENV                   —
             (                  —
             SLBL               —
             UNLD               —
             PDEV(2400)         —
             )                  —
          )                     —
          RECORDMODE            —
          TEMP
EXPORT                          —
          RECEIVE.CLUSTER       —
          INFILE(RECFIL)        —
          OUTFILE(RECTAPE       —
          ENV                   —
             (                  —
             SLBL               —
             UNLD               —
```

```
                        PDEV(2400)        -
                        )                 -
                      )                   -
                      RECORDMODE          -
                      TEMP
    /*
```

For OS:

```
//EXPORT    JOB   ACCTDATA,'MIKE BOUROS',CLASS=R
//INVAMS    EXEC  PGM=IDCAMS
//STEPCAT   DD    DSN=UCATLG01,DISP=SHR
//INVFIL    DD    DSN=INVENTRY.CLUSTER,DISP=SHR
//PURFIL    DD    DSN=PURCH.CLUSTER,DISP=SHR
//SALFIL    DD    DSN=SALES.CLUSTER,DISP=SHR
//RECFIL    DD    DSN=RECEIVE.CLUSTER,DISP=SHR
//INVTAPE   DD    DSN=INVENTRY.CLUSTER.EXPORT,DISP=NEW,
//                VOL=SER=111111,UNIT=TAPE,LABEL=(,SL),
//                DCB=(LRECL=200,BLKSIZE=4000,RECFM=FB)
//PURTAPE   DD    DSN=PURCH.CLUSTER.EXPORT,DISP=NEW,
//                VOL=SER=222222,UNIT=TAPE,LABEL=(,SL),
//                DCB=(LRECL=120,BLKSIZE=3600,RECFM=FB)
//SALTAPE   DD    DSN=SALES.CLUSTER.EXPORT,DISP=NEW,
//                VOL=SER=333333,UNIT=TAPE,LABEL=(,SL),
//                DCB=(LRECL=74,BLKSIZE=800,RECFM=VB)
//RECTAPE   DD    DSN=RECEIVE.CLUSTER.EXPORT,DISP=NEW,
//                VOL=SER=444444,UNIT=TAPE,LABEL=(,SL),
//                DCB=(LRECL=80,BLKSIZE=4000,RECFM=FB)
//SYSPRINT  DD    SYSOUT=A
//SYSIN     DD    *
            EXPORT                        -
                  INVENTRY.CLUSTER        -
                  OUTFILE(INVTAPE)        -
                  TEMPORARY
            EXPORT                        -
                  PURCH.CLUSTER           -
                  OUTFILE(PURTAPE)        -
                  TEMPORARY
            EXPORT                        -
                  SALES.CLUSTER           -
                  OUTFILE(SALTAPE)        -
                  TEMPORARY
            EXPORT                        -

                  RECEIVE.CLUSTER         -
```

```
                OUTFILE(RECTAPE)      -
                TEMPORARY
/*
```

8.3.5 EXAMPLE IMPORT COMMANDS

The following job streams can be used to **restore** a previously EXPORTED cluster:

For DOS:

```
IMPORT                                -
     INFILE(INVTAPE                   -
     ENV                              -
       (                              -
       SLBL                           -
       PDEV(2400)                     -
       )                              -
     )                                -
     OUTFILE(INVFIL)                  -
     CATALOG(UCATLG01)

IMPORT                                -
     INFILE(PURTAPE                   -
     ENV                              -
       (                              -
       SLBL                           -
       PDEV(2400)                     -
       )                              -
     )                                -
     OUTFILE(PURFIL)                  -
     CATALOG(UCATLG01)

IMPORT                                -
     INFILE(SALTAPE                   -
     ENV                              -
       (                              -
       SLBL                           -
       PDEV(2400)                     -
       )                              -
     )                                -
     OUTFILE(SALFIL)                  -
     CATALOG(UCATLG01)

IMPORT                                -
     INFILE(RECTAPE                   -
```

```
        ENV                          -
          (                          -
          SLBL                       -
          PDEV(2400)                 -
          )                          -
        )                            -
        OUTFILE(RECFIL)              -
        CATALOG(UCATLG01)
/*
```

For **OS** the Control cards would look like this:

```
IMPORT                               -
     INFILE(INVTAPE)                 -
     OUTFILE(INVFIL)                 -
     CATALOG(UCATLG01)
IMPORT                               -
     INFILE(PURTAPE)                 -
     OUTFILE(PURFIL)                 -
     CATALOG(UCATLG01)
IMPORT                               -
     INFILE(SALTAPE)                 -
     OUTFILE(SALFIL)                 -
     CATALOG(UCATLG01)
IMPORT                               -
     INFILE(RECTAPE)                 -
     OUTFILE(RECFIL)                 -
     CATALOG(UCATLG01)
```

Another way this could have been done for **OS** is the following: Instead of:

OUTFILE(INVFIL)

we could have put:

OUTDATASET(INVENTRY.CLUSTER)

If we did it the second way, we would not have required a DD card for **INVFIL**.

8.3.6 THE IMPORT COMMAND WITH JCL

For our IMPORT function the following JCL will be required:

For DOS:

```
// JOB IMPORT ACCTDATA
// DLBL IJSYSUC,'UCATLG01',,VSAM
// DLBL INVFIL,'INVENTRY.CLUSTER',,VSAM
// DLBL SALFIL,'SALES.CLUSTER',,VSAM
// DLBL PURFIL,'PURCH.CLUSTER',,VSAM
// DLBL RECFIL,'RECEIVE.CLUSTER',,VSAM
// TLBL INVTAPE,'INVENTRY.CLUSTER.EXPORT'
// TLBL SALTAPE,'SALES.CLUSTER.EXPORT'
// TLBL PURTAPE,'PURCH.CLUSTER.EXPORT'
// TLBL RECTAPE,'RECEIVE.CLUSTER.EXPORT'
// ASSGN SYS005,TAPE
// EXEC IDCAMS,SIZE=AUTO

                    CONTROL CARDS GO HERE

/*
```

FOR OS:

```
//IMPORT    JOB   ACCTDATA,'MIKE BOUROS',CLASS=R
//INVAMS    EXEC  PGM=IDCAMS
//STEPCAT   DD    DSN=UCATLG01,DISP=SHR
//INVFIL    DD    DSN=INVENTRY.CLUSTER,DISP=SHR
//PURFIL    DD    DSN=PURCH.CLUSTER,DISP=SHR
//SALFIL    DD    DSN=SALES.CLUSTER,DISP=SHR
//RECFIL    DD    DSN=RECEIVE.CLUSTER,DISP=SHR
//INVTAPE   DD    DSN=INVENTRY.CLUSTER.EXPORT,DISP=OLD
//PURTAPE   DD    DSN=PURCH.CLUSTER.EXPORT,DISP=OLD
//SALTAPE   DD    DSN=SALES.CLUSTER.EXPORT,DISP=OLD
//RECTAPE   DD    DSN=RECEIVE.CLUSTER.EXPORT,DISP=OLD
//SYSPRINT  DD    SYSOUT=A
//SYSIN     DD    *

                    CONTROL CARDS GO HERE

/*
```

Putting it all together:

For DOS:

```
// JOB IMPORT ACCTDATA
// DLBL IJSYSUC,'UCATLG01',,VSAM
```

```
// DLBL INVFIL,'INVENTRY.CLUSTER',,VSAM
// DLBL SALFIL,'SALES.CLUSTER',,VSAM
// DLBL PURFIL,'PURCH.CLUSTER',,VSAM
// DLBL RECFIL,'RECEIVE.CLUSTER',,VSAM
// TLBL INVTAPE,'INVENTRY.CLUSTER.EXPORT'
// TLBL SALTAPE,'SALES.CLUSTER.EXPORT'
// TLBL PURTAPE,'PURCH.CLUSTER.EXPORT'
// TLBL RECTAPE,'RECEIVE.CLUSTER.EXPORT'
// ASSGN SYS005,TAPE
// EXEC IDCAMS,SIZE=AUTO
      IMPORT                          -
            INFILE(INVTAPE            -
            ENV                       -
               (                      -
               SLBL                   -
               PDEV(2400)             -
               )                      -
            )                         -
            OUTFILE(INVFIL)           -
            CATALOG(UCATLG01)
      IMPORT                          -
            INFILE(PURTAPE            -
            ENV                       -
               (                      -
               SLBL                   -
               PDEV(2400)             -
               )                      -
            )                         -
            OUTFILE(PURFIL)           -
            CATALOG(UCATLG01)
      IMPORT                          -
            INFILE(SALTAPE            -
            ENV                       -
               (                      -
               SLBL                   -
               PDEV(2400)             -
               )                      -
            )                         -
            OUTFILE(SALFIL)           -
            CATALOG(UCATLG01)
      IMPORT                          -
            INFILE(RECTAPE            -
            ENV                       -
               (                      -
               SLBL                   -
               PDEV(2400)             -
```

```
            )                          -
        )                              -
        OUTFILE(RECFIL)                -
        CATALOG(UCATLG01)
/*
```

OS:

```
//IMPORT      JOB    ACCTDATA,'MIKE BOUROS',CLASS=R
//INVAMS      EXEC   PGM=IDCAMS
//STEPCAT     DD     DSN=UCATLG01,DISP=SHR
//INVFIL      DD     DSN=INVENTRY.CLUSTER,DISP=SHR
//PURFIL      DD     DSN=PURCH.CLUSTER,DISP=SHR
//SALFIL      DD     DSN=SALES.CLUSTER,DISP=SHR
//RECFIL      DD     DSN=RECEIVE.CLUSTER,DISP=SHR
//INVTAPE     DD     DSN=INVENTRY.CLUSTER.EXPORT,
//                     DISP=OLD
//PURTAPE     DD     DSN=PURCH.CLUSTER.EXPORT,DISP=OLD
//SALTAPE     DD     DSN=SALES.CLUSTER.EXPORT,DISP=OLD
//RECTAPE     DD     DSN=RECEIVE.CLUSTER.EXPORT,
//                     DISP=OLD
//SYSPRINT    DD     SYSOUT=A
//SYSIN       DD     *
              IMPORT                            -
                     INFILE(INVTAPE)            -
                     OUTFILE(INVFIL)            -
                     CATALOG(UCATLG01)
              IMPORT                            -
                     INFILE(PURTAPE)            -
                     OUTFILE(PURFIL)            -
                     CATALOG(UCATLG01)
              IMPORT                            -
                     INFILE(SALTAPE)            -
                     OUTFILE(SALFIL)            -
                     CATALOG(UCATLG01)
              IMPORT                            -
                     INFILE(RECTAPE)            -
                     OUTFILE(RECFIL)            -
                     CATALOG(UCATLG01)
/*
```

8.4 THE LISTCAT COMMAND

One of the most useful tools available for use with VSAM is the **LISTCAT** facility. LISTCAT can be used to perform any of the following functions:

List ALIAS entries (OS only)
List alternate index entries
List cluster entries
List data component entries
List Generation Data Group entries (OS only)
List index component entries
List non-VSAM entries
List Page Data Set space (OS only)
List paths
List space
List user catalog pointers

In addition to this, different **levels** of information can be requested by the following:

Name
Allocation
Volume
All

The following is the format of the LISTCAT command:

COMMAND	PARAMETERS	NOTES
LISTCAT		REQ'D
	[ENTRIES(en1 [/pass] en2 [/pass] ...] |	
	[LEVEL(number)]	OS
	[ALTERNATEINDEX]	
	[CLUSTER]	
	[DATA]	
	[INDEX]	
	[NONVSAM]	
	[PATH]	
	[SPACE]	
	[USERCATALOG]	
	[ALIAS]	OS
	[GENERATIONDATAGROUP]	OS
	[PAGESPACE]	OS
	[NAME] |	
	[VOLUME] |	

(Continued on p. 152)

COMMAND	PARAMETERS	NOTES
	[ALLOCATION] |	
	[HISTORY]	
	[ALL]	
	[NOTUSABLE]	
	[CREATION(days)]	
	[EXPIRATION(days)]	
	[OUTFILE(jcl-dname)]	OS
	[CATALOG(cname [/password])]	

8.4.1 THE LISTCAT PARAMETERS

EXPLANATION OF PARAMETERS

LISTCAT:

This command requests that Access Method Services list certain information found in the specified VSAM catalog. Its abbreviation is **LISTC**.

ENTRIES(en1 [/password] en2 [/password]...):

This parameter allows you to restrict the requested report (LISTCAT) to only those VSAM objects requested by this parameter. Any number of entries can be specified. Typically, this is used by the programmer to specify that information about one or more specific clusters be printed. Its abbreviation is **ENT**.

LEVEL(number): (OS only)

This parameter pertains to OS only. As stated in chapter 6, a VSAM catalog can also point to CVOLS. Information pertaining to data set **qualifiers** can be requested with this option. All entries at the specified qualifier level (no.) can be listed. In order to use this option, the CATALOG parameter must be omitted and no JOBCAT or STEPCAT cards can be submitted with your JCL. Its abbreviation is **LVL**.

ALTERNATEINDEX:

This parameter requests that alternate index entries be listed. The abbreviation for this is **AIX**.

CLUSTER:

This parameter requests that cluster entries be listed. The abbreviation for this is **CL**.

DATA:

This parameter requests that cluster data components be listed.

INDEX:

This parameter requests that cluster index components be listed. The abbreviation for this is **IX**.

NONVSAM:

This parameter requests that non-VSAM objects be listed. Its abbreviation is **NVSAM**.

PATH:

This parameter requests that alternate index path information be listed.

SPACE:

This parameter requests that VSAM space entries for the volumes controlled by this catalog be listed. The abbreviation for this is **SPC**.

USERCATALOG:

This parameter requests that VSAM user catalog connections be listed. The abbreviation for this is **UCAT**.

ALIAS: (OS ONLY)

This parameter is used by OS only. The purpose of this parameter is to list ALIAS entries found in the specified catalog. The purpose of originally defining the ALIAS is primarily to **associate** or **relate** a **qualifier** with a specific user catalog. For instance, in the following example the high-level qualifier "ABC" is associated with a user catalog named "UCAT.VOLA." From this point on, any data set having a high-level qualifier of "ABC" (e.g., DSN=ABC.PAYROLL.FILE) will be directed to this catalog. Furthermore, JOBCAT or STEPCAT JCL cards will not be required to locate the VSAM data set.

```
DEFINE ALIAS                  —
        (NAME(ABC)            —
        RELATE(UCAT.VOLA)     —
        CATALOG(MASTCAT/PASS) —
```

Another function of the ALIAS is to equate a data set name to another data set name. A data set could then be referred to by more than one name.

GENERATIONDATAGROUP: (OS ONLY)

This parameter is used by OS only. The information pertaining to generation data sets can be listed with this option. For DOS users especially who are not familiar with GDGs, chronological versions of a file can be managed by the operating system. Each new copy of a data set is cataloged and can be referred to later on by using the same data set name. The copies are distinguished by using a GDG number in addition to the data set name. For instance, a file called **INVENTRY.FILE** would be referred to as **INVENTRY.FILE(0)** if the current file was required, or **INVENTRY.FILE(-1)** for the previous version, **(-2)** the one before that, and so on. This parameter can be abbreviated **GDG**.

PAGESPACE: (OS ONLY)

This parameter is used by OS only. If the catalog specified is used to maintain space used for page data sets, you can list those catalog entries by specifying this parameter. Its abbreviation is **PGSPC**.

NAME | ALLOCATION | VOLUME | HISTORY | ALL:

With this parameter you can restrict the type of printout you receive from the LISTCAT. The most simple report is by NAME. The parameter will cause AMS to list only the NAME and type of object. An ALLOCATION request will print detailed information pertaining to index and data components only. If VOLUME is requested, information such as object name, owner-id, creation and expiration dates, volume serial numbers, device type, and Catalog Recovery Area volume identification can be listed. HISTORY (OS only) is similar to VOLUME but, in addition, information about the following can also be listed: GDGs, PAGESPACE, PATH, and NONVSAM. The **ALL** parameter will list all catalog entry information. Abbreviations for these can be **ALLOC**, **VOL**, and **HIST**. (NAME and ALL cannot be abbreviated.) NAME is the default.

NOTUSABLE:

Entries marked in the catalog as being **UNUSABLE** can be listed with this parameter. **UNUSABLE** entries are a result of a system failure of some sort that has left the entry in an incomplete form. In Chapter 11 certain recovery facilities and methods are discussed that might correct this problem. Its abbreviation is NUS.

EXIPRATION(days):

Entries listed can be restricted by use of this parameter. Only those entries made within the specified number of days will be printed. Its abbreviation is **EXPIR**.

CREATION(days):

Entries listed can be restricted by use of this parameter. Only those entries due to expire within the specified number of days will be printed. Its abbreviation is **CREAT**.

OUTFILE(jcl-dname): (OS ONLY)

In addition to a report being printed on SYSPRINT, you can direct AMS IDCAMS to write LISTCAT information to the data set identified by **jcl-dname**. This can be abbreviated **OFILE**.

In APPENDIX A you will find several examples of LISTCAT output. For the purposes of this chapter, however, we will set up some LISTCAT job streams for the inventory system we have defined.

8.4.2 SOME LISTCAT EXAMPLES

The JCL required for *all* the LISTCAT examples are as follows:

For DOS:

```
// JOB LISTCAT ACCTDATA
// DLBL IJSYSUC,'UCATLG01',,VSAM
// EXEC IDCAMS,SIZE=AUTO

                    CONTROL CARDS GO HERE

/*
```

For OS:

```
//LISTCAT      JOB     ACCTDATA,'MIKE BOUROS',CLASS=R
//AMS          EXEC    PGM=IDCAMS
//STEPCAT      DD      DSN=UCATLG01,DISP=SHR
//SYSPRINT     DD      SYSOUT=A
//SYSIN        DD      *

                    CONTROL CARDS GO HERE

/*
```

To list all the details pertaining to our inventory system clusters:

```
LISTCAT                       —
        ENT(                  —
        INVENTRY.CLUSTER      —
        PURCH.CLUSTER         —
        SALES.CLUSTER         —
        RECEIVE.CLUSTER       —
        )                     —
        ALL                   —
        CATALOG(UCATLG01)
```

To list only limited information about our clusters such as the VSAM names given to the cluster, data, and index components:

```
LISTCAT                       —
        ENT(                  —
        INVENTRY.CLUSTER      —
        PURCH.CLUSTER         —
```

```
            SALES.CLUSTER          —
            RECEIVE.CLUSTER        —
            )                      —
            CLUSTER                —
            ALL                    —
            CATALOG(UCATLG01)
```

To list the names of all the objects in catalog UCATLG01:

```
      LISTCAT                      —
            NAME                   —
            CATALOG(UCATLG01)
```

If we wished to list any non-VSAM objects that were contained in the catalog:

```
      LISTCAT                      —
            NONVSAM                —
            CATALOG(UCATLG01)
```

If we wanted to see all the space allocated for our clusters:

```
      LISTCAT                      —
            ENT(                   —
            INVENTRY.CLUSTER       —
            PURCH.CLUSTER          —
            SALES.CLUSTER          —
            RECEIVE.CLUSTER        —
            )                      —
            ALLOCATION             —
            CATALOG(UCATLG01)
```

8.5 THE DELETE COMMAND

We will on occasion be required to **delete** clusters and other objects in our system. The following is the format of the DELETE command:

COMMAND	PARAMETERS	NOTES
DELETE		REQ'D
	en1 [/pass] en2 [/pass] ...	
	[ALTERNATEINDEX] |	
	[CLUSTER] |	
	[NONVSAM] |	

COMMAND	PARAMETERS	NOTES
	[PATH]	
	[SPACE]	
	[USERCATALOG]	
	[MASTERCATALOG]	DOS
	[ALIAS]	OS
	[GENERATIONDATAGROUP]	OS
	[PAGESPACE]	OS
	[ERASE | NOERASE]	
	[FILE(jcl-dname)]	
	[FORCE | NOFORCE]	
	[PURGE | NOPURGE]	
	[SCRATCH | NOSCRATCH]	
	[CATALOG(cname [/password])]	

8.5.1 THE DELETE PARAMETERS

EXPLANATION OF PARAMETERS

DELETE:

This command requests that Access Method Services DELETE a VSAM object. The abbreviation for this is **DEL**.

ent1 [/pass] ent2 [/pass].... :

This parameter specifies either the name of the entry to be deleted or the volume serial number of the volume containing data space to be deleted. More than one entry can be specified at a time.

ALTERNATEINDEX:

This parameter specifies that the object to be deleted is an alternate index. Deletion of this object also causes the deletion of its components (data, index, and paths). Its abbreviation is **AIX**.

CLUSTER:

This parameter specifies that the object to be deleted is a cluster. Deletion of this object causes all its associated components to be deleted (data, index, alternate indices, and paths). This can be abbreviated **CL**.

MASTERCATALOG: (DOS ONLY)

This parameter specifies that the object to be deleted is the master catalog.

This object can only be deleted if empty. Its abbreviation can be **MCAT** or **MRCAT**.

NONVSAM:

This parameter specifies that the object to be deleted is a non-VSAM data set entry. If the file resides on a DASD device, VSAM will also remove the entry from the VTOC unless NOSCRATCH is specified. This parameter can be abbreviated **NVSAM**.

PATH:

This parameter specifies that the object to be deleted is an alternate index path. Note: after deletion, associated components remain intact (alternate index and base cluster).

SPACE:

This parameter specifies that the objects to be deleted are VSAM space(s). All empty VSAM space is removed from the volume designated and the ownership bit is removed from the VTOC. Data spaces can be deleted even if not empty by specifying FORCE, unless the volume also contains a user catalog. In that case, the UCAT must be deleted individually. Its abbreviation is **SPC**.

USERCATALOG:

This parameter specifies that the object to be deleted is a user catalog. When this parameter is specified, the entry for it in the master catalog is deleted along with any ALIAS entries (OS). If the UCAT is not empty, it cannot be deleted unless FORCE is specified. The abbreviation for this parameter is **UCAT**.

ALIAS: (OS ONLY)

This parameter specifies that the objects to be deleted are ALIAS entries.

GENERATIONDATAGROUP: (OS ONLY)

This parameter specifies that the objects to be deleted are Generation Data group entries. The abbreviation for this is **GDG**.

PAGESPACE:

This parameter specifies that the catalog entries for Page Space are to be deleted. Its abbreviation is **PGSPC**.

ERASE | NOERASE:

You can request that Access Method Services erase the space occupied by deleted entries. This is for security purposes and is useful when dealing with sensitive data. The area formerly occupied is overwritten with binary zeros. This can be abbreviated **ERAS** or **NERAS**, respectively.

FORCE | NOFORCE:

This specifies that even though a component to be deleted still contains objects or pointers, the entry is to be deleted by force. Associated objects will not be deleted; however, they may no longer be accessible after FORCE is used. The default for this is NOFORCE. Its abbreviations can be **FRC** and **NFRS**, respectively.

PURGE | NOPURGE:

This specifies that even though a component has not yet reached its expiration date, it is to be deleted if PURGE is specified. The default is NOPURGE. This can be abbreviated **PRG** and **NPRG**.

SCRATCH | NOSCRATCH:

If SCRATCH is specified, the VTOC entry for a non-VSAM data set will be deleted. This parameter can be abbreviated **SCR** and **NSCR**, respectively. SCRATCH is the default.

FILE(jcl-name):

This parameter is required by DOS for most delete functions. It points to the object you wish to delete such as a cluster or user catalog.

Catalog(cname [/password]:

This specifies the name of the catalog in which the entry exists for the object being deleted. Its abbreviation is **CAT**.

8.5.2 THE DELETE COMMANDS WITH JCL

The JCL required for *all* the DELETE examples are as follows:

For DOS:

```
// JOB DELETE ACCTDATA
// DLBL IJSYSUC,'UCATLG01',,VSAM
// DLBL INVFIL,'INVENTRY,CLUSTER',,VSAM
// DLBL SALFIL,'SALES.CLUSTER',,VSAM
// DLBL PURFIL,'PURCH.CLUSTER',,VSAM
// DLBL RECFIL,'RECEIVE.CLUSTER',,VSAM
// EXEC IDCAMS,SIZE=AUTO

                 CONTROL CARDS GO HERE

/*
```

For OS:

```
//DELETE     JOB    ACCTDATA,'MIKE BOUROS',CLASS=R
//AMS        EXEC   PGM=IDCAMS
//STEPCAT    DD     DSN=UCTALG01,DISP=SHR
//INVFIL     DD     DSN=INVENTRY.CLUSTER,DISP=SHR
```

```
//PURFIL      DD    DSN=PURCH.CLUSTER,DISP=SHR
//SALFIL      DD    DSN=SALES.CLUSTER,DISP=SHR
//RECFIL      DD    DSN=RECEIVE.CLUSTER,DISP=SHR
//SYSPRINT    DD    SYSOUT=A
//SYSIN       DD    *

                CONTROL CARDS GO HERE

/*
```

To DELETE all our data clusters:

```
DELETE                          -
        INVENTRY.CLUSTER        -
        FILE(INVFIL)            -
        PURGE                   -
        CLUSTER                 -
        CATALOG(UCATLG01)

DELETE                          -
        PURCH.CLUSTER           -
        FILE(PURFIL)            -
        PURGE                   -
        CLUSTER                 -
        CATALOG(UCATLG01)

DELETE                          -
        SALES.CLUSTER           -
        FILE(SALFIL)            -
        PURGE                   -
        CLUSTER                 -
        CATALOG(UCATLG01)

DELETE                          -
        RECEIVE.CLUSTER         -
        FILE(RECFIL)            -     Not req'd OS
        PURGE                   -
        CLUSTER                 -
        CATALOG(UCATLG01)
```

To DELETE the VSAM user catalog on volume VSAM02:

```
DELETE                          -
        UCATLG01                -
        USERCATALOG             -
        PURGE
```

8.6 THE VERIFY COMMAND

The next AMS command we will study is the VERIFY command. The purpose of this command is to **reset** a data set that was not closed properly.

During the operation of any system, it may happen that because of either a hardware or software failure, open VSAM data sets will not get closed. When this occurs certain status information such as records read, added, or deleted will be inaccurate. This is because this information is updated in the catalog at file **close** time. In addition to this, the high-used RBA field that keeps track of the logical end-of-file never gets updated for the same reason. VSAM will not allow the data set to be opened until this problem is resolved.

The purpose of the VERIFY function is to correct this problem. This function actually examines the old or previous HIGH-USED RBA then chases the data until an end-of-file record is located. The HIGH-USED RBA is then updated.

At this time, the latest releases of VSAM are beginning to dynamically invoke the VERIFY function at open time if the file was never closed. This new capability may do away with the need for this facility in the future.

The format of the VERIFY command is as follows.

COMMAND	PARAMETERS	NOTES
VERIFY		REQ'D
	DATASET(ename)	R-DOS
	FILE(jcl-dname)	R-DOS

For OS DATASET and FILE are mutually exclusive.

8.6.1 THE VERIFY PARAMETERS

EXPLANATION OF PARAMETERS

VERIFY:

This command requests that Access Method Services reset the catalog entries for a cluster. This parameter can be abbreviated **VFY**.

DATASET(ename [/password]):

This parameter is optional for OS but required for DOS. If this parameter is not used in OS, the FILE parameter must be used. In an OS environment if the

DATASET parameter is used, the data set (ename) is dynamically allocated. This causes a DISP=OLD to be assumed and sometimes causes the VERIFY function to cancel if another region/partition is accessing the cluster. In situations where multiple address spaces are always accessing the same cluster, the FILE parameter and DISP=SHR will usually be preferable. Its abbreviation is **DS**.

FILE(jcl-dname):

This parameter is required by DOS. It specifies the name (jcl-dname) of the DLBL or DD JCL card.

8.6.2 THE VERIFY COMMAND WITH JCL

The AMS control cards required to perform a VERIFY function for all four of our inventory system data sets would look like this:

For DOS:

```
VERIFY                                  -
          DATASET(INVENTRY.CLUSTER)     -
          FILE(INVFIL)
VERIFY                                  -
          DATASET(PURCH.CLUSTER)        -
          FILE(PURFIL)
VERIFY                                  -
          DATASET(SALES.CLUSTER)        -
          FILE(SALFIL)
VERIFY                                  -
          DATASET(RECEIVE.CLUSTER)      -
          FILE(RECFIL)
```

For OS:

```
VERIFY DATASET(INVENTRY.CLUSTER)
VERIFY DATASET(PURCH.CLUSTER)
VERIFY DATASET(SALES.CLUSTER)
VERIFY DATASET(RECEIVE.CLUSTER)
```

Or:

```
VERIFY FILE(INVFIL)
VERIFY FILE(PURFIL)
VERIFY FILE(SALFIL)
VERIFY FILE(RECFIL)
```

The JCL required for the **VERIFY** function is as follows:

For DOS:

```
// JOB VERIFY ACCTDATA
// DLBL IJSYSUC,'UCATLG01',,VSAM
// DLBL INVFIL,'INVENTRY.CLUSTER',,VSAM
// DLBL SALFIL,'SALES.CLUSTER',,VSAM
// DLBL PURFIL,'PURCH.CLUSTER',,VSAM
// DLBL RECFIL,'RECEIVE.CLUSTER',,VSAM
// EXEC IDCAMS,SIZE=AUTO
          VERIFY                                  —
                DATASET(INVENTRY.CLUSTER)         —
                FILE(INVFIL)
          VERIFY                                  —
                DATASET(PURCH.CLUSTER)            —
                FILE(PURFIL)
          VERIFY                                  —
                DATASET(SALES.CLUSTER)            —
                FILE(SALFIL)
          VERIFY                                  —
                DATASET(RECEIVE.CLUSTER)          —
                FILE(RECFIL)
/*
```

For OS:

```
//VERIFY     JOB     ACCTDATA,'MIKE BOUROS',CLASS=R
//AMS        EXEC    PGM=IDCAMS
//STEPCAT    DD      DSN=UCATLG01,DISP=SHR
//SYSPRINT   DD      SYSOUT=A
//SYSIN      DD      *
             VERIFY DATASET(INVENTRY.CLUSTER)
             VERIFY DATASET(PURCH.CLUSTER)
             VERIFY DATASET(SALES.CLUSTER)
             VERIFY DATASET(RECEIVE.CLUSTER)
/*
```

Or:

```
//VERIFY     JOB     ACCTDATA,'MIKE BOUROS',CLASS=R
//AMS        EXEC    PGM=IDCAMS
//STEPCAT    DD      DSN=UCATLG01,DISP=SHR
//INVFIL     DD      DSN=INVENTRY.CLUSTER,DISP=SHR
//PURFIL     DD      DSN=PURCH.CLUSTER,DISP=SHR
```

```
//SALFIL       DD     DSN=SALES.CLUSTER,DISP=SHR
//RECFIL       DD     DSN=RECEIVE.CLUSTER,DISP=SHR
//SYSPRINT     DD     SYSOUT=A
//SYSIN        DD     *
                      VERIFY FILE(INVENTRY.CLUSTER)
                      VERIFY FILE(PURCH.CLUSTER)
                      VERIFY FILE(SALES.CLUSTER)
                      VERIFY FILE(RECEIVE.CLUSTER)
/*
```

8.7 THE PRINT COMMAND

The next function discussed is the AMS PRINT function.

The **PRINT** command is used to list or dump records contained in a VSAM data set. Records can be displayed in character, hexadecimal, or both. The format is as follows:

COMMAND	PARAMETERS	NOTES
PRINT		REQ'D
	INFILE(jcl-dname [/pass]) |	R-DOS
	[INDATASET(ename [/pass])]	O-OS
	[ENVIRONMENT(	O-DOS
	BLOCKSIZE(size)	O-DOS
	[HINDEXDEVICE(dtype)]	O-DOS
	[NOLABEL | STDLABEL]	O-DOS
	[NOREWIND| REWIND | UNLOAD]	O-DOS
	[PRIMEDATADEVICE(dtype)]	O-DOS
	[RECORDFORMAT(format)]	O-DOS
	[RECORDSIZE(size)]	O-DOS
	)	O-DOS
	[CHARACTER | DUMP | HEX]	
	[FROMADDRESS(address)] |	
	[FROMKEY(key)] |	
	[FROMNUMBER(number)] |	
	[SKIP(count)]	
	[TOADDRESS(address)] |	
	[TOKEY(key)] |	
	[COUNT(count)]	
	[OUTFILE(jcl-dname)]	OS

8.7.1 THE PRINT PARAMETERS

EXPLANATION OF PARAMETERS

PRINT:

This command requests that Access Method Services print data records from a data cluster.

INDATASET(ename [/password]): (OS ONLY)

This parameter can be used at OS installations only. It allows you to specify to AMS the name of the data set (ename) to be used as INPUT to this function. This parameter can be abbreviated **IDS**.

INFILE(jcl-dname [/password]):

This entry allows you to specify to AMS the name of the DD (OS) or DLBL (DOS) JCL card that points to the input file. This parameter is optional for OS but required for DOS. It can be abbreviated **IFILE**. Example:

PRINT INFILE(**INPFILE**)

// DLBL **INPFILE**,'INPUT.FILE'   DOS

//**INPFILE**   DD   DSN=INPUT.FILE,DISP=OLD   OS

ENVIRONMENT(subparameters): (DOS ONLY)

This parameter pertains to DOS only. It describes the characteristics of the input file if it is a non-VSAM file. This parameter is not required for VSAM files. It can be abbreviated **ENV**.

BLOCKSIZE(bsize): (DOS ONLY)

This parameter is valid for DOS systems only. It is a subparameter of the ENVIRONMENT command. With this parameter the size (bsize) of the block is specified for the input file. It can be abbreviated **BLKSZ**.

HINDEXDEVICE(dtype): (DOS ONLY)

This parameter is valid for DOS systems only. It is an optional subparameter of the ENVIRONMENT command. This parameter is specified for ISAM files only and describes the device type (dtype) on which the highest level index is found (e.g., 2314, 3330, 3340). This parameter can be abbreviated **HDEV**.

NOLABEL | STDLABEL: (DOS ONLY)

This parameter is valid for DOS systems only. It is an optional subparameter of the ENVIRONMENT command. This parameter indicates to AMS whether an input file contains standard labels. This parameter can be abbreviated **NLBL** or **SLBL**, respectively.

NOREWIND | REWIND | UNLOAD: (DOS ONLY)

This parameter is valid for DOS systems only. It is an optional subparameter of the ENVIRONMENT command. This parameter indicates to AMS input tape control options. Default is NOREWIND. This parameter can be abbreviated **NREW**, **REW**, or **UNLD**, respectively.

PRIMEDATADEVICE(pdev): (DOS ONLY)

This parameter is valid for DOS systems only. It is an optional subparameter of the ENVIRONMENT command. This parameter indicates to AMS the input device type (pdev). This parameter is required for ISAM and tape files only. A device type of 2400 must be used for tape files and an ASSGN card using SYS004 as the programmer-logical unit. This parameter can be abbreviated **PDEV**.

RECORDFORMAT(format): (DOS ONLY)

This parameter is valid for DOS systems only. It is a required subparameter of the ENVIRONMENT command. This parameter indicates to AMS the type of non-VSAM record being used. The valid record formats are as follows:

FIXUNB	or	F	Fixed unblocked
FIXBLK	or	FB	Fixed blocked
SPNUNB	or	S	Spanned unblocked
SPNBLK	or	SB	Spanned blocked
VARUNB	or	V	Variable unblocked
VARBLK	or	VB	Variable blocked
UNDEF	or	U	Undefined

This parameter can be abbreviated **RECFM**.

RECORDSIZE(rsize): (DOS ONLY)

This parameter is valid for DOS systems only. It is an optional subparameter of the ENVIRONMENT command. This parameter indicates to AMS the size of the logical record for FIXUNB and FIXBLK non-VSAM files. This parameter specifies the **maximum** record size for SPNBLK, SPNUNB, and UNDEF files. It is not required for VARUNB or VARBLK files. This parameter can be abbreviated **RECSZ**.

OUTFILE(jcl-dname [/password]) (OS ONLY):

This entry allows you to specify to AMS the name of the DD (OS) JCL card that points to an output data set that will be used to hold a copy of printed file. This is in addition to the SYSPRINT data set. This parameter can be abbreviated **OFILE**.

CHARACTER | DUMP | HEX:

This specifies the formatting to take place on the printed output. Default is DUMP. CHARACTER format will not show hexadecimal representations of data. HEX will not show character representations of data. DUMP shows both. **CHAR** is the only abbreviation.

FROMADDRESS(faddress):
FROMKEY(fkey):
FROMNUMBER(fnumber):

With this parameter you can specify to Access Method Services the point within an input file at which you would like to begin your print operation. The specification can be made as either a key (KEY), relative byte address-RBA(ADDRESS), or relative record number-RRN(NUMBER). If this parameter is omitted, a PRINT operation will always begin at the first record. Its abbreviations can be **FADDR**, **FKEY**, or **FNUM**, respectively.

SKIP(number):

This parameter allows you to specify the number of records that AMS is to SKIP over before beginning a PRINT operation.

COUNT(number):

This parameter allows you to specify the number of records that AMS is to list before ending the PRINT operation.

TOADDRESS(taddress):
TOKEY(tkey):
TONUMBER(tnumber):

With this parameter, you can specify to Access Method Services the point within an input file at which you would like to end your PRINT operation. The specification can be made as either a key (KEY), relative byte address-RBA(ADDRESS), or relative record number-RRN(NUMBER). If this parameter is omitted, a PRINT operation will always end at the last record. Its abbreviations can be **TADDR** and **TNUM**, respectively.

8.7.2 SAMPLE PRINT COMMANDS WITH JCL

Some examples of PRINT functions are as follows.

To PRINT the first 50 records from each data set (**OS or DOS**):

```
PRINT                                  —
          INFILE(INVENTRY.CLUSTER)     —
          COUNT (50)
PRINT                                  —
          INFILE(PURCH.CLUSTER)        —
          COUNT (50)
```

```
PRINT                              —
        INFILE(SALES.CLUSTER)      —
        COUNT (50)
PRINT                              —
        INFILE(RECEIVE.CLUSTER)    —
        COUNT (50)
```

Or for **OS** only:

```
PRINT DATASET(INVENTRY.CLUSTER)
PRINT DATASET(PURCH.CLUSTER)
PRINT DATASET(SALES.CLUSTER)
PRINT DATASET(RECEIVE.CLUSTER)
```

The JCL required for the PRINT function are as follows:

For DOS:

```
// JOB PRINT ACCTDATA
// DLBL IJSYSUC,'UCATLG01',,VSAM
// DLBL INVFIL,'INVENTRY.CLUSTER',,VSAM
// DLBL SALFIL,'SALES.CLUSTER',,VSAM
// DLBL PURFIL,'PURCH.CLUSTER',,VSAM
// DLBL RECFIL,'RECEIVE.CLUSTER',,VSAM
// EXEC IDCAMS,SIZE=AUTO
            PRINT                      —
                    INFILE(INVFIL)     —
                    COUNT (50)
            PRINT                      —
                    INFILE(PURFIL)     —
                    COUNT (50)
            PRINT                      —
                    INFILE(SALfil)     —
                    COUNT (50)
            PRINT                      —
                    INFILE(RECFIL)     —
                    COUNT (50)
/*
```

For OS:

```
//VERIFY     JOB     ACCTDATA,'MIKE BOUROS',CLASS=R
//AMS        EXEC    PGM=IDCAMS
//STEPCAT    DD      DSN=UCATLG01,DISP=SHR
```

```
//SYSPRINT     DD       SYSOUT=A
//SYSIN        DD       *
               PRINT DATASET(INVENTRY.CLUSTER)
               PRINT DATASET(PURCH.CLUSTER)
               PRINT DATASET(SALES.CLUSTER)
               PRINT DATASET(RECEIVE.CLUSTER)
/*
```

Or:

```
//VERIFY       JOB      ACCTDATA,'MIKE BOUROS',CLASS=R
//AMS          EXEC     PGM=IDCAMS
//STEPCAT      DD       DSN=UCATLG01,DISP=SHR
//INVFIL       DD       DSN=INVENTRY.CLUSTER,DISP=SHR
//PURFIL       DD       DSN=PURCH.CLUSTER,DISP=SHR
//SALFIL       DD       DSN=SALES.CLUSTER,DISP=SHR
//RECFIL       DD       DSN=RECEIVE.CLUSTER,DISP=SHR
//SYSPRINT     DD       SYSOUT=A
//SYSIN        DD       *
               PRINT
                    INFILE(INVFIL)    —
                    COUNT (50)
               PRINT                  —
                    INFILE(PURFIL)    —
                    COUNT (50)
               PRINT                  —
                    INFILE(SALfil)    —
                    COUNT (50)
               PRINT                  —
                    INFILE(RECFIL)    —
                    COUNT (50)
/*
```

If we wanted to **SKIP** the first 25 records, then print the next 50 in CHARACTER:

```
PRINT                  —
     INFILE(INVFIL)    —
     SKIP(25)          —
     CHARACTER         —
     COUNT (50)
```

To select a range of records to PRINT:

```
PRINT                    —
        INFILE(INVFIL)   —
        SKIP(25)         —
        CHARACTER        —
        FROMKEY(AAAAA)   —
        TOKEY(CCCCC)
```

The preceding would list all records starting at AAAAA and ending with CCCCC. If no record with key AAAAA exists, the next highest record will be the first printed.

8.8 THE AMS ALTER COMMAND

Occasionally, it will be necessary to make modifications to some of the parameters we have previously defined for some VSAM object. When this happens we basically have two choices, either DELETE and reDEFINE the object **or** modify the definition of an existing object through the use of the **ALTER** command.

The ALTER command allows us to handily modify parameters while leaving the data undisturbed. Not all parameters can be altered. Obviously, VSAM is not going to allow us to change an existing cluster from KSDS to ESDS, nor will it allow us to change a cluster definition from SUBALLOCATION to UNIQUE.

The options that can be changed, however, can be very useful. Following is the format of the ALTER command. You should already be familiar with most of the parameters but you should also notice some new ones.

COMMAND	PARAMETERS	NOTES
ALTER		REQ'D
	ename [/password]	
	[ADDVOLUMES(volser [volser...])]	
	[ATTEMPTS(number)]	
	[AUTHORIZATION(entrypoint [string])]	
	[BUFFERSPACE(size)]	
	[CODE(code)]	
	[CONTROLPW(password)]	
	[DESTAGEWAIT | <u>NODESTAGEWAIT</u>]	OS
	[EMPTY | NOEMPTY]	OS
	[ERASE | <u>NOERASE</u>]	
	[EXCEPTIONEXIT(modname)]	

COMMAND	PARAMETERS	NOTES

```
[FILE(jcl-dname)]
[FOR( days ) | TO( date)]
[FREESPACE( cipct capct)]
[KEYS( len offset)]
[MASTERPW( password ) ]
[NEWNAME( NEWNAME ) ]
[NULLIFY(
    [AUTHORIZATION(MODULE | STRING) ]
    [CODE ]
    [CONTROLPW ]
    [EXCEPTIONEXIT ]
    [MASTERPW ]
    [OWNER ]
    READPW ]
    RETENTION ]
    [UPDATEPW ] ) ]
[OWNER( owner id ) ]
[READPW( password ) ]
[RECORDSIZE( avg. max.)]
[REMOVEVOLUMES( volser [ volser... ] ) ]
[SHAREOPTIONS( opt1 opt2)
[SCRATCH | NOSCRATCH ]
[STAGE | BIND | CYLINDERFAULT]                    OS
[UNIQUEKEY | NONUNIQUEKEY ]
[UPDATE | NOUPDATE ]
[UPDATEPW( password ) ]
[WRITECHECK | NOWRITECHECK ]
                                                  REQ'D
[CATALOG( cname [/PASSWORD ] ) ]
```

8.8.1 THE ALTER COMMAND PARAMETERS

EXPLANATION OF PARAMETERS

ALTER

This AMS command specifies that you wish to ALTER one or more parameters previously defined for a VSAM object.

ename [/password]:

This specifies the name of entry to be altered.

ATTEMPTS(number):

This parameter is used only in those cases where the cluster is password protected. The number of attempts the operator can make before IDCAMS aborts is specified here. If ATTEMPTS(0) is specified, the operator is not allowed to enter a password from a system console. Password protection is discussed in Chapter 12. This parameter can be abbreviated **ATT**.

AUTHORIZATION(entrypoint/string):

This parameter specifies the name of a routine (entrypoint) to which control is passed every time this cluster is accessed. This routine is called a **user exit**; it is usually written by the systems programmer at the installation in which the catalog will be used. For more specifics about writing a user exit routine, see Chapter 12. In addition to passing control to the user exit, a character **string** of up to 256 characters in length can also be passed to the routine. The characters passed can be specified as either character or hexadecimal values. See Chapter 12 for more information on this subject. This parameter can be abbreviated **AUTH**. Example:

```
AUTHORIZATION(CHECKRTN authdata) or
AUTHORIZATION(CHECKRTN X'C1E4E3C8C4C1E3C1')
```

BUFFERSPACE(size):

This specifies the space to be provided for buffers when the cluster is in use. For a KSDS file, the space allotted should be large enough to contain at least two data control intervals and one index control interval. If enough BUFFERSPACE is allocated for this cluster, the entire index set plus one sequence set CI could be brought into main storage (KSDS). The term **index set** refers to those parts of the index hierarchically higher than the sequence set. If this parameter is left out, VSAM will compute the BUFFERSPACE required. This parameter can be abbreviated **BUFSP** or **BUFSPC**, respectively.

CATALOG(cname [/password]):

This parameter allows us to specify the name of the catalog containing the entry to be altered. This parameter can be abbreviated **CAT**.

CODE(code):

This parameter is used for those objects that are password protected. The designated **code** is used in lieu of the object name when prompting the operator for the password. This might be used in those cases where it might not be desirable for an operator to know the actual names of the objects being accessed (e.g., a payroll application).

CONTROLPW(password):

A special method of file access called **control interval access** enables an assembler language program to optionally read or write entire CIs at a time rather than individual records (Chapter 16). With this parameter you can control the access to the cluster by specifying a password. The entire subject of passwords is covered in Chapter 12. This parameter can be abbreviated **CTLPW**.

DESTAGEWAIT | NODESTAGEWAIT (OS ONLY)

This parameter pertains only to the OS operating system using the Mass Storage System (MSS). A VSAM object stored on MSS must first be **staged**, that is, copied to a 3330/3350-type volume before it can be used. When the object is no longer needed (e.g., the application program closes the file), the volume can then be **DESTAGED**. This parameter allows you to specify whether the application should wait for the conclusion of the destaging (DESTAGEWAIT) operation or whether it can be done asynchronously (NODESTAGEWAIT). NO-DESTAGEWAIT is the default. For more information on this subject, see Chapter 14. This parameter can be abbreviated **DSTGW** or **NDSTGW**, respectively.

EMPTY | NOEMPTY: (OS ONLY)

This specifies the action to take place when the maximum number of generation data sets has been cataloged. Specification of EMPTY directs VSAM to uncatalog **all** data sets. NOEMPTY directs VSAM to uncatalog only the oldest entry. There is no default. Its abbreviations can be **EMP** or **NEMP**.

ERASE | NOERASE:

For sensitive data, the specification of ERASE will cause VSAM to erase the entire area occupied by the cluster when the entry is deleted from the catalog. The extent formerly occupied by this cluster will be overwritten with binary zeros (low-value). The abbreviation for this parameter is **ERAS** (ERASE) or **NERAS** (NOERASE).

EXCEPTIONEXIT(modname):

This parameter specifies the name of an exit routine written by the user to which control is given whenever an unusual error takes place. This is usually an I/O error. This exit routine is link edited to your load (OS) or core-image (DOS) library. To find out more about an EXIT routine such as this, see the *IBM VSAM Programmer's Guide* and also Chapter 16.

FOR(days) TO(date):

With this parameter you can specify the retention period for this cluster. It can be specified either in days or by date. If the specification is made in days, you must use the FOR parameter. The days may be specified as any value between 0 and 1830. Any value higher than this will force a retention through the year 1999. In order to specify a specific date use the TO parameter. A specific date is specified in the form yyddd, where yy = year and ddd is the Julian day of the year (001–366). For example, 84365 is interpreted the 365th day of 1984.

FILE(jcl-dname):

This parameter is required by DOS only but can also be used in OS. It is used to point to the // DLBL JCL card (DOS) or a DD JCL card (OS). The name specified here must match the name specified by the DLBL/DD card. The following illustrates the association between the JCL and the FILE (jcl-name):

// DLBL **CLDEF** ..... DOS
//**CLDEF** DD .... OS
FILE(**CLDEF**)

FREESPACE(cipct capct):

This parameter pertains only to KSDS clusters. The amount of FREESPACE to be left in a control interval or control area can be specified here. When a cluster is initially loaded or during record insertions made in **sequential insert mode**, VSAM will maintain the FREESPACE specified with this parameter. Both **cipct** (CI%) and **capct** (CA %) are specified as percentages of space to be *left* in the CI/CA. Specification of (0 0) allows no FREESPACE to be reserved in the CI/CA. There is one exception to the way that this parameter is handled by VSAM, that is, when a specification of (100 100) is made. In this case only one record per CI and one CI per CA will contain data. This parameter can be abbreviated **FSPC**.

INHIBIT | NOINHIBIT:

Specifies whether the entry can be accessed for read-only or for all purposes. If INHIBIT is specified, the entry can be accessed for read purposes only. An entry previously set to INHIBIT with the EXPORT command can be reset by using NOINHIBIT. Its abbreviations can be **INH** or **UNUNH**, respectively.

KEYS(len offset):

This parameter pertains to KSDS clusters and alternate indices only and can be specified only if the object is empty. It specifies the length (len) and location (offset) of the key within a data record. The maximum length of a key is 64 bytes. The offset is specified as relative to zero. For example, a cluster containing records with a key length of 16 and beginning in the first byte of the record would be specified as:

KEYS(16 0)

MASTERPW:

This parameter specifies a password that is to be used for the cluster being defined. Unless this parameter is specified, the associate parameters CODE, ATTEMPTS, and AUTHORIZATION are of no significance. The password must be one to eight characters in length, and can contain alpha, numeric, or special characters. When using special characters the entire password should be contained within apostrophes. The password can also be specified in hexadecimal. Examples:

MASTERPW(MIKEB) or
MASTERPW('MIKEB') or
MASTERPW(X'D4C9D2C5C2')

Passwords are discussed more thoroughly in Chapter 12. The abbreviation for this is **MRPW**.

NEWNAME(newname):

With this parameter you can rename the entry being ALTERed. Its abbreviation can be **NEWNM**.

NULLIFY(options...):

This specifies that certain options previously selected are to be reset (nullified). The following options can be nullified: AUTHORIZATION, CODE, CONTROLPW, MASTERPW, EXCEPTIONEXIT, OWNER, READPW, RETENTION(previous TO or FOR parameter settings), and UPDATEPW.

OWNER(owner id):

This parameter is used for documentation purposes only. It specifies the name of the owner of the cluster. The **owner id** can contain one to eight characters and follows the same rules described under MASTERPW.

READPW(password):

This specifies the password to be used whenever the cluster is accessed for **read** purposes. This parameter can be abbreviated **RDPW**.

RECORDSIZE(avg. max.):

This parameter specifies in bytes the average (**avg.**) and maximum (**max.**) size of records in the data component. If **avg.** and **max.** are equal, VSAM understands this to be a file of fixed length records. When avg. and max. are different, VSAM understands this cluster to be a file of variable length records. If the size specified is larger than what has been specified for the CI size, you must specify SPANNED records. This parameter can be abbreviated **RECSZ**.

REMOVEVOLUMES(volser [volser]...):

This allows you to "remove" volume serial numbers previously defined for CANDIDATE or SPACE purposes as long as they are not being used. The abbreviation for this is **RVOL**.

SCRATCH | NOSCRATCH: (OS ONLY)

This specifies whether generation data sets are to be removed from the VTOC when the VSAM catalog entry is deleted. Its abbreviations can be **SCR** or **NSCR**.

SHAREOPTIONS(opt1 opt2):

This parameter specifies how a cluster is be shared between partitions or regions (opt1). For OS installations only, the second option (opt2) specifies how this cluster is to be shared across systems in multi-CPU environments. For **opt1** you must code one of the following:

CROSS-PARTITION/REGION OPTIONS:

1. This specifies that the data set can be shared between any number of users for read purposes, or only one user for read and write processing.
2. This code allows any number of users to be reading the data set, and one user to write to the data set at any given time.
3. With this option a cluster can be shared by any number of users for both read and write purposes. Neither VSAM nor the operating system does anything in order to ensure the integrity of the data set. If two users are writing to this cluster at the same time, there is a good chance that the cluster will be destroyed. When using this option it is up to the user to ensure that this does not happen. This could possibly be accomplished through proper scheduling and through the use of ENQ and DEQ (enqueue and dequeue) macros. See Chapter 14 for a more detailed explanation of this facility.
4. With this option VSAM can offer some protection and assistance when a date set is to be shared for both read and write purposes by multiple partitions or regions. When using this option VSAM will retrieve a fresh copy of the control interval containing the desired record (random read) even if a copy of the record is presently in the CPU. This helps ensure read integrity. When records are written to the data set the first partition/region to issue the write will get exclusive control over the data set until the write operation is completed. There is one major restriction when using this option: no record additions can be made that could cause a control area split. VSAM will not permit record additions in this case, and will instead pass a return code pack to the application program. This restriction is meant to prevent you from changing the HIGH-USED RBA field. See Chapters 7 and 14 for further information.

CROSS-SYSTEM(OS ONLY):

1. Not currently used.
2. Not currently used.

3. This function is to cross-system what **3** is to cross-partition/region. VSAM will allow you to perform any kind of operation but delegates all responsibility to you. Improper use of this option can result in destroyed data sets and program check interruptions within VSAM.

4. With this cross-system option VSAM expects you to use OS RESERVE and DEQ macros in order to hardware RESERVE (software enqueue) and hardware release (software dequeue) a data set. A hardware reserve is actually a special channel command that causes a CPU to **seize** a particular DASD device causing a second CPU to be locked out in a true hardware sense. In order to accomplish this, a RESERVE macro is issued. A DEQ macro is required to return the DASD device to an **available to anyone** state. This is performed with a DEQ macro that issues a hardware command (CCW) called RELEASE. More about the use of these macros is covered in Chapter 14. Another service that VSAM performs under this option is to prevent the occurrence of a CA or CI split that results in a CA split. This is done because when a CA split takes place, a new CA is acquired from the end of the data set. This cannot be allowed to take place because it would then change the HIGH-USED RBA (the indicator that marks the end of the data set). If this happened on one system, there is currently no way for the other system to find out about it. More about this appears in Chapter 14.

The abbreviation for this option is **SHR**.

STAGE | BIND | CYLINDERFAULT: OS ONLY

This option pertains only to users of the MSS (Mass Storage Systems). When STAGE is specified, the cluster is to be staged to a DASD device when the data set is opened. If the entire cluster cannot be staged at that time because of heavy staging activity, the *data* is staged as the program needs it. The BIND parameter is similar to STAGE; it ensures, however, that the data, once staged, is **bound** to the DASD device to which it was staged until the cluster is closed. If CYLINDERFAULT is specified, the cluster is not staged when the data set is opened. Rather, the data is staged as it is required. The entire operation of these options very closely resembles the paging operation that takes place in memory.

UNIQUEKEY | NONUNIQUEKEY:

This entry pertains to alternate index entries only. It specifies whether alternate key values will be UNIQUE. If NONUNIQUEKEY is specified, any number of replicated keys can exist. An example of this would be found in a payroll system. Although the employee number is unique, department number alternate index records might occur for each employee in a department. Its abbreviations can be **UNQK** or **NUNQK**, respectively.

UPDATE | NOUPDATE:

This specifies whether the UPGRADE set belonging to the base cluster of a path is to be UPDATED. See Chapter 9 for further information. Its abbreviations can be **UPD** or **NUPD**, respectively.

UPDATEPW(password):

This specifies the password to be used any time this cluster is **updated**, that is, records added, deleted, or changed. See the rules described under MASTERPW for a description of the password format.

UPGRADE | NOUPGRADE:

For alternate indices, this parameter specifies to VSAM whether the Index is to be kept updated along with the update of the base cluster. The specification of this parameter causes the VSAM AIX to be placed in the **upgrade set** belonging to the base cluster. Its abbreviations can be **UPG** or **NUPG**, respectively.

WRITECHECK | NOWRITECHECK

If WRITECHECK is specified, a special verification function is performed on the data just written to verify that it was written correctly. A special I/O operation called a **soft-read** is performed to accomplish this. When WRITECHECK is specified, VSAM constructs a special channel program for the I/O operation that, when chained to a WRITE operation, allows the soft-read operation. In a soft-read the data, although read, is not actually transferred back to the CPU. Unless high volume data makes this prohibitive, WRITECHECK should be specified. Although more time is required to perform this than is required to merely write, the time involved is less than the time it would take to write and read using a normal read operation. This option can be abbreviated **WCK** or **NWCK**, respectively.

8.8.2 ALTER COMMAND WITH JCL

In the following example we ALTER the specification for a hypothetical data set (HYPO.THET). The AMS commands to change a previous FREESPACE requirement would look something like this:

```
ALTER HYPO.THET/SECRET
      FREESPACE( 20 10 )
      CATALOG(USERCAT.NO1)
```

In this example notice that our data set uses a password **SECRET**.

Commands to ALTER the SHAREOPTIONS in our data set might look like this:

```
ALTER    HYPO.THET/SECRET          —
         SHAREOPTIONS( 4 4 )       —
```

```
            FILE(HYPO)                      —
            CATALOG(USERCAT.NO1)
```

The JCL for the preceding would look something like this:

For DOS:

```
// JOB ALTER ACCTDATA
// DLBL IJSYSUC,'USERCAT.NO1',,VSAM
// DLBL HYPO,'HYPO.THET',,VSAM
// EXEC IDCAMS,SIZE=AUTO

                 CONTROL CARDS GO HERE

/*
```

For OS:

```
//ALTER       JOB     ACCTDATA,'MIKE BOUROS',CLASS=R
//AMS         EXEC    PGM=IDCAMS
//SYSPRINT    DD      SYSOUT=A
//SYSIN       DD      *

                 CONTROL CARDS GO HERE

/*
```

Putting it all together:

For DOS:

```
// JOB ALTER ACCTDATA
// DLBL IJSYSUC,'USERCAT.NO1',,VSAM
// DLBL HYPO,'HYPO.THET',,VSAM
// EXEC IDCAMS,SIZE=AUTO
   ALTER   HYPO.THET/SECRET           —
           SHAREOPTIONS( 4 4 )        —
           FILE(HYPO)                 —
           CATALOG(USERCAT.NO1)
/*
```

For OS:

```
//ALTER       JOB     ACCTDATA,'MIKE BOUROS',CLASS=R
//AMS         EXEC    PGM=IDCAMS
```

```
//SYSPRINT     DD        SYSOUT=A
//SYSIN        DD        *
     ALTER   HYPO.THET/SECRET              —
             SHAREOPTIONS( 4 4 )           —
             CATALOG(USERCAT.NO1)
/*
```

8.9 THE CATALOG RECOVERY AREA COMMANDS

There are four commands that are used for Catalog Recovery Area functions:

```
LISTCRA
RESETCAT
IMPORTRA
EXPORTRA
```

LISTCRA is used to display the contents of the CRA. You can also **COMPARE** the CRA to the catalog with this option; differences will be highlighted. **RESETCAT** allows the catalog information to be changed so that it is in agreement with the information in the CRA. **IMPORTRA** and **EXPORTRA** allow exporting and importing, using the information in the Catalog Recovery Area. This process causes the catalog information to be reset.

If a master catalog is password protected, all of these options require that the master catalog's master password be specified. This is to protect against the use of these powerful commands by unauthorized personnel.

8.9.1 THE LISTCRA COMMAND

The format of the **LISTCRA** command is as follows.

COMMAND	PARAMETERS	NOTES
LISTCRA		REQ'D
	INFILE(jcl-dname [/pass])	
	[CATALOG(cname [/pass])]	
	[COMPARE | NOCOMPARE]	
	[DUMP | NAME | SEQUENTIALDUMP]	
	[INVOLUMES(volid.....)]	DOS
	[MASTERPW(pass)]	
	[OUTFILE(jcl-dname)]	OS

8.9.1.1 The LISTCRA Parameters

EXPLANATION OF PARAMETERS

LISTCRA:

This identifies this command as the **List Catalog Recovery Area** command.

CATALOG(cname [/pass]):

This parameter indicates the name of the catalog that owns the volume stated in the INFILE parameter. This parameter is required when using the COMPARE option with either NAME or DUMP. This parameter cannot be used with the SEQUENTIALDUMP option.

COMPARE | NOCOMPARE:

This specifies whether the catalog and the Catalog Recovery Areas are to be compared. If COMPARE is used, only those items that do not compare are listed. When NOCOMPARE is used, all the information in the CRA is printed. COMPARE cannot be used with SEQUENTIALDUMP. **NOCOMPARE** is the default.

DUMP | NAME | SEQUENTIALDUMP:

This specifies the printing options for this run. DUMP lists each entry in character and hexadecimal. NAME lists in character only. For both the NAME and DUMP options, entries are sorted and listed alphabetically. The SEQUENTIALDUMP lists entries in the order in which they occur in the CRA. The default is **NAME**.

INVOLUMES(volid....): (DOS ONLY)

This specifies the volume serial number of one or more volumes from which the CRA information is to be printed.

MASTERPW(pass):

If the master catalog is password protected, you must specify the master password here. The abbreviation for this is **MRPW**.

OUTFILE(jcl-dname):

This specifies the name of a DD statement identifying a data set that is to receive the printed output instead of SYSPRINT. This parameter is optional. If left out, the output is directed to SYSPRINT.

8.9.1.2 Sample LISTCRA Jobstream

Some **examples of the LISTCRA command are as follows**:

For DOS:

```
// JOB LISTCRA ACCTDATA
// DLBL IJSYSUC,'USERCAT.NO1',,VSAM
// ASSGN SYS006,VOL=VSAM01,SHR
// DLBL INNAME,'UCATLG01',,VSAM
// EXTENT SYS006
// EXEC IDCAMS,SIZE=AUTO
     LISTCRA                              —
               INFILE(INNAME)             —
               CATALOG(UCATLG01)          —
               COMPARE                    —
               NAME                       —
               INVOLUMES(VSAM01)          —
               MASTERPW(MASTERPW)
/*
```

For OS:

```
//LISTCRA      JOB       ACCTDATA,'MIKE BOUROS',CLASS=R
//AMS          EXEC      PGM=IDCAMS
//STEPCAT      DD        DSN=UCATLG01,DISP=OLD
//INNAME       DD        DSN=UCATLG01,DISP=OLD
//SYSPRINT     DD        SYSOUT=A
//SYSIN        DD        *
     LISTCRA                              —
               INFILE(INNAME)             —
               CATALOG(UCAT01)            —
               COMPARE                    —
               NAME                       —
               MASTERPW(MASTERPW)
/*
```

In this example the CRA information belonging to UCATLG01 will be printed on SYSPRINT (OS) or SYSLST (DOS). Since **COMPARE** was specified, only mismatching entries will be listed.

8.9.2 THE RESETCAT COMMAND

When it has been determined that the information in a catalog is in error, the catalog can be **reset** to agree with information found in the CRA. This is accomplished with the **RESETCAT** command. The format of the **RESETCAT** command is as follows.

COMMAND	PARAMETERS	NOTES
RESETCAT		REQ'D
	[CATALOG(cname [/pass] [dname])]	
	[CRAFILES((jcl-dname [ALL | NONE]) ....)	
	[CRAVOLUMES(volid [devtype])..)]	OS
	[CRAVOLUMES(volid [ALL | NONE])..)]	DOS
	[IGNORE | NOIGNORE]	
	[MASTERPW(pass)]	
	[WORKFILE(jcl-dname [/pass])]	
	[WORKVOLUMES(volid [/pass].....)]	DOS
	[WORKCAT(cname [/pass])]	

8.9.2.1 The RESETCAT Parameters

EXPLANATION OF PARAMETERS

RESETCAT:

This command directs AMS to **reset** catalog information, to agree with information found in the catalog's CRA.

CATALOG(cname [/pass]):

This parameter indicates the name of the catalog that is to be reset.

CRAFILES((jcl-dname [ALL | NONE]) ....)

This parameter performs a function similar to the CRAVOLUMES parameter. When specifying **NONE**, information in the CRA of the volume identified by jcl-dname will not be used to reset the catalog. This is useful when a catalog owns several volumes that have CRAs. It may be necessary to mount volumes on occasion even though a reset is not requested (**NONE**).

CRAVOLUMES(volid [devtype])..)]: (OS)
CRAVOLUMES((volid [ALL | NONE])..)]: (DOS)

This specifies the volume serial number of one or more volumes from which the CRA information is to be obtained. For OS, specify the device types as well as the volid. For DOS, **ALL** or **NONE** specifies whether information in the associated volid is to be used to reset the catalog. This is useful when the catalog owns multiple volumes. Even if the CRA information in some of the volumes will not be used to reset the catalog, it will still be necessary on occasion to have **all** the volumes mounted.

IGNORE | NOIGNORE:

This informs VSAM of the action to take if errors are encountered. VSAM will attempt to continue processing even though information in the CRA is in error.

It will even attempt to continue when I/O errors are encountered in either the catalog or the CRA.

MASTERPW(pass):

This specifies the master catalog's master password. This is required when the master catalog is password protected.

WORKCAT(cname [/pass]):

This specifies the name of the catalog used for the work file. See the WORKFILE parameter.

WORKFILE(jcl-dname [/pass]):

This specifies the name of a DD (OS) or DLBL (DOS) statement that identifies a VSAM data set that can be used as a work file.

WORKVOLUMES(volid [/pass].....): (DOS ONLY)

This specifies the volume serial numbers of the volumes used for work files.

MASTERPW(pass):

If the master catalog is password protected, you must specify the **master** password here.

8.9.2.2 Sample RESETCAT Jobstream

For DOS:

```
// JOB RESETCAT ACCTDATA
// DLBL IJSYSUC,'USERCAT.NO1',,VSAM
// DLBL WORK,'WORK',,VSAM
// ASSGN SYS006,VOL=VSAM01,SHR
// DLBL CRAVOL,,,VSAM
// EXTENT SYS006
// EXEC IDCAMS,SIZE=AUTO
   RESETCAT                                     —
            CATALOG(UCATLG01 IJSYSUC)           —
            CRAFILES(CRAVOL)                    —
            IGNORE                              —
            MASTERPW(MASTERPW)                  —
            WORKFILE(WORK)                      —
            WORKCAT(UCATLG01)                   —
            WORKVOLUMES(VSAM01)
/*
```

For OS:

```
//RESETCAT   JOB    ACCTDATA,'MIKE BOUROS',CLASS=R
//AMS        EXEC   PGM=IDCAMS
```

```
//STEPCAT     DD     DSN=UCATLG01,DISP=OLD
//WORK        DD     DSN=WORK,DISP=OLD,
//                   VOL=SER=VSAM02,
//                   UNIT=3350
//CRAVOL      DD     DISP=OLD,VOL=SER=VSAM01
//DDUCAT      DD     DISP-OLD,VOL=SER=VSAM01
//SYSPRINT    DD     SYSOUT=A
//SYSIN       DD     *
    RESETCAT                                  —
            CATALOG(UCATLG01 DDUCAT)          —
            CRAFILES(CRAVOL)                  —
            IGNORE                            —
            MASTERPW(MASTERPW)                —
            WORKFILE(WORK)                    —
            WORKCAT(UCATLG01)
/*
```

In this example the information in catalog **UCATLG01** will be reset with the information found in the Catalog Recovery Area. A work file is established during this process which is identified by the WORK DD or DLBL statement.

8.9.3 THE EXPORTRA COMMAND

When a catalog has been damaged, it may be impossible to retrieve data from one or more clusters or other objects. If a Catalog Recovery Area was defined for this catalog, it is very possible that the data can be retrieved by using the CRA instead.

In order to retrieve the data, the **EXPORTRA** command is used. To restore this data later on, use the **IMPORTRA** command instead of the **IMPORT** command. The format of the **EXPORTRA** command is as follows.

COMMAND	PARAMETERS	NOTES
EXPORTRA		REQ'D
	[OUTFILE(jcl-dname)	
	[CIMODE | RECORDMODE]	DOS
	[CRA((jcl-dname1	
	ALL [INFILE(jcl-dname2]	|
	ENTRIES(ename [jcl-dname3]...)	|
	NONE)])	
	[(jcl-dname1.......)]	

(Continued on p. 186)

COMMAND	PARAMETERS	NOTES
	[ENVIRONMENT(	DOS
	BLOCKSIZE(size)	DOS
	[NOLABEL | STDLABEL]	DOS
	[NOREWIND | REWIND | UNLOAD]	DOS
	[PRIMEDATADEVICE(dtype)]	DOS
	)	DOS
	[FORCE | NOFORCE]	
	[MASTERPW(pass)]	

8.9.3.1 The EXPORTRA Parameters

EXPLANATION OF PARAMETERS

EXPORTRA:

This command instructs VSAM to export one or more objects by using the Catalog Recovery Area entry information rather than the catalog's.

OUTFILE(jcl-dname):

This specifies the name of the DD (OS) or DLBL/TLBL statement identifying the sequential volume to which the exported data is to be written. The output device may be either tape or DASD.

CIMODE | RECORDMODE:

When **CIMODE** is specified, VSAM will export an object one control interval at a time. If this is not specified, backup is by logical record (**RECORDMODE**). Default is CIMODE.

CRA(jcl-dname1..ALL | ENTRIES | NONE...):

This parameter identifies the Catalog Recovery Area to be used. It also specifies the objects to be exported. **ALL** specifies that all of the objects in the CRA are to be exported. Specific objects can be exported by specifying the **ENTRIES** parameter. When **NONE** is specified, no exporting will take place for any of the objects in the CRA. This parameter may be necessary when several volumes are owned by a single catalog and are referenced.

CRAVOLUMES(volid [ALL | NONE])..)]: (DOS)

This specifies the volume serial number of one or more volumes from which the CRA information is to be obtained. For DOS **ALL** or **NONE** specifies whether objects are to be exported from the associated volid. This is useful when the catalog owns multiple volumes. Even if the CRA information in some of the volumes will not be used, it will still be necessary on occasion to have all the volumes mounted.

ENVIRONMENT(subparameters): (DOS ONLY)

This parameter pertains to DOS only. It describes the characteristics of the output file. This parameter can be abbreviated **ENV**.

BLOCKSIZE(bsize): (DOS ONLY)

This parameer is valid for DOS systems only. It is a subparameter of the ENVIRONMENT command and is required when ENVIRONMENT is used. With this parameter the size (bsize) of the block is specified for the output file. If not specified, the default is 2048. It can be abbreviated **BLKSZ**.

NOLABEL | STDLABEL: (DOS ONLY)

This parameter is valid for DOS systems only. It is an optional subparameter of the ENVIRONMENT command. This parameter indicates to AMS whether an output file contains standard labels. This parameter can be abbreviated **NLBL** or **SLBL**, respectively.

NOREWIND | REWIND | UNLOAD: (DOS ONLY)

This parameter is valid for DOS systems only. It is an optional subparameter of the ENVIRONMENT command. This parameter indicates to AMS output tape control options. Default is NOREWIND. This parameter can be abbreviated **NREW**, **REW**, or **UNLD**, respectively.

PRIMEDATADEVICE(pdev): (DOS ONLY)

This parameter is valid for DOS systems only. It is an optional subparameter of the ENVIRONMENT command. This parameter indicates to AMS the output device type (pdev). A device type of 2400 must be used for tape files and an ASSGN card using SYS005 as the programmer-logical unit. This parameter can be abbreviated **PDEV**.

FORCE | NOFORCE:

FORCE specifies that the catalog entry's copy be copied from the CRA even though the copy itself might not be accurate. This option will override time-stamp errors. Specification of **NOFORCE** causes AMS to terminate processing when an error condition such as this occurs. **NOFORCE** is the default.

MASTERPW(pass):

If the master catalog is password protected, you must specify the **master** password here.

8.9.3.2 Sample EXPORTRA Jobstream

For DOS:

```
// JOB EXPORTRA ACCTDATA
// DLBL IJSYSUC,'USERCAT.NO1',,VSAM
// DLBL WORK,'WORK',,VSAM
// ASSGN SYS006,VOL=VSAM01,SHR
// DLBL VOLVSAM1,,,VSAM
```

```
// EXTENT SYS006
// ASSGN SYS005,TAPE
// TLBL SYS005,'BACKUP'
// EXEC IDCAMS,SIZE=AUTO
   EXPORTRA
              OUTFILE(TAPEOUT)              —
              CIMODE                        —
              CRAVOLUMES( VSAM01 ALL)       —
              ENVIRONMENT(                  —
                   BLOCKSIZE(8192)          —
                   STDLABEL                 —
                   UNLOAD                   —
                   PDEV(2400)               —
                   )                        —
              FORCE                         —
              MASTERPW(MASTERPW)            —
/*
```

For OS:

```
//EXPORTRA   JOB    ACCTDATA,'MIKE BOUROS',CLASS=R
//AMS        EXEC   PGM=IDCAMS
//TAPEOUT    DD     DSN=BACKUP,LABEL=(,SL),DISP
//           DD        =(NEW,KEEP),
//           DD     UNIT=2400,VOL=SER=111111,
//                  DCB=(BLKSIZE=8192)
//VOLVSAM1   DD     DISP=OLD,VOL=SER=VSAM01
//SYSPRINT   DD     SYSOUT=A
//SYSIN      DD     *
                EXPORTRA
                         OUTFILE(TAPEOUT)          —
                         CRA( (VOLVSAM1 ALL) )     —
                         FORCE                     —
                         MASTERPW(MASTERPW)
/*
```

In this example, **ALL** of the objects belonging to catalog VSAM01 will be exported to tape. If any errors are encountered because of an out-of-synch condition, VSAM will attempt to continue.

8.9.4 THE IMPORTRA COMMAND

The **IMPORTRA** command is used to restore VSAM objects copied using the **EXPORTRA** parameter. The format of this command is as follows.

```
COMMAND          PARAMETERS                                   NOTES
------------------------------------------------------------------------
IMPORTRA                                                      REQ'D
                 INFILE
                 (
                 jcl-dname
                   [ENVIRONMENT                               R-DOS
                    (                                         DOS
                    BLOCKSIZE( bsize )                        R-DOS
                    [NOLABEL | STDLABEL ]                     DOS
                    [ NOREWIND | REWIND | UNLOAD ]            DOS
                    [PRIMEDATADEVICE( pdev) ]                 DOS
                   )
                 )

                 OUTFILE( dname [/password] )                 REQ'D
                 [OBJECTS
                 (
                    ( ename
                    [FILE( dname ) ]
                    [USECLASS( prim [sec] ) ]                 DOS
                    [VOLUMES( vol1 [vol2...] ) ] |
                       DEFAULTVOLUMES
                 [SAVRAC | NOSAVRAC ]
                 [CATALOG( cname [/password] )
```

8.9.4.1 The IMPORTRA Parameters

EXPLANATION OF PARAMETERS

IMPORTRA:

This command indicates to Access Method Services that you wish to restore a back-up copy of the VSAM object. The back-up copy used as input to this command must have been previously copied using **EXPORTRA**.

OBJECTS:

This parameter is used to specify changes to be made to the VSAM object when being restored. Its abbreviation can be **OBJ**.

VOLUMES(volser volser...):

This parameter specifies the volume serial number of the device that contains the OBJECT. Its abbreviation can be **VOL**.

ENVIRONMENT(subparameters): (DOS ONLY)

For DOS this parameter identifies the file characteristics that cannot be defined through JCL. This parameter can be abbreviated **ENV**.

BLOCKSIZE(bsize): (DOS ONLY)

This parameter is valid for DOS systems only. It is a subparameter of the ENVIRONMENT command and is required if ENV is used. With this parameter the size (bsize) of the block is specified for the input data set. It can be abbreviated **BLKSZ**.

NOLABEL | STDLABEL: (DOS ONLY)

This parameter is valid for DOS systems only. It is an optional subparameter of the ENVIRONMENT command. This parameter indicates to AMS whether an input file contains standard labels. Default is STDLABEL. This parameter can be abbreviated **NLBL** or **SLBL**, respectively.

NOREWIND | REWIND | UNLOAD: (DOS ONLY)

This parameter is valid for DOS systems only. It is an optional subparameter of the ENVIRONMENT parameter. This parameter indicates to AMS input tape control options. Default is NOREWIND. This parameter can be abbreviated **NREW**, **REW**, or **UNLD**, respectively.

PRIMEDATADEVICE(pdev): (DOS ONLY)

This parameter is valid for DOS systems only. It is an optional subparameter of the ENVIRONMENT command. This parameter indicates to AMS the input device type (pdev). A device type of 2400 must be used for tape files and an ASSGN card using SYS004 as the programmer-logical unit. This parameter can be abbreviated **PDEV**.

OUTFILE(jcl-dname [/password]):

This entry allows you to specify to AMS the name of the DD (OS) or DLBL (DOS) JCL card that points to the output volume. The output volume is the one that will receive the imported object. See also the INFILE parameter. This parameter can be abbreviated **OFILE**.

OBJECTS(name):

This parameter allows specification of new or changed attributes to be made to the object being imported. Its abbreviation can be **OBJ**.

FILE(dname):

This specifies the name of the DLBL (DOS) or DD (OS) statement that identifies the volume being imported. This parameter is required when the object is defined with the UNIQUE attribute. Two FILE parameters will be required to define the Index and Data components.

VOLUMES(volser1 [volser2]....):

This specifies the VOLUMES that are to receive the object. This can be abbreviated **VOL**.

SAVRAC | NOSAVRAC: (OS ONLY)

This parameter pertains to those objects protected by the RACF (Resources Access Control Facility) feature. RACF is not part of VSAM. It is used for security purposes and works *with* VSAM. Specification of SAVRAC allows retention of existing RACF profiles. Default is NOSAVRAC.

USECLASS (prim [sec]: (DOS ONLY)

This parameter allows the modification of the USECLASS for the object being imported. For a more thorough discussion of this subject see the DEFINE command. Its abbreviation can be **USCL**.

8.9.4.2 Sample IMPORTRA Jobstream

For DOS:

```
// JOB IMPORTRA ACCTDATA
// DLBL IJSYSUC,'USERCAT.NO1',,VSAM
// DLBL WORK,'WORK',,VSAM
// ASSGN SYS006,VOL=VSAM01,SHR
// DLBL VOLVSAM1,,,VSAM
// EXTENT SYS006
// ASSGN SYS005,TAPE
// TLBL SYS005,'BACKUP'
// EXEC IDCAMS,SIZE=AUTO
     IMPORTRA
                  OUTFILE(TAPEOUT)              —
                  CIMODE                        —
                  CRAVOLUMES( VSAM01 ALL)       —
                  ENVIRONMENT(                  —
                       BLOCKSIZE(8192)          —
                       STDLABEL                 —
                       UNLOAD                   —
                       PDEV(2400)               —
                       )                        —
                  FORCE                         —
                  MASTERPW(MASTERPW)            —
/*
```

For OS:

```
//IMPORTRA   JOB    ACCTDATA,'MIKE BOUROS',CLASS=R
//AMS        EXEC   PGM=IDCAMS
//TAPEIN     DD     DSN=BACKUP,LABEL=(,SL),DISP=OLD
//           DD     UNIT=2400,VOL=SER=111111,
//           DD     DCB=(BLKSIZE=8192)
//VSAMOBJ    DD     DISP=OLD,VOL=SER=VSAM01,UNIT=3350
//           DD     DSN=UCATLG01
```

```
//SYSPRINT   DD      SYSOUT=A
//SYSIN      DD      *
   IMPORTRA
             INFILE(TAPEIN)          —
             OUTFILE(VSAMOBJ)        —
             CATALOG(UCATLG01)       —
             MASTERPW(MASTERPW)      —
/*
```

In this example an object copied previously using an EXPORTRA is now restored. The object will be imported into the volume identified by the **OUTFILE** parameter. The master catalog is password protected; therefore, the master catalog master password is required.

8.10 USING MODELS WITH AMS

One of the parameters we have glossed over in previous chapters is the **MODEL** command. This parameter can be used when DEFINing any of the following VSAM objects:

Clusters
Alternate indices
Paths
User catalogs
Page space

When defining a VSAM object, the MODEL parameter allows you to point AMS to a previously defined entry in order to obtain its parameter information. This allows you to supply AMS specifications with a minimum amount of coding. Several clusters can be defined, for instance (whether real or dummy), and later referenced again and again. Certain installation standards might be established and followed by using this method. MODEL is useful in defining test files that will behave exactly like certain production files. When using the MODEL parameter, specific parameters can be overridden by simply supplying these parameters during the object definition.

8.10.1 EXAMPLES USING MODELS

Following are some examples of the use of the MODEL parameter:

```
DEFINE  CLUSTER                        —
        (NAME                          —
        (NEW.CLUSTER)                  —
        MODEL(OLD.CLUSTER)             —
        KEYS(12 0)                     —
        RECORDSIZE(200 200) )          —
        CATALOG(USERCAT.NO1)
```

In this example all the parameters specified for **OLD.CLUSTER** will apply also to **NEW.CLUSTER** except the KEYS and RECORDSIZE parameters are overridden.

```
DEFINE  CLUSTER                        —
        (NAME                          —
        (NEW.CLUSTER)                  —
        MODEL(OLD.CLUSTER)             —
        SHAREOPTIONS( 2 3 ) )          —
        CATALOG(USERCAT.NO1)           —
```

In the preceding only the SHAREOPTIONS parameter will be overridden.

TEST YOUR UNDERSTANDING

1. Explain two uses for the REPRO command.
2. How can REPRO be used to select test data?
3. What does EXPORT DISCONNECT do?
4. What is the difference between REPRO and EXPORT?
5. Name some of the ways in which LISTCAT can be used.
6. When would you use the FORCE option of DELETE?
7. What function does VERIFY perform?
8. Name the three types of PRINT format available.
9. How is the ALTER command used?
10. Explain the purpose and use of the MODEL parameter.
11. What are the differences between the LISTCAT and LISTCRA commands?
12. What is the purpose of the RESETCAT command?
13. How and when are the EXPORTRA and IMPORTRA used?

chapter 9

ACCESS METHOD SERVICES—ALTERNATE INDICES

9.1 WHAT IS AN ALTERNATE INDEX?

Before getting into the AMS commands necessary for the definition, creation, and maintenance of an alternate index, it is first necessary to explain just what an alternate index is.

In Chapter 7 one of the VSAM data sets we defined was a purchase order file. The **key** for this file was the purchase order number. Along with the purchase order number, many other valuable data fields are stored in each purchase order record. One of the more important fields is the vendor number. If we were required to be able to access every purchase order by vendor number, how would we accomplish this?

Basically, the solution would be to collect all the vendor numbers from the purchase orders we have on file and create another file containing just the vendor number and the purchase order number. We would then sort this file by vendor number. From this point on, whenever the need arose to find all the PO's for a given vendor number, we would only have to pull out our vendor cross-reference file to find them. This file fulfills the basic requirements for what is commonly called an alternate index.

Before VSAM was introduced, the only indexed method available was ISAM. ISAM does not support any form of alternate index. How did one proceed to utilize the **features** of an alternate index when ISAM was the only access method available?

One way was to duplicate the entire file, sort it into vendor number sequence, and then load a new file. This, of course, would satisfy our users, but it certainly, because of the duplication of data, would not do our conscience much good. Unfortunately, this method was all too often resorted to in the past because it was quick and did not require even a fraction of the work required by other solutions.

A second method that was utilized involved the creation of a second file (usually also ISAM) that contained as its key a field such as vendor number, which became its primary file key. Along with this, another field was always placed in the record that served as a **pointer** to the primary file. This pointer field was, in fact, the actual key of the primary file record. The end result was that the base file could be accessed by both the primary or **base** index as well as by some **alternate** index.

9.2 DOING IT THE OLD WAY

If you have been a programmer for any length of time, you may have been involved in the development of major applications that operated this way. Before the advent of VSAM when ISAM was king, you had no alternative but to build your own alternate indices. This undertaking would often become a project in itself. Since alternate indices are not supported by ISAM, all the functions now taken for granted as existing in VSAM had to be programmed into the application system.

Programs had to be written that extracted the keys and pointers from the prime ISAM file. They had to be sorted and a second ISAM file had to be created. This ISAM file served as the alternate index to the prime ISAM file. If duplicate keys were possible, a **sequence** field had to be appended to the end of the key and would be incremented in order to make each record unique (ISAM does not allow duplicate keys under any circumstances).

Once the alternate index file was created, what would happen if we decided to add new records to the base file? If the **add** program was not written to update the alternate index file as well, the files would end up out of synch, at least until the alternate index file was re-created.

This could present a problem: not everyone could accept waiting until tomorrow to find out if any additional POs existed for a certain vendor, especially when one finds out that they have been refusing to take back bad merchandise.

9.3 VSAM TO THE RESCUE

It must be obvious to you by now that I have been picking on ISAM. At the same time I have not been saying the same nasty things about VSAM, the reason, of course, being that all these functions which had to be performed through brute-force programming are now automatic with VSAM if you choose to use them.

VSAM will allow you to specify an alternate index (abbreviated AIX) through the IDCAMS define command. With this definition you can specify whether the AIX is to be updated each time the base cluster is updated. You can also specify whether duplicate keys are allowed for the AIX (duplicates are not allowed in the base cluster index). In addition to this, **multiple** alternate indices can be created and maintained by VSAM.

9.4 IDCAMS COMMANDS FOR ALTERNATE INDICES

There are three commands used for the definition, creation, and access of data through VSAM AIXs. They are as follows:

DEFINE ALTERNATEINDEX (or DEFINE AIX)
BLDINDEX
DEFINE PATH

The steps required to create an alternate index are illustrated in the following.

1. **CREATE BASE CLUSTER** — Establish base cluster. Only KSDS and ESDS data sets can have an alternate index.

2.	**DEFINE ALTERNATE INDEX**	Use IDCAMS to define the alternate index in the catalog.
3.	**RUN IDCAMS BLDINDEX**	Use the IDCAMS function to load the AIX cluster.*
4.	**DEFINE PATH**	DEFINE a PATH using IDCAMS to direct VSAM to the base cluster through the AIX.*

DATA CAN NOW BE ACCESSED

DEFINE ALTERNATEINDEX:

The purpose of this command is to **DEFINE** the characteristics of an **alternate index** and to **relate** this index to a base cluster. Since an AIX is, in effect, a KSDS cluster, many of the parameters used to define a cluster are also available to define an alternate index. This step does **not** actually put any entries into the alternate index itself. It just makes a catalog entry for the AIX.

BLDINDEX:

This command is used to build alternate indices from data contained in the base cluster. Before this can be run, the base cluster must have been previously loaded and the AIX must already have been defined. Using the data found in the base cluster, records are created that will form the key and pointer records for the AIX. The records are then sorted and loaded to the AIX data set. The **BLDINDEX** facility can automatically define two ESDS data sets to be used as sort work areas. These data sets are deleted at the end of the BLDINDEX run.

* Steps 3 and 4 may be interchanged.

DEFINE PATH:

It has been stated that an AIX is essentially a KSDS cluster. As such, it can be **opened** and **read** by an application program. Although this capability may come in handy at one time or another, it is certainly not the main purpose of the alternate index. In order to direct VSAM to **use the AIX to access the base cluster**, you must indicate this to VSAM through the **DEFINE PATH** facility. A PATH is not a physical structure such as are clusters, catalogs, or alternate indices. The PATH definition simply places an entry in the appropriate catalog.

The PATH then is the only way in which an **application program** accesses base cluster data in an alternate sequence. It never accesses the AIX directly as a data set to accomplish this.

If you were thoroughly aware of the structure of the AIX, you **could** write a program to do so, however.

9.4.1 DEFINING THE ALTERNATE INDEX

Following is the format of the DEFINE ALTERNATEINDEX command. We shall continue to use the two volumes that we have defined for our purchase order application.

<table>
<tr><th>COMMAND</th><th>PARAMETER</th><th>NOTES</th></tr>
<tr><td></td><td>The following parameters apply to both the INDEX and DATA components.</td><td></td></tr>
<tr><td>DEFINE</td><td>ALTERNATEINDEX</td><td>REQ'D</td></tr>
<tr><td></td><td>NAME(aixname)</td><td>REQ'D</td></tr>
<tr><td></td><td>CYLINDERS(prime [sec]) |</td><td></td></tr>
<tr><td></td><td>BLOCKS(prime [sec]) |</td><td></td></tr>
<tr><td></td><td>TRACKS(prime [sec]) |</td><td></td></tr>
<tr><td></td><td>RECORDS(prime [sec])</td><td></td></tr>
<tr><td></td><td>[ERASE | NOERASE]</td><td></td></tr>
<tr><td></td><td>[EXCEPTIONEXIT(modname)]</td><td></td></tr>
<tr><td></td><td>[FILE(jcl-dname)]</td><td></td></tr>
<tr><td></td><td>[ATTEMPTS(number)</td><td></td></tr>
<tr><td></td><td>[AUTHORIZATION(entrypoint [string])]</td><td></td></tr>
<tr><td></td><td>[BUFFERSPACE(size)]</td><td></td></tr>
<tr><td></td><td>[CODE(code)]</td><td></td></tr>
<tr><td></td><td>[CONTROLINTERVALSIZE(size)]</td><td></td></tr>
<tr><td></td><td>[CONTROLPW(password)]</td><td></td></tr>
<tr><td></td><td>[DESTAGEWAIT | NODESTAGEWAIT]</td><td>OS</td></tr>
<tr><td></td><td>[FOR(days) | TO(date)]</td><td></td></tr>
<tr><td></td><td>[FREESPACE(cipct capct)]</td><td></td></tr>
</table>

COMMAND	PARAMETERS	NOTES
	[IMBED | NOIMBED]	
	[KEYRANGES(lkey hkey) (lkey hkey).....]	
	[KEYS(len offset)]	
	[MASTERPW(password)]	
	[MODEL(ename [/pass] [cname[/pass]])]	
	[ORDERED | UNORDERED]	
	[OWNER(owner id)]	
	[READPW(password)]	
	[RECORDSIZE(avg. max.)]	
	[RELATE(r-ename [/password])]	
	[REPLICATE | NOREPLICATE]	
	[REUSE | NOREUSE]	
	[SHAREOPTIONS(opt1 opt2)	
	[STAGE | BIND] CYLINDERFAULT]	OS
	[UNIQUE | SUBALLOCATION | NOALLOCATION]	
	[UNIQUEKEY | NONUNIQUEKEY]	
	[UPDATEPW(password)]	
	[UPGRADE | NOUPGRADE]	
	[USECLASS(prim sec)]	
	[VOLUMES(vol1 vol2...) | DEFAULTVOLUMES]	
	[WRITECHECK | NOWRITECHECK]	
	)	REQ'D

The following parameters pertain to the optional DEFINITION of the DATA component.

COMMAND	PARAMETERS	NOTES
[DATA		
	(	
	NAME(dname)	REQ'D
	CYLINDERS(prime [sec])]	
	BLOCKS(prime [sec]) |	
	TRACKS(prime [sec]) |	
	RECORDS(prime [sec])	
	[ERASE | NOERASE]	
	[EXCEPTIONEXIT(modname)]	
	[FILE(jcl-dname)]	
	[ATTEMPTS(number)	
	[AUTHORIZATION(entrypoint [string])]	
	[BUFFERSPACE(size)]	
	[CODE(code)]	
	[CONTROLINTERVALSIZE(size)]	

(Continued on p. 200)

COMMAND	PARAMETERS	NOTES
	[CONTROLPW(password)]	
	[DESTAGEWAIT | NODESTAGEWAIT]	OS
	[FREESPACE(cipct capct)]	
	[KEYRANGES(lkey hkey) (lkey hkey).....]	
	[KEYS(len offset)]	
	[MASTERPW(password)]	
	[MODEL(ename [/pass] [cname[/pass]])]	
	[ORDERED | UNORDERED]	
	[OWNER(owner id)]	
	[READPW(password)]	
	[RECORDSIZE(avg. max.)]	
	[REUSE | NOREUSE]	
	[SHAREOPTIONS(opt1 opt2)	
	[STAGE | BIND | CYLINDERFAULT]	OS
	[UNIQUE | SUBALLOCATION | NOALLOCATION]	
	[UNIQUEKEY | NONUNIQUEKEY]	
	[UPDATEPW(password)]	
	[USECLASS(prim sec)]	
	[VOLUMES(vol1 vol2...) | DEFAULTVOLUMES]	
	[WRITECHECK | NOWRITECHECK]	
	)]	

The following parameters pertain to the optional DEFINITION of the INDEX component.

COMMAND	PARAMETERS	NOTES
[INDEX		
	NAME(iname)	REQ'D
	CYLINDERS(prime [sec]) |	
	BLOCKS(prime [sec]) |	
	TRACKS(prime [sec]) |	
	RECORDS(prime [sec])	
	[EXCEPTIONEXIT(modname)]	
	[FILE(jcl-dname)]	
	[ATTEMPTS(number)	
	[AUTHORIZATION(entrypoint [string])]	
	[CODE(code)]	
	[CONTROLINTERVALSIZE(size)]	
	[CONTROLPW(password)]	
	[DESTAGEWAIT | NODESTAGEWAIT]	OS
	[IMBED | NOIMBED]	
	[MASTERPW(password)]	

COMMAND	PARAMETERS	NOTES
	[MODEL(ename [/pass] [cname[/pass]])]	
	[ORDERED | UNORDERED]	
	[OWNER(owner id)]	
	[READPW(password)]	
	[REPLICATE | NOREPLICATE]	
	[REUSE | NOREUSE]	
	[SHAREOPTIONS(opt1 opt2)	
	[STAGE | BIND | CYLINDERFAULT]	OS
	[UNIQUE | SUBALLOCATION | NOALLOCATION]	
	[UPDATEPW(password)]	
	[VOLUMES(vol1 vol2...) | DEFAULTVOLUMES]	
	[WRITECHECK | NOWRITECHECK]	
	)]	

9.4.2 EXPLANATION OF AIX PARAMETERS

EXPLANATION OF PARAMETERS

DEFINE ALTERNATEINDEX:

This AMS command specifies that you wish to define to IDCAMS the characteristics of a VSAM alternate index. This command can be abbreviated **DEF AIX**.

NAME(aixname):

This entry allows you to give a name to the AIX being defined. The name can be up to 44 characters in length and can be any combination of characters, numbers, or the special symbols @, #, and $. The name must begin with a character, and if greater than eight characters, must be broken into segments of one to eight digits separated by periods, for example:

DEFINE AIX(PURCH.AIX.VENDOR)

CYLINDERS/TRACKS/RECORDS/BLOCKS(prime sec):

The purpose of this parameter is twofold: to allocate the initial (prime) space for the AIX, and to specify the dynamic secondary (sec) allocation to be made in the event that the primary space allocation becomes exhausted. The space allocation can be specified in CYLINDERS, TRACKS, RECORDS, or BLOCKS. The first three entries are used for CKD devices. The first two entries are the ones most commonly used, especially CYLINDERS. For FBA devices, the allocation must be specified in BLOCKS. The abbreviation for CYLINDERS is **CYL**, TRACKS is **TRK**, RECORDS is **REC**, and BLOCKS is **BLK**.

ERASE | NOERASE]:

For sensitive data, the specification of ERASE will cause VSAM to erase the entire area occupied by the AIX when the entry is deleted from the catalog. The extent formerly occupied by this cluster will be overwritten with binary zeros (low-value). The abbreviation for this parameter is **ERAS** (ERASE) or **NERAS** (NOERASE).

EXCEPTIONEXIT(modname):

This parameter specifies the name of an exit routine written by the user to which control is given whenever an unusual error condition takes place. This is usually an I/O error. This exit routine is Link Edited to your Load (OS) or Core-Image (DOS) library. To find out more about this EXIT routine, see the *IBM VSAM Programmer's Guide*. Also see Chapter 14. Its abbreviation is **EEXT**.

FOR(days) TO (date):

With this parameter you can specify the retention period for this AIX. It can be specified either in days or by date. If the specification is made in days, you must use the FOR parameter. The days may be specified as any value between 0 and 1830. Any value higher than this will force a retention through the year 1999. In order to specify a specific date use the TO parameter. A specific date is specified in the form yyddd, where yy = year and ddd is the Julian day of the year (001–366). Example 84365 is interpreted the 365th day of 1984.

FILE(jcl-dname):

This parameter is used to point to the // DLBL JCL card (DOS) or a DD JCL card (OS). The name specified here must match the name specified by the DLBL/DD card. The following illustrates the association between the JCL and the FILE (jcl-name):

```
// DLBL AIXDEF ........      DOS
//AIXDEF DD ............     OS
       FILE(AIXDEF)
```

This parameter is required only for UNIQUE AIXs.

ATTEMPTS(number):

This parameter is used only in those cases where the cluster is password protected. The number of attempts the operator can make before IDCAMS aborts is specified here. If ATTEMPTS(0) is specified, the operator is not allowed to enter a password from a system console. See the chapter on security (Chapter 12) for a more thorough explanation. This parameter can be abbreviated **ATT**.

AUTHORIZATION(entrypoint/string):

This parameter specifies the name of a routine (entrypoint) to which control is passed every time this cluster is accessed. This routine is called a **user exit** or **user verification routine**. It is usually written by the systems programmer at the installation in which the AIX will be used. In addition to passing control to the user-exit, a character string up to 256 characters in length can also be passed to the routine. The characters passed can be specified as either character or hexadecimal values. For the specifics in writing a user exit see chapter 12. This parameter can be abbreviated **AUTH**. Example:

```
AUTHORIZATION(CHECKRTN authdata) or
AUTHORIZATION(CHECKRTN X'C1E4E3C8C4C1E3C1')
```

BUFFERSPACE(size):

This specifies the space to be provided for buffers when this cluster is in use. The specification to be used for both the data and index components should be large enough to contain at least two data control intervals and one index control interval if this is a KSDS file. If this parameter is left out, VSAM will compute the BUFFERSPACE required. For more information on this subject, see Chapter 17. This parameter can be abbreviated **BUFSP** or **BUFSPC**.

CODE(code):

This parameter is used for those clusters that are password protected. The designated **code** is used in lieu of the AIX name when prompting the operator for the password. See Chapter 12 for more information.

CONTROLINTERVALSIZE(cisize):

With this parameter you can establish or set the size (cisize) of the control interval. The CI size for the index and data components can be specified separately. For the index, the allowable CI for the data component must be a multiple of 512 or 2048 and can be any size between 512 and 32768. For the size of the AIX CIs it is usually best to let VSAM calculate this for you, at least for the index component. For more information on this subject, see Chapters 13 and 17. See also RECORDSIZE. This parameter can be abbreviated **CISZ** or **CNVSZ**.

CONTROLPW(password):

A special method of file access called **control interval access** enables a program to read or write entire CIs at a time rather than individual records. With this parameter you can control the access to the AIX cluster by specifying a password. The entire subject of passwords is covered in Chapter 12. This parameter can be abbreviated **CTLPW**.

DESTAGEWAIT | NODESTAGEWAIT (OS ONLY)

This parameter pertains only to the OS operating system using the Mass Storage System (MSS). A VSAM object stored on an MSS system must be first STAGED, that is, copied to a 3330-type volume before it can be used. When the object is no longer needed (i.e., the application program closes the file) the volume can then be **DESTAGED**. This parameter allows you to specify whether the application should wait for the conclusion of the DESTAGing (DESTAGEWAIT) operation or whether it can be done asynchronously (NODESTAGEWAIT). NODESTAGEWAIT is the default. This parameter can be abbreviated **DSTGW** or **NDSTGW**, respectively.

FREESPACE(cipct capct):

The amount of FREESPACE to be left in a control interval or control area can be specified here. Both **cipct** (CI%) and **capct** (CA %) are specified as percentages of space to be *left* in the CI/CA of the alternate index being built. Specification of (0 0) allows no FREESPACE to be reserved in the CI/CA. There is one exception to the way that this parameter is handled by VSAM: when a specification of (100 100) is made. VSAM allows only one record per CI, and only one CI per CA will contain data. This parameter can be abbreviated **FSPC**.

IMBED | NOIMBED:

This option allows you to decide where you would like the AIX sequence set placed. The sequence set is the lowest level of the VSAM index structure. If you specify the IMBED option, VSAM will place the sequence set on the first track of the control area to which it belongs. This means that the sequence set will be located physically adjacent to the data it services. This is usually beneficial if the data access will primarily be sequential. With this option the sequence set is replicated as many times as it will fit on the first track of the control area. If NOIMBED is specified, the sequence set remains with the rest of the index. This parameter can be abbreviated **IMBD** (IMBED) or **NIMBD** (NOIMBED).

KEYRANGES(Lkey1 Hkey1 Lkey2 Hkey2......):

This option allows you to place portions of the alternate indices' data components on different volumes. This parameter is used in conjunction with the VOLUMES parameter. Each preceding KEYRANGE specified coresponds to the respective volume serial number coded in the VOLUMES parameter. Up to 123 KEYRANGES can be specified. **Lkey** pertains to the low key of a given range and **Hkey** pertains to the high key of the same range. If you cannot contain *all* the records of a given KEYRANGE on a particular volume and the number of VOLUMES exceeds the KEYRANGES, the excess data records will overflow onto the extra VOLUMES without any consideration given to the keys. If the number of VOLUMES is less than the KEYRANGES specified, the excess records will be placed on the last VOLUME specified. This parameter can be abbreviated **KRNG**.

KEYS (len offset):

This parameter defines the location and length of the key to be used for the alternate index. This value is obtained from the base cluster record. The maximum length of a key is 64 bytes. The offset is specified as relative to zero. For example, an AIX containing records with a key length of 6 and beginning in the eleventh byte of the record would be specified as:

KEYS(6 10)

MASTERPW:

This parameter specifies a password that is to be used for the AIX being defined. This parameter allows access to all AMS operations for this entry. Unless this parameter is specified, the associate parameters CODE, ATTEMPTS, and AUTHORIZATION are of no value. The password must be one to eight characters in length, and can contain alpha, numeric, or special characters. When using special characters, the entire password should be contained within apostrophes. The password can also be specified in hexadecimal. Examples:

MASTERPW(MIKEB)
MASTERPW('MIKEB')
MASTERPW(X'D4C9D2C5C2')

See Chapter 12 for more information. The abbreviation for this is **MRPW**.

MODEL(ename / password cname / password):

This parameter allows you to point VSAM to some other object that you have already defined to obtain and fill in parameters that you optionally omit. This parameter can be used to refer to *any* VSAM object. The ename parameter here refers to an AIX being used for the model. The cname parameter is used to name the catalog in which the AIX being referenced is defined.

ORDERED | UNORDERED:

This parameter is used in conjunction with the VOLUMES parameter. It specifies whether the volumes are to be used in the ORDER specified. When KEYRANGES is also specified, the first range of keys is placed on the first volume, the second range on the second volume, and so on. This differs slightly from the use of KEYRANGES without the ORDERED parameter in that VSAM has more flexibility in placing the data records when UNORDERED is specified. UNORDERED is the default. These parameters can be abbreviated **ORD** and **UNORD**, respectively.

OWNER(owner id):

This parameter is used for documentation purposes only. It specifies the name of the OWNER of the AIX. The **owner id** must be specified as one to eight characters and follow the same rules described under MASTERPW.

READPW(password):

This specifies the password to be used whenever the AIX is accessed for **read** purposes. As mentioned earlier in this chapter, an alternate index can be accessed in the same manner as a KSDS cluster can be accessed. This parameter can be abbreviated **RDPW**.

RECORDSIZE(avg. max.):

This parameter specifies in bytes the average (**avg.**) and maximum (**max.**) size of an alternate index data component. If avg. and max. are equal, VSAM understands this to be a file of fixed length records. When avg. and max. are different, VSAM understands this cluster to be a file of variable length records. The formula to compute the recordsize is as follows:

$$RECSZ = 5 + ALK + (N \times BKL)$$

where:

AKL is the length of the AIX key.

BKL is the length of the base cluster key if KSDS or **4** if an ESDS.

N is equal to 1 if UNIQUEKEY has been specified. N is equal to the number of records in the base cluster that can have the same alternate key.

This parameter can be abbreviated **RECSZ**.

RELATE(r-ename [/password])]:

This parameter points AMS to the base cluster for which this AIX is being created, **r-ename** is the name of a KSDS or ESDS cluster to which the alternate index will point. The abbreviation for this parameter is **REL**.

REPLICATE | NOREPLICATE:

With this option you can tell VSAM to REPLICATE the index entries (KSDS only) as many times as they will fit on one track. This, of course, reduces the rotational delay because a shorter time is required for the correct index record to be in position to pass under the read/write head. This parameter can be abbreviated **REPL** or **NREPL**, respectively.

REUSE | NOREUSE:

If REUSE is specified, when the AIX cluster is **opened** it is opened as an output file with DISP=NEW (as opposed to input or I/O), and the HIGH-USED RBA (end of file pointer) is reset to zero as if *no* records exist on this file. For all practical purposes, once the HIGH-USED RBA pointer is reset to zero, old records on this file are no longer accessible. If NOREUSE is used, the AIX would have to be DELETEd and redefined each time it is to be re-created. This parameter is abbreviated **RUS** or **NRUS**, respectively.

SHAREOPTIONS(opt1 opt2):

This parameter specifies how an AIX cluster is to be shared between partitions or regions (opt1). For OS installations only, the second option (opt2) specifies how this cluster is to be shared across systems, that is, in multi-CPU environments. For opt1 you must code one of the following:

CROSS-PARTITION/REGION OPTIONS:

1. This specifies that the AIX set can be shared between any number of users for **read** purposes or only one user for read and write processing.

2. This code allows any number of users to be reading the AIX and one user to WRITE to the data set at any given time.

3. With this option a cluster can be shared by any number of users for both read and write purposes. Neither VSAM nor the operating system does anything in order to ensure the integrity of the cluster. If two users are writing to this object at the same time, there is a good chance that the cluster will be destroyed. When using this option, it is up to the user to ensure that this does not happen. This could possibly be accomplished through proper scheduling and through the use of ENQ and DEQ (enqueue and dequeue) macros.

4. With this option VSAM can offer some protection and assistance when a cluster is to be shared for both read and write purposes by multiple partitions or regions. When using this option VSAM will retrieve a fresh copy of the control interval containing the desired record (random read) even if a copy of the record is presently in the CPU. This helps ensure read integrity. When records are written to the data set, the first partition/region to issue the **write** will get exclusive control over the data set until the write operation is completed.

CROSS-SYSTEM (OS ONLY):

1. Not currently used.
2. Not currently used.
3. This function is to cross-system what **3** is to cross-partition/region. VSAM will allow you to perform any kind of operation but delegates all responsibility to you. Improper use of this option can result in destroyed clusters and possibly program check interruptions within VSAM.

4. This option is similar to option **4** which is used for cross-partition/region. With this cross-system option VSAM expects you to use OS RESERVE and DEQ macros in order to hardware RESERVE (software enqueue) and hardware release (software dequeue) a data set. A hardware reserve is actually a special channel command that causes a CPU to **seize** a particular DASD device causing a second CPU to be locked out in a true hardware sense. In order to perform this a RESERVE macro is issued. A DEQ macro is required to return the DASD device to an **available to anyone** state. This is performed with a DEQ macro that issues a hardware command (CCW) called RELEASE. Another service that VSAM performs under this option is to prevent the occurrence of a CA or CI split that results in a CA split. This is because when a CA

split takes place a new CA is acquired from the end of the data set. This cannot be allowed to occur because it would then change the HIGH-USED RBA, in other words, the indicator that marks the end of the data set. If this happened on one system, there is currently no way for the other system to find out about it. The abbreviation for this option is **SHR**.

STAGE | BIND | CYLINDERFAULT: (OS ONLY)

This option pertains only to users of the MSS (Mass Storage Systems). When STAGE is specified the cluster is to be staged to a DASD device when the data set is opened. If the cluster cannot be staged at that time because of heavy staging activity, the data is staged as the program needs it. The BIND parameter is similar to STAGE; it ensures, however, that the data, once staged is **bound** to the DASD device it was staged to until the cluster is closed. If CYLINDERFAULT is specified, the cluster is not staged when the data set is opened; rather, the data is staged as it is required. These operations in some ways resemble the paging operation that takes place in memory.

UNIQUE | SUBALLOCATION | NONALLOCATION

This parameter identifies the type of space that this AIX is to occupy. If UNIQUE is specified, it will be the only object contained within the space that is acquired for it. When this option is specified,the space that contains this object is created at the same time the AIX is defined. If SUBALLOCATION is specified, the space used to contain the cluster is obtained from space already in existence on the volume or volumes pointed to by the VOLUMES parameter. If NOALLOCATION is specified, no allocation is made for the AIX but the AIX name is added to the catalog, this capability could come in handy when defining MODELs. UNIQUE can be abbreviated **UNQ**. SUBALLOCATED can be abbreviated **SUBAL**. There is no abbreviation for NOALLOCATION.

UNIQUEKEY | NONUNIQUEKEY:

Specifies whether this alternate index can contain duplicate keys or if only UNIQUE keys will be supported. If NONUNIQUEKEY is specified, duplicate keys will be allowed in the AIX. This parameter is abbreviated **UNQK** or **NUNQK**, respectively.

UPDATEPW(password):

Specifies the password to be used any time this AIX is **updated**: that is, records added, deleted, or changed. See the rules described under MASTERPW for a description of the password format. Its abbreviation is **UPDPW**.

UPGRADE | NOUPGRADE:

This specifies whether this AIX is to be updated every time an addition, update, or deletion takes place on the base cluster. If NOUPGRADE is specified, the AIX is never updated after it is created. This parameter can be abbreviated **UPG** or **NUPG**, respectively.

VOLUMES(vol1 vol2....) | DEFAULTVOLUMES:

This designates the VOLUMES upon which this AIX is to be placed; **vol1 vol2**... are the serial numbers with which the DASD volumes were initialized. The data and index components can be located on separate VOLUMES if desired. DEFAULTVOLUMES is used in conjunction with the MODEL parameter. It specifies to VSAM that the information pertaining to VOLUMES should be obtained from the MODEL. This parameter can be abbreviated **VOL**.

WRITECHECK | NOWRITECHECK

If WRITECHECK is specified, a special verification function is performed on the data just written to verify that it was written correctly. A special I/O operation called a **soft-read** is performed to accomplish this. When WRITECHECK is specified, VSAM constructs a special channel program for the I/O operation that, when chained to a WRITE operation, allows the soft-read operation. In a soft-read the data, although read, is not actually transferred back to the CPU. Unless high volume data makes this prohibitive, WRITECHECK should be specified. Although more time is required to perform this than is required to merely write, the time involved is less than the time it would take to write and read using a normal read operation. This option can be abbreviated **WCK** or **NWCK**, respectively.

9.4.3 EXAMPLES OF DEFINING ALTERNATE INDICES

```
DEFINE ALTERNATEINDEX        —
    NAME(PUR.AIX.VENDOR)     —
    RELATE(PUR.CLUSTER)      —
    CYL(5 1)                 —
    KEYS(6 29)               —
    NONUNIQUEKEY             —
    UPGRADE                  —
    VOL(VSAM02)              —
    )                        —
    CATALOG(UCATLG01)        —
```

In this example we are defining an alternate index named **PUR.AIX.VENDOR**. This AIX is used as a pointer to the base cluster **PUR.CLUSTER**. The vendor number is located in the thirtieth position of the purchase order record and is six bytes in length. Duplicate records are allowed (NONUNIQUEKEY). This AIX will be updated whenever the base cluster is updated.

9.4.4 THE JOB CONTROL REQUIREMENTS FOR AIX DEFINITION

The Job Control for the preceding would look something like this:

For DOS:

```
// JOB PURAIX ACCTDATA
// DLBL IJSYSUC,'UCATLG01',,VSAM
// EXTENT SYS006,VSAM02
// EXEC IDCAMS,SIZE=AUTO

                    CONTROL CARDS GO HERE

/*
```

For **OS** the JCL might look like this:

```
//PURAIX      JOB     ACCTDATA,'MIKE BOUROS',CLASS=R
//PURAMS      EXEC    PGM=IDCAMS
//STEPCAT     DD      DSN=UCATLG01,DISP=SHR (OPTIONAL)
//SYSPRINT    DD      SYSOUT=A
//SYSIN       DD      *

                    CONTROL CARDS GO HERE

/*
```

Now putting it all together:

For DOS:

```
// JOB PURAIX ACCTDATA
// DLBL IJSYSUC,'UCATLG01',,VSAM
// EXTENT SYS006,VSAM02
// EXEC IDCAMS,SIZE=AUTO
     DEFINE ALTERNATEINDEX          -
          (                         -
          NAME(PUR.AIX.VENDOR)      -
          RELATE(PUR.CLUSTER)       -
          CYL(5 1)                  -
          KEYS(6 29)                -
          NONUNIQUEKEY              -
          UPGRADE                   -
          VOL(VSAM02)               -
          )                         -
          CATALOG(UCATLG01)         -
/*
```

For **OS**:

```
//PURAIX     JOB    ACCTDATA,'MIKE BOUROS',CLASS=R
//PURAMS     EXEC   PGM=IDCAMS
//STEPCAT    DD     DSN=UCATLG01,DISP=SHR (OPTIONAL)
//SYSPRINT   DD     SYSOUT=A
//SYSIN      DD     *
         DEFINE ALTERNATEINDEX          —
                 (                      —
                 NAME(PUR.AIX.VENDOR)   —
                 RELATE(PUR.CLUSTER)    —
                 CYL(5 1)               —
                 KEYS(6 29)             —
                 NONUNIQUEKEY           —
                 UPGRADE                —
                 VOL(VSAM02)            —
                 )                      —
                 CATALOG(UCATLG01)      —
/*
```

Now let us change and/or add some options:

```
DEFINE ALTERNATEINDEX           —
      NAME(PUR.AIX.VENDOR)      —
      RELATE(PUR.CLUSTER)       —
      CYL(5 1)                  —
      KEYS(6 29)                —
      FILE(AIXJCL)              —
      UNIQUE                    —
      UNIQUEKEY                 —
      UPGRADE                   —
      VOL(VSAM02)               —
      WRITECHECK                —
      )                         —
      CATALOG(UCATLG01)         —
```

Some of the parameters have been changed from the previous example. The AIX being defined will be created in a UNIQUE space. No duplicate alternate key values will be allowed (UNIQUEKEY). The AIX will be updated whenever the base cluster is updated (UPGRADE). A write-verify will be performed.

Now putting it all together:

For DOS:

```
// JOB PURAIX ACCTDATA
// DLBL IJSYSUC,'UCATLG01',,VSAM
// EXTENT SYS006,VSAM02
// DLBL AIXJCL,'PUR.AIX.VENDOR',,VSAM
// EXEC IDCAMS,SIZE=AUTO
        DEFINE ALTERNATEINDEX          —
              (                        —
              NAME(PUR.AIX.VENDOR)     —
              RELATE(PUR.CLUSTER)      —
              CYL(5 1)                 —
              KEYS(6 29)               —
              FILE(AIXJCL)             —
              UNIQUE                   —
              UNIQUEKEY                —
              UPGRADE                  —
              VOL(VSAM02)              —
              WRITECHECK               —
              )                        —
              CATALOG(UCATLG01)
/*
```

For **OS**:

```
//PURAIX      JOB     ACCTDATA,'MIKE BOUROS',CLASS=R
//PURAMS      EXEC    PGM=IDCAMS
//STEPCAT     DD      DSN=UCATLG01,DISP=SHR (OPTIONAL)
//AIXJCL      DD      DSN=PUR.AIX.VENDOR,DISP=NEW,
//                    VOL=SER=VSAM02,UNIT=3350,
//                    SPACE=(CYL(40))
//SYSPRINT    DD      SYSOUT=A
//SYSIN       DD      *
        DEFINE ALTERNATEINDEX          —
              (                        —
              NAME(PUR.AIX.VENDOR)     —
              RELATE(PUR.CLUSTER)      —
              CYL(5 1)                 —
              KEYS(6 29)               —
              FILE(AIXJCL)             —
              UNIQUE                   —
              UNIQUEKEY                —
              UPGRADE                  —
              VOL(VSAM02)              —
              WRITECHECK               —
```

```
            )                                   —
            CATALOG(UCATLG01)
/*
```

9.5 BUILDING THE ALTERNATE INDEX

At this point we have defined the characteristics of our alternate index. The next step in our strategy is to now actually create the AIX cluster. It is possible to define the PATH information through AMS at this time; for our purposes, however, the index (BLDINDEX) will be built next. Do not forget that the base cluster must contain data for this step to work.

COMMAND	PARAMETERS	NOTES
BLDINDEX		REQ'D
	INDATASET(ename [/password]) |	REQ'D
	INFILE(jcl-dname [/password])	REQ'D
	OUTDATASET(ename [/password]) |	REQ'D
	OUTFILE(jcl-dname [/password])	REQ'D
	[EXTERNALSORT | INTERNALSORT]	
	[WORKFILES(jcl-dname1 jcl-dname2)	
	[WORKVOLUMES(volser volser .....)	DOS
	[CATALOG(cname [/password])]	

9.5.1 THE BLDINDEX PARAMETERS

EXPLANATION OF PARAMETERS

INDATASET:

This specifies the name of the base cluster or path that points to the base cluster for the alternate index being created. This parameter and INFILE are mutually exclusive. Its abbreviation is **IDS**.

INFILE:

This parameter names the DLBL (DOS) or DD (OS) JCL card that identifies the base cluster or the PATH to the base cluster. Its abbreviation is **IFILE**.

OUTDATASET:

This parameter specifies the name of the AIX entry or the PATH that points to the AIX entry to be loaded. The abbreviation for this is **ODS**.

OUTFILE:

This parameter names the DLBL (DOS) or DD (OS) JCL card that identifies the AIX entry or the PATH to the base entry. Its abbreviation is **OFILE**.

EXTERNALSORT | INTERNALSORT:

This specifies whether the sort required to order the keys for the AIX being loaded is to be done in virtual storage or on DASD. If the virtual storage available is insufficient, IDCAMS will attempt to allocate available work files dynamically. This is done using the standard default IDCUT1 and IDCUT2 JCL statements (see WORKFILES). If EXTERNALSORT is specified, name the JCL statements in the WORKFILES parameter unless you are using the standard defaults. Its abbreviations can be **ESORT** or **ISORT**, respectively.

WORKFILES (jcl-dname1 jcl-dname2):

This statement identifies the DD (OS) or DLBL (DOS) names used for work files when an exernal sort is performed. If the default names IDCUT1 and IDCUT2 are coded on the JCL cards, this parameter (WORKFILES) is not required. If these defaults are used, VSAM dynamically defines two ESDS data sets for sort work purposes. When DD or DLBL names are used that are different than the standard default, those names must be specified both here and in the JCL. Furthermore, you must define those data sets as ESDS data sets using IDCAMS. This parameter is abbreviated **WFILE**.

WORKVOLUMES: (DOS ONLY)

This parameter allows you to specify up to 10 volume serial numbers from which space can be suballocated for sorting purposes. This parameter is abbreviated **WVOL**.

9.5.2 BLDINDEX EXAMPLES

The following is a very simple form of the statements required for the BLDINDEX function:

```
BLDINDEX INDATASET( PUR.CLUSTER )        —
         OUTDATASET( PUR.AIX.VENDOR)     —
         CATALOG(UCATLG01)
```

In this example the input to the BLDINDEX operation comes from the base cluster **PUR.CLUSTER**. The sorted output will load the AIX **PUR.AIX.VENDOR**.

To add external workfiles:

```
BLDINDEX INDATASET( PUR.CLUSTER )        —
         OUTDATASET( PUR.AIX.VENDOR)     —
```

```
                EXTERNALSORT                         —
                CATALOG(UCATLG01)
```

To add external workfiles using other than IDCUT1/IDCUT2:

```
       BLDINDEX INDATASET( PUR.CLUSTER )             —
                OUTDATASET( PUR.AIX.VENDOR)          —
                EXTERNALSORT                         —
                WORKFILES( WORK1 WORK2)              —
                WORKVOLUMES( VSAM01 VSAM02 )         — *
                CATALOG(UCATLG01)
```

9.5.3 THE BLDINDEX JCL REQUIREMENTS

For DOS:

```
// JOB BLDINDEX ACCTDATA
// DLBL IJSYSUC,'UCATLG01',,VSAM
// EXTENT SYS006,VSAM02
// DLBL WORK1,'SORT.WORK.NO1',,VSAM
// DLBL WORK2,'SORT.WORK.NO2',,VSAM
// EXEC IDCAMS,SIZE=AUTO

                 CONTROL CARDS GO HERE

/*
```

For **OS**:

```
//BLDINDEX     JOB      ACCTDATA,'MIKE BOUROS',CLASS=R
//AMS          EXEC     PGM=IDCAMS
//STEPCAT      DD       DSN=UCATLG01,DISP=SHR (OPTIONAL)
//WORK1        DD       DSN=SORT.WORK.NO1,DISP=SHR
//WORK2        DD       DSN=SORT.WORK.NO2,DISP=SHR
//SYSPRINT     DD       SYSOUT=A
//SYSIN        DD       *

                 CONTROL CARDS GO HERE

/*
```

Now putting it all together:

* DOS only.

For DOS:

```
// JOB BLDINDEX ACCTDATA
// DLBL IJSYSUC,'UCATLG01',,VSAM
// DLBL WORK1,'SORT.WORK.NO1',,VSAM
// DLBL WORK2,'SORT.WORK.NO2',,VSAM
// EXEC IDCAMS,SIZE=AUTO
     BLDINDEX INDATASET( PUR.CLUSTER )            —
              OUTDATASET( PUR.AIX.VENDOR)         —
              EXTERNALSORT                        —
              WORKFILES( WORK1 WORK2)             —
              WORKVOLUMES( VSAM01 VSAM02 )        —
              CATALOG(UCATLG01)
/*
```

For **OS**:

```
//BLDINDEX    JOB     ACCTDATA,'MIKE BOUROS',CLASS=R
//AMS         EXEC    PGM=IDCAMS
//STEPCAT     DD      DSN=UCATLG01,DISP=SHR (OPTIONAL)
//WORK1       DD      DSN=SORT.WORK.NO1,DISP=SHR
//WORK2       DD      DSN=SORT.WORK.NO2,DISP=SHR
//SYSPRINT    DD      SYSOUT=A
//SYSIN       DD      *
     BLDINDEX INDATASET( PUR.CLUSTER )            —
              OUTDATASET( PUR.AIX.VENDOR)         —
              EXTERNALSORT                        —
              WORKFILES( WORK1 WORK2)             —
              CATALOG(UCATLG01)
/*
```

9.6 THE AMS PATH COMMAND

The **primary** function of the PATH command is to direct VSAM **through the AIX to the base cluster**. Another capability provided by this function is to allow access to a base cluster directly from a PATH by simply using a PATH name. In this case there is no intermediate AIX. When used in this manner, it allows a sort of **ALIAS** capability in that more than one name can be used to reference the same base cluster.

As stated previously, when used in its normal fashion, **PATH** serves to point us through an AIX to our base cluster. **Using this facility allows us to write programs that utilize the PATH name as if it were the name**

of a base cluster. One difference between accessing a base cluster and using a PATH, however, is that random retrieval by means of a PATH is by **key only**; that is, no access to records can be made by RBA using this PATH. Of course, RBA access is still allowable when the base cluster is accessed directly. Whenever a PATH name is used in an **OPEN** macro/command within an application program, **both the AIX and base clusters are opened**. Finally, if AIX updating (UPGRADE) was defined, it can be overridden by the PATH **NOUPDATE** parameter.

COMMAND	PARAMETERS	NOTES
DEFINE	**PATH**	REQ'D
	(	REQ'D
	NAME(pathname)	REQ'D
	PATHENTRY(p-ename [/password])	REQ'D
	[FILE(jcl-dname)]	
	[ATTEMPTS(number)	
	[CODE(code)]	
	[CONTROLPW(password)]	
	[FOR(days) | TO(date)]	
	[MASTERPW(password)]	
	[MODEN(ename [/pass] [cname[/pass]])]	
	[ORDERED | <u>UNORDERED</u>]	
	[OWNER(owner id)]	
	[UPDATEPW(password)]	
	[<u>UPDATE</u> | NOUPDATE]	
	)	REQ'D
	[CATALOG(cname [/password])	

9.6.1 EXPLANATION OF PATH PARAMETERS

EXPLANATION OF PARAMETERS

DEFINE PATH

This AMS command specifies that you wish to define to VSAM the characteristics of a VSAM PATH. This command defines a gateway to a target base cluster either directly or through an AIX.

NAME(pathname):

This entry allows you to give a name to the PATH being defined. The name can be up to 44 characters in length and can be any combination of characters, numbers, or the special symbols @, #, and $. The name must begin with a character and, if greater than eight digits, must be broken into segments of one to eight digits separated by periods; for example:

DEFINE PATH(PUR.PATH.VENDOR)

PATHENTRY(p-ename [/password]):

When a PATH is to be provided through an AIX to its base cluster, the name of the AIX is coded here. If the PATH is to be direct to the base cluster, code the name of the base cluster here. If a base cluster name is used, the name placed in the NAME parameter provides an **alias** name by which the base cluster can be accessed. This parameter can be abbreviated **PENT**.

FOR(days) TO (date):

With this parameter you can specify the retention period for this PATH. It can be specified either in days or by date. If the specification is made in days, you must use the FOR parameter. The days may be specified as any value between 0 and 1830. Any value higher than this will force a retention through the year 1999. In order to specify a specific date use the TO parameter. A specific date is specified in the form yyddd, where yy = year and ddd is the Julian day of the year (001–366). Example 84365 is interpreted the 365th day of 1984.

FILE(jcl-dname):

This parameter is used to point to the // DLBL JCL card (DOS) or a DD JCL card (OS). The name specified here must match the name specified by the DLBL/DD card. The following illustrates the association between the JCL and the FILE(jcl-name):

```
// DLBL PATHDEF .........      DOS
//PATHDEF DD .............     OS
      FILE(PATHDEF)
```

This parameter is required when the PATH being defined is for an AIX or base cluster that is itself defined in a catalog containing the **recoverable** attribute. This parameter points to a DD (OS) or DLBL (DOS) JCL card that names the cluster. This is the same cluster (AIX or base) named in the PATHENTRY parameter.

ATTEMPTS(number):

This parameter is used only in those cases where the PATH is password protected.The number of attempts the operator can make before IDCAMS aborts is specified here. If ATTEMPTS(0) is specified, the operator is not allowed to enter a password from a system console. See Chapter 12 for a more thorough explanation. This parameter can be abbreviated **ATT**.

AUTHORIZATION(entrypoint/string):

This parameter specifies the name of a routine (entrypoint) to which control is passed every time this PATH is accessed. This routine is called a **user exit or**

user verification routine. It is usually written by the systems programmer at the installation in which the AIX will be used. For the specifics in writing a user exit routine, see Chapter 12. In addition to passing control to the user-exit, a character string up to 256 characters in length can also be passed to the routine. The characters passed can be specified as either character or hexadecimal values. This parameter can be abbreviated **AUTH**. Example:

AUTHORIZATION(CHECKRTN authdata) or
AUTHORIZATION(CHECKRTN X'C1E4E3C8C1E3C1')

CODE(code):

This parameter is used for those PATHs that are password protected. The designated **code** is used in lieu of the PATH name when prompting the operator for the password.

CONTROLPW(password):

A special method of file access called **control interval access** enables a program to read or write entire CIs at a time rather than individual records. With this parameter you can control the access to the base cluster by specifying a password. The entire subject of passwords is covered in Chapter 12. This parameter can be abbreviated **CTLPW**.

MASTERPW:

This parameter specifies a password that is to be used for the PATH being defined. This parameter allows access to all AMS operations for this entry. Unless this parameter is specified, the associate parameters CODE, ATTEMPTS, and AUTHORIZATION are of no significance. The password must be one to eight characters in length, and can contain alpha, numeric, or special characters. When using special characters the entire password should be contained within apostrophes. The password can also be specified in hexadecimal. Examples:

MASTERPW(MIKEB)
MASTERPW('MIKEB')
MASTERPW(X'D4C9D2C5C2')

See Chapter 12 for more information. The abbreviation for this is **MRPW**.

MODEL(ename / password cname / password):

This parameter allows you to point VSAM to some other PATH that you have already defined to obtain and fill in parameters that you optionally omit. This parameter can be used to refer to any VSAM object; in this example the object is a PATH. The ename or parameter refers to the PATH being used for the model. The cname parameter is used to name the catalog in which the cluster being referenced is defined.

OWNER(owner id):

This parameter is used for documentation purposes only. It specifies the name of the OWNER of the PATH. The **owner id** must be specified as one to eight characters and follow the same rules described under MASTERPW.

READPW(password):

This specifies the password to be used whenever the PATH is accessed for **read** purposes. This parameter can be abbreviated **RDPW**.

UPDATEPW(password):

This specifies the password to be used any time this PATH is **updated**: that is, records added, deleted, or changed. See the rules described under **MASTERPW** for a description of the password format. Its abbreviation is **UPDPW**.

UPDATE | NOUPDATE

This specifies whether updates will be allowed to be made for any alternate indices **related** to the base cluster. If NOUPDATE is specified, no updating of alternate indices will take place even if the UPGRADE attribute was defined for them. When UPDATE is specified, the associated AIX is updated every time an addition, update, or deletion takes place on the base cluster. This parameter can be abbreviated **UPG** or **NUPG**, respectively.

CATALOG(cname [/password]):

This specifies the name of the CATALOG containing the AIX or base cluster named in the PATHENTRY parameter. This can be abbreviated **CAT**.

9.6.2 EXAMPLES USING THE DEFINE PATH COMMAND

A simple example is as follows:

```
DEFINE PATH                               —
       (                                  —
       NAME(PUR.PATH.VENDOR)              —
       PATHENTRY(PUR.AIX.VENDOR)          —
       )                                  —
       CATALOG(UCATLG01)
```

In the preceding, a PATH has been defined and given the name **PUR.PATH.VENDOR**. It will point to the base cluster (**PUR.CLUSTER**) through the alternate index defined and built previously as **PUR.AIX.VENDOR**. UPDATE is the default parameter.

9.6.3 USING JCL WITH THE PATH COMMAND

For DOS:

```
// JOB DEFPATH ACCTDATA
// DLBL IJSYSUC,'UCATLG01',,VSAM
// EXTENT SYS006,VSAM02
// EXEC IDCAMS,SIZE=AUTO
```

```
                    CONTROL CARDS GO HERE

/*
```

For **OS**:

```
//DEFPATH     JOB    ACCTDATA,'MIKE BOUROS',CLASS=R
//AMS         EXEC   PGM=IDCAMS
//STEPCAT     DD     DSN=UCATLG01,DISP=SHR (OPTIONAL)
//SYSPRINT    DD     SYSOUT=A
//SYSIN       DD     *

                    CONTROL CARDS GO HERE

/*
```

Putting it all together:

For DOS:

```
// JOB DEFPATH ACCTDATA
// DLBL IJSYSUC,'UCATLG01',,VSAM
// EXTENT SYS006,VSAM02
// EXEC IDCAMS,SIZE=AUTO
   DEFINE PATH                              —
          (                                 —
          NAME(PUR.PATH.VENDOR)             —
          PATHENTRY(PUR.AIX.VENDOR)         —
          )                                 —
          CATALOG(UCATLG01)
/*
```

For **OS**:

```
//DEFPATH     JOB    ACCTDATA,'MIKE BOUROS',CLASS=R
//AMS         EXEC   PGM=IDCAMS
//STEPCAT     DD     DSN=UCATLG01,DISP=SHR (OPTIONAL)
//SYSPRINT    DD     SYSOUT=A
//SYSIN       DD     *
   DEFINE PATH                              —
          (                                 —
          NAME(PUR.PATH.VENDOR)             —
          PATHENTRY(PUR.AIX.VENDOR)         —
          )                                 —
          CATALOG(UCATLG01)
/*
```

Actual examples of AIX and PATH definitions are found in Appendix A.

TEST YOUR UNDERSTANDING

1. Explain the purpose and function of an alternate index.
2. Explain the logical steps involved in creating an AIX. Is there more than one order/method that can be adopted?
3. What does the RELATE parameter do?
4. Explain the purpose of the AIX UPGRADE parameter.
5. When is the WORKFILES parameter required when using the BLDINDEX command?
6. What actually gets sorted when the BLDINDEX command is used?
7. What is the purpose of a PATH?
8. Name the two types of PATHs and explain how they are used.

chapter 10

ACCESS METHOD SERVICES— SPECIAL AMS FACILITIES

The facilities presented in this chapter are available for the OS operating system only. VSE users may wish to skip this chapter if desired.

This chapter is the fourth and final chapter on Access Method Services. Up until this point we have concentrated on those facilities that fall within the realm of the application programmer (although some of the functions discussed would be performed only by systems programmers or data base administrators). The purpose of this chapter is to introduce readers to those facilities that are almost never accessible to the average programmer, primarily because some of them affect not applications, but the operating environment itself.

10.1 THE AMS SYSTEM-CLASS FACILITIES

The facilities discussed in this chapter include the following:

For Cache storage:

SETCACHE
BINDDATA
LISTDATA

For the MSS (Mass Storage System):

DEFINE

Special data sets:

DEFINE PAGESPACE
DEFINE GENERATIONDATAGROUP
DEFINE ALIAS

Other:

CNVCAT
CHKLST

10.2 CACHE STORAGE FACILITIES

Cache memory is the term normally applied to that ultra high-speed memory utilized by most mainframes. It is **not** the memory used for regular operating system operations such as that allocated for partitions or regions; application programs do not run in cache storage. One of the uses of cache memory is to provide a work area in which the mainframe can fetch, decode, and execute machine language instructions in high-speed memory. This ability allows the computer to operate at a speed much higher than that attained with regular main storage memory. Although the concept is the same, the term **cache**, however, has a different meaning when used by Access Method Services.

The IBM 3880 Storage Controller contains the apparatus to control certain DASD devices such as the IBM 3350 and 3380 disk drives. Besides providing functions found on all disk controllers, the 3880 can optionally utilize a 3880 cache memory facility.

There are two different uses for the cache depending on the 3880 model. The 3880 Model 11 cache is used as a paging device. Paging operations that would normally be performed on DASD can be done in cache. The 3880 model 13 had a slightly different purpose. Data written or read to or from certain specific DASD extents can be duplicated dynamically in cache. The real performance gains occur with read operations. When an existing record is contained within a cache extent, it is immediately made available to the CPU with no need to wait for a DASD operation. When a write operation takes place on data duplicated in cache, the channel is informed that the operation is complete even though the actual operation has not yet been carried out on disk. In either case, there is a great improvement in speed.

The 3880 utilizes anywhere from four to eight megabytes of cache memory **within the controller**. Through AMS you can allocate certain DASD extents for use in cache memory. Statistics pertaining to the usage of memory as well as all I/O operations performed are also kept in cache.

The **SETCACHE** command is used by Access Method Services to enable or disable access to cache facilities for either certain volumes or for an entire 3880 **subsystem**. The **BINDDATA** command is used to designate that the usage of specific volume extents be established or terminated in cache. The **LISTDATA** command requests AMS to print statistics or counts kept in cache memory. The cache memory facilities of the IBM 3380 are available under OS only. The following is the format of the SETCACHE command.

10.3 THE SETCACHE COMMAND

COMMAND	PARAMETERS	NOTES
SETCACHE		REQ'D
	FILE (dname) | VOLUME (volser)	REQ'D
	UNIT (device-type)	REQ'D
	<u>DEVICE</u> | SUBSYSTEM	
	<u>ON</u> | OFF	

10.3.1 THE SETCACHE PARAMETERS

EXPLANATION OF PARAMETERS

SETCACHE:

This command indicates to Access Method Services that you wish to enable or disable the cache facility for either the entire subsystem or for a specific volume. There is no abbreviation for this parameter.

FILE(dname) | VOLUME (volser):

This entry allows you to specify to AMS the specific volume within the subsystem. This can be specified by either the FILE or VOLUME parameter. If VOLUME is used, you must code the UNIT parameter in order to specify the device type. If FILE is used, a DD JCL card is required that points to the particular volume. The VOLUME parameter is abbreviated **VOL**; there is no abbreviation for FILE. Example:

```
                            SETCACHE FILE(VOLPTR)
//VOLPTR      DD      VOL=SER=VSAM02,UNIT=3350
```

UNIT(device type):

This specifies the DASD device type. It is required when using the VOLUME parameter. Example:

```
UNIT (3350)
```

DEVICE | SUBSYSTEM:

This parameter specifies whether the entire subsystem or a particular volume is to be enabled or disabled. Its abbreviations can be **DEV** for DEVICE, and **SUBSYS** or **SSYS** for SUBSYSTEM.

ON | OFF:

This specifies whether the cache facility is to be enabled (ON) or disabled (OFF) for a specific volume or for the entire subsystem.

10.3.2 SOME EXAMPLES OF SETCACHE

The following is an example of the IDCAMS control statements necessary to perform the SETCACHE operation:

```
SETCACHE                    —
          FILE(CACHEVOL)    —
          DEVICE            —
          ON
```

In the preceding the FILE was used instead of VOLUME. This will require a DD card with a matching name. The CACHE facility will be enabled (ON) for a specific volume (DEVICE) rather than the entire subsystem.

```
SETCACHE                    —
          VOLUME(VSAM02)    —
          UNIT(3350)        —
```

```
SUBSYSTEM          —
ON
```

This example illustrates how an entire subsystem (SUBSYSTEM) can be enabled (ON). Specification of any volume in the subsystem identifies the subsystem to be enabled when SUBSYSTEM is specified.

10.3.3 SAMPLE SETCACHE WITH JCL

The JCL required for the preceding would look like this:

```
//SETCACHE     JOB     ACCTDATA, 'MIKE BOUROS',CLASS=R
//AMS          EXEC    PGM=IDCAMS
//CACHEVOL     DD      VOL=SER=VSAM02,UNIT=3350,
//                     DISP=SHR
//SYSPRINT     DD      SYSOUT=A
//SYSIN        DD      *

                  CONTROL CARDS GO HERE

/*
```

Putting it all together:

Example using FILE:

```
//SETCACHE     JOB     ACCTDATA, 'MIKE BOUROS',CLASS=R
//AMS          EXEC    PGM=IDCAMS
//CACHEVOL     DD      VOL=SER=VSAM02,UNIT=3350,
//                     DISP=SHR
//SYSPRINT     DD      SYSOUT=A
//SYSIN        DD      *
               SETCACHE                  —
                    FILE(CACHEVOL)       —
                    DEVICE               —
                    ON

/*
```

Example using VOLUME:

```
//SETCACHE     JOB     ACCTDATA, 'MIKE BOUROS',CLASS=R
//AMS          EXEC    PGM=IDCAMS
```

```
//SYSPRINT    DD    SYSOUT=A
//SYSIN       DD    *
                    SETCACHE                  —
                          VOLUME(VSAM02)      —
                          UNIT(3350)          —
                          SUBSYSTEM           —
                          ON

/*
```

In the first example the cache facility is enabled for a single volume only (VSAM02). In the second example the facility is made available for the entire subsystem.

10.4 THE BINDDATA FACILITY

BINDDATA is the command used by AMS to designate a section of DASD that is to reside in cache memory. You can also free up cache memory being used for this purpose with the **TERMINATE** parameter.

If the **FILE** parameter is used to **ESTABLISH** a cache area, you can specify the UNIT parameter on the DD card and omit it from the AMS command parameters. If no DD card is provided, the **VOLUME** and **UNIT** parameters must be used instead. Cache space can be freed (unbound) by specifying TERMINATE and either the **DEVICE** or **SUBSYSTEM** parameter, depending upon whether all or selective cache space is to be released.

The following is the format of the BINDDATA command.

10.4.1 THE BINDDATA COMMAND

COMMAND	PARAMETERS	NOTES
BINDDATA		REQ'D
	ESTABLISH | TERMINATE	REQ'D
	FILE (dname) | VOLUME (volser)	REQ'D
	UNIT (device-type)	
	LOWCCHH(cchh)	REQ'D
	HIGHCCHH(cchh)	REQ'D
	DEVICE | SUBSYSTEM	

10.4.2 THE BINDDATA PARAMETERS

EXPLANATION OF PARAMETERS

BINDDATA:

This command indicates to Access Method Services that you wish to set on (ESTABLISH) or off (TERMINATE) the cache facility for either the entire subsystem or for a specific volume. This can be abbreviated **BDATA**.

ESTABLISH | TERMINATE

The ESTABLISH parameter causes the controller to copy the tracks defined with the LOWCCHH and HIGHCCHH parameters into cache memory. Future references to these areas will actually be directed to the cache area. TERMINATE reverses this process.

FILE(dname) | VOLUME (volser):

This entry allows you to specify to AMS the specific volume within the subsystem. This can be specified by either the FILE or VOLUME parameter. If VOLUME is used, you must code the UNIT parameter in order to specify the device type. If FILE is used, a DD JCL card is required that points to the particular volume. The VOLUME parameter is abbreviated VOL. There is no abbreviation for FILE. Example:

BINDDATA FILE(**VOLPTR**)

//**VOLPTR** DD VOL=SER=VSAM02,UNIT=3350

UNIT(device type):

This specifies the DASD device type. It is required when using the VOLUME parameter. Example:

UNIT(3350)

DEVICE | SUBSYSTEM:

With this parameter one specifies whether the entire subsystem or a particular volume is to be bound or unbound. Its abbreviations can be **DEV** for DEVICE, and **SUBSYS** or **SSYS** for SUBSYSTEM.

LOWCCHH(cccchhhh):

With this parameter you specify the lower (starting) track of an extent. For **cccchhhh** you specify the cylinder (cccc) and head (hhhh) address of the first track to be bound or unbound. This parameter must be specified in hexadecimal: the first four digits representing the cylinder, the next four representing the head. This parameter can be abbreviated **LCCHH**.

HIGHCCHH(ccchhhh):

With this parameter you specify the upper (ending) track of an extent. For **ccchhhh** you specify the cylinder (cccc) and head (hhhh) address of the last track to be bound or unbound. This parameter must be specified in hexadecimal: the first four digits representing the cylinder, the next four representing the head. This parameter can be abbreviated **HCCHH**.

10.4.3 EXAMPLE BINDDATA USAGE

```
BINDDATA    ESTABLISH                 —
            VOLUME( VSAM02 )          —
            UNIT( 3350 )              —
            LOWCCHH (00010000)        —
            HIGHCCHH (0001001D)
```

or:

```
BINDDATA    ESTABLISH                 —
            FILE( BDFILE )            —
            LOWCCHH (00010000)        —
            HIGHCCHH (0001001D)
```

In the preceding example we specify to AMS that we wish to ESTABLISH or bind a specific extent currently contained on volume VSAM02 into cache. The starting location is cylinder 1 track 0 or physical track 30. The ending address is cylinder 1 track 29. The DASD type used for this is an IBM 3350. This type of DASD contains 30 tracks per cylinder.

10.4.4 BINDATA WITH JCL

```
//BINDDATA     JOB        ACCTDATA, 'MIKE BOUROS',CLASS=R
//AMS          EXEC       PGM=IDCAMS
//BDFILE       DD         VOL=SER=VSAM02,UNIT=3350,DISP=SHR
//SYSPRINT     DD         SYSOUT=A
//SYSIN        DD         *
               BINDDATA     ESTABLISH              —
                            FILE( BDFILE )         —
                            LOWCCHH (00010000)     —
                            HIGHCCHH (0001001D)

/*
```

We could have also coded:

```
//BINDDATA     JOB      ACCTDATA, 'MIKE BOUROS',CLASS=R
//AMS          EXEC     PGM=IDCAMS
//SYSPRINT     DD       SYSOUT=A
//SYSIN        DD       *
               BINDDATA    ESTABLISH               -
                           VOLUME( VSAM02 )        -
                           UNIT( 3350 )            -
                           LOWCCHH (00010000)      -
                           HIGHCCHH (0001001D)

/*
```

10.5 THE LISTDATA FACILITY

The purpose of the **LISTDATA** facility is to provide information on the utilization of cache memory. With this function the I/O activity counts and cache status can be printed out for review. The format of this command is found in the following.

10.5.1 THE LISTDATA COMMAND

COMMAND	PARAMETERS	NOTES
LISTDATA		REQ'D
	COUNTS | STATUS	REQ'D
	FILE (dname) | VOLUME (volser)	REQ'D
	UNIT (device-type)	
	DEVICE | SUBSYSTEM | <u>ALL</u>	
	LEGEND | <u>NOLEGEND</u>	
	OUTFILE (dname) | OUTDATASET (dset)	

10.5.2 THE LISTDATA PARAMETERS

EXPLANATION OF PARAMETERS

LISTDATA:

This command indicates to Access Method Services that you wish to print status and/or count information contained within cache memory. This information is maintained by the controller and is updated whenever an event occurs that affects the monitored information. This command can be abbreviated **LDATA**.

COUNTS | STATUS:

Specific information pertaining to cache usage can be provided for with this parameter. COUNTS provides information about I/O operations performed against data contained in cache. STATUS provides information about the overall usage of cache memory such as the amount of memory used or remaining, or the assignment of cache memory blocks. Its abbreviations can be **CNT** or **STAT**.

FILE(dname) | VOLUME (volser):

This entry allows you to indicate to AMS a specific volume within the subsystem. This can be specified by either the FILE or VOLUME parameter. If VOLUME is used, you must code the UNIT parameter in order to specify the device type. If FILE is used, a DD JCL card is required that points to the particular volume. The VOLUME parameter is abbreviated **VOL**; there is no abbreviation for FILE. Example:

LISTDATA FILE(**VOLPTR**)

//**VOLPTR** DD VOL=SER=VSAM02,UNIT=3350

UNIT(device type):

This specifies the DASD device type. It is required when using the VOLUME parameter. Example:

UNIT(3350)

DEVICE | SUBSYSTEM | ALL:

With this parameter one specifies whether information pertaining to all subsystems, one specific subsystem, or a particular volume is to be printed. The default is ALL. Its abbreviations can be **DEV** for DEVICE and **SUBSYS** or **SSYS** for SUBSYSTEM.

LEGEND | NOLEGEND:

If LEGEND is specified, information about the abbreviations used as well as headings is provided in the printed report. NOLEGEND is the default. This parameter can be abbreviated **LGND** or **NOLGND**.

OUTFILE (dname) | OUTDATASET (dset):

The output of the LISTDATA command is normally sent to SYSPRINT. You can, however, direct the output to a data set instead. This allows the data to be used as input to another program if so desired. If OUTFILE is used, dname is the name of a DD card. In order to use OUTDATASET, the data set name (dset) must already have been cataloged. Its abbreviations can be **OFILE** for the OUTFILE parameter, and **ODS** or **OUTDS** for OUTDATASET.

10.5.3 EXAMPLE LISTDATA USAGE

```
LISTDATA    COUNTS                 —
            VOLUME( VSAM02 )       —
            UNIT( 3350 )           —
            DEVICE                 —
            LEGEND
```

In the preceding example cache information has been requested that pertains to a specific volume. The output will go to SYSPRINT. A legend will be printed on the report.

```
LISTDATA    STATUS                           —
            ALL                              —
            NOLEGEND                         —
            OUTDATASET ( LSTAT.REPORT.INFO )
```

In this example status information about all cache devices connected to this mainframe is requested. The output will be directed to a specific data set that has previously been cataloged.

10.5.4 LISTDATA WITH JCL

For the first example:

```
//LISTDATA     JOB      ACCTDATA, 'MIKE BOUROS',CLASS=R
//AMS          EXEC     PGM=IDCAMS
//SYSPRINT     DD       SYSOUT=A
//SYSIN        DD       *
               LISTDATA     COUNTS                 —
                            VOLUME( VSAM02 )       —
                            UNIT( 3350 )           —
                            DEVICE                 —
                            LEGEND

/*
```

For the second example:

```
//LISTDATA     JOB      ACCTDATA, 'MIKE BOUROS',CLASS=R
//AMS          EXEC     PGM=IDCAMS
//SYSPRINT     DD       SYSOUT=A
//SYSIN        DD       *
```

```
LISTDATA    STATUS                                   —
            ALL                                      —
            NOLEGEND                                 —
            OUTDATASET ( LSTAT.REPORT.INFO )
/*
```

10.6 THE MASS STORAGE SYSTEM (MSS)

The **IBM 3850 MASS STORAGE SYSTEM** or **MSS** was introduced by IBM in 1974. The purpose of MSS is to offer an alternative solution to problems involving the storing of vast quantities of data. Prior to 1974 large-volume data was stored mostly on tape.

There are, of course, problems and tradeoffs with this. Tape, for instance, is very inexpensive. The logistical problems with tape, however, are readily apparent. Tape files require a great deal of manual handling. Tape reels are almost never used to near capacity. In many applications only a small portion of a reel is used; furthermore, only in rare cases does a tape volume contain more than one data set. Holding large quantities of data on DASD is cost prohibitive. Neither solution seems fitting in some cases. The Mass Storage System provides a means of satisfying both requirements. The IBM 3850 is a device that allows the storing of upward of 236 gigabytes (236 billion bytes). The device itself cannot be classified as either a tape device or a true DASD device.

The MSS consists of a honeycomb assembly (see Figure 10.1), containing many **slots** (up to 4720 for model A13, B13). Each slot contains a cartridge which, in turn, contains data. Each cartridge has a 50-MB (50 megabyte) capacity. Unlike a disk or drum device, the MSS is not addressed directly by a program. Before data can be processed it must first be **staged**. The staging of data stored on the MSS involves first copying it to either an IBM 3330 or 3350 disk device. This disk device is sometimes referred to as a **virtual volume**. The staging operation is controlled by the operating system by means of a program called the **Hierarchical Storage Manager (HSM)**. HSM is also responsible for keeping track of everything stored in MSS. When the program completes the processing of data, it is then **destaged**, or copied back to the MSS from the virtual volume.

Access Method Services gives you some degree of control over the staging and destaging process. This is accomplished through parameters provided with the **DEFINE** command used for certain VSAM objects (cluster, space, etc.). These parameters are **STAGE**, **BIND**, **CYLINDER-FAULT**, **DESTAGEWAIT**, and **NODESTAGEWAIT**.

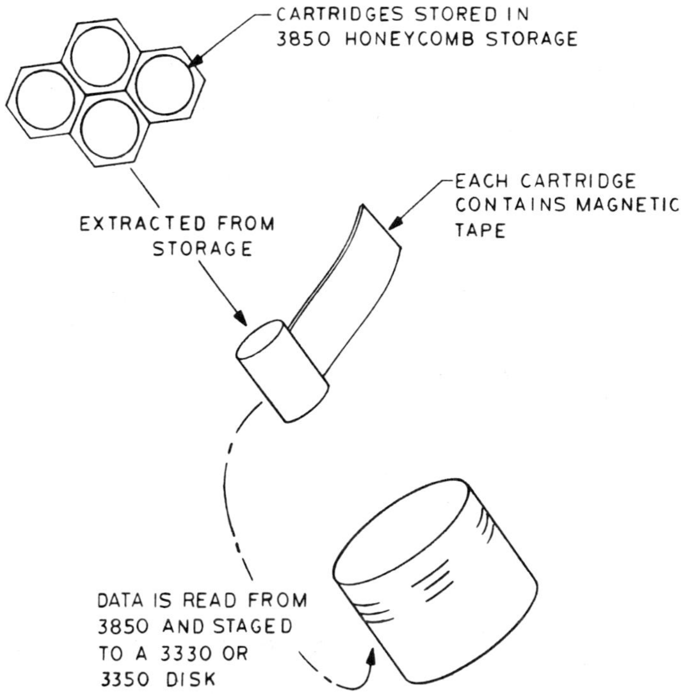

Figure 10.1 The 3850 mass storage system.

A master catalog cannot be contained on MSS. Furthermore, a user catalog contained on an MSS is automatically staged and held (bound) until no longer needed. All these parameters are covered in Chapter 7 (Access Method Services—Part One). The subject of MSS is mentioned here only because the facilities for its usage are not usually placed in the hands of the application programmer.

10.7 THE DEFINE PAGESPACE FACILITY

The DEFINE PAGESPACE command is used to define page data sets. Page data sets contain the operating system's virtual storage. When a page data set is defined through this facility, AMS defines and formats an ESDS for this purpose. A page data set must reside on a single volume. This volume must not be on a Mass Storage System. Each page is 4096 bytes. The theoretical page space limit is 65,535 page slots. This, however, may change with MVS/XA.

There are two ways in which OS/VS2 (MVS) can use the page data set. The first method is used primarily for normal batch processing programs running in virtual storage. This method is referred to as **demand paging**. Using this technique, pages are transferred in or out according to usage. Pages (parts of a program or data) not referenced very often are eligible to be paged out if the real main storage is required for another function. When a page is referenced that is not currently in main storage, it is then paged in.

The second paging technique involves something called **swapping**. This method is used primarily for certain interactive online systems such as TSO, although sometimes a very low-usage CICS system may be made eligible for swapping. Swapping differs from demand paging in that all of the referenced pages of an address space (region) are written to a swap data set when a swap operation takes place. This operation then can frequently free up a lot of main storage for other usage. The decision to designate an application as swappable or not is sometimes difficult and is almost always made by the systems programmer. A swap data set is defined separately from the standard page data set.

10.7.1 THE DEFINE PAGESPACE COMMAND

```
COMMAND        PARAMETERS                                      NOTES
---------------------------------------------------------------------
DEFINE         PAGESPACE                                       REQ'D
               (                                               REQ'D
               NAME( pname )                                   REQ'D
                   CYLINDERS( prime [ sec ] )   |
                   BLOCKS( prime [ sec ] )      |
                   TRACKS( prime [ sec ] )      |
                   RECORDS( prime [ sec ] )
               [FILE(jcl-dname)]
               VOLUME(volser no.)                              REQ'D
               [ATTEMPTS( number)
               [CODE( code ) ]
               [CONTROLPW ( password )]
               [FOR( days ) | TO( date ) ]
               [MASTERPW( password ) ]
               [MODEL(ename [/pass] [ cname[/pass]] ) ]
               [OWNER( owner id ) ]
               [READPW( password ) ]
               [SWAP | NOSWAP ]
               [UPDATEPW( password ) ]
               [ UNIQUE | SUBALLOCATION ]
               )                                               REQ'D
               [CATALOG( cname ) ]
```

10.7.2 THE DEFINE PAGESPACE PARAMETERS

EXPLANATION OF PARAMETERS

DEFINE PAGESPACE:

This AMS command specifies that you wish to **DEFINE** to VSAM a page data set. A page data set is used to contain the operating system's **virtual storage**. This command can be abbreviated **DEF PGSPC**.

NAME(pname):

This entry allows you to give a name to the page data set being defined. The name can be up to 44 characters in length and can be any combination of characters, numbers, or the special symbols @, #, and $. The name must begin with a character and, if greater than eight digits, must be broken into segments of one to eight digits separated by periods, for example:

DEF PGSPC(PAGE.DATA.SET.SYSTEM.A)

CYLINDERS/TRACKS/RECORDS/BLOCKS(prime/sec):

This parameter specifies the amount of space desired for the page data set. The space allocation can be specified in either CYLINDERS, TRACKS, RECORDS, or BLOCKS. The first three entries are used for CKD devices. The first two entries are the ones most commonly used, especially CYLINDERS. For FBA devices the allocation must be specified in BLOCKS. The abbreviation for CYLINDERS is **CYL**, TRACKS is **TRK**, RECORDS is **REC**, and BLOCKS is **BLK**.

FILE(jcl-dname):

This parameter is used to point to the DD card that identifies the volume upon which the page data set is to reside. The following illustrates the relationship between the JCL and the FILE(jcl-name):

```
//PNAME     DD     VOL=SER=SYSRES,UNIT=3350
                  FILE(PNAME)
```

VOLUME(volser no.):

This designates the volume upon which the page data set is to be placed; **volser no.** is the serial number with which the volume was initialized. It can be abbreviated **VOL**.

ATTEMPTS(number):

This parameter is used only in those cases where the page data set is password protected. The **number** of attempts the operator can make before IDCAMS aborts is specified here. If ATTEMPTS(0) is specified, the operator is not allowed to enter a password from a system console. Password protection is discussed in Chapter 12. This parameter can be abbreviated **ATT**.

AUTHORIZATION(entrypoint/string):

This parameter specifies the name of a routine (entrypoint) to which control is passed when an attempt is made to access this object. This routine (see Chapter 12 for details) is called a **User Verification Routine (USVR)**. It is usually written by the systems programmer. For the specifics in writing a USVR, you are directed to Chapter 12 of this book. In addition to passing control to the user-exit, a character string up to 256 characters in length can also be passed to the routine. The characters passed can be specified as either character or hexadecimal values. This parameter can be abbreviated **AUTH**. Example:

AUTHORIZATION(CHECKRTN authdata) or
AUTHORIZATION(CHECKRTN X'C1E4E3C8C4C1E3C1')

CODE(code):

This parameter is used when page data sets are password protected. The designated **code** is used in lieu of the data set name when prompting the operator for the password. See also Chapter 12.

CONTROLPW(password):

A password can be specified for the page data set on the control interval level. This is a system class data set, however, and cannot be opened by an application program. This parameter can be abbreviated **CTLPW**.

FOR(days) TO (date):

With this parameter you can specify the retention period for this page data set. It can be specified either in days or by date. If the specification is made in days, you must use the **FOR** parameter. The days may be specified as any value between 0 and 1830. Any value higher than this will force a retention through the year 1999. In order to specify a specific date use the **TO** parameter. A specific date is specified in the form yyddd, where yy = year and ddd is the Julian day of the year (001–366). Example 87365 is interpreted as being the 365th day of 1987. If no value is specified with either the FOR or TO parameter, the entry can be deleted at any time.

MASTERPW:

This parameter specifies a password that is to be used for the page data space. Unless this parameter is specified, the associate parameters CODE, ATTEMPTS, and AUTHORIZATION are of no significance. The password must be one to eight characters in length, and can contain alpha, numeric, or special characters. When using special characters the entire password should be contained within apostrophes. The password can also be specified in hexadecimal. Examples:

MASTERPW(MIKEB)
MASTERPW('MIKEB')
MASTERPW(X'D4C9D2C5C2')

The abbreviation is **MRPW**.

MODEL(ename / password cname / password):

This parameter allows you to point VSAM to some other object that you have already defined in order to obtain and fill in parameters that you optionally omit. In our current example we are referring specifically to another page data set. The ename parameter refers to a page data set that is being used for the model.

OWNER(owner id):

This parameter is used for documentation purposes only. It specifies the name of the OWNER of the page data set. The **owner id**, if used, must be one to eight characters in length and follows the same rules described under MASTERPW.

READPW(password):

This specifies the password to be used whenever the page data space is accessed for read purposes. Since a page space is a **system** data set, it cannot be accessed by an application program. This parameter can be abbreviated **RDPW**.

SWAP | NOSWAP:

This defines the usage of this page space. It can be a regular or **swap** data set. The abbreviation for NONSWAP only is **NSWAP**.

UNIQUE | SUBALLOCATION:

This specifies whether this page space is to be suballocated from an existing VSAM space or if it is to be the only object contained in its own space. Its abbreviations can be **UNQ** or **SUBAL**, respectively.

UPDATEPW(password):

This specifies the password to be used whenever the page data space is accessed for update purposes. Since a page space is a **system** data set, it cannot be accessed by an application program. This parameter can be abbreviated **UPDPW**.

CATALOG(cname):

This specifies the name of the catalog in which the page space entry is to be made. Its abbreviation is: **CAT**.

10.7.3 EXAMPLE DEF PAGESPACE USAGE

```
DEFINE PAGESPACE              —
          (                   —
          NAME(PAGE.DATA.SET) —
          CYLINDERS(50)       —
          FILE( PSPACE )      —
          VOLUME(SYSPAG)      —
          SWAP                —
```

```
TO(99365)            —
UNIQUE               —
)                    —
CATALOG(SYSTEM.CAT)
```

In this example a page space has been defined that is 50 cylinders long. The specific volume is pointed to by the FILE parameter. The data set will occupy an extent by itself (UNIQUE). The entry for the SWAP space will be made in catalog SYSTEM.CAT. The page data set is to be retained until the year 1999.

10.7.4 DEF PAGESPACE WITH JCL

For the preceding example, the JCL could be coded as follows:

```
//PAGEDSET    JOB     ACCTDATA, 'MIKE BOUROS',CLASS=R
//AMS         EXEC    PGM=IDCAMS
//PSPACE      DD      VOL=SER=SYSPAG,UNIT=3350
//SYSPRINT    DD      SYSOUT=A
//SYSIN       DD      *
              DEFINE PAGESPACE              —
                        (                   —
                        NAME(PAGE.DATA.SET) —
                        CYLINDERS(50)       —
                        FILE( PSPACE )      —
                        VOLUME(SYSPAG)      —
                        SWAP                —
                        TO(99365)           —
                        UNIQUE              —
                        )                   —
                        CATALOG(SYSTEM.CAT)

/*
```

10.8 THE DEFINE GENERATIONDATAGROUP FACILITY

Data sets designated as **Generation Data Groups (GDG)** can be defined and controlled using this facility. A GDG is a set of non-VSAM data sets known by the same data set name. For each iteration of a data set, a relative reference number is used to identify it from other GDG data sets. For instance, the GDG entries for a payroll detail file might look something like this:

PAYROLL.WEEKLY.DETAIL(−2)	Two iterations or versions ago
PAYROLL.WEEKLY.DETAIL(−1)	One iteration or version ago
PAYROLL.WEEKLY.DETAIL(0)	Current version
PAYROLL.WEEKLY.DETAIL(+1)	Next iteration or version

In this particular case the file PAYROLL.WEEKLY.DETAIL(−2) represents data from the payroll period three weeks prior; (−1) represents data from two weeks prior payroll; (0) represents the last processed payroll (current). The creation of a GDG entry is as follows:

```
//PROG        EXEC   PGM=ANYPROG
//GDGCREAT    DD     DSN=PAYROLL.WEEKLY.DETAIL(+1),
//                   DISP=(NEW,CATLG),.........etc.
```

After this entry is cataloged, the current version (0) becomes accessable as (−1); the file being cataloged as (+1) then becomes the new (0). Through AMS you can regulate (LIMIT) the number of entries maintained.

10.8.1 THE DEFINE GENERATIONDATAGROUP COMMAND

COMMAND	PARAMETERS	NOTES
DEFINE	**GENERATIONDATAGROUP**	REQ'D
	(	REQ'D
	NAME(gname)	REQ'D
	LIMIT(limit)	
	[EMPTY | NOEMPTY]	
	[OWNER(owner id)]	
	[SCRATCH | NOSCRATCH]	
	[TO(date) | FOR(days)]	
	)	
	[CATALOG(cname [/password])]	

10.8.2 THE DEFINE GENERATIONDATAGROUP PARAMETERS

EXPLANATION OF PARAMETERS

DEFINE GENERATIONDATAGROUP

This AMS command specifies that you wish to **DEFINE** to AMS a Generation Data Group. The abbreviation for this is **DEF GDG**.

NAME(gname):

This entry allows you to give a name (gname) to the generation data group being defined. The name can be up to 44 characters in length and can be any combination of characters, numbers, or the special symbols @, #, and $. The name must begin with a character and, if greater than eight digits, must be broken into segments of one to eight digits separated by periods, for example:

DEF GDG(PAYROLL.WEEKLY.DETAIL)

LIMIT(limit):

This specifies the maximum number of data sets, up to 255, to be maintained by this GDG. This parameter can be abbreviated **LIM**.

EMPTY | NOEMPTY:

This specifies the response to be taken when the maximum (LIMIT) number of data sets has been reached. EMPTY specifies that all the catalog entries for these GDG data sets are to be deleted. When NOEMPTY is specified, only the oldest entry is deleted. The default for this is NOEMPTY. Its abbreviations can be **EMP** or **NEMP**, respectively.

OWNER(owner id):

This entry is used for documentation purposes only. The owner's name is placed here. This information is available for viewing with the LISTCAT command.

SCRATCH | NOSCRATCH:

With this parameter you can specify the disposition of the data set when its entry is deleted from the catalog. Scratch causes the removal and actual deletion of the data set from the volume's VTOC; this is in addition to the deletion of the VSAM catalog entry. NOSCRATCH allows the data set to remain in the VTOC even though the entry is deleted from the VSAM catalog. The default is NOSCRATCH. Its abbreviations can be **SCR** or **NSCR**, respectively.

TO (date) | FOR(days):

With this parameter you can specify the retention period for the GDG. It can be specified either in days or by date. If the specification is made in days, you must use the **FOR** parameter. The days may be specified as any value between 0 and 1830. Any value higher than this will force a retention through the year 1999. In order to specify a specific date use the **TO** parameter. A specific date is specified in the form yyddd, where yy = year and ddd is the Julian day of the year (001–366). Example 87365 is interpreted as being the 365th day of 1987. If no value is specified with either the FOR or TO parameter, the entry can be deleted at any time.

10.8.3 EXAMPLE DEF GDG USAGE

```
DEFINE GDG                               —
          (                              —
          NAME(PAYROLL.WEEKLY.DETAIL)    —
```

```
LIMIT(15)                         -
NOEMPTY                           -
SCRATCH                           -
TO( 99365 )                       -
)                                 -
CATALOG(PAYROLL.CAT)
```

In this example we have defined a GDG with a maximum (LIMIT) of 15 entries for a payroll system. When the limit has been reached, only the oldest entry is to be deleted (NOEMPTY). In addition to this, the data set itself is to be deleted (SCRATCH) from the VTOC on the volume on which it resides. The GDG entry itself will not expire until the year 1999.

10.8.4 DEF GDG WITH JCL

For the preceding example the JCL coding could be as follows:

```
//DEFGDG      JOB     ACCTDATA, 'MIKE BOUROS',CLASS=R
//AMS         EXEC    PGM=IDCAMS
//SYSPRINT    DD      SYSOUT=A
//SYSIN       DD      *
                DEFINE GDG                                  -
                        (                                   -
                        NAME(PAYROLL.WEEKLY.DETAIL)         -
                        LIMIT(15)                           -
                        NOEMPTY                             -
                        SCRATCH                             -
                        TO( 99365 )                         -
                        )                                   -
                        CATALOG(PAYROLL.CAT)

/*
```

10.9 THE DEFINE ALIAS FACILITY

The **ALIAS** command provides two facilities. The first is to provide a method of **assigning alternate names** to non-VSAM data sets. It allows you to use another name by which you can reference the same data set.

A second function of ALIAS is to provide a way in which to **define a high level qualifier in the Master catalog which would, in turn, point us to a specific user catalog**. For example, let us assume that we have a data set defined in user catalog OPTIONS.CAT, called OPTIONS.-

DAILY.TRADES, which is part of an options trading system. Up until this time we have used a STEPCAT DD card to point VSAM to the proper user catalog. This means that every job stream accessing this data set has a STEPCAT DD card. If in the future we wish to move this data set to another catalog it would require modifying all the job streams.

There is an alternative to JOBCAT or STEPCAT cards. We could define an ALIAS entry pointing our high-level qualifier (OPTIONS) to the proper user catalog. Once this is done, the STEPCAT or JOBCAT card is no longer required. When a data set cannot be found in the current catalog, a search is made for an ALIAS entry that matches the high-level qualifier. When a match is found, a search will then take place for that data set in the catalog being referenced in the alias.

10.9.1 THE DEFINE ALIAS COMMAND

COMMAND	PARAMETERS	NOTES
DEFINE	**ALIAS**	REQ'D
	(	REQ'D
	NAME(alias name)	REQ'D
	RELATE(ename)	
	)	REQ'D
	[CATALOG(cname [/password])]	

10.9.2 THE DEFINE ALIAS PARAMETERS

EXPLANATION OF PARAMETERS

DEFINE ALIAS:

This AMS command specifies that you wish to **DEFINE** to AMS an ALIAS entry. An alias can be defined only for non-VSAM data sets or for connectors pointing to a user catalog from the master catalog. The abbreviation for this is **DEF ALIAS**.

NAME(alias name):

This entry allows you to specify an alias by which a data set can be located. The alias can be either an alternate data set name or a high-level qualifier that points to a user catalog. If it is an alternate name, it can be up to 44 characters in length and can be any combination of characters, numbers, or the special symbols @, #, and $. The name must begin with a character and, if greater than eight digits, must be broken into segments of one to eight digits separated by periods, for example:

DEF ALIAS(OPTIONS.CURRENT.TRADES)

RELATE(ename):

This specifies the name of the user catalog or data set for which the alias is being defined. Its abbreviation is **REL**.

CATALOG(cname [/password]):

For non-VSAM entries **cname** specifies the name of the catalog in which the entry is found. If a user catalog pointer is being defined, the name of the master catalog goes in **cname**. Its abbreviation is **CAT**.

10.9.3 EXAMPLE DEF ALIAS USAGE

Example one—the user catalog alias:

```
DEFINE ALIAS                          —
          (                           —
          NAME(OPTIONS)               —
          RELATE(UCAT.OPTIONS)        —
          )                           —
          CATALOG(MASTER.CAT)
```

In this example we have **related** the high-level qualifier **OPTIONS** to user catalog **UCAT.OPTIONS**. The entry is made in the master catalog **MASTER.CAT**. Henceforth, any search for a data set name beginning with the high level qualifier OPTIONS will be automatically directed to UCAT.OPTIONS.

Example two—the alternate name alias:

```
DEFINE ALIAS                                  —
          (                                   —
          NAME(OPTIONS.CURRENT.TRADES)        —
          RELATE(OPTIONS.DAILY.TRADES)        —
          )                                   —
          CATALOG(OPTIONS.CAT)
```

In the preceding example an alternate data set name OPTIONS.-CURRENT.TRADES is assigned as an alias of OPTIONS.DAILY.-TRADES. The data set entry resides in user catalog OPTIONS.CAT and the alias entry will be placed there as well.

10.9.4 DEF ALIAS WITH JCL

For the first example:

```
//DEFALIAS     JOB      ACCTDATA,'MIKE BOUROS',CLASS=R
//AMS          EXEC     PGM=IDCAMS
//SYSPRINT     DD       SYSOUT=A
//SYSIN        DD       *
               DEFINE ALIAS                               -
                          (                               -
                          NAME(OPTIONS)                   -
                          RELATE(UCAT.OPTIONS)            -
                          )                               -
                          CATALOG(MASTER.CAT)

/*
```

For the second example:

```
//DEFALIAS     JOB      ACCTDATA,'MIKE BOUROS',CLASS=R
//AMS          EXEC     PGM=IDCAMS
//STEPCAT      DD       DSN=OPTIONS.CAT,DISP=SHR
//SYSPRINT     DD       SYSOUT=A
//SYSIN        DD       *
               DEFINE ALIAS                                     -
                          (                                     -
                          NAME(OPTIONS.CURRENT.TRADES)          -
                          RELATE(OPTIONS.DAILY.TRADES)          -
                          )                                     -
                          CATALOG(OPTIONS.CAT)

/*
```

10.10 THE CNVCAT FUNCTION

The purpose of the **CNVCAT** function is to **convert** non-VSAM OS catalog (CVOLS) entries to VSAM catalog entries. OS CVOL entries in one CVOL can point to a second CVOL. This type of entry is referred to as a control volume pointer entry (CVPE). Besides normal entry conversion, AMS makes provision for CVPEs as well.

Although the conversion of **regular** CVOL entries occurs on an entry-for-entry basis, there is a difference in the way in which CVPEs are handled. Instead of the entries in one VSAM user catalog pointing to a second user catalog, the CVOL pointers are actually added as aliases in the master catalog. This is why the MASTERCATALOG parameter is required. In addition to this, the CVOLEQUATES parameter is used in the pointing (alias) process.

10.10.1 THE CNVCAT COMMAND

COMMAND	PARAMETERS	NOTES
CNVCAT	INFILE(dname) | INDATASET(ename)	REQ'D
	[CATALOG(cname [/password)]	
	[CVOLEQUATES(cname vol....cname vol)]	
	[LIST | NOLIST]	
	MASTERCATALOG(mname [/password])]	

10.10.2 THE CNVCAT PARAMETERS

EXPLANATION OF PARAMETERS

CNVCAT:

This command indicates to Access Method Services that OS catalog (CVOL) entries are to be converted to VSAM catalog entries. This parameter can be abbreviated **CNVTC**.

INFILE(dname) | INDATASET(ename):

The purpose of this parameter is to point to the **OS CVOL** to be used as **input** to the conversion process. If INFILE is used, a DD card must be provided and the ddname must match the INFILE(dname) parameter. If INDATASET is used, the catalog is dynamically allocated. Its abbreviations can be **IFILE** or **IDS**, respectively.

CATALOG(cname [/password]):

This parameter specifies the name (cname) of the VSAM catalog that is to be the **recipient** of the conversion process. This parameter is abbreviated **CAT**.

CVOLEQUATES(cname vol......cname vol):

This parameter sets up the apparatus for the alias process. The cname subparameter identifies the name of the VSAM user catalog that will be pointed to and that will contain the entries. The vol subparameter contains the present CVPE which points to another CVOL. Let us take the example in which the OS catalog on volume 111111 has entries pointing to the CVOL on 222222. If the 222222 entries have already been converted (CNVCAT) and now reside in

USER.CAT02, it will then be necessary to convert the 111111 entries so that they will point to the VSAM catalog USER.CAT02. In order to accomplish this, an entry would be set up as follows:

CVOLEQUATES(USER.CAT02 222222)

Since this process is handled in the same way in which alias pointers are set up from the master catalog to user catalogs, the MASTERCATALOG parameter is required when using this parameter. This parameter can be abbreviated **CVEQU**.

LIST | NOLIST:

This specifies whether the entries converted during this process are to listed. The abbreviation for NOLIST is **NLIST**; LIST cannot be abbreviated.

MASTERCATALOG(mname):

This parameter is required only when using the CVOLEQUATES parameter. It specifies the name and password (when required) of the master catalog. This parameter can be abbreviated **MCAT**.

10.10.3 EXAMPLE CNVCAT USAGE

Using the example described under the CVOLEQUATES parameter, we now set up the commands and JCL required to convert the CVOL entries on volumes 111111 and 222222. In addition to this, there are entries in the CVOL on 111111 that point to 222222. These must be converted as well. When converting OS CVOLS that point to other OS CVOLS, the last catalog in the chain should be converted first. The steps then to be taken in our example are as follows:

Convert the OS CVOL on volume 222222
Convert the CVPEs on 111111 to point to 222222
Convert the regular entries on 111111

Step One

Convert the OS catalog entries on volume 222222 to VSAM entries in user catalog USER.CAT02.

```
//CNVCAT1     JOB     ACCTDATA,'MIKE BOUROS',CLASS=R
//AMS         EXEC    PGM=IDCAMS
//OSCATLG     DD      VOL=SER=222222,DISP=OLD,
//                    DSN=SYSCTLG
//SYSPRINT    DD      SYSOUT=A
//SYSIN       DD      *
                   CNVCAT     INFILE(OSCATLG)         —
```

```
                                         CATALOG(USER.CAT02)      —
                                         LIST

/*
```

In this example the entries in the OS catalog on 222222 will be converted and placed in VSAM catalog USER.CAT02.

Step Two

Convert the pointer entries in the OS catalog on 111111 that point to 222222.

```
//CNVCAT2     JOB      ACCTDATA,'MIKE BOUROS',CLASS=R
//AMS         EXEC     PGM=IDCAMS
//OSCATLG     DD       VOL=SER=111111,DISP=OLD,
//                     DSN=SYSCTLG
//SYSPRINT    DD       SYSOUT=A
//SYSIN       DD       *
                     CNVCAT    INFILE(OSCATLG)            —
                               CATALOG(USER.CAT02)        —
                               CVOLEQUATES
                               (USER.CAT02 222222)        —
                               MASTERCATALOG(MCAT)        —
                               LIST
/*
```

In the preceding example the entries in the OS catalog on 111111 that point to 222222 will be added as pointers in the VSAM master catalog. These entries will point to USER.CAT02.

Step Three

Convert the OS catalog entries on volume 111111 to VSAM entries in user catalog USER.CAT02.

```
//CNVCAT3     JOB      ACCTDATA,'MIKE BOUROS',CLASS=R
//AMS         EXEC     PGM=IDCAMS
//OSCATLG     DD       VOL=SER=111111,DISP=OLD,
//                     DSN=SYSCTLG
//SYSPRINT    DD       SYSOUT=A
//SYSIN       DD       *
                     CNVCAT    INFILE(OSCATLG)            —
                               CATALOG(USER.CAT02)        —
                               LIST

/*
```

In this example the entries in the OS catalog on 111111 will be converted and placed in VSAM catalog USER.CAT02.

10.11 THE CHKLIST FUNCTION

It is difficult to see how the **CHKLIST** facility found a place in Access Method Services. It has only one function: to provide information about the usage of **tape** data sets that were recorded during a checkpoint operation.

The operating system checkpoint/restart facility allows checkpoint data to be written to either sequential or partitioned data sets. Along with other items, information about tape data sets that have been opened by the application is kept in the checkpoint records. The following tape-related information can be printed out with the CHKLIST facility:

DDNAME
Volume serial number of the tape volume
The sequence number of the volume (multivolume)
The data set name
The unit on which the tape volume was mounted

10.11.1 THE CHKLIST COMMAND

COMMAND	PARAMETERS	NOTES
CHKLIST	INFILE(dname)	REQ'D
	[OUTFILE(dname)]	
	[CHECKID (id id id ....)]	

10.11.2 THE CHKLIST PARAMETERS

EXPLANATION OF PARAMETERS

CHKLIST:

This command indicates to Access Method Services that you wish to print tape data set information found within one or more checkpoint records. Its abbreviation is **CKLST**.

INFILE(dname):

This parameter indicates the name of the DD card that points to the checkpoint data set. This data set can be a sequential or partitioned data set. Its abbreviation is **IFILE**.

OUTFILE(dname):

This specifies the name of the DD statement that points to a data set other than SYSPRINT that is to receive the output report. Its abbreviation is **OFILE**.

CHECKID(id id id ....):

This specifies the ids of one or more checkpoints found within the checkpoint data set. The id field can be up to 16 characters in length. If this field is omitted, information for **all** checkpoints is printed. The abbreviation for this is **CHKID**.

10.11.3 EXAMPLE CHKLIST USAGE

In the following example we print the tape data set data for all checkpoints in a checkpoint data set.

```
//CHKLIST     JOB     ACCTDATA,'MIKE BOUROS',CLASS=R
//AMS         EXEC    PGM=IDCAMS
//CHKPOINT    DD      DSN=CHECK.POINT.DS,DISP=OLD
//SYSPRINT    DD      SYSOUT=A
//SYSIN       DD      *
                     CHKLIST     INFILE(CHKPOINT)

/*
```

In the next example we print out the checkpoint information for only one checkpoint: number 14.

```
//CHKLIST     JOB     ACCTDATA,'MIKE BOUROS',CLASS=R
//AMS         EXEC    PGM=IDCAMS
//CHKPOINT    DD      DSN=CHECK.POINT.DS,DISP=OLD
//SYSPRINT    DD      SYSOUT=A
//SYSIN       DD      *
                     CHKLIST     INFILE(CHKPOINT)
                                 CHECKID(C0000014)

/*
```

TEST YOUR UNDERSTANDING

1. Explain the usage and purpose of cache memory on the IBM 3880 controller models 11 and 13.

2. What is the main purpose of the MSS?
3. What is the function of the DEF PAGESPACE command? What are the two distinct usages of page space?
4. Explain the purpose of a Generation Data Group.
5. What does the LIMIT parameter of the DEF GDG command do?
6. How does the DEF ALIAS command work? What two functions does it provide?
7. Explain the purpose of the CNVCAT command. How should the conversion process proceed?
8. What is the function of the CHKLIST command?

chapter 11

BACK-UP AND DISASTER RECOVERY

11.1 BACK-UP AND RECOVERY

Of all of the subjects discussed in this book perhaps the most important of all is the recovery from a seemingly hopeless disaster. There are several **tools** available that can be utilized for this purpose. Some of these tools are used to restore an entire copy of a data set, whereas others concentrate on the **repair** of a damaged file. The following functions are available for restoration:

IDCAMS—REPRO
IDCAMS—EXPORT/IMPORT
IEHDASDR (OS)
VSAM BACKUP/RESTORE (DOS)
Vendor written software packages
Specially written application programs

The following are available for reconstruction:

IDCAMS—EXPORTCRA/IMPORTCRA
IDCAMS—LISTCRA
IDCAMS—RESETCAT
IDCAMS—VERIFY
IDCAMS—DELETE(FORCE)
IDCAMS—ALTER REMOVEVOLUMES
Vendor written software

11.2 SUMMARY OF BACK-UP/RESTORE RECONSTRUCTION FUNCTIONS

Although some of these functions have been covered in previous chapters, a brief review of each of these facilities is in order.

REPRO:

This Access Method Services command is without doubt very widely used as a **backup** function. This command allows a VSAM file to be copied to another VSAM file or to a sequential data set (e.g., tape or disk). With this facility a back-up copy can be made of the file that can also be read by non-VSAM programs. This capability is often used to prepare a data file for use in another system. REPRO can also be used to back-up or copy a catalog. When used in this manner it is sometimes referred to as **unloading** a catalog.

EXPORT/IMPORT:

This function is somewhat similar to a REPRO in that it is used to copy (EXPORT) an existing VSAM object. When the object is a data set, the difference between this and REPRO exists in the direct usability of the backed-up copy. EXPORTed copies of VSAM data sets are not readily readable by application programs as are files backed up using REPRO. EXPORTed files are written with the expectation of being read only by the IMPORT function of AMS.

IEHDASDR:

This utility is used in OS installations to copy a DASD volume either entirely or in part. The copy process takes place track by track (CKD) or block by block (FBA). If a restoration is required at some point in the future, the volume can be restored in the same manner so that both physically and logically the volume looks identical to the way it looked before the failure.

VSAM BACKUP/RESTORE:

This function is available for DOS installations only. See Chapter 14 for a discussion on this subject.

Vendor Written Software:

Regardless of whether the installation runs under OS or DOS, several specially designed packages have been developed specifically to back up and restore VSAM files. The difference between a package like this and IEHDASDR might simply be the amount of time it takes to back up a VSAM file. Most vendor-written packages have been specially developed with a view toward speed. This can become vital at an installation that backs up all or most of their VSAM volumes on a frequent basis.

Specially Written Applications:

Application programs can also be used to back up a VSAM data set. The program will simply read the entire file sequentially. Normally, applications are not written specifically for this purpose; usually there is another reason that this file is backed up sequentially. For instance, if an application program must pass through the entire file, say, for report purposes, it would be more efficient to write a copy of each record to a sequential data set for back-up, rather than run a separate REPRO or EXPORT for this. An application written in assembler can also retrieve data by control interval (Chapter 16).

EXPORTRA/IMPORTRA:

With these AMS comamnds, data sets controlled by catalogs containing errors can often be saved. The data pertaining to cluster location and other information will be taken from the catalog recovery area rather than the damaged catalog when an EXPORTRA operation is performed. In all other aspects, this command is functionally the same as the standard EXPORT command. Objects backed up using EXPORTRA must be restored using IMPORTRA instead of IMPORT. The use of this function presupposes, of course, that the catalog in question was created with a CRA.

LISTCRA:

If you suspect that you might be having catalog problems, this command could be of some help. With this command you can have AMS **COMPARE** all or some of the catalog entries against the entries contained in the various catalog recovery areas (if more than one exists). The output of this program is a printed report showing discrepancies. If a discrepancy exists, you might choose to run either a RESETCAT or an IDCAMS EXPORTRA/IMPORTRA set. It might be safest to do both. For example, first run an EXPORTCRA. Follow this with a RESETCAT. If the volume is in very bad shape, IDCAMS might abend. If it does, EXPORTRA will render you a good data set to fall back upon. If it does not abend, the RESETCAT probably did its job. You should run LISTCRA once more to be sure that there are no more discrepancies.

VERIFY:

This is probably the most widely used of all AMS functions. When a job setup ends abnormally, any VSAM data sets that might have been opened are not closed. When this happens, VSAM will refuse to open the data set for processing the next time around. One of the reasons for this is that VSAM can no longer be sure where the end of the data set is. This information is kept in a catalog field called the HIGH-USED RBA. This field points to the last **data** byte in the file. When records are added to this data set this pointer will be updated to reflect the new end-of-file (assuming it changes). This is done, however, only when the data set is closed. When the data set is first opened, another catalog field called the **Open Indicator** is set on to indicate that the cluster has been opened. This indicator is turned off when the file is closed. VSAM checks this field at Open time. If already on, VSAM assumes that the cluster was never closed, and stops further processing. To correct this situation, run the VERIFY function. This function forces VSAM to start at the HIGH-USED RBA field (never updated) and to **chase** down the data until it encounters end-of-file. At this point the HIGH-USED RBA and **Open Indicator** fields are updated. In the latest releases of VSAM the VERIFY function is being incorporated into the **Open** routine so that the VERIFY can be done automatically when required.

DELETE FORCE:

At times it might be difficult to get rid of a troublesome cluster. For instance, when encountering catalog problems, suppose you decided to run an EXPORTRA. You now have the cluster backed up. You would like to restore the cluster and reset the catalog entry. To get rid of the old cluster, you would run an IDCAMS DELETE, naming the cluster. It fails. In order to override AMS you can make IDCAMS DELETE the cluster by specifying the **FORCE** parameter in addition to the cluster name.

ALTER REMOVEVOLUMES:

There are two uses for this command. The first is to allow you to remove entries made in the catalog for CANDIDATE volumes providing they are not being used. The second function is the more valuable of the two from a recovery point of view. REMOVEVOLUMES allows you to specify volumes from which all VSAM data spaces are to be removed along with VSAM ownership without accessing the user catalog that **owns** the volumes. This use of the REMOVEVOLUMES parameter requires that you specify the name of the master catalog along with the password if applicable. Also you *must* use the FILE parameter.

Vendor Written Software:

Specially written software can be purchased or leased from a software development firm. This type of software can come in very handy if the need arises to reconstruct a data set. In addition, vital information can be printed about the data set that is not available or difficult to interpret using LISTCAT.

11.3 DISASTER AND RECOVERY PROCEDURES

Following is a list of some of the most common problems that can occur with VSAM and the section in which a solution can be found.

PROBLEM	SECTION
Data set not closed	11.3.1
Data set cannot be opened	11.3.2
Data invalid (garbage)	11.3.3
Duplicate data	11.3.4
Read/Write I/O errors	11.3.5
Cannot open catalog	11.3.6
Catalog unusable	11.3.7
Unusable noncatalog volume	11.3.8
Physical damage to catalog.	11.3.9

11.3.1 DATA SET NOT CLOSED

The result of not closing a data set is that the **open indicator** is not reset, nor is the **HIGH-USED RBA** updated to point to the correct end-of-file.

Solution:

Use IDCAMS **VERIFY**.

11.3.2 DATA SET CANNOT BE OPENED

The simplest reason that the data set cannot be opened is that it was not closed or closed properly. If this is the case, use IDCAMS **VERIFY**. If this is not the case, there is a high probability that the catalog is damaged.

Solution:

Use **LISTCAT** and **LISTCRA(COMPARE)** to see if anything unusual can be detected and possibly the extent of the damage. If the **COMPARE** picks up differences, first try a **RESETCAT**. If that does not work, try an **EXPORTRA** followed immediately by an **IMPORTRA**. If this does not work, you will have to restore a back-up copy. In that case use **DELETE** followed by **IMPORT** or **DELETE**, **DEFINE**, and **REPRO**.

11.3.3 DATA INVALID (GARBAGE)

There are basically four reasons for this:

Power failure
DASD overwritten

Catalog error
Volume restore

When a power failure occurs it can sometimes cause invalid data to be written on the DASD surface. This type of error can occur during the processing of data or during a catalog update.

Another similar type of problem can occur when a movable DASD volume is **swapped** during its use. This type of problem can occur more readily in DOS installations where the volume serial number is not reread following an **attention** interrupt which occurs any time a drive is made ready. This type of problem is more common in those installations that use removable disks, but it also can happen when the DASD address is changed by the swapping of address plugs. The reason that any of these items can cause trouble is this: once the data set or catalog is opened, there is normally no reason to reverify, once again, the volume serial number. Swapping, therefore, can cause the new volume to be overwritten somewhere within the extents of the object that was originally opened.

If a catalog becomes damaged or overwritten it can end up pointing to an incorrect DASD address. This can certainly render incorrect or unreadable data.

Finally, if a volume is restored using **IEHDASDR** or a similar utility, the catalog can end up out of synch with the restored volume.

Solution:

1. Use **LISTCAT** and **LISTCRA COMPARE** to check for obvious damage.
2. If the data area has not been overwritten, try using the **RESETCAT**.
3. If RESETCAT does not work, try an **EXPORTRA** followed immediately by an **IMPORTRA**.
4. If there are minor problems in the data area (you cannot access one or two records), examine the solution as outlined in Section 11.3.5).
5. If these all fail, you will have to restore a previous back-up copy using **DELETE** and **IMPORT** or a **DELETE**, **DEFINE**, and **REPRO**.

11.3.4 DUPLICATE DATA

This problem is usually caused by an incomplete CI split. In other words, some condition occurs (machine check, operator cancel, etc.) during a CI split that prevents it from completing. Some of the more recently released versions of VSAM will correct this problem automatically. See Chapter 14 and Appendix B for more information.

Solution:

1. **REPRO** to a temporary data set.
2. Restore to the original using **DELETE**, **DEFINE**, and **REPRO**.
3. The restoring **REPRO** will not allow duplicate records to be written to the cluster.

11.3.5 READ/WRITE I/O ERRORS

When a record cannot be accessed because of an I/O error, the data set can be saved (except for that record) by backing the unaffected area(s) to temporary data sets.

Solution:

There are basically two techniques that can be used to accomplish this. The first method involves **REPRO**ing the file to a temporary data set in the following stages: (1) the part of the file that occurs before the I/O error record, and (2) the part that occurs after the record in question. This can be accomplished by using the **FROM** and **TO** options of **REPRO**. Whether OS or DOS, two temporary data sets can be used for this. For OS a DISP=MOD can be used on the DD statement if only one data set is desired. If this method is used, you would restore by first using the **DELETE** and **DEFINE** commands and then following up by restoring the temporary data set(s) using a REPRO (or two REPROs). The second method involves the use of an **alternate index**. If an Alternate Index entry exists for every record in the base cluster, the data can be accessed by writing an application that retrieves all but the errant record using the AIX sequence. The output (a temporary data set) can then be sorted and restored.

11.3.6 CANNOT OPEN CATALOG

The correction of a catalog problem such as this can be tedious and often very involved and difficult. There are, however, several options available. You should first review them all before setting out to rebuild or restore the catalog.

Solution:

Before anything else is attempted, first run an IDCAMS **RESETCAT**. If this does not work, proceed to one of the following solutions. To play it safe, you should use the IDCAMS **EXPORTRA** facility on all volumes owned by the catalog in question. The first method then involves the following sequence:

1. **ALTER REMOVEVOLUMES** to disassociate the volumes and their respective spaces.
2. **DISCONNECT** (EXPORT parameter) the user catalog from the master catalog.
3. **DEFINE** the catalog.
4. **DEFINE SPACE** on all the volumes involved.
5. **IMPORTRA** all data sets previously **EXPORTRA**ed.

If an unloaded catalog copy is available (REPRO) it might be desirable to attempt to restore this instead of performing the foregoing procedure. A good reason for this is that the catalog might contain a great deal of information about data sets other than those that are standard VSAM clusters. For instance, entries might exist for NONVSAM, PAGE, and Generation Data Sets. To use this method, the following steps should be followed:

1. **EXPORTRA** the catalog volume data sets.
2. **DISCONNECT** (EXPORT parameter) the user catalog from the master catalog.
3. **DEFINE** the catalog.
4. **REPRO** the unloaded catalog back.
5. **DEFINE SPACE** on the catalog volume.
6. **IMPORTRA** all data sets previously **EXPORTRA**ed.
7. Run the IDCAMS LISTCRA(COMPARE) to search for nonmatching entries.

For mismatches on the catalog volume, use EXPORTRA followed immediately by IMPORTRA for each data set. For mismatches on noncatalog volumes do the following:

1. **EXPORTRA** the catalog volume data sets.
2. **DELETE(FORCE)** to erase all traces of the old entry.
3. **DEFINE SPACE** on the volume.
4. **IMPORTRA** all data sets previously **EXPORTRA**ed.

11.3.7 CATALOG UNUSABLE

If there are problems accessing more than one data set on a given catalog, there is a good chance that the catalog has somehow been corrupted. To verify that some problem exists, use both the LISTCAT and LISTCRA facilities.

Solution:

If only a few data sets are affected, the simplest solution would be to EXPORTRA, then immediately IMPORTRA those data sets in question. If there are more than a few bad data sets, you might want to consider restoring an unloaded catalog if one is available (see Section 11.3.6). You can also try a RESETCAT.

11.3.8 UNUSABLE NONCATALOG VOLUME

A noncatalog volume is a volume containing VSAM spaces but no catalog.

Solution:

1. **EXPORTRA** all the data sets on the volume.
2. **DELETE(FORCE)** to erase all traces of the old entry.
3. **DEFINE SPACE** on the volume.
4. **IMPORTRA** all data sets previously **EXPORTRA**ed.

11.3.9 PHYSICAL DAMAGE TO CATALOG

Physical damage can involve only a small part of a track or can involve the entire volume; both possibilities are discussed in the following.

Solution:

For partial damage:

1. **EXPORTRA** the data sets on **all** owned volumes.
2. **ALTER REMOVEVOLUMES** to disassociate the volumes and their respective spaces.
3. **DISCONNECT** (EXPORT parameter) the user catalog from the master catalog.
4. Assign Alternate Track(s).
5. **DEFINE** the catalog.

6. **DEFINE SPACE** on all the volumes involved.
7. **IMPORTRA** all data sets previously **EXPORTRA**ed.

If the entire volume is damaged:

1. Initialize another volume with the same serial number using **IEHDASDR** (OS) or **ICKDSF** (DOS).
2. If entire volume back-up is available, restore it. Use the LISTCRA facility and handle mismatches as outlined in Section 11.3.6.

If an unloaded copy of the catalog is available, restore it as follows:

1. Initialize another volume with the same serial number using **IEHDASDR** (OS) or **ICKDSF** (DOS).
2. **DEFINE** the catalog.
3. **DEFINE SPACE** on all the volumes involved.
4. **REPRO** the copy of the catalog.
5. **DELETE**, **DEFINE**, and **REPRO**, or **DELETE** and **IMPORT** any data sets previously backed up for this volume.
6. Use a **LISTCRA(COMPARE)** to check for mismatches.
7. Resolve mismatches as outlined in Section 11.3.6.

In Chapter 14 you will be reading about another option available currently under the MVS operating system only, the **Integrated Catalog Facility**. Many of the problems discussed here are eliminated when using this facility. Furthermore, recovery from almost any type of failure is greatly simplified.

TEST YOUR UNDERSTANDING

1. Name some of the facilities used to back-up VSAM data sets and other objects.
2. How is RESETCAT used?
3. How does ALTER REMOVEVOLUMES work?
4. What does the VERIFY command do?
5. What does the LISTCRA function do?
6. Explain EXPORT DISCONNECT.
7. Are data sets created by EXPORT and REPRO formatted the same?

chapter 12

SECURITY AND PASSWORDS

12.1 TYPES OF SECURITY AVAILABLE

Through the use of Access Method Services, parameters for various security-related options can be specified. They are as follows:

AUTHORIZATION parameter
ERASE parameter
CODE parameter
Passwords

12.2 THE AUTHORIZATION PARAMETER

The **AUTHORIZATION** parameter can be specified when using a DEFINE command for a VSAM object. It can also be used in the ALTER command when modifying an object's characteristics. The use of this parameter causes a **User Security Verification Routine** (**USVR**) to be executed every time the VSAM object is accessed.

The USVR is an assembly language subroutine that is assembled and link edited to your load (OS) or core-image (DOS) library. When control is passed to the USVR, certain general registers will be preset as follows:

REG	SETTING
1	Address of a parameter list. This is not the typical AMS parameter list.
14	Address of VSAM return point.
15	Contains the base address of the USVR upon entry. Upon exit it must be loaded with a condition code – zero for successful processing.

Control is passed to the authorization routine by VSAM. To accomplish this, VSAM uses an assembler branch and link instruction as follows:

```
BALR 14,15
```

The parameter list points to the following:

44-byte object name
8-byte CODE parameter or zeros
8-byte owner id
AUTHORIZATION string of up to 255 bytes

If the program (an application or IDCAMS) is to be allowed to access the data, a zero is placed in register 15 by the authorization routine. If access is to be denied, a nonzero value will be placed in register 15 by the authorization routine instead. The authorization routine then returns control to the application by branching to the address found in register 14.

See the ALTER and the various DEFINE commands (in the chapters on Access Method Services) for further discussion on the use of the AUTHORIZATION parameter.

12.3 THE ERASE PARAMETER

In order to protect sensitive data contained in a VSAM object, you can use the **ERASE** parameter. When a VSAM object has been defined with the ERASE attribute, the space formerly occupied by that object will be overwritten with binary zeros when the object is deleted. Without this facility, deleted space can later be allocated and used for a different purpose. The data in this case would remain in that place even though the object no longer exists (at least logically). ERASE ensures that the data is truly erased, so that it cannot be accessed at a later time by some non-VSAM utility.

See the ERASE parameter in the DEFINE and ALTER commands (in the chapters on Access Method Services) for further discussion on the use of this parameter.

12.4 THE RACF FACILITY

In reality, the **Resource Access and Control Facility** (**RACF**) is not part of VSAM. The control of system resources by RACF is not limited to VSAM; it is not even limited to data sets. The VSAM protection facilities (AUTHORIZATION and passwords) are bypassed when RACF is used. The ERASE parameter remains in effect, however.

When using RACF facilities you may still want to consider using standard VSAM passwords. Although the passwords provide no function when RACF is used, the passwords could remain with the data if it is ever moved to another system.

12.5 THE CODE PARAMETER

The **CODE** parameter is a function of the DEFINE or ALTER command. Its purpose is to **hide** the identity of a VSAM data set or other object when the console operator is prompted for a password.

When a password is required for a data set, for instance, and one has not been provided through AMS statements or in the application program, the need for a password can be directed to the console operator (of the operating system). When that occurs, the data set name would normally appear on the display, and the operator would respond with the password.

For security purposes there are two problems with this. You may not want even the system operator to know what passwords are assigned to specific data sets. In addition, it is not desirable that protected data set names appear in hard copy (of the console display), even if the passwords are not revealed.

Use of the CODE parameter satisfies both requirements. When specified to AMS (DEFINE or ALTER), it causes VSAM to substitute an eight-byte code for the object name. The system operator is prompted to respond to this code and not the data set name for the password. The operator need not ever know which codes are associated with which VSAM object.

12.6 VSAM PASSWORDS

VSAM offers optional protection of its resources through the password facility. Passwords can be utilized by AMS and by application programs for access to data sets. There are **four levels** of password protection. Shown from the highest to the lowest, they are as follows.

Level 1—Total access (MASTERPW parameter) allows any valid operation to take place on the object protected. The following functions can be performed:

Read
Update
Insert
Delete
Control interval access

Level 2—Control Interval access (CONTROLPW parameter) allows the following operations to be performed directly on Control Intervals:

Read a control interval
Write a control interval

Level 3—Update access (UPDATEPW parameter) allows the following operations:

Read
Update
Insert
Delete

Level 4—Read access (READPW parameter) allows only read operations to be performed.

Passwords on higher levels permit operations on all lower levels. If a low-level password exists, a master password must also exist. For the DEFINE and ALTER commands only, the highest level password will be propagated upward to the master password level. If you specified UPDATEPW only, for instance, it will also become the CONTROLPW and MASTERPW. Password protection can be defined for clusters, catalogs, alternate indices, paths, and page spaces (OS only). In addition to this, the data and index components of clusters and alternate indices can be protected as well.

When a cluster has password protection but no passwords have been defined for its individual components, access can be made to the data and index components directly at any time; they are not protected. If, however, these components are also specified with passwords, the same access restrictions apply. The same password values can be used for a cluster and for its components.

There are times when the passwords required for a VSAM command will apply to the catalog and other times when they apply to other components. The catalog is affected whenever an object is defined (DEFINE), altered (ALTER), deleted (DELETE), or listed (LISTCAT).

If passwords are defined for noncatalog objects (i.e., clusters), they **must** also be specified in the catalog. If this is not done, no checking is performed in the catalog's entry for that file.

Passwords are one to eight bytes in length. Characters can be alpha, numeric, or special characters. The password can also be specified in hexadecimal.

Passwords submitted when none are required are ignored.

12.6.1 USING THE PASSWORDS

If the master catalog is password protected, the only times that its password must be specified are when defining or altering a user catalog entry.

A catalog is a VSAM KSDS data set. One of the things that makes catalog password processing different is the fact that unlike a cluster, for example, catalogs contain self-defining entries. In other words, a catalog contains entries defining its own extent, whether a catalog recovery area is present, and so forth.

Some of the things you should know about password requirements:

1. To define an entry in a catalog, the update or higher level password is required.

2. For catalog entries that are altered (ALTER), the master password of the catalog is required unless the entry is a GDG or non-VSAM entry. In this case the update level password is good enough.
3. For catalog entries that are to be deleted, the master password (MASTERPW) of the catalog or the master password of the entry is required unless the entry is a GDG or non-VSAM entry, in which case the update (UPDATEPW) level password is good enough.
4. To delete a nonempty VSAM data space, the master password is required. To delete an empty VSAM data space, the UPDATEPW password can be used.
5. To delete a user catalog, its master password must be given.
6. To list (LISTC) the passwords of an entry, the master password for that entry or the catalog is required.
7. Catalog entries that are password protected can be listed by specifying the read password (READPW).
8. When importing an object, you can specify both the update password of the catalog (CATALOG parameter) **and** the update password of the data set (OFILE or ODS). If the master password of the catalog is specified, both password requirements will be satisfied.
9. Password protection by AMS is not available for non-VSAM data sets. This can, however, be accomplished through JCL.

For information on how application programs access data sets using passwords, see Chapters 15 and 16.

TEST YOUR UNDERSTANDING

1. Name the different security facilities available to VSAM.
2. What is the AUTHORIZATION function? What must you do to make it work?
3. How do passwords work? Name the four levels of password protection.
4. What is RACF?
5. What password facilities are available for non-VSAM data sets?
6. How does the CODE parameter work?

chapter 13

SPACE CALCULATIONS

13.1 TYPES OF SPACE CALCULATIONS

In this chapter we concentrate on the calculations required to compute space for the following:

Clusters and alternate indices
Catalogs
Indices

13.2 CLUSTERS AND ALTERNATE INDICES

In this section the steps required in order to compute the space requirements for a VSAM cluster or alternate index are examined. Calculations for alternate indices are computed in the same manner as KSDS clusters. The steps required for this process are as follows:

1. Determine the size of the control area.
2. Determine the number of **physical** blocks per track (if more than one) used to house a control interval, and the size of the control interval.

3. Compute the number of records per CI.
4. Calculate the number of records per cylinder.

13.2.1 DETERMINING THE SIZE OF THE CONTROL AREA

If a cluster is to be suballocated from an existing VSAM space, the size of the CA is determined by examining the initial space allocation parameters. If these parameters were stated in cylinders, the control area size will be one cylinder. The CA size can **never** be greater than one cylinder. For suballocated VSAM spaces, if the allocation was not made in cylinders, the lesser of the primary or secondary allocation determines the size of the CA. For unique clusters, the CA size is always equal to one cylinder. When unsure of the CA size, this value can be obtained by running a LISTCAT on the volume to be used.

13.2.2 DETERMINING CI SIZE

VSAM calculates the number of physical blocks it will use to store control intervals. The calculation is based upon track capacity, record and CI sizes. You do not have direct control over this. It can be somewhat manipulated, however, through your choice of record and CI sizes. In a good number of cases the size of the CI and the size of the physical block it resides in is the same. In any event, before the space requirements can be calculated, this factor must be determined. Once again, this can be determined by viewing a LISTCAT.

13.2.3 COMPUTING THE NUMBER OF RECORDS PER CI

The following factors must be taken into account before the number of records per CI can be determined. They are as follows:

Size of the CI
Record size (or average size if variable)
Amount of freespace (KSDS) desired per CI

The formula for computing this is as follows:

For fixed length records:

$$\mathbf{RECCI} = \frac{\mathbf{CISZ} - \mathbf{10}}{\mathbf{RECLEN} \times (\mathbf{1} - \mathbf{FSPCTCI})}$$

For variable length records:

$$\textbf{RECCI} = \frac{\textbf{CISZ} - (\textbf{4} + (\textbf{N} \times \textbf{3}))}{\textbf{RECLEN} \times (\textbf{1} - \textbf{FSPCTCI})}$$

Where:

RECCI	=	Number of records per control interval
CISZ	=	Size of the control interval
RECLEN	=	Record length (or avg. if variable)
FSPCTCI	=	CI freespace percentage in decimal
N	=	Estimated number of records per CI. The purpose of this field is to determine the byte requirements for RDFs. An average should be used.

The decimal part of RECCI should be truncated.

Example:

For a fixed length file with records of 250 bytes, CI freespace of 20%, and a CI size of 4096:

$$\text{RECCI} = (\textbf{4096} - 10)/\textbf{250} \times (1-\textbf{.20})$$
$$\text{RECCI} = \textbf{13.07}$$
$$\text{RECCI} = \textbf{13}$$

For variable length:

$$\text{RECCI} = (\textbf{4096} - (4 + (\textbf{12} \times 3))/\textbf{250} \times (1.-\textbf{.20})$$
$$\text{RECCI} = \textbf{12.97}$$
$$\text{RECCI} = \textbf{12}$$

13.2.4 COMPUTING THE NUMBER OF RECORDS PER CYLINDER

Computing the number of records per cylinder is a two-step process. First, the number of records per CA must be computed, and then the number of CAs per cylinder must be calculated.

In the preceding example we computed the number of records in a CI. Multiplying this by the number of physical blocks per track gives us the number of records per track. Multiplying that number by the number of tracks in a CA will give us the number of records per CA with no CA freespace. The formula for this follows:

$$\mathbf{RECCA = (PHYBLK \times RECCI \times TRKCA) \times (1 - FSPCTCA)}$$

Where:

RECCA	=	Number of records per CA
PHYBLK	=	Number of physical blocks per track
RECCI	=	Number of records in a CI
TRKCA	=	Number of tracks in a CA
FSPCTCA	=	Amount of freespace desired for the CA

Example:

RECCA	=	(**3** × **16** × **3**) × (1 − **.25**)
RECCA	=	**108** records per CA

In order to compute the number of records on a cylinder, use the following formula:

$$\mathbf{RECCYL = RECCA \times NOCACYL}$$

Where:

RECCYL	=	Number of records on a cylinder
RECCA	=	Number of records in a control area
NOCACYL	=	Number of control areas per cylinder

Example:

RECCYL	=	**108** × **6.3**
RECCYL	=	**680.4**
RECCYL	=	**680**

This example refers to an IBM 3330. The 3330 has 19 tracks per cylinder. Using a CA size of 3 tracks that gives us 6.3 CAs per cylinder.

Let us now calculate the number of cylinders required to hold 30,000 records.

SPACE = **30000 / 680**
SPACE = **44.12**
SPACE = **45** cylinders (rounded upward)

A final note: If the sequence set IMBED option is used, reduce the number of records in a CA by the percentage of space used by the sequence set (always one track).

13.3 CALCULATING CATALOG SPACE

In order to calculate the size of a catalog, estimates must be made on the number of entries required for each entry type. The following worksheet is to be used in conjunction with the table in Figure 13.1:

WORKSHEET FOR COMPUTING THE SIZE OF A CATALOG

ENTRY TYPE	FORMULA	ESTIMATE
Alternate Indices		
Number of alternate indices	× 3	
Path, nonVSAM, GDG, Alias, PGSPACE		
Number of entries for each	× 1	
Key Sequenced Data Sets		
Number of KSDS clusters	× 3	
Spread across: 3–7 volumes	× 1	
8–12 volumes	× 2	
13–17 volumes	× 3	
For each KSDS and AIX with space on more than two volumes	+ 1	
For each additional 1–5 vols	+ 1	
No. of KSDS clusters with AIXs to be upgraded	× 4	
Entry Sequenced Data Sets		
Number of ESDS clusters	× 2	
Number of ESDS cluster with AIXs to be upgraded	× 3	
Relative Record Data Set		
Number of RRDS clusters	× 2	

(Continued on p. 274)

RRDS and ESDS Clusters For each cluster with space on more than 5 vols, add 1 for each additional group of 1 to 5 vols .... 6 to 13 volumes .... 14 to 21 volumes	 + 1 × 1 × 2	
Volume Ownership Number of volumes owned: If 2305 .... 2314/2319 .... 3330–1/3340/3344/3370 .... 3330–11/3350/3380	 × 2 × 3 × 4 × 6	
Data Spaces For each group of four data spaces on a volume	 + 1	
Basic Requirement		10
	TOTAL:	

To compute the catalog size in tracks, use the following formula:

$$\text{CATTRKS} = \text{FACTORA} \times \text{TOT} + \text{FACTORB}$$

Where:

CATTRKS = Number of tracks required for the catalog
FACTORA = From Figure 13.1 according to device type
FACTORB = From Figure 13.1 according to device type
TOT = Total computed from work sheet

13.4 COMPUTING THE SIZE OF THE INDEX

The following formula can be used to calculate the **approximate** size of the index component. This computation is the most difficult one to calculate because of the variables involved. Key compression is one of them, freespace is another. The following formula should give you reasonably good results.

DEVICE TYPE	FACTOR A	FACTOR B
2305-1	0.1	5
2305-2	0.09	3
2314/2319	0.1364	5
3330-1/3330-11	0.09	3
3340/3344	0.125	5
3350	0.0667	3
3370	0.0389	3
3380	0.0264	3

Figure 13.1 Catalog space parameters.

13.4.1 FORMULA FOR COMPUTING THE INDEX COMPONENT

NOCIBYT = (HDR + CTL + (3 × NFSPCCI) + (TCICA × 5) + 30)

Where:

HDR	=	Number of bytes in the index CI header (24)
CTL	=	Number of bytes in CIDF and RDF (Index CI only has one RDF)
NFSPCCI	=	Number of freespace CIs in the CA
TCICA	=	Total control intervals in the CA; this can be computed as follows: CISZ / TRKCAP * CASZ. Truncate the result of CISZ / TRKCAP
CISZ	=	Size of one control interval
TRKCAP	=	Track capacity in bytes, device-dependent
CASZ	=	Size of the control area
NOCIBYT	=	Number of bytes in an index CI

The following formula can be substituted for the preceding one.

NOCIBYT = (24 + 8 + (3 × NFSPCCI) + (TCICA × 5) + 30)

This formula will compute the **minimum** number of bytes required for an index control interval. The CI size for the index component must be one of the following sizes: 512, 1024, 2048, or 4096.

After computing the number of bytes required for the index record, pick the CI size into which it will fit. By the way, the index of the CI is considered to have only one record in it. Because of this, there is only one RDF present in the control interval.

All you now need do is approximate the number of records the cluster will contain. Once this is ascertained, you simply divide the number by NOCIBYT in order to determine the number of control intervals required for the entire file. Taking this result, divide this by the number of CIs that can fit in a track, and you will have your answer.

TEST YOUR UNDERSTANDING

1. Compute the space requirements in cylinders for a cluster that will contain 80,000 records. The device type is a 3350, the record size (fixed) is 320 bytes, and freespace requirements will be 20% for the CI and 15% for the CA.
2. Run a LISTCAT at your installation showing all entries. Based upon this, compute what the catalog space requirements should be and compare this to what is allocated in the LISTCAT. Use the worksheet and table in this chapter.

chapter **14**

VSAM—ADVANCED PROCESSING OPTIONS

14.1 VSAM—ADVANCED OPTIONS

This chapter presents topics of special interest to systems planners. The subjects covered here are as follows:

Cross-system (multimainframe) data set sharing
Sharing buffers and other resources
Control interval processing
Catalog access and processing
Index access and processing
VSE advanced VSAM options
VSE SAM feature
VSE Back-up/Restore feature

The Integrated Catalog Facility of DF/EF MVS
The ISAM interface

14.2 CROSS-SYSTEM (MULTIMAINFRAME) DATA SET SHARING

If you have already been involved with data set sharing across mainframes, you are aware, no doubt, of the difficulties that can arise. VSAM on one system does not know what VSAM on another system is doing. If you restrict your cross-system requirements to read-only functions, this **might** not pose any problem to you. However, even read-only access can involve problems at times.

When a VSAM data set is opened, information from the catalog is brought into main storage and placed in VSAM control blocks. This includes fields such as HIGH-USED RBA and statistical information such as the number of records read, added, updated, and deleted, and the total number of records on file. This information is updated in main storage while the application is processing the data set. When the data set is closed, the information is written back to the catalog. The statistics will always be different after processing. If the file was expanded, the HIGH-USED RBA (end-of-file indicator) will also have changed.

When the statistics or HIGH-USED RBA on one mainframe changes in main storage, the change is not effected on the second system. This condition can pose problems for all types of processing including read-only applications that are being run concurrently with update applications.

The entire index set of a cluster might be brought into main storage if sufficient space exists (see Chapter 17). If the application on one system is allowed to modify a data set in any way, it will not be reflected on the other system.

Index records on one system could theoretically contain pointers to whole groups of records that have just been deleted by the application on another system. There is no way for the other application to know this.

There is another problem that can arise. Let us take the case where there is an application on system **A** that is updating (adding, changing, deleting) records, while the application on system **B** is read-only. Let us assume that application **B** opens the data set first. Application **A** now opens the data set, processes it, and closes it while application **B** is still using it. Application **B** now closes the data set. Which statistics and HIGH-USED RBA data will the catalog entry then contain? If you answered "the system that closed the data set last," you were correct! **The information maintained in main-storage always replaces the catalog information when the data set is closed.**

If this situation were to occur, it might seem as though the data set were never updated. Records added to the data set outside (past the HIGH-USED-RBA) those in freespace areas would be totally inaccessible. This is because a new control area would be obtained from the end of the data set if a CA split occurred. The HIGH-USED-RBA would be reset by application **B** to point to the end-of-file RBA that existed before the additions were made. If this situation were allowed to continue, the data set would become totally corrupted and would have to be reconstructed.

What is the solution to this? Unfortunately, there are no clear-cut solutions. It becomes a matter of application requirements. There **are** tools you can use, however, to ensure data set integrity. They are as follows:

Procedural/operational restrictions

Cross-system data set sharing using SHAREOPTIONS(4 4) and RESERVE/DEQ

Global Resource Serialization option (MVS only)

System Lock File (DOS/VSE)

Vendor-supplied or user-developed software

14.2.1 PROCEDURAL/OPERATIONAL RESTRICTIONS

Of all the possible solutions available, application segregation is the best. Whenever possible, those applications that modify data sets should be isolated and run only **when there is no possibility of data set access by another system**. This solution will ensure data set integrity.

This solution is probably the one relied upon by most multicomputer installations. It is the safest and best method. Unfortunately, there are sometimes applications that require data set updating throughout the day. In this case, the procedural or operational solution is not adequate.

14.2.2 CROSS-SYSTEM SHARING USING RESERVE/DEQ AND SHAREOPTIONS(4 4)

In Chapter 7 we were introduced to the concept of data set sharing by the AMS SHAREOPTIONS parameter. This parameter allows us to select options for sharing data sets among partitions or regions and across systems. The parameter format looks like this:

SHAREOPTIONS(cross-partition/region cross-system)

The following is a summary of the capabilities provided.

CROSS REGION/PARTITION

Value	Description
1	Allows any number of applications to **read** the data set **or** only one application to open the data set for **update** processing.
2	Allows any number of applications to read the data set **and** one application to update the data set.
3	Allows unrestricted use of the data set. VSAM, however, does nothing to protect you; you are on your own. You should use the ENQ (enqueue) and DEQ (dequeue) macros with this option in order to protect the data set. ENQ allows you, through operating system software, to put a **hold** on a resource. DEQ allows you to **release** it (more about this follows).
4	VSAM provides unrestricted access to data sets. Some protection is provided, however. The HIGH-USED-RBA is not allowed to change. Control interval splits are allowed as long as they do not result in control area splits. Control area splits cause VSAM to allocate new control areas beyond the HIGH-USED-RBA and, therefore, are not allowed with this option. Another function provided for this option is **read refresh**. Each time a read is issued, a new copy of the record is brought in from the DASD device, even if a copy of that record already resides in main-storage.

CROSS SYSTEM

Value	Description
1	Not currently used.
2	Not currently used.

Value	Description
3	Similar to cross region option 3. VSAM provides no assistance whatsoever. You are on your own. You should use the OS RESERVE and DEQ macros with this option (see the following).
4	With this option VSAM requires that you use the OS RESERVE and DEQ macros in order to ensure data set integrity.

14.2.2.1 How the ENQ, RESERVE, and DEQ Macros Work

If you are not already familiar with the concept of ENQ/DEQ, it can be somewhat difficult at first to grasp. First, this facility is not restricted to VSAM. The ENQ macro allows you to reserve any resource for your exclusive use.[1] **If you issue an ENQ for a certain resource and the resource is not already enqueued, you will receive exclusive control of that resource.** If, however, the resource is already enqueued, your application or task will be placed into a **wait** state until the resource is released by the application or task that first enqueued it.[2]

As sophisticated as this all sounds, the mechanism for ENQ/DEQ is actually quite simple; in fact, it is nothing more than a switch setting and testing facility. Whenever you ENQ a resource, the operating system places the **name** or **address** of the resource in a table, which we will call the ENQ table. Before placing the entry into the resource table, however, the table is first checked to see if an exact match on that entry already exists. If it does, the entry is not added to the table again. Rather, the task or application is placed in a wait state until that entry is removed from the table by the application that placed it there originally. The removal is usually accomplished with a **DEQ** macro. An entry will also be removed if, for some reason, the originating task is cancelled or abends. There may be many tasks waiting on the ENQ table. They are queued up serially waiting their turn at the resource.

So far nothing has been said about data sets or how they are protected. Look at the following illustration.

```
1.    MYPROG    START
                  .
                  .
2.                ENQ     INVNTORY
                  .
                  .
3.                PUT     RPL=VSAMRPL (Add rec. to file)
                  .
```

```
                              .
4.                            DEQ      INVNTORY
                              .
                              .
5.                            END
```

In this example a VSAM data set is protected by ENQ/DEQ. The PUT operation could allow for record additions using SHR (4 4) **as long as enough freespace has been provided**. If the addition of a record would cause a control area split, the addition would be suppressed and a **return code** would be passed back to the program.

Step 1 in the preceding example placed the word **INVNTORY** in the ENQ table. The next ENQ issued to access this data set would cause the operating system to *try* to place the word in the table as well. If it was already there, the application would have to wait its turn. **If** all applications accessing this data set use this convention, the data set could be protected. Notice, however, that the word **if** is used. There is nothing that forces an application to use this convention. If there is some concern that an application program might circumvent this protection scheme, you might want to also utilize additional security measures such as passwords, or even the RACF facility (Chapter 12).

In a cross-system situation any application can access a shared data set that has been defined with SHAREOPTIONS 3 or 4. Imagine the damage that can be caused by two applications updating the same control interval at the same time. The ENQ table pertains to one mainframe only. **The operating system in one mainframe is not aware of ENQ entries in another mainframe.**

If the convention previously discussed can be maintained, however, similar protection can be extended to cross-system data sets as well by use of the **RESERVE** and **DEQ** macros. The RESERVE macro is composed of two parts:

Software ENQ
Hardware Reserve Command (CCW)

The first part of the RESERVE macro functions identically to the ENQ. The second part (**Reserve CCW**) requires some explanation.

Exclusive control of the **entire volume** could be facilitated through the use of a hardware **Reserve** command. This command is executed by the operating system. The execution of this command causes the seizure of the volume for exclusive use, providing that the other mainframe does not itself already have exclusive control of this volume. The successful execution of this command causes an actual hardware lockout to take place. The second system **cannot** access the volume. The obvious disadvantage of this facility is that the **entire volume** is unavailable to the other system. This could be a major problem if the volume is frequently accessed.

Another hardware command, **Release**, places the volume toggle back in the middle position. This position allows either system to gain control of the volume. The issuance of a Release command causes an interrupt in the locked-out system, thereby notifying it of its availability. The RESERVE macro incorporates the hardware Reserve command as well as the ENQ. DEQ incorporates the hardware Release command as well as DEQ.

There is one quirk about the RESERVE macro that you should know. The hardware Reserve does not actually take place until the first I/O operation against that volume takes place. It does not take place when the macro is issued, as is commonly supposed. By I/O is meant any I/O operation, including the I/O that takes place when an OPEN verb or macro is issued by the program.

The RESERVE, ENQ, and DEQ macros can only be written in the assembler language. Subroutines invoking the macros could, however, be written in assembler and **called** from programs written in a higher level language.

A word to the systems programmer. If the RESERVE macro is to be used, be sure you specify **shared** when coding the device for the I/O GEN. The UCB must have the shared attribute for RESERVE to work. If it is omitted, the operating system treats the RESERVE like an ENQ macro.

There is another facility available that greatly resembles the features found in these macros but provides **global** ENQ support. This facility is called **Global Resource Serialization**.

14.2.3 GLOBAL RESOURCE SERIALIZATION

There are two requirements for using Global Resource Serialization (**GRS**). It must be an MVS installation, and the mainframes sharing data sets must be able to communicate to each other by means of channel-to-channel adapters. I suspect that this type of information will eventually be passed along by means of communication facilities. GRS allows you to define system resources that require global protection. Each system sharing the data sets (or other resource) must use this convention in order for it to be successful.

Every time a GRS resource is enqueued by one system, all other systems are notified, by channel-to-channel adapter, of this request. If the resource is not already enqueued on any system, the application or task will then be given exclusive global control of it. ENQ and DEQ information is constantly being passed between mainframes using GRS. One advantage of GRS over RESERVE/DEQ is that whole volumes are not locked out when using this method.

In order to use GRS you must define its use as well as the resources it is to protect. This information is provided to MVS in SYS1.PARMLIB in member (GRSCFGxx). For further information on this subject you are directed to the *IBM System Programming Library* reference on *Performance and Tuning*.

14.2.4 THE SYSTEM LOCK FILE (DOS/VSE)

Some of the conventions previously discussed are OS options only. They cannot be used in a VSE environment. DOS provides another option, however, the **System Lock File (SLF)**. This facility allows the sharing of resources by placing an ENQ table (in a sense) on DASD. All accesses to a protected resource are first checked in the SLF. The same philosophy discussed under ENQ applies here as well. Entries to be protected are first defined in the SLF. There is, of course, additional I/O involved using this method, but it works!

14.2.5 VENDOR-SUPPLIED AND USER-DEVELOPED SOFTWARE

It is worth mentioning at this point that there is at least one vendor-developed software product on the market that supports cross-system resource sharing. It allows the use of a System Lock File mechanism in an OS environment. You could, of course, code your own routines to accomplish this, but you would have to do this for each application. The vendor-provided software allows for much greater flexibility.

14.3 SHARING BUFFERS AND OTHER RESOURCES

One of VSAM's greatest drawbacks is the amount of virtual storage it requires to operate. VSAM uses so much storage, in fact, that it sometimes seems as though virtual storage was invented just to support VSAM. A healthy MVS system running several CICS regions could require several megabytes of storage just for VSAM buffers. A good percentage of space allocated for buffers either is never used, or is used only a small percentage of the time.

There are two facilities available to allow for the sharing of VSAM buffers, **Local Shared Resources (LSR)** and **Global Shared Resources (GSR)**. GSR, an MVS-only option, allows the sharing of VSAM buffer space among all regions, if desired. LSR allows for data set buffer sharing in a single region or partition. The LSR option is available for MVS, VS1, and DOS/VSE. You can also use this facility for online processing by using the LSR option of CICS (SHARECTL). In order to facilitate this, VSAM provides the following buffer control macros:

BLDVRP—Build VSAM buffer pool
DLVRP—Delete VSAM buffer pool
WRTBFR—Write buffer
SCHBFR—Search buffer
MRKBFR—Mark buffer

Before you can share buffers you must first establish a buffer pool. A buffer pool is an area of storage that is segmented to provide a specific number of buffers. Buffers are obtained from the pool when needed and returned when no longer needed. Once returned to the pool, the buffer is then free to be used for another purpose. The **BLDVRP** macro is used to define the number of buffers, the buffer size, the type (LSR/GSR), whether the buffer is to be constructed in pageable or nonpageable storage, whether VSAM control blocks are included, and the number of file position pointers to be maintained (see the discussion on concurrent positioning in Chapter 16). You can also define several different sizes of buffers and the amount of each size. Buffers are assigned numbers after the pool is established, beginning with number 1. The second buffer number is 2, and so forth.

Storage obtained for GSR buffers in the common area of virtual storage must be obtained by issuing a **GETMAIN** macro for storage in subpool 241. MVS systems can have both LSR and GSR resource pools.

After a buffer pool is established, you can attach your **Access Method Control Block (ACB)** to the pool at open time by using the ACB **MACRF** parameter and by specifying either LSR or GSR. If different size buffers are available in the pool, the most appropriate size is selected. The ACB macro is described in Chapter 16.

VSAM offers facilities to allow for buffer space optimization as well as improved access response time. For example, if you have a data set that is being continuously updated and inquired against, you might want to consider using the **deferred-PUT** option. Deferred-PUT accomplishes the following: (1) it cuts down the number of I/Os performed since a CI is not written out until full, and (2) it greatly decreases response time because it has the most recent copy of a record available in storage if a retrieval of that record is requested.

VSAM provides a special macro **WRTBFR** that allows you to write out any buffers containing records **marked** with the deferred-PUT attribute. You do not have to use the WRTBFR macro when using deferred-PUT. If buffer pool space becomes tight, deferred-PUT and other marked records (MRKBFR) sitting in buffers are first written out to provide buffers for other functions. Remaining marked buffers are automatically written out when a file is closed.

There is another way in which to **mark** a buffer for output, the **MRKBFR** macro. Any buffer flagged with a MRKBFR macro is written out whenever a WRTBFR macro is executed. WRTBFR then causes both deferred-PUT and MRKBFR-flagged buffers to be output to DASD.

Another macro that can be very useful is the **SCHBFR** (search buffer) macro. With this facility you may request that VSAM search its buffers in order to determine whether a specific record is contained therein. When using this macro, you provide it with two parameters: the RBA of the record (or control interval) and the range of buffers to be searched (from–to). If the RBA is located, you are notified. You are not, however, given exclusive control over it; in other words, other tasks or regions have equal access to it. The RBA of the control interval is provided when the application is performing control interval processing. You can return the buffer pool space to the system by executing the **DLVRP** macro.

14.4 CONTROL INTERVAL PROCESSING

You can request **control interval** processing in your ACB. This option allows you to treat whole control intervals as though they were records. When using this option, you are on your own; VSAM does not examine any control interval you write back to ensure that it is still valid. You are responsible for making whatever adjustments are required if the contents of the CI are altered. Records already existing can be altered and written back without problems, as long as the length or position of the record has not been modified. If you wish to alter record sizes you will have to alter the CIDF and RDF control fields as well. For the most part you should stay away from file updating functions with CI processing, especially if the data set is a KSDS.

14.4.1 NORMAL CONTROL INTERVAL PROCESSING

In order to specify control interval processing in your ACB, you must code the MACRF parameter specifying the **CNV** option. If you intend to modify control intervals, you must be in move (**MVE**) mode. The SCHBFR, MRKBFR, and WRTBFR macros can also be used with this option.

14.4.2 IMPROVED CONTROL INTERVAL PROCESSING

Another interval control processing option is **improved interval control** access (MACRF = ICI). If you can adhere to the restrictions, this option offers several performance improvements. One of the improvements involves **page fixing** the area used for VSAM's buffers and control blocks. Page fixing means that the operating system will dedicate real storage for the virtual page being fixed. When real storage is dedicated like this, no paging will take place. This improves performance because no I/O will ever take place for paging reasons. A second improvement is made because VSAM will spend less time checking your macro and parameters.

The restrictions on its use are as follows:

1. The control interval used must be equal in size to the physical record in which it resides.
2. The cluster may be RRDS, ESDS, or KSDS. If KSDS is used, only the index or data component can be accessed at one time.
3. The index component of a KSDS cannot be replicated.
4. Chained RPLs may not be used (more about this in Chapter 16).
5. The macros used must be GET, GET (for update), or PUT (for update). POINT cannot be used.
6. The I/O operation may not be asynchronous; the CHECK or ENDREQ (see Chapter 16) macros may not be used. See Chapter 16 for more information on asynchronous processing using the CHECK macro.

14.5 CATALOG ACCESS AND PROCESSING

VSAM catalogs are KSDS data sets. They can be accessed in the same manner as any other KSDS data set. When processing in this manner, the catalog name must be specified in the DD (OS) or DLBL (DOS) JCL card.

After opening the catalog as you would any KSDS data set, the catalog records may be read. The control interval of the catalog's data component is always 512 bytes in length. The format for these records is found in the various VSAM **Diagnostic** or **Program Logic** manuals.

The **SHOWCAT** macro offers another way in which you can access catalog information. This macro enables you to access a catalog without first defining an ACB (Chapter 16) and without first opening the catalog for processing like a data set. When the SHOWCAT macro is issued the first time without specifying an ACB, an ACB will be created and its address returned to you.

Entries in a catalog are interrelated in that more than one entry is required to describe an object and its associated objects. One entry may point to one or more other entries. A PATH, for instance, may point to an alternate index which, in turn, would point to a base cluster. The base cluster would, in turn, point to its index and data components. Associated with the base component is the **upgrade set**, which points to other alternate indices that get updated whenever record processing that affects them (insertions and deletions) takes place.

SHOWCAT enables you to follow these entries through the catalog. After you issue the first SHOWCAT, VSAM returns the control interval numbers of catalog records that belong to the objects contained therein. You can then issue subsequent SHOWCAT macros to retrieve the remaining records by supplying the CI numbers returned with the first SHOWCAT.

The following is the format of the SHOWCAT macro.

```
SHOWCAT     [ACB=address]
            AREA=address
            CI=address | NAME=address
```

ACB:

This parameter specifies the address of an Access Control Block that describes the catalog. This parameter is optional; if omitted, VSAM will supply one for you the first time the SHOWCAT macro is issued.

AREA:

Points to a specific address in which the catalog information is to be returned. This area must be large enough to accommodate the largest size record or the record will be truncated.

CI | NAME:

The CI parameter points to an area that contains a field three bytes in length. This field contains a control interval number that is used to point to catalog entries. You can alternatively supply VSAM with the name of the object for which information is to be retrieved. The address pointed to by the NAME parameter must be 44 bytes long and contain the name of the object.

14.6 INDEX ACCESS AND PROCESSING

The index component of a KSDS can be accessed in one of two ways:

By opening only the index component and using the standard macros (GET, PUT, etc.)

By using the GETIX and PUTIX macros after opening the index

When accessing by means of the standard macros, you may retrieve individual index records by supplying an RBA. You may also access the control intervals directly using control interval access (MACRF= CNV). In addition to this, records can also be accessed sequentially.

The GETIX and PUTIX macros use control interval access only. The search argument for GETIX is the RBA of the control interval. The format of the GETIX and PUTIX is identical to that of the GET and PUT macros. GET and PUT are described in Chapter 16.

14.7 VSE ADVANCED OPTIONS

DOS/VSE now has some new VSAM features not found in OS. The most notable of these are the following:

Open with automatic verify

Multiple catalog space ownership on a single volume

14.7.1 OPEN WITH AUTOMATIC VERIFY

VSAM always checks the status of a data set at open time. In the past a VERIFY was required if the data set had not been closed after processing. If this condition existed, the application could not continue.

As of Release 3.0 of VSE/VSAM, the VERIFY function will be performed automatically by VSAM whenever a **not-closed** condition is detected.

14.7.2 MULTIPLE CATALOG SPACE OWNERSHIP

As of VSE/VSAM Release 3.0, multiple catalogs can now own VSAM space on a single DASD volume. There are some restrictions, however:

Only one catalog may reside on the volume

Only one of the catalogs sharing space on the volume can have a Catalog Recovery Area

If a VSAM data set resides on several volumes, each of those data spaces must be owned by a single catalog.

The **volume ownership-bit** in the VTOC no longer indicates that a volume is owned by a single catalog. It now indicates that **one or more** catalogs own the volume.

14.8 VSE/VSAM SAM FEATURE

DOS/VSE does not support any form of dynamic space allocation for non-VSAM data sets. This has forced many DOS installations to purchase vendor-supplied software to accomplish this. In an attempt to address this need, IBM offers an **optional** alternative to DOS users, the VSAM **Space Management for SAM Feature**—a Program Product. The **VSAM/SAM** feature is invoked whenever you use VSAM parameters on your DLBL JCL card **and** a DTF is used by the application program instead of an ACB. This is true regardless of the language used. A COBOL compiler will compile a machine language program containing a DTF instead of an ACB if VSAM parameters are not specified in the SELECT clause.

VSAM can obtain the space required for a SAM file from a suballocated VSAM space. A special VSAM/SAM space need not be defined.

The VSAM/SAM data set resembles an ESDS data set but is slightly different. The space is allocated by control intervals and control areas as is done with a standard KSDS. The control intervals in the VSAM/SAM space, however, have an unusual trait in that **control intervals can cross control area boundaries**.

The primary space allocation is taken from the RECORDS= and RECSIZE= parameters of the DLBL card. The secondary allocation is assumed to be 20% of the primary allocation. Another feature supported by this option is **file extension**. This allows you to add records to the end of an existing VSAM/SAM data set by specification in the DISP parameter. This is similar to the DISP=MOD parameter in OS. Finally, the data set is closed automatically if this is not done by the application when the job step ends.

14.9 VSE/VSAM BACKUP/RESTORE FEATURE

The **Backup/Restore** Program Product allows for high-speed back-up and restoration of VSAM data sets. One of the ways in which the high-speed capability is accomplished is through its support of the IBM 8809 Magnetic Tape Streaming feature.

Each time a block is written to a standard tape drive, the motor on the drive must start up and shut down as each I/O operation is completed. This is why these drives are sometimes referred to as start/stop devices. Tape streaming allows for continuous operation of the drive, whether or not data is being written to it. This is identical to the continuous operation of a standard tape recorder. Operation in this manner is much faster. A second reason that Back-up/Restore provides for fast back-up is that large blocks of data are read and written during its operation. Data is not retrieved by logical record.

Another nice feature of this facility allows for file reorganization whenever a data set is copied and restored.

14.10 THE INTEGRATED CATALOG FACILITY OF DF/EF MVS

The Integrated Catalog Facility (ICF) is part of the Data Facility Extended Function (DF/EF). It is a Program Product currently offered for the MVS operating system environment only. The purpose of this facility is to improve processing efficiency and to simplify catalog and data set recovery when disaster strikes. The ICF catalog offers significant performance improvements over that of the VSAM catalog, and equal or better performance than that of the OS CVOL. The DF/EF feature greatly modifies the standard structure of VSAM. The most drastic changes are found in the catalog structure used by DF/EF.

A DF/EF catalog replaces the standard VSAM catalog and is composed of two parts, the **Basic Catalog Structure (BCS)** and the **VSAM Volume Data Set (VVDS)**. VSAM catalogs can coexist on the same volume as an ICF catalog (see Figure 14.1).

The **BCS** contains volume, security, and other information for VSAM data sets and for the catalog itself. **It contains information that is not subject to change during file processing.** It also contains extent information for non-VSAM data sets.

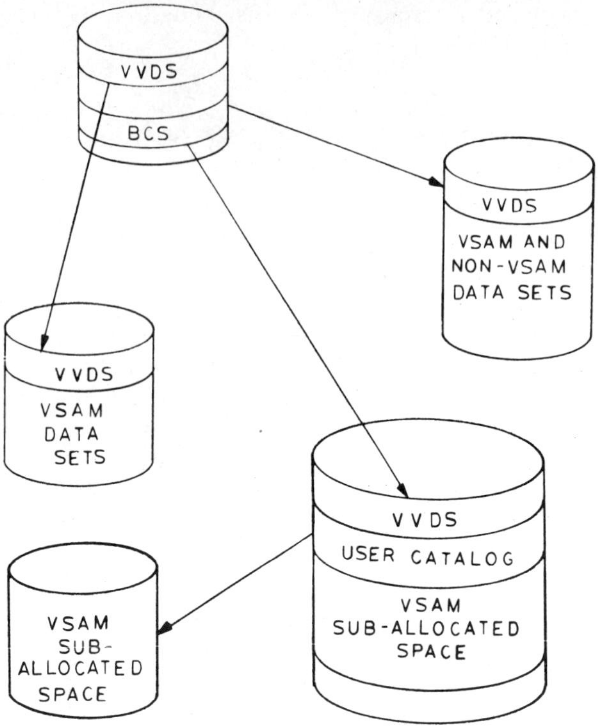

VVDS=VSAM VOLUME DATA SET
BCS=BASIC CATALOG STRUCTURE

Figure 14.1

The **VVDS** contains information such as data set characteristics, back-pointers to any catalogs that own space on that volume (up to 36), and information about any BCS catalog on the volume. **The catalog information that is most dynamic is located in the VVDS.** This reduces contention for catalog access as is the case with VSAM catalogs.

The ICF catalog utilizes a standard KSDS for the BCS and an ESDS for the VVDS.

Another major difference lies in the area of VSAM space allocation. With the ICF facility, there is no concept of Unique or Suballocated data spaces. Allocation of data sets is handled by DADSM (DASD Storage Management). The VTOC reflects all data set usage including VSAM data sets. In order to improve processing time further, related catalog records, such as a cluster, and its associated alternate index(es), are grouped together in what are known as **sphere records**. This simple modification reduces head movement and I/O operations when the catalog is being accessed. The data stored in the BCS are not comprised of fixed length records as is the VSAM catalog, but of KSDS spanned records. In addition to this, the catalog can be **tuned** to meet performance requirements.

Because the recovery from catalog and data set damage is greatly simplified, **the Catalog Recovery Area is not used with ICF VSAM**. Compatibility, however, with standard VSAM is maintained and operation can continue as in the past. DF/EF allows for gradual conversion.

The concept of volume ownership does not exist with the Integrated Catalog Facility. Multiple BCSs may exist on a single volume, and can coexist with VSAM catalogs and OS CVOLS. Only one VVDS, however, may reside on a volume. Master and user catalogs continue to exist for ICF catalogs. A BCS may be either a master or user catalog. Only one master catalog can exist, however.

14.10.1 DEFINING THE ICF CATALOG

In order to define an ICF catalog, the DEFINE USERCATALOG command is used with the **ICFCATALOG** parameter. This creates the BCS. If a VVDS does not exist on the volume already, one will be created at that time. If a data set is created on a volume that does not contain a VVDS, one will be dynamically created as long as the data set belongs to a BCS catalog.

14.10.2 CONVERSION CONSIDERATIONS

The CNVCAT command can be used to convert existing OS CVOLS to VSAM or ICF catalogs. VSAM catalogs can be converted to ICF catalogs with this AMS command. Space must be provided for both the BCS and VVDS.

An **alternate master catalog** facility is available in another program product, **Data Facility Device Support** (DF/DS). This facility allows you to utilize a VSAM master catalog as your main catalog while a second VSAM catalog functions as an alternate. At some predetermined point you could then convert your alternate to an ICF catalog and use that catalog instead. Since the system always looks to member SYSCATLG in SYS1.PARMLIB (SYS1.NUCLEUS was formerly used for this) for the master catalog name, you would have to alter this to substitute the name of the new master catalog.

Another conversion consideration involves the use of DEFINE SPACE. If you utilize an ICF, you will have trouble with this command. VSAM space is not supported with ICF catalogs. Job steps containing DEFINE SPACE commands will fail if used.

14.10.3 DISASTER RECOVERY

The simpler the recovery procedure, the more likely you will recover successfully when disaster strikes. There are basically two methods that you can follow:

Method 1

Periodical backup of the BCS using EXPORT.

Volume backup of all volumes references by this catalog. This will back up all the data sets and the VVDS that points to them.

Method 2

Periodical back-up of the BCS using EXPORT.

Critical data sets may be exported.

If you suspect a problem between a BCS and the VVDS, run the AMS **DIAGNOSE** command. DIAGNOSE is an AMS ICF command, and as such is not found in standard VSAM. DIAGNOSE provides a report showing where the BCS and VVDS differ. A damaged VVDS can be reset entirely by IMPORTING the affected data sets or all the data sets, if need be, on the volume.

Another method of recovery involves volume restoration and IMPORT of the BCS. Restoring the preceding is simple because the BCS contains information that changes only infrequently. To restore the BCS use the AMS IMPORT command. Restore the VVDS and data sets with the same non-VSAM volume restore utility used to back it up. A VVDS may not be restored by itself. This data set is too dynamic; it gets updated every time a data set on that volume is opened, closed, or extended.

14.10.4 ICF SUMMARY

There are at least six reference manuals available from IBM on this subject. The material presented here is simply a brief overview. From the foregoing, however, it should be apparent that IBM has been hard at work improving VSAM to meet the changing user environment. In the years ahead we will be seeing even greater change, especially in the area of data set sharing between mainframes. Perhaps we will one day see a VSAM MACHINE that resembles the dedicated database mini-computers now coming into being.

14.11 THE ISAM INTERFACE

IBM offers a facility to assist users in converting from ISAM to VSAM. It is called the **ISAM Interface**. The ISAM Interface is like an invisible helper that is always there, always ready to assist you during your conversion to VSAM. It allows you to forgo the rewriting of ISAM applications until some later date. To exercise it, you simply create a VSAM data set and change your JCL card to reflect that this is now a VSAM data set.

Whenever you issue an OPEN command or macro, the ISAM Interface routine determines whether you are using an ACB (Access Control Block). The ACB is always used for VSAM data sets. It provides a function similar to the DCB (OS) or DTF (DOS). If the control block used is a DCB or DTF, the interface then determines the data set you would like to access. If it is found to be a VSAM data set, the interface routine will take over, translating the application's ISAM requests to VSAM requests. This operation is completely transparent to you. You should, however, use this facility only until you are able to convert the application entirely to VSAM. The interface routine requires a certain amount of additional system overhead.

NOTES

1. There is a parameter for the ENQ macro that allows a **shared** entry to be placed in the enqueue table. Shared entries of the ENQ macro are discussed in the *System Programmer's Library—Supervisor Macros* reference.
2. Parameters can be coded on the ENQ macro to allow the operating system to pass a return code back to the application if the resource is not available. When this feature is used, the application is not placed in a wait state if the object is already enqueued.

TEST YOUR UNDERSTANDING

1. Explain the various methods that can be utilized when sharing VSAM data sets between mainframes.

2. How do the ENQ and DEQ macros work?
3. What is the difference between ENQ and RESERVE?
4. What is GSR? LSR? What operating systems support each?
5. What does the MRKBFR macro do?
6. How does deferred-PUT work?
7. Explain the two different kinds of control interval access that are available. What are the differences?
8. Explain the two ways in which catalog information can be accessed.
9. Explain the methods of access for the index component of a KSDS.
10. Explain the following facilities and how they work: VSE/VSAM SAM feature; VSE/VSAM Back-up/Restore feature.
11. What are some of the differences between standard VSAM and the ICF?
12. What is the ISAM Interface routine?

chapter **15**

ACCESSING VSAM THROUGH COBOL AND PL/I

The two most widely used business application languages around today are **COBOL** and **PL/I**. The popularity of these two languages can be traced directly to both their simplicity and their power.

There are other programming languages that are gaining wide appeal such as **C** and **PASCAL**. These are not, however, **record-oriented** languages. They deal primarily with **strings** (bytes of data chained together).

The business world revolves around **files** of data in which individual **records** are stored, rather than one-line messages. Although COBOL and PL/I programs are capable of manipulating string data, they have been developed primarily for record handling.

Writing VSAM applications in COBOL or PL/I is easy. The languages each contain facilities that greatly simplify coding. If after reading this chapter you are not totally convinced of this fact, a quick glance at Chapter 16 (VSAM assembler coding) will help convince you.

15.1 THE STRUCTURE OF COBOL AND PL/I

In order to access or create a VSAM data set, the data set must first be **defined** in the COBOL or PL/I program. Following definition, the data set must then be **connected** to the application. The file can now be **accessed**, allowing records to be processed.

15.2 FILE DEFINITION IN COBOL AND PL/I

The file definition section of the application program informs the compiler that the program will be accessing a data set. There is, typically, one file definition for each data set to be accessed. I say typically because PL/I does allow a variable to be referenced in order to connect the program to a DD (OS) or DLBL (DOS) statement. This is not usually done, however. COBOL allows only constants to be used.

15.2.1 DEFINING THE FILE IN COBOL

A COBOL program is composed of four major parts known as divisions. These divisions are as follows:

IDENTIFICATION DIVISION
ENVIRONMENT DIVISION
DATA DIVISION
PROCEDURE DIVISION

All of the definition, connection, and processing options take place in the ENVIRONMENT and PROCEDURE DIVISIONS. The definition of the file mostly takes place in the ENVIRONMENT DIVISION. The only item not defined here is whether the file will be accessed as INPUT, OUTPUT, or both (I–O); this is done in the PROCEDURE DIVISION.

15.2.1.1 The ENVIRONMENT DIVISION—Definition Statements

The following are the statements used for defining a VSAM file:

ENVIRONMENT DIVISION.
FILE-CONTROL.
  SELECT filename ASSIGN TO dname
  ORGANIZATION IS SEQUENTIAL | INDEXED | RELATIVE

ACCESS IS SEQUENTIAL | RANDOM | DYNAMIC (ESDS, KSDS, RRDS)
[RECORD KEY IS key-field] (For KSDS only)
[RELATIVE KEY IS key-field] (For RRDS only)
[PASSWORD IS password-field]
[FILE STATUS IS status-field]

EXPLANATION OF STATEMENTS

SELECT filename ASSIGN TO dname:

This statement pairs up the internal file name to an actual DD or DLBL statement. The internal file name is the name used in all OPEN, CLOSE, START, READ, and DELETE verbs.* It is also the name used in the file definition (**FD**) statement that describes the records contained in the file. Example:

In the program:

```
SELECT PAYROLL-FILE ASSIGN TO PAYDD.
FD PAYROLL-FILE ........................etc.
OPEN INPUT PAYROLL-FILE ............etc.
READ PAYROLL-FILE .....................etc.
CLOSE PAYROLL-FILE ...................etc.
```

In the JCL:

```
//PAYDD    DD    DSN= PAYROLL.MASTER,DISP=OLD    (OS)
```

or:

```
// DLBL    PAYDD,'PAYROLL.MASTER',,VSAM    (DOS)
```

ORGANIZATION IS SEQUENTIAL | INDEXED | RELATIVE:

This designates the type of VSAM data set to be accessed; **SEQUENTIAL** signifies an **ESDS**; **INDEXED** defines a **KSDS**; **RELATIVE** signifies an **RRSD**.

ACCESS (MODE) IS SEQUENTIAL | RANDOM | DYNAMIC:

This specifies how the data set is to be processed: sequentially, randomly, or both (DYNAMIC).

* For WRITE and REWRITE the FD record name is used.

RECORD KEY IS key-field:

This specifies the name of the field **within the record** that contains the record's key. This is not used for ESDS or RRDS data sets.

PASSWORD IS password-field:

This specifies the name of a field in which the data-set password is kept. This field is matched against the passwords that were designated for the cluster when it was DEFINED.

FILE STATUS IS status-field:

This specifies the name of a field that is available to receive status codes returned by VSAM. Status codes are presented to the program when an error occurs. The particular code indicates the exact nature of the problem. The application programmer is expected to check the FILE STATUS field after every VSAM verb.

15.2.1.2 The PROCEDURE DIVISION Verbs

The COBOL verbs available for use with VSAM files are as follows:

OPEN —Connect an application program to a data set
START —Request that VSAM position a data set for subsequent sequential access
READ —Retrieve a record from the data set
WRITE —Output a record to the data set
REWRITE—Replace a record within the data set
DELETE —Erase a record from the data set
CLOSE —Disconnect a data set from an application

15.3 CODING PROGRAMS IN COBOL FOR VSAM ACCESS

A COBOL program for accessing an ESDS cluster can be coded in the following manner.

15.3.1 SAMPLE ESDS RETRIEVAL PROGRAM

```
ENVIRONMENT DIVISION.
FILE-CONTROL.
    SELECT PAYROLL-FILE ASSIGN TO PAYDD
    ORGANIZATION IS SEQUENTIAL
    ACCESS IS SEQUENTIAL
    PASSWORD IS WS-PASSWORD
    FILE STATUS IS PAYROLL-STATUS-CODE.
```

```
DATA DIVISION.
FILE SECTION.
FD     PAYROLL-FILE.......


WORKING-STORAGE SECTION.
01     PAYROLL-STATUS-CODE      PICTURE 99 VALUE ZEROS.

01     WS-PASSWORD      PICTURE X(8) VALUE 'SECRET '.
IDENTIFICATION DIVISION.
000-HOUSEKEEPING.
    OPEN INPUT PAYROLL-FILE.
    IF PAYROLL-STATUS-CODE NOT EQUAL TO ZEROS
             PERFORM 900-STATUS-ERROR-ON-OPEN
             CALL 'ABEND' USING CONDCODE.

    .
    READ PAYROLL-FILE, AT END GO TO 500-END-OF-JOB.
    IF PAYROLL-STATUS-CODE IS NOT EQUAL TO ZEROS
                PERFORM 910-STATUS-ERROR-ON-READ
                CALL 'ABEND' USING CONDCODE.

    .
500-END-OF-JOB.
    CLOSE PAYROLL-FILE.
    IF PAYROLL-STATUS-CODE NOT EQUAL TO ZEROS
            PERFORM 920-STATUS-ERROR-ON-CLOSE
            CALL 'ABEND' USING CONDCODE.
900-STATUS-ERROR-ON-OPEN.
    DISPLAY 'OPEN ERROR ON PAYROLL MASTER, STATUS CODE '
           PAYROLL-STATUS-CODE.
    CLOSE PAYROLL-FILE.
910-STATUS-ERROR-ON-READ.
    DISPLAY 'READ ERROR ON PAYROLL MASTER, STATUS CODE '
           PAYROLL-STATUS-CODE.
    CLOSE PAYROLL-FILE.
920-STATUS-ERROR-ON-CLOSE.
    DISPLAY 'CLOSE ERROR ON PAYROLL MASTER, STATUS CODE '
           PAYROLL-STATUS-CODE.
    CLOSE PAYROLL-FILE.
```

In this example and ESDS cluster is read sequentially and processed. If any error condition occurs, VSAM returns the reason in the status code field PAYROLL-STATUS-CODE. The ABEND subroutine causes the program to cancel and, in addition, sets a condition code (OS only). Finally, a password is used for file access.

15.3.2 SAMPLE NON-ESDS RETRIEVAL PROGRAM

In order to access a non-Entry Sequenced Data Set for input, code your application in this manner:

For a KSDS:

```
ENVIRONMENT DIVISION.
FILE-CONTROL.
    SELECT PAYROLL-FILE ASSIGN TO PAYDD
    ORGANIZATION IS INDEXED
    ACCESS IS SEQUENTIAL
    RECORD KEY IS PAY-KEY
    FILE STATUS IS PAYROLL-STATUS-CODE.

DATA DIVISION.
FILE SECTION.
FD      PAYROLL-FILE.......
01      PAY-REC.
    03      PAY-KEY      PICTURE 9(6).
WORKING-STORAGE SECTION.
01      PAYROLL-STATUS-CODE      PICTURE 99 VALUE ZEROS.

IDENTIFICATION DIVISION.
000-HOUSEKEEPING.
    OPEN INPUT PAYROLL-FILE.
    IF PAYROLL-STATUS-CODE NOT EQUAL TO ZEROS
              PERFORM 900-STATUS-ERROR-ON-OPEN
              CALL 'ABEND' USING CONDCODE.
    READ PAYROLL-FILE, AT END GO TO 500-END-OF-JOB.
    IF PAYROLL-STATUS-CODE IS NOT EQUAL TO ZEROS
                 PERFORM 910-STATUS-ERROR-ON-READ
                 CALL 'ABEND' USING CONDCODE.

500-END-OF-JOB.
    CLOSE PAYROLL-FILE.
    IF PAYROLL-STATUS-CODE NOT EQUAL TO ZEROS
              PERFORM 920-STATUS-ERROR-ON-CLOSE
              CALL 'ABEND' USING CONDCODE.
900-STATUS-ERROR-ON-OPEN.
    DISPLAY 'OPEN ERROR ON PAYROLL MASTER, STATUS CODE '
            PAYROLL-STATUS-CODE.
    CLOSE PAYROLL-FILE.
910-STATUS-ERROR-ON-READ.
    DISPLAY 'READ ERROR ON PAYROLL MASTER, STATUS CODE '
            PAYROLL-STATUS-CODE.
    CLOSE PAYROLL-FILE.
```

```
920-STATUS-ERROR-ON-CLOSE.
    DISPLAY 'CLOSE ERROR ON PAYROLL MASTER, STATUS CODE '
                PAYROLL-STATUS-CODE.
    CLOSE PAYROLL-FILE.
```

The preceding example differs very little from the previous example. The areas that differ are highlighted. To convert this program to RRDS change the ORGANIZATION to RELATIVE, replace the RECORD KEY statement with RELATIVE KEY.

15.3.3 LOADING (CREATING) A KSDS CLUSTER

In the following example, a KSDS cluster is created.

```
ENVIRONMENT DIVISION.
FILE-CONTROL.
    SELECT PAYROLL-FILE ASSIGN TO PAYDD
    ORGANIZATION IS INDEXED
    ACCESS IS SEQUENTIAL
    RECORD KEY IS PAY-KEY
    FILE STATUS IS PAYROLL-STATUS-CODE.

DATA DIVISION.
FILE SECTION.
FD     PAYROLL-FILE.......
01     PAY-REC.
    03     PAY-KEY     PICTURE 9(6).

WORKING-STORAGE SECTION.
01     PAYROLL-STATUS-CODE     PICTURE 99 VALUE ZEROS.

IDENTIFICATION DIVISION.
000-HOUSEKEEPING.
    OPEN INPUT TRANSACTIONS, OUTPUT PAYROLL-FILE.
    IF PAYROLL-STATUS-CODE NOT EQUAL TO ZEROS
            PERFORM 900-STATUS-ERROR-ON-OPEN
            CALL 'ABEND' USING CONDCODE.
    .
    READ TRANSACTION, AT END GO TO 500-END-OF-JOB
    .
    WRITE PAY-REC, INVALID KEY PERFORM 600-DUP-OR-OOS.
    IF PAYROLL-STATUS-CODE IS NOT EQUAL TO ZEROS
              PERFORM 910-STATUS-ERROR-ON-WRITE
              CALL 'ABEND' USING CONDCODE.
```

```
500-END-OF-JOB.
    CLOSE PAYROLL-FILE, TRANSACTIONS.
    IF PAYROLL-STATUS-CODE NOT EQUAL TO ZEROS
            PERFORM 920-STATUS-ERROR-ON-CLOSE
            CALL 'ABEND' USING CONDCODE.
* DUPLICATE OR OUT OF SEQUENCE ROUTINE
600-DUP-OR-OOS.
    ..........
900-STATUS-ERROR-ON-OPEN.
    DISPLAY 'OPEN ERROR ON PAYROLL MASTER, STATUS CODE '
            PAYROLL-STATUS-CODE.
    CLOSE PAYROLL-FILE.
910-STATUS-ERROR-ON-WRITE.
    DISPLAY 'WRITE ERROR ON PAYROLL MASTER, STATUS CODE '
            PAYROLL-STATUS-CODE.
    CLOSE PAYROLL-FILE.
920-STATUS-ERROR-ON-CLOSE.
    DISPLAY 'CLOSE ERROR ON PAYROLL MASTER, STATUS CODE '
            PAYROLL-STATUS-CODE.
    CLOSE PAYROLL-FILE.
```

In this example a sequential data set (TRANSACTIONS) is read and the records are output to a KSDS. For a **load** operation, the data set must be OPENed for OUTPUT. In the example found in Section 15.3.2, a **START** command could be used sometime after OPEN. This would allow the program to position itself for sequential reading at a point other than the beginning of the file. Repositioning can occur as often as desired during processing.

15.3.4 RANDOM RETRIEVAL, ADDITION, AND DELETION

In the following example, a KSDS cluster is updated.

```
ENVIRONMENT DIVISION.
FILE-CONTROL.
    SELECT PAYROLL-FILE ASSIGN TO PAYDD
    ORGANIZATION IS INDEXED
    ACCESS IS INDEXED
    RECORD KEY IS PAY-KEY
    FILE STATUS IS PAYROLL-STATUS-CODE.

DATA DIVISION.
FILE SECTION.
FD    PAYROLL-FILE.......
```

```
01      PAY-REC.
    03      PAY-KEY      PICTURE 9(6).
    .
WORKING-STORAGE SECTION.
01      PAYROLL-STATUS-CODE      PICTURE 99 VALUE ZEROS.

IDENTIFICATION DIVISION.
000-HOUSEKEEPING.
    OPEN INPUT TRANSACTIONS, I-O PAYROLL-FILE.
    IF PAYROLL-STATUS-CODE NOT EQUAL TO ZEROS
                PERFORM 900-STATUS-ERROR-ON-OPEN
                CALL 'ABEND' USING CONDCODE.
100-READ-TRANSACTION.
    READ TRANSACTION, AT END GO TO 500-END-OF-JOB.
    MOVE TRANSACTION-KEY TO PAY-KEY.
    READ PAYROLL-FILE, INVALID KEY PERFORM 650-NOT-FOUND.
    IF PAYROLL-STATUS-CODE IS NOT EQUAL TO ZEROS
                  PERFORM 910-STATUS-ERROR-ON-READ
                  CALL 'ABEND' USING CONDCODE.
    IF TRANSACTION-CODE = 'C' PERFORM 200-CHANGES-ROUTINE.
    IF TRANSACTION-CODE = 'D' PERFORM 300-DELETE-RECORD.
    IF TRANSACTION-CODE = 'A' PERFORM 400-ADD-RECORD.
    GO TO 100-READ-TRANSACTION.
200-CHANGES-ROUTINE.
    .
    REWRITE PAY-REC.
    IF PAYROLL-STATUS-CODE IS NOT EQUAL TO ZEROS
                  PERFORM 905-STATUS-ERROR-ON-REWRITE
                  CALL 'ABEND' USING CONDCODE.
300-DELETE-RECORD.
    DELETE PAYROLL-FILE RECORD.
    IF PAYROLL-STATUS-CODE IS NOT EQUAL TO ZEROS
                 PERFORM 925-STATUS-ERROR-ON-DELETE
                 CALL 'ABEND' USING CONDCODE.
400-ADD-RECORD.
    WRITE PAY-REC.
    IF PAYROLL-STATUS-CODE IS NOT EQUAL TO ZEROS
                 PERFORM 915-STATUS-ERROR-ON-WRITE
                 CALL 'ABEND' USING CONDCODE.
500-END-OF-JOB.
    CLOSE PAYROLL-FILE, TRANSACTIONS.
    IF PAYROLL-STATUS-CODE NOT EQUAL TO ZEROS
               PERFORM 920-STATUS-ERROR-ON-CLOSE
               CALL 'ABEND' USING CONDCODE.
900-STATUS-ERROR-ON-OPEN.
```

```
         DISPLAY 'OPEN ERROR ON PAYROLL MASTER, STATUS CODE '
                 PAYROLL-STATUS-CODE.
         CLOSE PAYROLL-FILE.
     905-STATUS-ERROR-ON-REWRITE.
         DISPLAY 'REWRITE ERROR ON PAYROLL MASTER, STATUS CODE '
                 PAYROLL-STATUS-CODE.
         CLOSE PAYROLL-FILE.
     910-STATUS-ERROR-ON-READ.
         DISPLAY 'READ ERROR ON PAYROLL MASTER, STATUS CODE '
                 PAYROLL-STATUS-CODE.
         CLOSE PAYROLL-FILE.
     915-STATUS-ERROR-ON-WRITE.
         DISPLAY 'WRITE ERROR ON PAYROLL MASTER, STATUS CODE '
                 PAYROLL-STATUS-CODE.
         CLOSE PAYROLL-FILE.
     920-STATUS-ERROR-ON-CLOSE.
         DISPLAY 'CLOSE ERROR ON PAYROLL MASTER, STATUS CODE '
                 PAYROLL-STATUS-CODE.
         CLOSE PAYROLL-FILE.
     925-STATUS-ERROR-ON-DELETE.
         DISPLAY 'DELETE ERROR ON PAYROLL MASTER, STATUS CODE '
                 PAYROLL-STATUS-CODE.
         CLOSE PAYROLL-FILE.
```

In the preceding example, a sequential transaction file is read. Records containing a code **C** will be changed and rewritten, and records containing a **D** will cause the corresponding payroll record to be deleted. When code **A** is encountered, the record is added to the payroll file. If a record is not found, a message will be displayed to that effect.

Special note: A COBOL program can access a file for both sequential and random access. When this feature is desired, the file must be opened as **DYNAMIC** instead of INPUT or OUTPUT as the case may be. Further information can be found in the appropriate language publication.

15.4 DEFINING THE FILE IN PL/I

A VSAM file is defined in a PL/I program with a Declare statement (**DCL**).

15.4.1 THE DCL (DECLARE) STATEMENT

The format of the DCL statement (for VSAM) is as follows:

```
DCL filename FILE RECORD
             SEQUENTIAL | DIRECT
             KEYED
             OUTPUT | INPUT | UPDATE
             ENVIRONMENT(
                 BUFND(number)
                 BUFNI(number)
                 BUFSP(number)
                 VSAM
                 SIS
                 SKIP
                 REUSE
                 BKWD
                 PASSWORD(password-field) )
```

Note: the ENVIRONMENT parameter can be abbreviated **ENV**.

EXPLANATION OF THE DECLARATION FIELDS

SEQUENTIAL | DIRECT:

This identifies the mode of processing. This statement is similar to the ORGANIZATION statement in COBOL.

KEYED:

Specifies whether the data set is to be processed sequentially or by key. **KEY** refers to any kind of key, whether the key is an RBA, an RRN, or a data key such as an employee number.

OUTPUT | INPUT | UPDATE:

This specifies the **mode** of processing: input, output, or both.

THE FOLLOWING ARE THE FIELDS OF THE **ENVIRONMENT** PARAMETER:

BUFND(number):

This allows you to specify the number of data control interval buffers.

BUFNI(number):

This allows specification of the number of index control interval buffers desired.

BUFSP(number):

This parameter allows you to specify the number of bytes desired for buffer space.

VSAM:

This parameter specifies that this is a VSAM file definition.

SIS:

This option allows you to specify that **sequential insert strategy** is to be used when adding records to a data set. See Chapter 5 for more information on this subject.

SKIP:

This allows records to be processed **skip-sequentially**. Skip-sequential allows the program to **skip** over large groups of records when retrieving records sequentially. When using this option, only forward skipping is allowed. See also Chapter 16 for more information.

REUSE:

This parameter specifies this data set to be a **reusable** cluster.

BKWD:

With this option, the cluster can be read backward. See also Chapter 16.

PASSWORD(password-field):

A password can be supplied either as a string constant or a string variable. This password is compared to the cluster password when the data set is opened. Cluster passwords are declared for the cluster when the cluster is initially defined through Access Method Services.

15.4.2 THE PL/I VERBS

OPEN —Connect an application program to a data set
READ —Retrieve a record from the data set
WRITE —Output a record to the data set
REWRITE—Replace a record within the data set
DELETE —Erase a record from the data set
CLOSE —Disconnect a data set from an application

15.5 CODING PROGRAMS IN PL/I FOR VSAM ACCESS

The following are examples of VSAM access through PL/I applications.

15.5.1 SAMPLE ESDS RETRIEVAL PROGRAM

```
VSAMSEQ : PROC OPTIONS(MAIN);
DCL     VSAMIN     FILE
                   RECORD
                   SEQUENTIAL
                   INPUT
                   ENV(VSAM);



/* IF VSAM RETURNS AN ERROR CODE PRINT A MESSAGE, ABEND
*/
ON UNDEFINEDFILE(VSAMIN) ..................
ON ENDFILE(VSAMIN) EOF-VSAMIN = '1'B;
OPEN FILE(VSAMIN);
      READ FILE(VSAMIN) INTO(INPUT-AREA);
      DO UNTIL EOF-VSAMIN;


          READ FILE(VSAMIN) INTO(INPUT-AREA);
      END;
      CLOSE FILE(VSAMIN);
END VSAMSEQ;
```

This program reads an ESDS data set and does some processing. If an error code is returned by VSAM, a message will be displayed and the program terminated.

15.5.2 SAMPLE NON-ESDS RETRIEVAL PROGRAM

```
VSAMKSEQ : PROC OPTIONS(MAIN);
DCL     VSAMIN     FILE
                   RECORD
                   SEQUENTIAL
                   KEYED
                   INPUT
                   ENV(VSAM);
```

```
.
.
/* IF VSAM RETURNS AN ERROR CODE PRINT A MESSAGE, ABEND
*/
ON UNDEFINEDFILE(VSAMIN) ..................
ON ENDFILE(VSAMIN) EOF-VSAMIN = '1'B;
OPEN FILE(VSAMIN);
      READ FILE(VSAMIN) INTO(INPUT-AREA);
      DO UNTIL EOF-VSAMIN;
         .
         READ FILE(VSAMIN) INTO(INPUT-AREA);
      END;
      CLOSE FILE(VSAMIN);
END VSAMKSEQ;
```

In this example records are retrieved sequentially from a KSDS or RRDS data set. Other than adding the **KEYED** statement, there is no difference between this example and the one preceding it.

15.5.3 LOADING (CREATING) A KSDS CLUSTER

```
VSAMLOAD : PROC OPTIONS(MAIN);
/* DEFINE VSAM OUTPUT FILE */
DCL     VSAMOUT     FILE
                    RECORD
                    SEQUENTIAL
                    KEYED
                    OUTPUT
                    ENV(VSAM);

/* DEFINE SEQUENTIAL INPUT CARD FILE /*
DCL     INPUTFL     FILE
                    RECORD
                    INPUT
                    ENV(MEDIUM(SYSIPT) );
   .

/* IF VSAM RETURNS AN ERROR CODE PRINT A MESSAGE, ABEND */
ON UNDEFINEDFILE(VSAMOUT) ..................
OPEN FILE(VSAMOUT), FILE(INPUTFL);
ON ENDFILE(INPUTFL) EOF-INPUTFL = '1'B;
READ FILE(INPUTFL) INTO(INPUT-AREA);

DO WHILE(¬EOF-INPUTFL);
   OUTPUT-AREA = INPUT-AREA, BY NAME;
   WRITE FILE(VSAMOUT) FROM(OUTPUT-AREA)
```

```
        KEYFROM(KEYFIELD);
        READ FILE(INPUTFL) INTO(INPUT-AREA);
    END;
    CLOSE FILE(VSAMOUT), FILE(INPUTFL);
    END VSAMLOAD;
```

In this example a sequential input file is read and records are used to create a KEYED VSAM file. The VSAM file can be a KSDS or an RRDS, depending on how it was defined to Access Method Services. The SYSIPT operand of the ENV statement is required for DOS only.

15.5.4 RANDOM RETRIEVAL, ADDITION, AND DELETION

```
VSAMUPDT : PROC OPTIONS(MAIN);
/* DEFINE VSAM UPDATE FILE */
DCL    VSAMIO      FILE
                   RECORD
                   DIRECT
                   KEYED
                   UPDATE
                   ENV(VSAM
                        BUFND(2)
                        BUFNI(2)
                        SIS
                        );

/* DEFINE SEQUENTIAL TRANSACTION FILE/*
DCL    INPUTFL     FILE
                   RECORD
                   INPUT
                   ENV(MEDIUM(SYSIPT) ),

       INPUT-RECORD     CHAR(80);
DCL    1    OUTPUT-AREA
         .
         .
/* IF VSAM RETURNS AN ERROR CODE PRINT A MESSAGE, ABEND */
ON UNDEFINEDFILE(VSAMOUT) ..................
OPEN FILE(VSAMIO), FILE(INPUTFL);
ON ENDFILE(INPUTFL) EOF-INPUTFL = '1'B;
READ FILE(INPUTFL) INTO(INPUT-AREA);

DO WHILE(¬EOF-INPUTFL);
```

```
      OUTPUT-AREA = INPUT-AREA, BY NAME;
      IF TRANCODE = 'A' DO;
        WRITE FILE(VSAMIO) FROM(OUTPUT-AREA) KEY(KEYFIELD);
        END;
      IF TRANCODE = 'C' DO;


        REWRITE FILE(VSAMIO) FROM(OUTPUT-AREA)
                             KEY(KEYFIELD);
        END;
      IF TRANCODE = 'D' DO;

        END;
       READ FILE(INPUTFL) INTO(INPUT-AREA);
    END;

    CLOSE FILE(VSAMOUT), FILE(INPUTFL);
    END VSAMUPDT;
```

In this example records are read from a transaction file (INPUTFL). These records cause additions, deletions, and changes to be made to a VSAM KSDS. You may have noticed that two buffers were specifically requested for the data and index control intervals. Sequential insert strategy (SIS) was also requested. These options are not available in COBOL.

In the preceding example you will notice an **ON UNDEFINEDFILE** was used. This facility works very much like the COBOL **FILE STATUS**. When VSAM encounters an unusual situation, a return code is passed back to the application by means of this facility.

The return codes for both COBOL and PL/I can be found in the various language reference manuals. The codes used by PL/I are different from those used by COBOL. Furthermore, the codes differ between the OS and DOS operating systems.

TEST YOUR UNDERSTANDING

1. Explain the statements used in a COBOL program to describe how a VSAM file is to be processed.

2. What is the difference between describing an ESDS and a KSDS in the COBOL ENVIRONMENT DIVISION?
3. Name a few of the VSAM processing options available to PL/I that are not accessible in COBOL.
4. What is the meaning of the SIS keyword in PL/I?
5. What is the FILE STATUS code field? How is it used?

chapter 16

USING VSAM IN ASSEMBLER LANGUAGE

It is very convenient to write VSAM applications in high-level languages such as COBOL or PL/I; programming is greatly simplified by using one of them. There are occasions, however, when one of VSAM's special facilities is required. When this occurs you have no choice but to write the code in assembler language. This chapter presents the capabilities available to the assembler programmer through the use of VSAM macros.

16.1 VSAM SPECIAL PROCESSING FEATURES

Special capabilities available only to the assembler programmer include the following:

Asynchronous processing
Chained RPLs
Performing IDCAMS functions from within the program
Usage of LSR (Chapter 14)

Mode switching
Enhanced access to the catalog, index, or CRA areas
Journaling and update routines
User exits

16.1.1 ASYNCHRONOUS PROCESSING

When compared to CPU processing speed, I/O operations take a **very** long time to complete. Most applications require that the I/O be completed before the program can do any further work. There are sometimes situations in which a great deal of work could be performed by the application **while** the I/O operation is in progress. VSAM, like other access methods, allows the assembler program to initiate an I/O operation such as a read while allowing the program to continue processing, rather than forcing it into a **wait** state. This is accomplished by specifying the **OPTCD=ASY** parameter of the **RPL** macro (see Section 16.2). This capability could be extended to high-level languages only through **called** assembler routines.

16.1.2 CHAINED RPLS

RPL chaining is the ability to initiate **multiple consecutive I/O operations** with a single macro request. When setting up for an I/O operation, the program can specify to VSAM the action to take place when the I/O operation is complete. VSAM can be instructed either to give control back to the application program at the point after which the macro was executed, or to begin another I/O operation automatically. This is accomplished through data transfer macros such as GET and PUT, and through the RPL (Request Parameter List) macro. The first I/O can be chained to the second, which can be chained to a third, and so forth.

GET and PUT macros always specify an RPL. One RPL is required for each read or write operation. When the processing of an RPL is complete, you can optionally point to another RPL with the **NXTRPL** operand. The effect is to initiate multiple I/O operations with a single GET or PUT (see Figure 16.1).

16.1.3 PERFORMING IDCAMS FUNCTIONS FROM WITHIN THE PROGRAM

Access Method Services commands can be executed from within an assembler program. This is accomplished differently for OS and for DOS/VSE. This topic is discussed in detail at the end of this chapter.

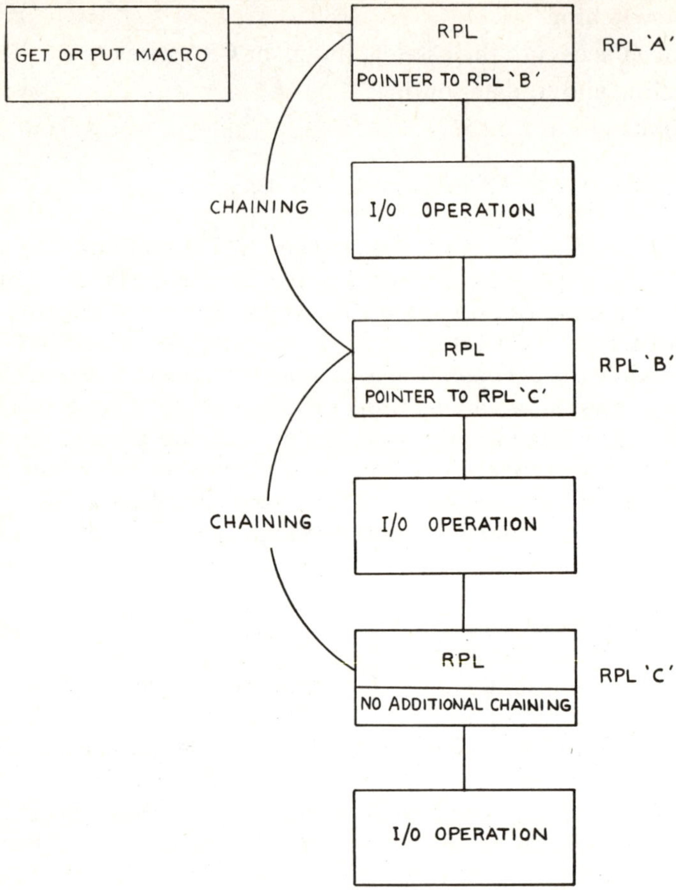

Figure 16.1 RPL chaining.

16.1.4 USING THE LSR FEATURE

You can make use of the **Local Shared Resource** buffering facilities by specifying this option in your **ACB** (Access Control Block). The LSR feature is explained in Chapter 14, and the ACB macro is described in Section 16.4.

16.1.5 MODE SWITCHING

The application program can switch processing states and options through the use of the **MODCB** macro. Without repetitive opening and closing of the data set, an application can, for instance, switch the processing of data between the sequential and the direct mode. This can be done as often as required. It is sometimes useful, for instance, to change the insert strategy between SIS (Sequential Insert Strategy) and NIS (Normal or Direct Insert Strategy). Sequential and direct insert are discussed in Chapter 5. There are other processing options you may wish to specify as well. The MODCB macro is explained later in this chapter.

16.1.6 ENHANCED ACCESS TO THE CATALOG, INDEX, AND CRA

Access to the catalog and CRA can be specified in the ACB macro using the **CATALOG** and **CRA** operands. In addition to this, the GETIX and PUTIX macros are available for accessing the index component of a KSDS. The GETIX and PUTIX macros are identical in format to GET and PUT, but are used exclusively for index processing.

16.1.7 USER-DEVELOPED JOURNALING AND UPDATE ROUTINES

User exits can be written and specified to VSAM to allow for journaling and to monitor file accesses. The method of coding these routines is explained near the end of this chapter. The **EXLST** (Exit List) macro defines to VSAM the routines to be used for these optional functions. The **JRNAD** parameter is used to specify the journaling routine address; the **UPAD** parameter specifies the address of the file update checking routine.

16.1.8 USER EXITS

In addition to the preceding routines, other user exits can be specified by the EXLST macro for problem handling and end-of-file notification. The **SYNAD** operand defines an exit to be used for the analyzing of physical errors, **LERAD** is used for analyzing logical errors, and **EODAD** describes the name of the routine to which control is passed when an end-of-file creation is encountered.

16.2 PROGRAM STRUCTURE

In order to write a VSAM application, at least two VSAM and three non-VSAM macros are required. The VSAM macros are: ACB and RPL. The non-VSAM macros are: OPEN and CLOSE, and GET or PUT.

The cornerstone of a VSAM program is the ACB. The VSAM Access Method Control Block provides functions similar to those of a DTF (DOS) or DCB (OS). The main purpose of the ACB is to connect the program to the data set you wish to process. Like the DCB/DTF, the ACB provides other facilities as well. These functions include: definition of I/O areas, buffer usage, input or output processing, sequential or direct access, exit handling, DD or DLBL name, and password protection. The ACB is connected to the application at **OPEN** time through the use of the OPEN macro.

The transfer of data in or out is controlled by the **GET** and **PUT** macros. Unlike other access methods, the GET or PUT macros do not point to the ACB directly. Rather, they point to an RPL macro which, in turn, points to an ACB.

The **RPL** fulfills two functions: to provide certain operand information not found in the ACB, and to provide an **override** facility that temporarily

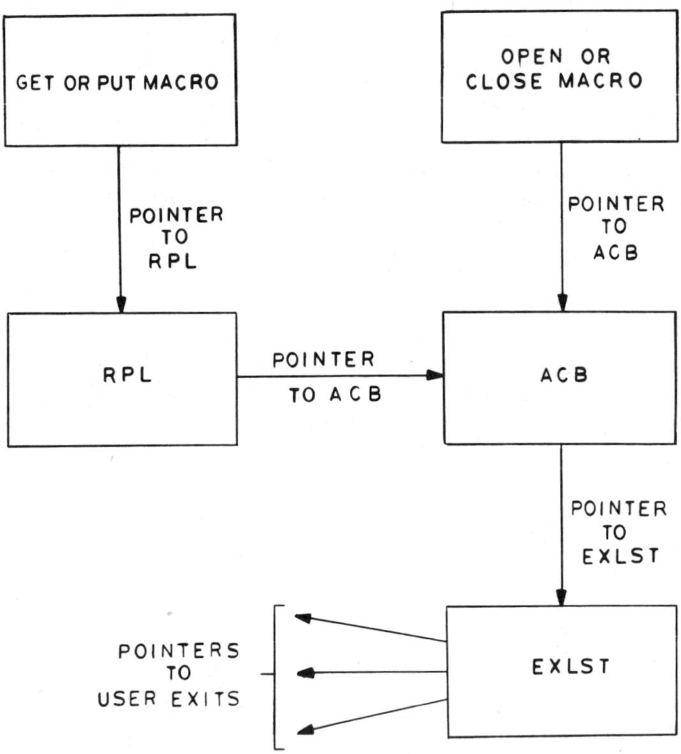

Figure 16.2 Relationship between VSAM macros.

modifies certain options specified in the ACB. Figure 16.2 shows the relationship between the various macros.

16.3 DESCRIBING THE MACROS

VSAM macros can be said to fall into two distinct categories: commonly used macros and seldom used macros.

16.3.1 COMMONLY USED VSAM MACROS

The following represent the more commonly used VSAM macros:

ACB —Access Control Block
RPL —Request Parameter List
GET —Read a record or control interval
PUT —Write a record or control interval
EXLST —List program exits
ERASE —Delete a record
POINT —Position a pointer within a data set
TESTCB —Test for successful completion of an event
SHOWCB—Examine VSAM control block information

16.3.2 LESS FREQUENTLY USED VSAM MACROS

CHECK —Test if an I/O operation has completed
CLOSE —TYPE=T, temporary close (OS)
TCLOSE—Temporary close (DOS)
ENDREQ—Terminate a positioning request
GENCB —Generate a VSAM control block (macro) dynamically
MODCB —Modify a VSAM control block (macro)

16.4 THE ACB MACRO

The format of the ACB macro is as follows:

```
[label]   ACB   [AM=VSAM]
                [,BSTRNO=number ]
                [,BUFND=number ]
```

```
[,BUFNI=number ]
[,CATALOG=YES | NO ]
[,CRA=SCRA | UCRA]
[,DDNAME=name on jcl card
[,MACRF=[ADR | CNV | KEY ]
        [,NFX | CFX ]
        [,DDN | DSN ]
        [,DFR | NDF ]
        [,DIR | SEQ | SKP ]
        [,ICI | NCI ]
        [,IN | OUT ]
        [,NIS | SIS ]
        [,NRM | AIX ]
        [,NRS | RST ]
        [,NSR | LSR ]
        [,NUB | UBF ]
[,MAREA=address ]
[,MLEN=length ]
[,PASSWD=address ]
[,PARMS=CLOSDSP=KEEP | DELETE | DATE ]
[,STRNO=number ]
```

16.4.1 EXPLANATION OF THE ACB PARAMETERS

Label:

This is the name given to the ACB for purposes of reference by the program. It is also the address of the ACB macro.

AM=VSAM:

This specifies the access method used for this ACB. The reason that you specify the access method is that this macro is also used by **VTAM**, the Virtual Telecommunications Access Method. VSAM is the default.

BSTRNO=number:

This specifies the number of strings initially allocated for access to the base cluster of a path. If not specified, the value defaults to the value specified in the STRNO parameter. This parameter is ignored if the object opened is not a path.

BUFND=number:
BUFNI=number:

BUFSP=number:

These parameters specify the number of buffers that VSAM will use for data (BUFND) and index (BUFNI) records. You can also specify the space (BUFSP) in bytes, used for buffers. These parameters are optional. If omitted, VSAM will use values specified in the catalog. These operands can be overridden with JCL statements.

CATALOG=YES | NO:

This parameter allows you to specify whether the catalog is opened as a catalog or a data set. Specifying **NO** allows the catalog to be processed like a data set using GET and PUT macros. If **YES** is specified, a special SVC (supervisor call) routine must be written to access the catalog. AMS uses SVC 26 to perform catalog access and modifications. Default is NO.

CRA=SCRA | UCRA:

The parameter allows you to access the Catalog Recovery Area. The data can be returned either in a user area (**UCRA**) or a system area (**SCRA**).

DDNAME=name:

This parameter states the name of the DD (OS) or DLBL (DOS) statement that describes the data set to be opened.

EXLST=address:

This specifies the name of the EXLST macro that contains the address of exits to be taken under certain circumstances. The specification is also the address of the EXLST.

MACRF=. Parameters follow:
ADR | CNV | KEY:

This specifies how the data are to be accessed: by RBA (**ADR**), by control interval (**CNV**), or by key (**KEY**). KEY is the default.

NFX | CFX:

This specifies whether VSAM control blocks and buffers should be page fixed (**CFX**) or not (**NFX**). Default is no page fix.

DDN | DSN: (OS ONLY)

With this option VSAM control blocks can be shared by subtasks on either a ddname or dsname basis. **DDN** is the default. This facility allows a certain **bonding** of ACBs by a common denominator, namely, a ddname or dsname. This operation causes integrity to be maintained among unrelated tasks. This facility can be especially useful when using SHAREOPTIONS(3).

DFR | NDF:

This specifies whether put requests will be **deferred** until either a WRTBFR macro is issued, or there is no longer any buffer space available. Default is **NDF**.

DIR | SEQ | SKP:

This parameter allows specification of VSAM's processing mode, direct (**DIR**), sequential (**SEQ**), or skip-sequential (**SKP**). Skip-sequential processing is a form of sequential access. The difference is that whole sections of records can be **skipped** over by specifying a new key. Skip-sequential only works in a forward direction. Once records are skipped over, you can continue sequential access. Record keys lower than the current key are invalid. Default is **SEQ**.

ICI | **NCI**:

This specifies, for control interval processing, whether normal or improved control interval processing will be used. If improved CI processing is selected, be sure to adhere to the restrictions for its use (see Chapter 14). Default is **NCI**.

IN | **OUT**:

This specifies whether the file is to be opened for input or output. **IN** is the default.

NIS | **SIS**:

This specifies the insertion strategy to be used: sequential (SIS) or direct (NIS). See Chapter 5 for details. Default is **NIS**.

NRM | **AIX**:

This parameter lets you specify whether the object to be accessed is an alternate index (**AIX**) or the object specified (path or file) in the DDNAME parameter. Default is **NRM**.

NRS | **RST**:

This specifies whether, for reusable data sets, the open routine is to reset the HIGH-USED RBA to zero (**RST**). If **NSR** is specified, no reset is performed.

NSR | **LSR**:

This specifies whether the Local Shared Resource facility is to be used (**LSR**) or not (**NSR**). See Chapter 14 for the discussion on LSR. Default is **NSR**.

NUB | **UBF**:

This states whether user buffering (**UBF**) or normal (nonuser) VSAM buffering (**NUB**) will be used. If UBF is specified, an entire control interval is placed in the area identified in the **AREA** parameter. Control interval processing **CNV** must also be specified for this option. Default is **NUB**.

MAREA=address:

This specifies the address of an area that will receive any OPEN, CLOSE, or TCLOSE messages. The application can examine these messages and take some action if required.

MLEN=length:

This specifies the length of MAREA previously defined.

PASSWD=:

This specifies the name of a field that contains the password. The first byte of the field contains the length of the password in binary; this is followed by the password itself.

PARMS=CLOSDSP=KEEP | DELETE | DATE: (DOS ONLY)

This specifies the final status of a reusable data set at CLOSE time. **KEEP** allows the file to be retained; **DELETE** deletes the file; **DATE** deletes the file if it is beyond the expiration date, otherwise it is kept.

STRNO=number:

This specifies the number of strings or position holders that VSAM is to reserve for use by the application. A position holder is required for each position pointer when concurrent data set positioning is used. If additional strings are required, VSAM will dynamically allocate them. Strings dynamically allocated may have an effect on processing time since the control blocks may not necessarily be contained within the same virtual page frame. This could cause page faults.

16.5 THE GET AND PUT MACROS

```
[label]    GET    RPL=address
[label]    PUT    RPL=address
```

16.5.1 EXPLANATION OF GET AND PUT PARAMETERS

Label:

This is the name given to the GET or PUT macro for purposes of reference by the program. It is also the address of the GET or PUT macro.

RPL=address:

This specifies the address of the RPL.

16.6 THE RPL MACRO

```
[label]    RPL    [ACB=address ]
                  [AM=VSAM]
                  [,AREA=address ]
                  [,AREALEN=length ]
                  [,ARG=address ]
                  [,ECB=address ]
                  [,KEYLEN=length ]
                  [,MSGAREA=address ]
                  [,MSGLEN=length ]
```

```
[,NXTRPL=address ]
[,OPTCD=[ADR | CNV | KEY ]
        [,DIR | SEQ | SKP ]
        [,ARD | LRD ]
        [,FWD | BWD ]
        [,SYN | ASY ]
        [,NSP | NUP | UPD ]
        [,KEQ | KGE ]
        [,FKS | GEN ]
        [,MVE | LOC ]
        [,NOWAITX | WAITX ]
[,RECLEN=length ]
[,TRANSID=number ]
```

16.6.1 EXPLANATION OF THE RPL OPERANDS

Label:

This is the name given to the RPL for purposes of reference by the program. It is also the address of the RPL macro.

AM=VSAM:

This specifies the access method used for this RPL. The reason that you specify the access method is that this macro is also used by **VTAM**, the Virtual Telecommunications Access Method. **VSAM** is the default.

AREA=address:

This parameter may serve one of the following purposes. First, it specifies a work area in which VSAM moves the data record. The data record is moved into this area when OPTCD=MVE (move mode) is specified. Second, if OPTCD=LOC (locate mode) is specified, the address of the record, within the VSAM buffer, is returned in this area.

AREALEN:

This parameter specifies the number of bytes set aside for the AREA parameter previously described.

ARG=address:

This specifies the address of the field containing the search argument for direct or skip-sequential retrieval. If a KEY is to be moved into this area, the field length must be large enough to contain the key. If retrieval is by RRN or RBA, a four-byte area is required.

ECB=address:

This allows specification of an Event Control Block. ECBs are not restricted to VSAM. They are used in all access methods to indicate when some event has completed. In our case it indicates the status of an I/O operation. It is also used for multitasking and in the telecommunication access methods. For further information on the ECB macro and its various uses, see the macro manuals available with your operating system.

KEYLEN = length:

This specifies the length of the key field. Maximum length of a key is 255 bytes. This field is not required for full key retrievals since the key length is known from information found in the catalog. When a generic search is required, you may want to specify only part of the key. In this case, you can specify the length here. There is an alternative to this; see the GEN operand.

MSGAREA = address:

This specifies the address of an area that will receive any messages encountered during data transfer. The application can examine these messages and take appropriate action if required.

MSGLEN = length:

This specifies the length of the MSGAREA previously defined.

NXTRPL = address:

This parameter allows you to chain RPLs together. When the I/O operation specified in the current RPL has completed, the I/O operation specified in the next RPL will be initiated. The second may point to a third and so forth. Multiple I/O operations can, therefore, be initiated by a single GET or PUT macro.

OPTCD = : Parameters follow:
ADR | CNV | KEY:

This specifies how the data is to be accessed: by RBA (**ADR**), by control interval (**CNV**), or by key (**KEY**). **KEY** is the default.

DIR | SEQ | SKP:

This parameter allows specification of VSAM's processing mode, direct (**DIR**), sequential (**SEQ**), or skip-sequential (**SKP**). Skip-sequential processing is a form of sequential access. The difference is that whole sections of records can be **skipped** over by specifying a new key. Skip-sequential only works in a forward direction. Record keys lower than the current key are invalid. Default is **SEQ**.

ARD | LRD:

This specifies the starting position for the record transfer operation, whether read or write. If **ARD** is specified, the user will supply an argument specifying the starting position within the file. **LRD** requests that VSAM set its pointers to the last record in the data set. If backward retrieval is desired, OPTCD = BWD must be specified. ARD is for forward, LRD for backward.

SYN | **ASY**:

This specifies whether the request will be processed as asynchronous (**ASY**) or synchronous (**SYN**). When ASY is requested, the program will not be forced into a wait state while an I/O is in progress. Processing and I/O can overlap with this option. This can, at times, drastically reduce the amount of time a program runs. The TESTCB macro can be used or the ECB tested to check whether the I/O operation has completed. The CHECK macro can also be used; in that case, the program will be placed into a wait state if the I/O operation has not completed. Caution is advised with the ASY option. SYN forces the program into a wait state until the I/O operation is completed. Default is **SYN**.

NSP | **NUP** | **UPD**:

When **NSP** is specified, VSAM will remember the current record position. This option is used only when OPTCD = DIR is specified. Using this parameter allows for subsequent sequential retrieval. **UPD** is used when retrieving records for update or deletion. VSAM keeps track of its position for sequential and direct GET requests. **NUP** specifies that records being retrieved will not be updated or deleted. New records may be added to the file, but no updating of existing records will take place. VSAM does not make any effort to remember its position with this option. Default is **NUP**.

KEQ | **KGE**:

This specifies the key matching process to be used by VSAM. If **KEY** is specified, the argument used (**AGR =**) must match the key of the record to be retrieved, regardless of whether the key is a key, an RBA, or an RRN. If **KGE** is specified, the **next higher** record is returned to the program if the argument key is not found. Default is **KEY**.

FKS | **GEN**:

This specifies whether a full key search (**FKS**) or a generic search (**GEN**) shall be performed. **FKS** is the default.

MVE | **LOC**:

This specifies whether the move (**MVE**) or locate (**LOC**) mode of operation is to be used. When MVE is specified, the data record is moved into the work area (AREA) from the I/O buffer. **LOC** allows you to address the record directly in the I/O buffer.

NOWAITX | **WAITX**:

If **NOWAITX** is specified, VSAM will never branch to the user's **UPAD** routine, even if the UPAD operand was specified in the EXLST macro. The UPAD routine gets control every time a file is accessed. If **WAITX** is specified, and OPTCD = SYN, VSAM will give control to the UPAD exit routine during the time the application would normally be in the wait state. **NOWAITX** is the default.

RECLEN = length:

This parameter must be used with the PUT macro. It specifies the length of the record to be written. This parameter is used for variable length record inserts.

TRANSID = number:

This parameter allows the specification of a transaction ID number. This number is related to deferred-PUT records when using LSR. The records can be then later identified and grouped logically and later output by specifying a **WRTBRF** macro. WRTBRF and LSR are explained in Chapter 14.

16.7 THE EXLST MACRO

The EXLST provides a means of establishing special user exit routines. The most useful and most widely used routine is the EODAD routine. VSAM passes control to the EODAD (end of data) routine whenever an end-of-file condition is encountered for an input file. The other special exits are described in the following. The format of the EXLST macro is as follows:

```
[label]    EXLST    [AM=VSAM]
                    [,EODAD=address [,A | N ] [,L ]
                    [,JRNAD=address [,A | N ] [,L ]
                    [,LERAD=address [,A | N ] [,L ]
                    [,SYNAD=address [,A | N ] [,L ]
                    [,UPAD=address [,A | N ] [,L ]
```

16.7.1 EXPLANATION OF THE EXLST PARAMETERS

Label:

This is the name given to the EXLST macro for purposes of reference by the program. It is also the address of the EXLST macro.

AM = VSAM:

This specifies the access method used for this EXLST macro. The reason that you specify the access method is that this macro is also used by **VTAM**, the Virtual Telecommunications Access Method. **VSAM** is the default.

EODAD = address:

This specifies the address of a routine to be entered when VSAM encounters an end-of-file condition during sequential retrieval.

JRNAD = address:

This specifies the address of a routine to be given control whenever an I/O operation is performed. This routine is used for **journaling** purposes. See Section 16.18 for more information.

LERAD=address:

This specifies the address of a routine to be given control whenever a **logical** error condition occurs. A logical error condition usually is encountered when macros are specified incorrectly or do not match the definition of the data set. See Section 16.18 for more information.

SYNAD=address:

This specifies the address of a routine to be given control whenever a **physical** error condition occurs. A physical error condition is caused by an I/O error. See Section 16.18 for more information.

UPAD=address:

This specifies the address of a routine to be given control during an I/O operation and at the point in which VSAM would normally issue a wait. This facility is invoked by specifying **OPTCD=(SYN,WAITX)**. See the user exit section for more information.

A | N:

This specifies whether the exit routine is active (**A**) or not active (**N**).

L:

For OS, **L** specifies the address of an eight-byte field that contains the name of the exit routine. The exit routine, in this case, will be stored in a partitioned data set identified by a JOBLIB or STEPLIB DD card, or resides in SYS1.LINKLIB. This option is not available for DOS.

16.8 SAMPLE VSAM PROGRAM USING ACB, RPL, GET, AND EXLST

This program reads a VSAM KSDS cluster sequentially.

```
START     OPEN    VSAMACB
          "
          "
GETREC    GET     RPL=VSAMRPL      POINT TO RPL FOR I/O
          "
          "
          "
          B       GETREC      GET NEXT RECORD
ENDFILE   CLOSE   VSAMACB       CLOSE THE FILE
          "
          "
          EOJ     (RETURN)      END OF JOB
VSAMRPL   RPL     ACB=VSAMACB,AREA=RECORD,                     +
```

```
                         AREALEN=100,                          +
                       OPTCD=(KEY,SEQ,MVE,NUP)
VSAMACB   ACB          BUFND=4,BUFNI=6,EXLST=EXITLIST,         +
                       MACRF=(KEY,SEQ),DDNAME=INVENTRY
EXITLIST  EXLST        EODAD=ENDFILE
RECORD    DS           CL100      WORK AREA FOR RECORD
          END
```

In this example a KSDS file is being accessed sequentially (OPTCD=SEQ and MACRF=SEQ). Move mode (MVE) causes VSAM to place the records read into the work area specified (RECORD). The program will continue to read records (GETREC routine) until an end-of-file condition occurs. At that time, the EODAD exit specified in the EXLST macro (ENDFILE) will be given control.

Notice the connections between the macros. OPEN and CLOSE point to the ACB. GET points to the RPL which, in turn, points to the ACB. The ACB points to the EXLST. The preceding example will work. However, if you have an error in one of the macros such as an incorrect dsname, or if the data set requires a VERIFY command, the application will probably abend. This is because no testing was performed to determine whether any of the macros executed successfully.

In order to test for a successful macro completion, you must place the following instruction behind the macro last executed:

LTR 15,15

After executing a macro, VSAM places a condition code in register 15. The preceding instruction loads the contents of one register into another register (in this case, into itself). It also sets a condition code in the PSW according to the value found in the register (zero or not zero). A zero return code is an indication of a normal macro completion.

The LTR instruction must be followed by a branch instruction to be effective. Example:

```
        LTR  15,15       LOAD AND TEST REG. 15
        BZ   GOOD        BRANCH IF ZERO TO 'GOOD'
  or
        LTR  15,15       LOAD AND TEST REF. 15
        BNZ  BAD         BRANCH NOT ZERO TO 'BAD'
```

Integrating the LTR with this example, it now looks like this:

```
START      OPEN    VSAMACB          *
           LTR     15,15            Q. GOOD OPEN RET.
```

```
                                          CODE
         BNZ    BADOPEN                     NO—ERROR
GETREC   GET    RPL=VSAMRPL             POINT TO RPL
         LTR    15,15                   Q. GOOD GET RET.
                                          CODE
         BNZ    BADGET                      NO—ERROR
         "
         B      GETREC                  GET NEXT RECORD
ENDFILE  CLOSE  VSAMACB                 CLOSE THE FILE
         LTR    15,15                   Q. GOOD CLOSE RET.
                                          CODE
         BNZ    BADOPEN                     NO—ERROR
         EOJ    (RETURN)                * END OF JOB
BADOPEN  ABEND  1,DUMP                  *
BADGET   ABEND  2,DUMP
BADCLOSE ABEND  3,DUMP
VASMRPL  RPL    ACB=VSAMACB,AREA=RECORD,
                AREALEN=100,                          +
                OPTCD=(KEY,SEQ,MVE,NUP)
VSAMACB  ACB    BUFND=4,BUFNI=6,EXLST=EXITLIST,       +
                MACRF=(KEY,SEQ),DDNAME=INVENTRY
EXITLIST EXLST  EODAD=ENDFILE
RECORD   DS     CL100          WORK AREA FOR RECORD
         END
```

The return code that VSAM places in register 15 contains one of the following hexadecimal values: 0, 4, 8, or 0C.

The Return Code Following OPEN:

0—Successful open of all data sets.

4—Successful open of all data sets, but at least one warning message was issued.

8—One or more data sets not opened successfully.

The Return Code Following CLOSE:

0—Successful close of all data sets.

4—Not all data sets closed properly.

8—Could not complete close because of lack of virtual storage.

The Return code Following GET or PUT:

0—Successful completion of operation.

* For DOS, substitute a DUMP macro instead of the ABEND macro. For OS use a RETURN instead of an EOJ macro.

4—Requested function not performed because of end of file encountered or RPL already active.

8—Could not complete due to logical error.

C—Could not complete due to physical error.

In addition to the preceding, the cause of a failure may be tested more specifically by using other VSAM macros such as **TESTCB** and **SHOWCB**. These are discussed shortly.

16.9 USING THE POINT AND ERASE MACROS

The **POINT** macro is used for sequential positioning. Positioning establishes a starting location for any subsequent read or write operation. A sequential read operation is often referred to as browsing.

You may browse a file in two ways: sequentially and skip-sequentially. When you browse a file skip-sequentially, you continue reading in a forward direction as you would when reading sequentially. The difference is that whole groups of records may be **skipped** over when using the skip-sequential method. This is accomplished through positioning by using the POINT macro.

You may also want to add records sequentially to your file. This, too, can be accomplished through the POINT macro. Before beginning the insert operation, you would first **point**, or position, VSAM to the correct location within the file.

ERASE deletes records in a KSDS and RRDS data set. Space deleted by the ERASE macro is freed to be used again. ESDS records cannot be erased.

16.9.1 THE FORMAT OF THE POINT AND ERASE MACROS

[label]	**POINT**	RPL = address
[label]	**ERASE**	RPL = address

16.9.2 EXPLANATION OF POINT AND ERASE PARAMETERS

Label:

This is the name given to the POINT or ERASE macro for purposes of reference by the program. It is also the address of the macro.

RPL = address:

This specifies the address of the RPL to be used for this operation.

16.9.3 SAMPLE PROGRAM USING POINT AND ERASE

The following illustrates the use of the POINT and ERASE macros:

```
START     OPEN     (VSAMACB,INPUT)   OPEN THE VSAM FILE
          LTR      15,15             Q. GOOD OPEN RET.
                                        CODE
          BNZ      BADOPEN              NO—ERROR
          OPEN     (SAMFILE,INPUT)   OPEN THE SAM INPUT
                                     FILE
GETREC    GET      SAMFILE,RECORD    GET RECORD FROM
                                     SAM
                                     KEY IN POS RE-
                                     CORD+10
          POINT    RPL=VSAMRPL       POSITION TO RECORD
          LTR      15,15             Q. GOOD POSITION
          BNZ      BADPOS               NO
          GET      RPL=VSAMRPL       RETRIEVE RECORD
          LTR      15,15             Q. GOOD GET
          BNZ      BADGET               NO, PROBABLY
                                        RECORD
                                        NOT FOUND
          CLC      CODE,=C'J'        Q. IS CODE = J
          BE       DELETE               YES—DELETE
                                        RECORD
          B        GETREC            GET NEXT RECORD
DELETE    ERASE    RPL=VSAMRPL       DELETE RECORD
          LTR      15,15             Q. GOOD DELETE
          BNZ      BADDEL               NO
          B        GETREC            GET NEXT SAM RECORD
ENDFILE   CLOSE    SAMFILE           CLOSE THE SAM FILE
          CLOSE    VSAMACB           CLOSE THE VSAM FILE
          LTR      15,15             Q. GOOD CLOSE RET.
                                     CODE
          BNZ      BADCLOSE             NO—ERROR
* TO END JOB USE EOJ MACRO IF DOS, RETURN MACRO IF OS
          RETURN   (14,12),RC=0      END OF JOB
BADOPEN   ABEND    1,DUMP            * (SEE NOTE)
BADGET    ABEND    2,DUMP
BADCLOSE  ABEND    3,DUMP
BADDEL    ABEND    4,DUMP
VSAMRPL   RPL      ACB=VSAMACB,AREA=RECORD,                 +
                   AREALEN=100,                             +
                   OPTCD=(KEY,DIR,MVE,UPD),                 +
                   ARG=CUSTOMER
```

```
VSAMACB  ACB      BUFND=4,BUFNI=6,DDNAME=INVENTRY,  +
                  MACRF=(KEY,DIR,OUT)
RECORD   DS       OCL100             WORK AREA FOR
                                     RECORD
         DS       CL10               UNUSED
CUSTOMER DS       CL8                CUSTOMER NO.
         DS       CL2                UNUSED
CODE     DS       C                  CUSTOMER CODE
         DS       CL59               UNUSED
SAMFILE  DCB      (OR DTF IF DOS)    EOFADDR=ENDFILE
         END
```

In this example records are read from a SAM input file. The customer number, which begins in position 10 of the SAM record, is used to retrieve a customer record from the VSAM file.

There is a problem with the preceding code: What happens if a record is not found on the VSAM file? Right now the program cancels using the ABEND macro because a nonzero return code is returned in register 15.

The **record not found** condition can be tested. In order to accomplish this you can use the **TESTCB** macro to examine the reason that the operation failed. VSAM returns information about a failed operation in a field in the RPL called the **FDBK** (feedback) field.

16.10 USING THE TESTCB MACRO

The **TESTCB** macro can be used to check information residing in the following VSAM macros:

ACB
RPL
EXLST

The result of the TESTCB is to set a condition code in the PSW. TESTCB allows a program to test fields within the ACB, RPL, and EXLST macros as if using an assembler instruction such as CLC, CLI, or TS. Example:

```
*  Test if no record found.
         TESTCB   RPL=VSAMRPL,FDBK=X'10'
         BE       NORECFND
```

There is an alternative method of obtaining this information. The actual data value for the fields tested can be obtained by use of the **SHOWCB** macro. SHOWCB is explained later in this chapter.

16.10.1 FORMAT OF THE TESTCB USED FOR ACBS

```
[label]     TESTCB     ACB=address
                       [,ERET=address ]
                       [,OBJECT=DATA | INDEX ]
                       [,ATRB=[([ESDS][,KSDS][,REPL][,RRDS]
                                [,SPAN][,SSWD][,WCK])              |
                       [ [ATRB=UNQ
                         [CATALOG=YES | NO
                         [CRA=SCRA | UCRA
                         [MACRF=([ADR][,AIX][,CFX][,CNV][,DDN]
                                  [,DFR][,DIR][,DSN][,ICI][,IN]
                                  [,KEY][,LSR][,NCI][,NDF][,NFX]
                                  [,NIS][,NRM][,NRS][,NSR][,NUB]
                                  [,OUT][,RST][,SEQ][,SIS][,SKP]
                                  [,UBF])      ]      ]
                       [OFLAGS=OPEN ]
                       [OPENOBJ=PATH | BASE | AIX ]
                       [ACBLEN=number ]
                       [AVSPAC=number ]
                       [BSTRNO=number ]
                       [BUFND=number ]
                       [BUFNI=number ]
                       [BUFSP=number ]
                       [CINV=number ]
                       [DDNAME=dname ]
                       [ENDRBA=number ]
                       [ERROR=number ]
                       [EXLST=address ]
                       [FS=number ]
                       [KEYLEN=number ]
                       [LRECL=number ]
                       [MAREA=address ]
                       [MLEN=number ]
                       [NCIS=number ]
                       [NDELR=number ]
                       [NEXCP=number ]
                       [NEXT=number ]
                       [NINSR=number ]
                       [NIXL=number ]
                       [NLOGR=number ]
```

```
[NRETR=number ]
[NSSS=number ]
[NUPDR=number ]
[PASSWD=address ]
[RKP=number ]
[STMST=address ]
[STRNO=number ]
```

16.10.2 EXPLANATION OF THE TESTCB–ACB PARAMETERS

Label:

This is the name given to the TESTCB for purposes of reference by the program. It is also the address of the TESTCB macro.

ACB=address:

This specifies that this TESTCB macro is to be used to test fields in an ACB macro.

ERET=address:

This parameter can specify the address of a routine to be given control if the program encounters a problem during the execution of the TESTCB macro.

OBJECT=DATA | INDEX:

This specifies for which component of the VSAM cluster the field is to be tested. Default is **DATA**.

ATRB=[,ESDS][,KSDS][,REPL][,RRDS][,SPAN][,SSWD][,WCK]:

With these parameters the attributes of a cluster can be tested. For instance, is the cluster type KSDS, RRDS, or ESDS? Are records SPANNED?

CATALOG=YES | NO:

This parameter allows you to determine whether the data set opened is a catalog.

CRA=SCRA | UCRA:

This allows you to check whether it was requested that Catalog Recovery Area control blocks be built in user or system space in main storage.

MACRF=([ADR][,AIX][,CFX][,CNV][,DDN]
[,DFR][,DIR][,DSN][,ICI][,IN]
[,KEY][,LSR][,NCI][,NDF][,NFX]
[,NIS][,NRM][,NRS][,NSR][,NUB]
[,OUT][,RST][,SEQ][,SIS][,SKP]
[,UBF]):

With these operands you can test to determine the parameters specified in the ACB macro. They can be tested singly or in groups.

OFLAGS=OPEN:

This allows you to test whether the data set has been opened.

OPENOBJ=PATH | BASE | AIX:

This parameter allows you to test to determine the type of object being accessed. This must take place after open.

ACBLEN=number:

This allows you to test the length of the ACB.

AVSPAC=number:

This allows you to test for the number of bytes available in the DATA or INDEX component.

BSTRNO=number:

This allows you to test for the number of strings initially allocated to access a base cluster by means of a PATH.

BUFND=number:

This allows testing for the number of buffers used that contain data buffers.

BUFNI=number:

This allows you to test for the number of buffers used that contain index buffers.

BUFSP=number:

This allows you to compare the number of bytes allocated for buffers.

CINV=number:

This allows you to test the size of a control interval.

DDNAME=dname:

This allows you to check the name of the data set used for this cluster.

ENDRBA=number:

This parameter lets you check the HIGH-USED RBA of a data set.

ERROR=number:

This allows comparison of the **code** returned by VSAM after the open or close of a data set.

EXLST=address:

This allows you to test the address of an EXLST.

FS=number:

This allows testing of the number of free control intervals per control area. This, of course, applies to the data component only.

KEYLEN = number:

This parameter allows you to test the length of the key used for this data set.

LRECL = number:

This allows testing of the length of the records in the index or data components.

MAREA = address:

This allows you to test the address of the message area.

MLEN = number:

This allows checking of length of the message area previously defined.

NCIS = number:

With this parameter you can check the number of control interval splits that have taken place.

NDELR = number:

This can be used to check the number of deletes that have taken place since the data set was created.

NEXCP = number:

This parameter gives you the ability to check the number of I/Os (EXCPs) that have taken place.

NEXT = number:

This allows you to test the number of extents allocated for the index or data component.

NINSR = number:

This allows you to test the number of records inserted into the file (data component).

NIXL = number:

This allows testing of the number of index levels for a KSDS.

NLOGR = number:

This allows you to test the number of records in the data component.

NRETR = number:

This allows you to test the number of records retrieved from the data set since it was created.

NSSS = number:

This allows testing of the number of control area splits.

NUPDR = number:

This allows testing of the number of record updates that have taken place since the data set was created.

PASSWD = address:

This allows checking of the address of the password.

RKP = number:

This allows testing of the relative key position within the data record.

STMST = address:

This allows testing of the system time-stamp.

STRNO = number:

This allows testing of the number of VSAM strings.

16.10.3 FORMAT OF THE TESTCB USED FOR RPLS

```
[label]  TESTCB  RPL=address
                 [,ERET=address ]
                 [,AIXFLAG=AIXPKP
                  AIXPC=number
                  FTNCD=number
                  I/O=COMPLETE
                  MACRF=([ADR][,ARD][,ASY][,BWD][,CNV]
                         [,DIR][,FKS][,FWD][,GEN][,KEQ]
                         [,KEY][,KGE][,LOC][,LRD][,MVE]
                         [,NSP][,NUP][,SEQ][,SKP][,SYN]
                         [,OUT][,RST][,SEQ][,SIS][,SKP]
                         [,UPD])      ]
                 ACB=address
                 AREA=address
                 AREALEN=number
                 ARG=address
                 ECB=address
                 FDBK=number
                 KEYLEN=number
                 MSGAREA=address
                 MSGLEN=length
                 NXTRPL=address
                 RBA=number
                 RECLEN=number
                 RPLLEN=number
                 TRANSID=NUMBER      ]
```

16.10.4 EXPLANATION OF THE TESTCB–RPL PARAMETERS

Label:

This is the name given to the TESTCB for purposes of reference by the program. It is also the address of the TESTCB macro.

RPL = address:

This specifies that this TESTCB macro is to be used to test fields in an RPL macro.

ERET = address:

This parameter can specify the address of a routine to be given control if the program encounters a problem during the execution of the TESTCB macro.

AIXFLAG = AIXPKP:

This specifies that prime key pointers, instead of RBA pointers, are used.

AIXPC = number:

This allows testing of the number of alternate index pointers.

FTNCD = number:

This allows testing of the **function code**, that is, the code return by VSAM when physical or logical errors occur.

I/O = COMPLETE:

This allows testing to determine if an asynchronous I/O operation has completed.

MACRF = ([ADR][,ARD][,ASY][,BWD][,CNV]
[,DIR][,FKS][,FWD][,GEN][,KEQ]
[,KEY][,KGE][,LOC][,LRD][,MVE]
[,NSP][,NUP][,SEQ][,SKP][,SYN]
[,OUT][,RST][,SEQ][,SIS][,SKP]
[,UPD]):

This parameter allows you to test which of the preceding options were specified in the RPL. These parameters can be tested either singly or in groups.

ACB = address:

This allows you to check the address of the ACB associated with the RPL being tested.

AREA = address:

This allows you to test the area used for the data record.

AREALEN = number:

This allows testing of the length of the area used for data records.

ARG = address:

This allows testing of the ARG field. ARG is used in conjunction with POINT.

ECB = address:

This allows checking of the ECB values. This can be used to test if the RPL I/O operation has completed.

FDBK=number:

This is perhaps the most important field to test using TESTCB. This area (FDBK) contains VSAM return codes. VSAM places a return code here indicating whether an error condition has occurred.

KEYLEN=number:

This allows testing of the key length used for the data set accessed by the RPL.

MSGAREA=address:

This allows testing of the message area. VSAM allows, if requested, error messages to be placed in this area. These are the same messages output to the system console or SYSPRINT (SYSLST).

MSGLEN=length:

This allows testing of the length of the message area.

NXTRPL=address:

This allows testing of the next RPL address. NXTRPL is used when chaining RPL I/O operations together.

RBA=number:

This parameter can be used to check the RBA of the record just processed or currently being processed.

RECLEN=number:

This parameter allows testing of the record length.

RPLLEN=number:

This allows checking of the RPL length.

TRANSID=NUMBER:

This allows checking of transaction number used in a buffer pool. See Chapters 14 and 17.

16.10.5 FORMAT OF THE TESTCB USED FOR EXLSTS

```
[label]  TESTCB  EXLST=address
                 [,ERET=address ]
                 EODAD=0 | ([address][,A | N ][,L])        |
                 JRNAD=0 | ([address][,A | N ][,L])        |
                 LERAD=0 | ([address][,A | N ][,L])        |
                 SYNAD=0 | ([address][,A | N ][,L])
                 [,EXLLEN=number ]
```

16.10.6 EXPLANATION OF THE TESTCB—EXLST PARAMETERS

Label:

This is the name given to the TESTCB for purposes of reference by the program. It is also the address of the TESTCB macro.

EXLST = address:

This specifies that this TESTCB macro is to be used to test fields in an EXLST macro.

ERET = address:

This parameter can specify the address of a routine to be given control if the program encounters a problem during the execution of the TESTCB macro.

EODAD = 0 | ([address][,A | N][,L])
JRNAD = 0 | ([address][,A | N][,L])
LERAD = 0 | ([address][,A | N][,L])
SYNAD = 0 | ([address][,A | N][,L]):

These allow testing to determine if an address is specified for an exit. If no entry is specified, an equal condition will occur when 0 is used (e.g., JRNAD = 0). You can also test specific addresses as well as whether the exit is active (**A**) or not (**N**). Finally, you can test if the address is the location (**L**) of an 8-byte field specifying the name of a PDS routine (see ACB).

EXLLEN = number:

This parameter can be used to test the length of an EXLST macro. If this parameter is used, do not use the EXLST = parameter.

16.10.7 EXAMPLE TESTCB USAGE

The following is an example of the TESTCB macro:

```
START    OPEN    (VSAMACB,INPUT)    OPEN THE VSAM FILE
         LTR     15,15              Q. GOOD OPEN RET.
                                       CODE
         BNZ     BADOPEN               NO—ERROR
         OPEN    (SAMFILE ,INPUT)   OPEN THE SAM INPUT
                                    FILE
GETREC   GET     SAMFILE,RECORD     GET RECORD FROM
                                    SAM
*                                   KEY IN POS
                                    RECORD + 10
         POINT   RPL = VSAMRPL      POSITION TO RECORD
         LTR     15,15              Q. GOOD POSITION
```

```
         BNZ      BADPOS                NO
         GET      RPL=VSAMRPL         RETRIEVE RECORD
         LTR      15,15               Q. GOOD GET
         BNZ      TSTNOREC               NO, PROBABLY
                                         RECORD
*                                        NOT FOUND
         CLC      CODE,=C'J'          Q. IS CODE = J
         BE       DELETE                 YES—DELETE
                                         RECORD
         B        GETREC              GET NEXT RECORD
DELETE   ERASE    RPL=VSAMRPL         DELETE RECORD
         LTR      15,15               Q. GOOD DELETE
         BNZ      BADDEL                 NO
         B        GETREC              GET NEXT SAM
                                      RECORD
ENDFILE  CLOSE    SAMFILE             CLOSE THE SAM FILE
         CLOSE    VSAMACB             CLOSE THE VSAM
                                      FILE
         LTR      15,15               Q. GOOD CLOSE RET.
                                         CODE
         BNZ      BADCLOSE               NO—ERROR
         RETURN   (14,12),RC=0        END OF JOB
BADOPEN  ABEND    1,DUMP              * (SEE NOTE)
TSTNOREC CH       15,=H'08'           Q. RETURN CODE OF
                                         8
         BNE      BADGET                 NO—OTHER
                                         ERROR
         TESTCB   RPL=VSAMRPL,FDBK=X'10' REC NOT
                  FOUND
         BE       GETREC        NO ERROR, NOT FOUND
BADGET   ABEND    2,DUMP
BADCLOSE ABEND    3,DUMP
BADDEL   ABEND    4,DUMP
VSAMRPL  RPL      ACB=VSAMACB,AREA=RECORD,          +
                  AREALEN=100,                      +
                  OPTCD=(KEY,DIR,MVE,NUP),          +
                  ARG=CUSTOMER
VSAMACB  ACB      BUFND=4,BUFNI=6,                  +
                  DDNAME=INVENTRY,                  +
                  MACRF=(KEY,DIR,OUT)
RECORD   DS       OCL100              WORK AREA FOR
                                      RECORD
         DS       CL10                UNUSED
CUSTOMER DS       CL8                 CUSTOMER NO.
         DS       CL2                 UNUSED
```

```
CODE        DS     C                     CUSTOMER CODE
            DS     CL59                  UNUSED
SAMFILE     DCB    (OR DTF IF DOS)       EOFADDR=ENDFILE
            END
```

Compare this example to the listing found in Section 16.9.3. The only changes are those involving the code to support the use of the TESTCB macro (boldface type).

For purposes of illustrating the use of the TESTCB macro, the **no record found** condition is not considered an error in this application.

If VSAM sets a return code other than 0 (in register 15), the RPL feedback (FDBK) field can be examined to further determine the cause of the problem. The various feedback function codes are defined in the *IBM DOS and OS VSAM Programmer's Guide*.

16.10.8 AN ALTERNATIVE TO TESTCB

There is another convenient way to accomplish the same functions available with the TESTCB macro, that is, through the **SHOWCB** macro. The SHOWCB allows you to retrieve various types of data into a work area specified by the AREA parameter. Once retrieved, it can then be examined and utilized.

16.11 THE SHOWCB MACRO

```
[label]  SHOWCB  ACB=address
                 ,AREA=address
                 ,LENGTH=length of area
                 [,OBJECT=DATA | INDEX ]
                 ,FIELDS=([ACBLEN][,AVSPAC][,BFRFND][,BSTRNO]
                          [,BUFND][,BUFNI][,BUFNO][,BUFRDS]
                          [,BUFSP][,CINV][,DDNAME][,ENDRBA]
                          [,HALCRBA][,ERROR][,EXLST][,FS]
                          [,KEYLEN][,LRECL][,MAREA][,MLEN]
                          [,NCIS][,NDELR][,NEXCP][,NEXT]
                          [,NINSR][,NIXL][,NLOGR][,NRETR]
                          [,NSSS][,NUIW][,NUPDR][,PASSWD]
                          [,RKP][,STMST][,STRMAX][,STRNO]
                          [,UIW] )
```

16.11.1 EXPLANATION OF THE SHOWCB–ACB PARAMETERS

Label:

This is the name given to the SHOWCB for purposes of reference by the program. It is also the address of the SHOWCB macro.

ACB=address:

This specifies that this SHOWCB macro is to be used to test fields in an ACB macro.

AREA=address:

This operand specifies the address of an area that will be used to contain the information returned by VSAM as a result of the execution of this macro.

LENGTH=length of area:

This operand specifies the length of the area that will receive the data to be returned.

OBJECT=DATA | INDEX:

This specifies for which component of the VSAM cluster the field is to be tested. Default is **DATA**.

DESCRIPTION OF OPERAND FIELDS FOLLOWS:

ACBLEN:

This allows you to retrieve into AREA the length of the ACB.

AVSPAC:

This allows you to retrieve the number of bytes available in the DATA or INDEX component.

BFRFND:

This allows retrieval of the number of times VSAM was able to locate a record already in buffer storage when a read operation was requested.

BSTRNO:

This allows you to retrieve into AREA the number of strings initially allocated to access a base cluster by a PATH.

BUFND:

This allows you to retrieve the number of buffers used to contain data records.

BUFNI:

This allows you to retrieve the number of buffers used to contain index records.

BUFNO:

This allows retrieval of a field that gives the number of I/Os issued for retrieval of control intervals into buffers.

BUFRDS:

This operand renders the number of times buffer reads were issued when sharing buffers. See also Chapter 14.

BUFSP:

This allows you to retrieve into AREA the number of bytes allocated for buffers.

CINV:

This allows you to retrieve the size of a control interval.

DDNAME:

This allows you to retrieve the name of the data set used for this cluster.

ENDRBA:

This parameter lets you retrieve the HIGH-USED RBA of a data set.

ERROR:

This allows retrieval of the **code** returned by VSAM after open or close of a data set.

EXLST:

This allows you to retrieve the address of an EXLST.

FS:

This allows you to retrieve into AREA the number of free control intervals per control area.

HALCRBA:

Specification of this operand allows retrieval of the HIGH-ALLOCATED RBA for the data set.

KEYLEN:

This allows retrieval of the length of the key used for this data set.

LRECL:

This allows retrieval of the length of records in the index or data components.

MAREA:

This allows you to obtain the address of the message area.

MLEN:

This allows retrieval of the length of the message area.

NCIS:

With this parameter, you can obtain the number of control interval splits that have taken place.

NDELR:

This can be used to obtain the number of deletes that have taken place since the data set was created.

NEXCP:

This parameter gives you the ability to retrieve the number of I/Os (EXCPs) that have taken place.

NEXT:

This allows you to obtain the number of extents allocated for the index or data component.

NINSR:

This allows you to obtain the number of records inserted into the file (data component).

NIXL:

This allows retrieval of the number of index levels for a KSDS.

NLOGR:

This allows you to obtain the number of records in the data component.

NRETR:

This allows you to obtain the number of records retrieved from the data set since it was created.

NSSS:

This allows retrieval of the number of control area splits.

NUIW:

This specifies the number of buffer writes that took place, but not by this task, when using the Local Shared Resource option. See also the UIW operand and the discussion on LSR buffer sharing in Chapter 14.

NUPDR:

This allows retrieval of the number of record updates that have taken place since the data set was created.

PASSWD:

This allows retrieval of the password.

RKP:

This allows you to obtain the relative key position in the data record.

STMST:

This allows retrieval of the system time-stamp.

STRMAX:

This operand allows retrieval of the number of concurrent string requests presently active.

STRNO:

This allows you to obtain the number of VSAM strings.

UIW:

This operand will return the number of writes initiated by this task. See also NUIW.

16.11.2 FORMAT OF THE SHOWCB USED FOR RPLS

```
[label]     SHOWCB RPL=address
                  ,AREA=address
                  ,LENGTH=length of area
                  ,FIELDS=([ACB][,AIXPC][,AREA][,AREALEN]
                          [,ARG][,ECB][,FDBK][,FTNCD]
                          [,KEYLEN][,MSGAREA][,MSGLEN]
                          [,NXTRPL][,RBA][,RECLEN]
                          [,RPLLEN][,TRANSID]
```

16.11.3 EXPLANATION OF THE SHOWCB–RPL PARAMETERS

Label:

This is the name given to the SHOWCB for purposes of reference by the program. It is also the address of the SHOWCB macro.

RPL = address:

This specifies that this SHOWCB macro is to be used to examine fields in an RPL macro.

AREA = area:

This specifies the address of an area that will receive information passed back as a result of the execution of the SHOWCB macro.

LENGTH = length of area:

This parameter states the length of the area defined by the AREA parameter.

OPERANDS FOR THE FIELD PARAMETER FOLLOW:

ACB:

This operand will return the address of the ACB associated with the RPL being addressed.

AIXPC:

This allows retrieval of the number of alternate index pointers.

AREA:

This allows you to obtain the address of the area used for the data record.

AREALEN:

This allows you to obtain the length of the area used for data records.

ARG:

This allows retrieval of the ARG field. ARG is used in conjunction with POINT.

ECB:

This allows you to obtain the address of the ECB (Event Control Block) associated with this RPL. This can be used to test if the RPL I/O operation has completed.

FTNCD:

This allows retrieval of the **function code**, that is, the code returned by VSAM when physical or logical errors occur.

FDBK:

This allows retrieval of the feedback code. This area (FDBK) contains VSAM return codes. VSAM places a return code here whenever an error condition occurs.

KEYLEN:

This allows you to obtain the key length used for the data set accessed by the RPL.

MSGAREA:

This allows you to obtain the address of the message area. VSAM allows messages to be placed in this area. These are the same messages output to the system console or SYSPRINT (SYSLST).

MSGLEN:

With this operand you can retrieve the length of the message area.

NXTRPL:

This allows you to access the address of the next RPL. NXTRPL is used when chaining RPL I/O operations together.

RBA:

This parameter can be used to retrieve the RBA of the record just processed, or currently being processed.

RECLEN:

This parameter allows you to obtain the length of the record.

RPLLEN:

This allows retrieval of the RPL length.

TRANSID:

This allows retrieval of the transaction number used in a buffer pool. See Chapters 14 and 17.

16.11.4 FORMAT OF THE SHOWCB USED FOR EXLSTS

```
[label]     SHOWCB EXLST=address
                   ,AREA=address
                   ,LENGTH=length of area
                   ,FIELDS=([EODAD][,EXLLEN][,JRNAD][,LERAD]
                           [,SYNAD]
```

16.11.5 EXPLANATION OF THE SHOWCB–EXLST PARAMETERS

Label:

This is the name given to the SHOWCB macro for purposes of reference by the program. It is also the address of the SHOWCB macro.

EXLST = address:

This specifies that this SHOWCB macro is to be used to examine fields in an EXLST macro.

AREA = area:

This specifies the address of an area that will receive information passed back as a result of the execution of the SHOWCB macro.

LENGTH = length of area:

This parameter states the length of the area defined by the AREA parameter.

OPERANDS FOR THE FIELD PARAMETER FOLLOW:

EODAD:
EXLLEN:

JRNAD:
LERAD:
SYNAD:

The addresses of the various exit routines can be obtained by specifying them in this macro. In addition, if EXLLEN is specified **instead of** EXLST, the **length** of the EXLST can be obtained.

16.11.6 EXAMPLES USING THE SHOWCB MACRO

The following illustrates the use of the **SHOWCB** macro. In this example records are read from a sequential SAM input file and added to a VSAM KSDS data set. The program checks for duplicate records and sends an error message to the printer if necessary.

```
START     OPEN    .....
GETSAM    GET     SAMFILE,SAMWORK    GET INPUT RECORD
          PUT     RPL=VSAMRPL        WRITE TO KSDS
          LTR     15,15              Q. WAS WRITE OK
          BNZ     BADPUT                NO

* CHECK IF DUPLICATE RECORD
CHKDUPRC SHOWCB RPL=VSAMRPL,AREA=REASON,LENGTH=4,     +
                FIELDS=FDBK
          CLI     REASON+3,X'08'     Q. DUPLICATE KEY
          BE      DUPKEY                YES-LIST
BADPUT    DUMP                       ABEND THE PROGRAM

DUPKEY    MVC     DUPNUM,KEY
          PUT     PRINTER,MESSAGE    OUTPUT DUP. MESSAGE
          B       GETSAM             GET NEXT RECORD.

REASON    DC      4X'00'             SET FDBK AREA
VSAMRPL   RPL     ACB=VSAMACB,BUFND=4,BUFSP=20000,         +
                  AREALEN=80,ARG=KEY,AREA=SAMWORK,         +
                  OPTCD=(KEY,SEQ,NUP,MVE)
VSAMACB   ACB     DDNAME=SAMFILE,MACRF=(KEY,SEQ,OUT)
SAMFILE   DTF     ......................
          END
```

In this example records are retrieved from a sequential input file and added to a VSAM file. After each PUT, register 15 is checked. A return code other than 0 indicates a problem with the write operation. In this example the application simply abends.

When register 15 contains a zero, the **FDBK** area must be checked to be sure that a duplicate record condition did not occur. This is the way it is done normally. A duplicate record is not considered a true error condition. When accessing the FDBK area, you must set aside 4 bytes. The last byte is checked for the feedback code.

16.11.7 SOME ADDITIONAL EXAMPLES OF SHOWCB

Example One

Obtain the relative byte address of a record after a GET operation:

```
SHOWCB    RPL=VSAMIN,AREA=FEEDBACK,LENGTH=4,FIELDS=RBA
```

This example places the four-byte RBA address in a field called FEEDBACK.

Example Two

Obtain the length of a variable length record.

```
SHOWCB    RPL=VSAMRPL,RECLEN=(0)
```

In this example you are requesting that VSAM obtain the record length and return it in register 0. The use of parentheses indicates to the macro that information is to be returned in a register. This is referred to as **special register notation**.

Example Three

Obtain the number of buffers used for data and index buffering, and the amount of buffer space allocated.

```
SHOWCB    ACB=VSAMACB,AREA=FEEDBACK,LENGTH=12,              +
          FIELDS=(BUFND,BUFNI,BUFSP)
```

In this example a 12-byte feedback area is set up to receive the information requested. Each field requires 4 bytes. Notice that multiple fields may be requested with the FIELDS operand. When it is used in this manner, parentheses are required.

Example Four

Obtain the address of an EXLST exit.

```
SHOWCB    EXLST=EXITLIST,AREA=EXITADDR,LENGTH=4,            +
          FIELDS=JRNAD
.
.
```

```
EXITLIST EXLST AM=VSAM,JRNAD=JOURNAL,EODAD=ENDOFILE
EXITADDR DS    F     FIELD TO RECEIVE JRNAD ADDRESS
```

This example obtains the address of the JRNAD exit routine specified in the EXLST macro.

16.12 THE CLOSE AND TCLOSE MACROS

Technically, the **CLOSE** macro is not a VSAM macro. CLOSE is used for all access methods. There is a special function that can be performed, however, that applies only to VSAM. By using the **CLOSE TYPE=T** (OS) and **TCLOSE** (DOS) macros, the data set statistics in the catalog can be updated (reset) without actually closing the data set. Another alternative would be to CLOSE the data set (no TYPE=T) and then OPEN it again, which takes more time.

Format of the OS version:

```
[label]    CLOSE    (filename),TYPE=T
```

Format of the DOS version:

```
[label]    TCLOSE    filename
```

16.13 THE MODCB MACRO

There are many options available when using VSAM macros. In addition to selection of specific parameters, VSAM gives you the ability to **modify** its control blocks during execution. The macros that can be modified are the ACB, RPL, and EXLST macros. This is accomplished through the use of the **MODCB** macro.

16.13.1 USING THE MODCB MACRO FOR MODIFYING AN ACB

The following is the format of the MODCB macro used to modify the ACB.

```
[label]    MODCB    ACB=address
                    [,BSTRNO=number ]
```

```
                    [,BUFND=number ]
                    [,BUFNI=number ]
                    [,CATALOG=YES | NO ]
                    [,CRA=SCRA | UCRA]
                    [,DDNAME=name on jcl statement ]
                    [,EXLST=address ]
                    [,MACRF=[ADR | CNV | KEY ]
                           [,NFX | CFX ]
                           [,DDN | DSN ]
                           [,DFR | NDF ]
                           [,DIR | SEQ | SKP ]
                           [,ICI | NCI ]
                           [,IN | OUT ]
                           [,NIS | SIS ]
                           [,NRM | AIX ]
                           [,NRS | RST ]
                           [,NSR | LSR ]
                           [,NUB | UBF ]
                    [,MAREA=address ]
                    [,MLEN=length ]
                    [,PASSWD=address ]
                    [,STRNO=number ]
```

In this macro, the EXLST operand allows you to modify an ACB to cause it to point to a different EXLST. For explanation of the rest of these parameters, see the ACB macro.

16.13.2 USING THE MODCB MACRO FOR MODIFYING AN RPL

The format of the MODCB macro used to modify an RPL is as follows.

```
[label]    MODCB    RPL=address
                    [ACB=address]
                    [,AREA=address ]
                    [,AREALEN=length ]
                    [,ARG=address ]
                    [,ECB=address ]
                    [,KEYLEN=length ]
                    [,MSGAREA=address ]
                    [,MSGLEN=length ]
                    [,NXTRPL=address ]
                    [,OPTCD=([ADR | CNV | KEY ]
                            [,DIR | SEQ | SKP ]
                            [,ARD | LRD ]
                            [,FWD | BWD ]
```

```
                    [,SYN | ASY ]
                    [,NSP | NUP | UPD ]
                    [,KEQ | KGE ]
                    [,FKS | GEN ]
                    [,MVE | LOC ]
                    [,NOWAITX | WAITX ] ) ]
            [,RECLEN=length ]
            [,TRANSID=number ]
```

Compare the macro parameters in this MODCB with the RPL macro. The only difference between the two is the addition of the ACB operand. This allows you to modify the ACB being pointed to by the RPL to a different ACB. The explanation for the other parameters can be bound under the RPL macro.

Finally, the MODCB macro can be used to modify a generated EXLST macro. The format is as follows.

16.13.3 USING THE MODCB MACRO FOR MODIFYING AN EXLST

```
[label]    MODCB    EXLST=address
                    [,EODAD=address [,A | N ] [,L ]
                    [,JRNAD=address [,A | N ] [,L ]
                    [,LERAD=address [,A | N ] [,L ]
                    [,SYNAD=address [,A | N ] [,L ]
```

16.13.4 EXAMPLE USES OF THE MODCB MACRO

In the following example variable length records are added to the data set. The length may be different for each record. The length is supplied to VSAM by altering the RPL using the MODCB macro.

16.13.4.1 Example 1, Modifying the RPL for Variable Records

```
START      OPEN     (VSAMACB,OUTPUT)
           .
           .
           LH       2,LENGTH            PUT LENGTH OF RECORD
                                          INTO R2
           MODCB    RPL=VSAMRPL,RECLEN=(2)
           LTR      15,15
           BNZ      BADMOD
           PUT      RPL=VSAMRPL
           .
```

```
         .
BADMOD   ABEND  1,DUMP
         .
RECORD   DS     CL500                  AREA FOR DATA RECORD
         .

VSAMACB  ACB    DDNAME=VSAMJCL,MACRF=(SEQ,KEY,              +
                OUT,NIS)
VSAMRPL  RPL    ACB=VSAMACB,AREA=RECORD,                    +
                AREALEN=500,
                OPTCD=(SEQ,KEY,MVE,NUP)
         END
```

In this example an area of 500 bytes is set aside to format and build a data record. The largest record will never exceed this length. Be sure that the actual length of the record is supplied to VSAM by the application program. Register 2 is used for this purpose.

When the RPL macro is assembled, the length of the record is set at 500 bytes. After issuing the MODCB macro, the RPL will reflect the length specified in register 2.

16.13.4.2 Example 2, Modifying the ACB, NIS to SIS

In the following example the processing mode for insert is switched from sequential insert strategy (SIS) to normal (direct) insert strategy (NIS).

```
START     OPEN    (VSAMACB,OUTPUT)

          PUT     RPL=VSAMRPL     PUT WITH NIS
          LTR     R15,R15         Q. WAS PUT OK
          BNZ     CHECKPUT           NO CHECK PUT
          MODCB   ACB=VSAMACB,                              +
                  MACRF=SIS       MODIFY ACB
          LTR     15,15
          BNZ     BADMOD
          PUT     RPL=VSAMRPL     PUT WITH SIS
          LTR     R15,R15         Q. WAS PUT OK
          BNZ     CHECKPUT           NO CHECK PUT

          .
*  CHECK IF DUPLICATE RECORD
CHECKPUT SHOWCB RPL=VSAMRPL,AREA=REASON,LENGTH=4,           +
                FIELDS=FDBK
          CLI     REASON+3,X'08'  Q. DUPLICATE KEY
          BE      ......................  YES–OK
```

```
BADPUT     ABEND    1,DUMP                  ABEND THE PROGRAM
BADMOD     ABEND    2,DUMP
REASON     DS       F
RECORD     DS       CL500                   AREA FOR DATA RECORD
VSAMACB    ACB      DDNAME=VSAMJCL,MACRF=(DIR,
                    KEY,OUT,NIS)
VSAMRPL    RPL      ACB=VSAMACB,AREA=RECORD,                  +
                    AREALEN=500,                              +
                    OPTCD=(DIR,KEY,MVE,NUP)
           END
```

16.13.4.3 Example 3, Modifying the EXLST Macro

In the following example the end-of-file address routine (EODAD) is modified to point to a different routine.

```
START      OPEN     (VSAMACB,INPUT)
GETREC     GET      RPL=                    GET A RECORD
                    VSAMRPL
           LTR      R15,R15                 Q. WAS GET OK
           BNZ      BADGET                     NO—ABEND
           MODCB    EXLST=XLIST,                              +
                    EODAD=EOF2              MODIFY EXLST
           LTR      15,15
           BNZ      ABEND
           B        GETREC
EOF1       .................................PERFORM SOME
                                            FUNCTION
EOF2       .................................PERFORM SOME
                                            FUNCTION
XLIST      EXLST    EODAD=EOF1
RECORD     DS       CL500                   AREA FOR DATA
                                            RECORD
VSAMACB    ACB      DDNAME=VSAMJCL,                           +
                    MACRF=(SEQ,KEY,IN),                       +
                    EXLST=XLIST
VSAMRPL    RPL      ACB=VSAMACB,AREA=RECORD,                  +
                    AREALEN=500,                              +
                    OPTCD=(SEQ,KEY,MVE)
```

In this example the EXLST used by the ACB initially points to a routine called EOF1. EOF1 is the EODAD (end of data) routine that will receive control when end-of-file is encountered. The EXLST address is modified using the MODCB macro to point to a different end-of-file routine, EOF2.

16.14 THE GENCB MACRO

Three of the macros introduced in this chapter are considered **control block** macros. These are the ACB, RPL, and EXLST macros. They are called control block macros because they generate control blocks in the assembler program rather than performing some action such as reading, writing, or testing. The format of control blocks sometimes changes with new releases of software. When this occurs, it is sometimes necessary to reassemble all the programs that use the older control block format in order to utilize the newer form. This is also useful when relocating a control block.

VSAM provides an easier way to meet this need: the **GENCB** macro. The GENCB macro causes **dynamic** generation of a VSAM control block **at execution time**. If you choose to generate an RPL macro dynamically, for instance, you would code a **GENCB BLK=RPL** macro instead of an **RPL** macro.

16.14.1 THE FORMAT OF THE GENCB BLK=ACB MACRO

The following is the format for the GENCB BLK=ACB macro:

```
[label]     GENCB     BLK=ACB
                      [,AM=VSAM ]
                      [,BSTRNO=number ]
                      [,BUFND=number ]
                      [,BUFNI=number ]
                      [,CATALOG=YES | NO ]
                      [,COPIES=number ]
                      [,CRA=SCRA | UCRA]
                      [,DDNAME=name on jcl card ]
                      [,LENGTH=length ]
                      [,MACRF=[ADR | CNV | KEY ]
                              [,NFX | CFX ]
                              [,DDN | DSN ]
                              [,DFR | NDF ]
                              [,DIR | SEQ | SKP ]
                              [,ICI | NCI ]
                              [,IN | OUT ]
                              [,NIS | SIS ]
                              [,NRM | AIX ]
                              [,NRS | RST ]
                              [,NSR | LSR ]
                              [,NUB | UBF ]
                      [,MAREA=address ]
```

```
[,MLEN=length ]
[,PASSWD=address ]
[,PARMS=CLOSDSP=KEEP | DELETE | DATE ]
[,STRNO=number ]
[,WAREA=address ]
```

Most of these operands are defined under the ACB macro discussed earlier in this chapter. There are, however, four new operands.

16.14.2 THE GENCB BLK=ACB OPERANDS

BLK=ACB:

Specification of this operand causes an ACB to be generated.

COPIES=number:

This specifies the number of control blocks of this type that are to be generated. The control blocks are generated serially, one after the other.

LENGTH=length:

This specifies the number of bytes being set aside for generation of the control block(s).

WAREA=address:

You may specify to VSAM the address where the control block is to be generated. If you do not supply this address, VSAM will obtain the storage for you from the virtual storage area in your partition or region. In this case the address of the control block is returned to you in register 1.

16.14.3 THE GENCB BLK=RPL MACRO

The following is the format for the GENCB BLK=RPL macro:

```
[label]     GENCB     BLK=RPL
                      [ACB=address ]
                      [,AM=VSAM ]
                      [,AREA=address ]
                      [,AREALEN=length ]
                      [,ARG=address ]
                      [,COPIES=number ]
                      [,ECB=address ]
                      [,KEYLEN=length ]
                      [,LENGTH=length ]
                      [,MSGAREA=address ]
                      [,MSGLEN=length ]
                      [,NXTRPL=address ]
```

```
[,OPTCD=[ADR | CNV | KEY ]
        [,DIR | SEQ | SKP ]
        [,ARD | LRD ]
        [,FWD | BWD ]
        [,SYN | ASY ]
        [,NSP | NUP | UPD ]
        [,KEQ | KGE ]
        [,FKS | GEN ]
        [,MVE | LOC ]
        [,NOWAITX | WAITX ]
[,RECLEN=length ]
[,TRANSID=number ]
[,WAREA=address ]
```

As in the ACB macro, most of the preceding operands are defined under the RPL macro discussed earlier in this chapter. There are, however, four new operands.

16.14.4 THE GENCB BLK=RPL OPERANDS

BLK=RPL:

Specification of this operand causes an RPL to be generated.

COPIES=number:

This specifies the number of control blocks of this type that are to be generated. The control blocks are generated serially, one after the other.

LENGTH=length:

This specifies the number of bytes being set aside for generation of the control block(s).

WAREA=address:

You may specify to VSAM the address where the control block is to be generated. If you do not supply this address, VSAM will obtain the storage for you from the vitual storage area in your partition or region. In this case the address of the control block is returned to you in register 1.

16.14.5 THE GENCB BLK=EXLST MACRO

The following is the format for the GENCB BLK=EXLST macro:

```
[label]   GENCB   BLK=EXLST
                  [AM=VSAM]
                  [,COPIES=number ]
                  [,EODAD=address [,A | N ] [,L ]
```

```
[,JRNAD=address [,A | N ] [,L ]
[,LENGTH=length ]
[,LERAD=address [,A | N ] [,L ]
[,SYNAD=address [,A | N ] [,L ]
[,UPAD=address [,A | N ] [,L ]
[,WAREA=address ]
```

This macro is identical in format to the EXLST macro. Except for the following, the definition of the various operands are explained under the EXLST macro.

16.14.6 THE GENCB BLK=EXLST OPERANDS

BLK=EXLST:

Specification of this operand causes an EXLST to be generated.

COPIES=number:

This specifies the number of control blocks of this type that are to be generated. The control blocks are generated serially, one after the other.

LENGTH=length:

This specifies the number of bytes being set aside for generation of the control block(s).

WAREA=address:

You may specify to VSAM the address where the control block is to be generated. If you do not supply this address, VSAM will obtain the storage for you from the vitual storage area in your partition or region. In this case the address of the control block is returned to you in register 1.

16.14.7 EXAMPLE OF THE GENCB MACRO

The following is the same program found in Section 16.13.4.3 except that it now uses GENCBs instead of the ACB, RPL, and EXLST.

***** BEFORE MODIFICATION *****

```
START     OPEN      (VSAMACB,INPUT)
GETREC    GET       RPL=VSAMRPL       GET RECORD
          LTR       R15,R15           Q. WAS GET OK
          BNZ       BADGET              NO—ABEND
          MODCB     EXLST=XLIST,      MODIFY EXLST
                    EODAD=EOF2
          LTR       15,15
```

```
               BNZ       BADMOD
               B         GETREC
EOF1           ..............................PERFORM SOME
                                               FUNCTION
EOF2           ..............................PERFORM SOME
                                               FUNCTION
XLIST          EXLST     EODAD=EOF1
BADMOD         ABEND     1,DUMP
RECORD         DS        CL500              AREA FOR DATA
                                              RECORD
VSAMACB        ACB       DDNAME=VSAMJCL,MACRF=
                           (SEQ,KEY,IN,),                +
                         EXLST=EOF1
VSAMRPL        RPL       ACB=VSAMACB,AREA=RECORD,
                           AREALEN=500,                  +
                         OPTCD=(SEQ,KEY,MVE)
               END
```

*** **AFTER MODIFICATION** ***

```
START          OPEN      (VSAMACB,INPUT)
VSAMACB        GENCB     BLK=ACB,                        +
                         DDNAME=VSAMJCL,
                         MACRF=(SEQ,KEY,IN),             +
                         EXLST=EOF1
               LR        2,1                  SAVE ADDRESS
                                              OF ACB

VSAMRPL        GENCB     BLK=RPL,                        +
                         ACB=VSAMACB,AREA=RECORD,        +
                         AREALEN=500,                    +
                         OPTCD=(SEQ,KEY,MVE)
               LR        3,1                  SAVE ADDRESS OF
                                              RPL

XLIST          GENCB     BLK=EXLST,EODAD=EOF1
               LR        4,1                  SAVE ADDRESS OF
                                              EXLST

START          OPEN      ((2),INPUT)
GETREC         GET       RPL=(3)              GET A RECORD
               LTR       R15,R15              Q. WAS GET OK
               BNZ       BADGET                 NO CHECK GET
               MODCB     EXLST=(4),           MODIFY EXLST
                         EODAD=EOF2
```

```
          LTR       15,15
          BNZ       BADMOD
          B         GETREC
EOF1      ...........................................PERFORM SOME
                                                     FUNCTION
EOF2      ...........................................PERFORM SOME
                                                     FUNCTION
BADMOD    ABEND     1,DUMP
RECORD    DS        CL500                            AREA FOR DATA
                                                     RECORD
          END
```

In this example the GENCB macros were moved before the rest of the program. This is because the VSAM control blocks had to be established before you could access them with OPEN, GET, and so on.

After the execution of each GENCB macro, the address of the macro is returned in register 1. In the preceding example, this address is saved in register 2 for the ACB, register 3 for the RPL, and register 4 for the EXLST macro.

16.15 THE CHECK MACRO

Earlier we discussed the **ASY** parameter of the RPL macro. This parameter allows you to continue other processing immediately after initiating an I/O operation. In other words, the application will not be placed in a **wait state** while awaiting completion of the I/O operation.

By using the TESTCB macro, or by testing the ECB, we can determine whether the I/O processing has completed. If the I/O has not completed, you can either continue to do some more work while waiting or you can force the application into a wait state. Forcing the application into the wait state is accomplished by using the **CHECK** macro.

16.15.1 THE FORMAT OF THE CHECK MACRO

The format of the check macro is as follows:

```
[label]     CHECK     RPL=address
```

16.15.2 EXAMPLE OF THE CHECK MACRO

```
START     OPEN     (VSAMACB,INPUT)
GETREC    GET      RPL=VSAMRPL       GET A RECORD
```

```
         LTR      R15,R15             Q. WAS GET OK
         BNZ      BADGET                 NO CHECK GET
         .
         .
* PERFORM SOME TASK HERE WHILE WAITING FOR I/O
* TO COMPLETE.
         .
         .
* ISSUE CHECK MACRO WHEN NO OTHER WORK CAN BE
* PERFORMED.
         CHECK    RPL=VSAMRPL
         B        GETREC
EOF1     ........ ............. PERFORM SOME FUNCTION
XLIST    EXLST    EODAD=EOF1
RECORD   DS       CL500               AREA FOR DATA RECORD
VSAMACB  ACB      DDNAME=VSAMJCL,MACRF=(SEQ,KEY,IN,),  +
                  EXLST=XLIST
VSAMRPL  RPL      ACB=VSAMACB,AREA=RECORD,             +
                  AREALEN=500,                         +
                  OPTCD=(SEQ,KEY,MVE,ASY)
         END
```

In this example the program issues a GET macro against an RPL which specifies **ASY** (asyncrhonous I/O). The program performs some task until it no longer has any work to do. At that time the program issues a **CHECK** macro. To determine whether there is a need to issue a CHECK macro, a TESTCB macro can be issued. If the I/O is already complete, the CHECK macro need not be executed.

16.16 CONCURRENT POSITIONING

Every time you retrieve a record with the **intent** to update or when you are browsing a file, VSAM maintains position holders, or pointers, to the location from which the records were retrieved. There position pointers are also called **place holders** or **strings**.

When **multiple** records are retrieved for update, or when performing both direct (random) and sequential processing, VSAM can maintain string pointers for each outstanding position. This is referred to as **concurrent positioning**.

When **NSP** is specified in the RPL and **OPTCD=DIR**, VSAM will **remember** a position **for sequential access**. This option allows for direct access (no update) followed by sequential processing.

When **UPD** is specified in the RPL, VSAM maintains position holders for any sequential or direct GET requests. If a PUT or ERASE is issued, positioning is released. For the **NUP** option, no positioning is maintained. If multiple update requests are outstanding, for instance, when **OPTCD=UPD**, this is called concurrent positioning. VSAM will maintain position holders or strings for each record. The number of string pointers you would like VSAM to maintain at any given time is specified by the **STRNO** operand of the ACB macro.

If at any time during program processing you wish to **release** the positioning for a record, you can accomplish this by using the **ENDREQ** macro.

16.17 THE ENDREQ MACRO

By using the **ENDREQ** macro, VSAM will release the positioning established by a previous request. This is accomplished by pointing VSAM to the RPL used for positioning. The following is the format of the ENDREQ macro:

```
[label]     ENDREQ   RPL=address
```

16.17.1 EXAMPLE USAGE OF THE ENDREQ MACRO

The following illustrates the usage of the ENDREQ macro.

```
START      OPEN     (VSAMACB,INPUT)
GETREC     GET      RPL=VSAMRPL          GET FOR UPDATE
           LTR      R15,R15              Q. WAS GET OK
           BNZ      BADGET                  NO CHECK GET
           "                             NOW, FOR SOME
                                         REASON
           "                             FORGET ABOUT
                                         UPDATE
           ENDREQ   RPL=VSAMRPL
           B        GETREC
EOF1       ....     ......               PERFORM SOME
                                         FUNCTION
XLIST      EXLST    EODAD=EOF1
RECORD     DS       CL500                AREA FOR DATA
                                         RECORD
VSAMACB    ACB      DDNAME=VSAMJCL,
                    MACRF=(SEQ,KEY,IN,),                  +
                    EXLST=XLIST
VSAMRPL    RPL      ACB=VSAMACB,AREA=RECORD,
```

```
                    AREALEN=500,                    +
                  OPTCD=(SEQ,KEY,MVE,UPD)
          END
```

In this example the application retrieves a record for update, then decides against it for some reason. The **ENDREQ** macro is issued to release positioning for that record. If a PUT is issued instead, positioning is released automatically.

16.18 USER EXITS

User exit routines can be defined for the following exits:

EODAD—End of file exit
JRNAD—Journaling exit
LERAD—Logical error exit
SYNAD—Physical error exit
UPAD—Record update exit
USVR—User verification unit

For each of these exit routines VSAM sets up certain general registers before entry to the routine. The contents of the registers depend on the routine being used. In general, register usage is as follows:

1. Register 1, address of a parameter list, prepared by VSAM, to be examined by the exit routine. Information in the parameter list will vary according to the exit to which control is passed.
2. Register 14, the address to return to when completed.
3. Register 15, the entry point address for this exit, also the base address.

16.19 PERFORMING AMS FUNCTIONS FROM WITHIN THE APPLICATION

Access Method Services functions can be accessed from an application program written in assembler. The functions available are those performed by invoking the **IDCAMS** program.

This function is available whether the operating system is OS or DOS. The method of accomplishing the function, however, is different.

16.19.1 INVOKING ACCESS METHOD SERVICES FROM A DOS APPLICATION

In DOS, AMS is invoked by using the CDLOAD macro. The format for this is as follows:

```
CDLOAD address
```

in which address specifies an eight-byte character string defined as follows:

```
        CDLOAD   NAME
NAME    DC       CL8'IDCAMS'
```

This macro returns the address of the entry point to IDCAMS in register 1. The following steps should then be taken:

1. Add 6 to the address in register 1. Place the result in register 15.

```
LA    15,6(1)
```

2. Place the address of a register save area into register 13. The save area must be 18 fullwords in length.

```
        LA  13,SAVEAREA
SAVAREA DS  18F
```

3. Load into register 14 the address of a point in your program to which control is to be passed when IDCAMS has completed its function.
4. Place the address of the **argument list** in register 1.
5. Branch to the address in register 15.

The **argument list** is a group of four fullwords that control certain functions during execution. Some of these functions include: specifying the address of the **options list**, controlling I/O operations during execution, identifying the DDNAME of the file you wish to control, and certain printer-related options.

The options list contains the format and parameters of the AMS **PARM** command. The PARM command is used primarily for debugging; it controls the format of the printed output. When the IDCAMS program is invoked, it will read AMS control statements for the standard input device, **SYSIPT** for DOS, **SYSIN** for OS.

A condition code is returned by IDCAMS in register 15. The meaning of the condition code is the same as that provided when using a stand-alone IDCAMS job stream.

16.19.2 INVOKING ACCESS METHOD SERVICES FROM AN OS APPLICATION

The parameter list and register usage is identical for both operating systems. The manner of invocation is different, however. For OS, IDCAMS is invoked as follows:

```
[label ]     LOAD EP=IDCAMS | EPLOC=address
```

Followed by:

```
LR      15,0
CALL    (15),(F1,F2,F3,F4),VL
```

Where: F1,F2,F3,F4 are the four full words mentioned under DOS. Register usage and condition code settings are also as defined under DOS.

16.20 SOME SAMPLE VSAM ASSEMBLER PROGRAMS

The following are sample VSAM assembler programs that can be used as models.

16.20.1 EXAMPLE VSAM ASSEMBLER ROUTINE FOR SEQUENTIAL RETRIEVAL

The following is an example showing sequential retrieval for a VSAM data set:

```
START     OPEN      (VSAMACB,INPUT)
GETREC    GET       RPL=VSAMRPL         GET RECORD
          LTR       R15,R15             Q. WAS GET OK
          BNZ       BADGET                 NO CHECK GET
          "                             PROCESSING HERE
          B         GETREC              GET NEXT RECORD
EOF1      RETURN    (14,12),RC=0        NORMAL END OF JOB
XLIST     EXLST     EODAD=EOF1
RECORD    DS        CL500               AREA FOR DATA
                                        RECORD
```

```
VSAMACB  ACB     DDNAME=VSAMJCL,                            +
                 MACRF=(SEQ,KEY,IN,),                       +
                 EXLST=XLIST
VSAMRPL  RPL     ACB=VSAMACB,AREA=RECORD,                   +
                 AREALEN=500,                               +
                 OPTCD=(SEQ,KEY,MVE,NUP)
         END
```

16.20.2 EXAMPLE VSAM ASSEMBLER ROUTINE, SKIP-SEQUENTIAL

The following example illustrates the skip-sequential method of access.

```
START    OPEN    (VSAMACB,INPUT)
         "                             SOME PROCESSING
                                         HERE
GETNXT   MVC     KEY,SOMETHING         MOVE IN SOME KEY
         GET     RPL=VSAMRPL           GET FOR UPDATE
         LTR     R15,R15               Q. WAS GET OK
         BNZ     BADGET                   NO CHECK GET
         "                             PROCESSING HERE
         B       GETNXT                GET NEXT RECORD
EOF1     RETURN  (14,12),RC=0          NORMAL END OF JOB
XLIST    EXLST   EODAD=EOF1
RECORD   DS      CL500                 AREA FOR DATA
                                         RECORD
KEY      DS      .....                 SIZE OF KEY
VSAMACB  ACB     DDNAME=VSAMJCL,                            +
                 MACRF=(SKP,KEY,IN,),                       +
                 EXLST=XLIST
VSAMRPL  RPL     ACB=VSAMACB,AREA=RECORD,                   +
                 AREALEN=500,                               +
                 OPTCD=(SKP,KEY,MVE,NUP,FKS,KGE),           +
                 ARG=KEY
         END
```

16.20.3 EXAMPLE VSAM ASSEMBLER ROUTINE, DIRECT RETRIEVAL

The following illustrates direct (random) retrieval:

```
START    OPEN    (VSAMACB,INPUT)
         "                             SOME PROCESSING
                                         HERE
```

```
GETNXT    MVC     RBA,ADDRESS              MOVE IN THE RBA
          GET     RPL=VSAMRPL              GET FOR UPDATE
          LTR     R15,R15                  Q. WAS GET OK
          BNZ     BADGET                      NO CHECK GET
          SHOWCB  RPL=VSAMRPL,AREA=FEEDBACK,                    +
                  AREALEN=4,                                    +
                  FIELDS=FDBK
          CLI     FDBK+3,X'10'             Q. NO RECORD FOUND
          BE      NOTFOUND                    YES
          "                                PROCESSING
          B       GETNXT                   GET ANOTHER RECORD
EOJ       CLOSE   (VSAMACB)
          RETURN  (14,12),RC=0             NORMAL END OF JOB
BADGET    ABEND   1,DUMP
RECORD    DS      CL250                    AREA FOR DATA
                                             RECORD
RBA       DS      CL4                      RBA USED AS KEY
VSAMACB   ACB     DDNAME=VSAMJCL,MACRF=(DIR,ADR,IN,)
VSAMRPL   RPL     ACB=VSAMACB,AREA=RECORD,                      +
                  AREALEN=250,                                  +
                  OPTCD=(DIR,ADR,MVE,NUP,KEQ),ARG=RBA
          END
```

16.20.4 EXAMPLE VSAM ASSEMBLER ROUTINE, CREATE A NEW FILE

The following illustrates the creation of a VSAM KSDS cluster.

```
START     OPEN    (VSAMACB,OUTPUT)
          OPEN    (SAM,INPUT)
GETREC    GET     SAM,RECORD               GET RECORD
          "                                PROCESSING HERE
          PUT     RPL=VSAMRPL              OUTPUT RECORD
          LTR     15,15                    Q. PUT OK
          BNZ     CHECK                       NO
          B       GETREC                   GET NEXT RECORD
EOF1      CLOSE   (VSAMACB)
          CLOSE   (SAM)
          RETURN  (14,12),RC=0             NORMAL END OF JOB
CHECK     ............
XLIST     EXLST   EODAD=EOF1
RECORD    DS      CL500                    AREA FOR DATA
                                             RECORD
VSAMACB   ACB     DDNAME=VSAMJCL,MACRF=(SEQ,OUT)
VSAMRPL   RPL     ACB=VSAMACB,AREA=RECORD,                      +
```

```
                        AREALEN=500,                          +
                        OPTCD=(SEQ,KEY,MVE,NUP)
 SAM         DCB        EODAD=EOF1
             END
```

TEST YOUR UNDERSTANDING

1. Explain the purpose of the ACB macro; the RPL macro.
2. What is the TESTCB macro used for?
3. How are the TESTCB and SHOWCB macros used?
4. What is an EXLST?
5. How can a VSAM macro be modified during execution?
6. What is asynchronous processing? How can it be used in VSAM?
7. What does it mean to chain RPLs? How is this accomplished?
8. Explain concurrent positioning.
9. How can IDCAMS be invoked from an application?
10. Explain the purpose of the GENCB macro.

chapter 17

PERFORMANCE AND TUNING

17.1 VSAM TUNING AND PERFORMANCE OPTIONS

This chapter presents some of the options available for fine-tuning both VSAM and, in a sense, your operating system. The items discussed include the following:

Control interval size
Control area size
Buffer size and usage
Index options
CI and CA freespace
KSDS reorganization

17.2 CONTROL INTERVAL SIZE

Of all the tuning options available, the size of the control interval is the most critical. The size of the data CI determines how much DASD space it uses, how much is wasted, the amount of buffer space the operating system must allocate, and the speed at which data can be processed.

The following are factors to be considered when choosing the size of the data control interval.

1. A larger CI size is often the most economical in terms of space usage versus wasted space. For smaller size records, the larger the CI, the smaller the percentage of space that is wasted.
2. For sequential file processing, larger control intervals will result in fewer I/O operations, thereby improving speed. There are reasons for this: the first involves physical access to the data. The selection CI size will influence the size of the physical record VSAM uses to house control intervals (see Chapter 13). Fewer I/O operations require fewer accesses to the disk. Read/write head movement and rotational delay take much more time than does the actual data transfer. The second reason involves index accesses. A larger data CI allows for more data records in that CI. This results in fewer index CIs. If an index set is not brought into memory (see Section 17.5), larger data CIs will result in fewer index CI accesses. Once again, you must bear in mind that this applies to sequentially accessed files only.
3. Another sequential processing consideration involves the use of **spanned** records. As you recall, spanned records are records that occupy more than one control interval. The last CI used to hold the last part of a spanned record will probably contain unused freespace. This freespace cannot be used by VSAM. If a lot of freespace is left, it will result in inefficient use of DASD space. Optimally, a spanned record will be spread across several small control intervals, or take up most of one CI.
4. For random file processing, a smaller CI (contained within a smaller **physical** record) would probably be the better processing choice. This is because transfer from disk to main storage of fewer bytes takes slightly less time. Furthermore, a smaller CI size would require less buffer space, thereby reducing system overhead.

For many applications, you will require both random and sequential access and will have to make some compromise on option choices. You will have to determine what factors are most important to you: speed, DASD space, or system overhead (buffers). If you are having difficulty determining the size of the CI, a good size all around is 4096. This not only nicely fits most data processing needs, but is also the same size as a virtual storage page frame in the OS and VM operating systems (DOS supports a 2048-byte page frame).

17.3 CONTROL AREA SIZE

The maximum (MAX-CA) size of a control area is one cylinder. The number of bytes in a cylinder is, of course, dependent upon the actual device. For instance, a 3330 cylinder is comprised of 19 tracks, and a 3350 cylinder is comprised of 30. The maximum size of the control area on a 3350 is much larger than the maximum CA size on a 3330. Whether the CA on one device is larger than the CA on another is not determined entirely by the number of tracks in a cylinder, however; for instance, a 3330 contains 19 tracks per cylinder whereas a 3380 contains 15. The number of bytes that can be held on a 3330 track is 13,030 whereas the number of bytes that can be contained on a 3380 track is 47,476. MAX-CA, therefore, is much greater on the 3380. You do not have much control over CA size selection. If the VSAM space defined on a volume was allocated in **cylinders**, the CA size will always be one cylinder. If a unique space was defined, the CA size will also be one cylinder. If you desire a control area size of less than one cylinder, VSAM will calculate the CA size. There are some things you can do to influence VSAM's choice of CA size. The determining factors that you can manipulate are the size of the index record and the size you specify for the VSAM space allocation.

One factor that you have no control over is the device type. VSAM also takes this into consideration when calculating the size of the CA (see Chapter 13 for more information on this). For better performance, control areas should not cross cylinder boundaries. It is best when whole CAs occupy a cylinder.

One of the more important factors when choosing CA size is the impact of CA splits. When a control area split takes place, a new control area is allocated at the end of the file. It is then preformatted by VSAM. Following this, approximately half (direct insert mode) the data from the full CA will be moved to the new CA. The time to perform all this will vary depending on the CA size. Obviously, a control area of two tracks will require less time to format and move data to than will a CA of one cylinder. The tradeoffs are space versus processing time.

Smaller CAs require more space. This is because there are more index CIs required to be used as pointers. Furthermore, if imbedding is used, the first track of each control area is used to store the sequence set. The more CAs there are, the more tracks will be used to store the sequence set when the IMBED option is used.

Although the benefits or faults of each option can be discussed hypothetically, CA size selection must be based entirely upon the requirements of the application and the resources of the system.

17.4 BUFFER SIZE AND USAGE

There are several factors to be taken into consideration when choosing buffer size and usage:

Size of the control intervals
Number of data buffers to be allocated
Number of index buffers to be allocated
Amount of storage area available for all buffers
Whether an in-memory index set is desired
Number of **concurrent positioning** requests (also referred to as strings) that can be issued
Type of access (random or sequential) to take place

17.4.1 DEFINITION OF BUFFER SPACE USAGE

Buffer space is used for control interval processing. It can be subdefined for the following:

Number of bytes that can be used (**BUFSP**)
Number of index buffers (**BUFNI**)
Number of data buffers (**BUFND**)
Number of concurrent positioning requests or strings (**STRNO**) allowed

There are three ways in which you can specify these options to VSAM: through the AMS DEFINE command, through JCL (OS only), and in the application program (see Chapters 15 and 16).

When defined through AMS, the parameters selected specify the **minimum** requirements to VSAM. If you do not specify these parameters, VSAM will force a minimum of one index and two data control interval buffers.

OS JCL can be used to specify buffer options. The AMP parameter of the DD card is used for this. The subparameters BUFSP, BUFND, BUFNI, and STRNO can be specified here. If used, these parameters will override the specifications provided to AMS through the DEFINE command. The same parameters BUFSP, BUFND, BUFNI, and STRNO can also be specified when coding the ACB macro in an application program (see Chapter 16).

17.4.2 BUFFERING CONSIDERATIONS

VSAM buffers usually occupy pageable storage space. Buffers can also utilize real fixed storage space. Even virtual storage blocks require real storage when being used. In either case, these are issues that must be considered when deciding processing options. The decision is one of processing speed versus system resources.

Generally, a minimum of four data buffers is recommended when sequential processing is used. It is sometimes advantageous to use more buffers, especially when an application is likely to retrieve records that happen to be in the buffer already. This greatly improves retrieval time. If an application is likely to access records recently processed (when mixed sequential and random processing is done), it might be beneficial to allocate more buffer space for data control intervals. If a read command is issued by an application, VSAM will first check to see if the record already exists in one of the data buffers. If so, no I/O operation is required, and the record is passed directly from the buffer to the application.

When sequential retrieval is used, extra buffer space for index control interval buffers does not help greatly, however, because the horizontal pointer in the sequence set is used instead of the index itself when determining the next control interval to be retrieved. Only one sequence set record at a time is kept in the buffer area.

If enough buffer space is allocated for a KSDS, VSAM will utilize the space by bringing in more index set control intervals. If enough space is available, the entire index set plus one sequence set record can be brought into memory.

Another consideration for determining buffer space is the number of concurrent data set positioning requests. An application may read more than one record with **update intent**. When this occurs, the program is said to have **exclusive control** over that record. With exclusive control, no other application can have access to that record for update until it is rewritten or otherwise released by the application. A buffer may be required for each read-for-update if the data records reside in different control intervals. Besides requiring additional buffer space for this, some space is required to contain position pointers. The number of such pointers is controlled by the STRNO parameter.

In addition to specifying the preceding, the **number of bytes** desired for buffer space can be specified as well. This can allow VSAM some flexibility in the usage of buffer space. For instance, by specifying BUFND = 2 and BUFSP = 30000 you are telling VSAM that you want to use two buffers for data CIs, but say nothing about how the rest of the space is used. This allows VSAM to use the remaining space as it sees fit. Most likely, it will be used for index set control intervals.

Finally, extra buffers will be required when using paths or alternate indices. At least one additional buffer is required for both the index and data control interval buffers for an alternate index.

For additional system options for buffer handling, see Chapter 14, the discussion on local and global shared resources.

17.5 INDEX OPTIONS

We have already discussed how, by using buffer space, VSAM can bring an entire index set into main storage. There are alternatives to this that can be considered as well:

Index and data component separation
Imbedding
Replication

In most installations, at least one of these options is utilized.

17.5.1 INDEX AND DATA COMPONENT SEPARATION

Lightly utilized DASD **volumes** are good candidates for index and data component separation. This is usually a good thing to do because without it (or some other option) the read/write head would require constant movement between the index and data components.

Separation allows for minimal head movement during record retrieval. Since the entire index often takes up less than one cylinder of space, once the read/write head is positioned to the right cylinder there is no further need to move the head during record retrieval. This is especially useful when processing a file randomly. If you have several other data sets on the same volume, the advantage will be reduced according to the activity of the read/write head.

Some installations place their indices on drum. This, of course, requires no head movement at all. Some disk devices (3340) have a few cylinders of fixed head area, in addition to the larger movable head area, in which indices could be stored. If such a device is available to you, you might consider placing the index in the fixed head area, while placing the data component in the movable area.

The separation option is worth considering when random processing is be to utilized most of the time for a particular data set, and buffer space is at a premium. Another variation of this is to define an imbedded sequence set and to separate the index and data components as well.

17.5.2 IMBEDDING

Imbedding causes the sequence set level of the index to be created on the first track of each control area. This option is an excellent choice when data set processing is primarily sequential. The sequence set is automatically replicated on the first CA track, as many copies as will fit. This improves sequence set retrieval time since a record will not have as far to travel before it is positioned under the read/write head. Imbedding, therefore, can also be advantageous when retrieving records randomly.

There are some tradeoffs when using imbedding. The most obvious is the amount of extra space required, far more than when the sequence set is kept with the rest of the index. This is especially true if you are using small control areas. Another disadvantage, although not a great one, is that additions to a file may cause more frequent changes to the sequence set pointers. If this occurs, all replicated records will have to be updated as well.

17.5.3 REPLICATION

Replication applies only to the **index set**. The index set is the name given to that part of the index not included in, and higher than, the sequence set.

With this option you can request that VSAM replicate each index set CI as many times as it will fit on one track. This will cost you something in DASD space. The number of records in the index set are usually so few, however, that the cost in space is usually not too bad. You might have noticed that the terms CI and record have been used interchangeably when referring to the index. This is because there is always only one record in an index CI. Each record, however, contains many pointer fields. If you will not be allocating enough buffer space to contain the entire index set, replication would be a good option.

If desired, both imbedding and replication can be used.

17.6 CI AND CA FREESPACE

The concept of freespace is one of the best features of VSAM. Freespace can be reserved in control intervals as well as control areas. You may request that VSAM reserve a certain percentage of each CA and CI when the cluster is defined through AMS. Decisions on freespace must be determined by the application itself. Below are some guidelines for determining the usage of freespace.

ADDITION OF RECORDS

If you are expecting that several small groups of records will be inserted into CIs that have closely related keys, it is usually best to allow for a large CI freespace percentage. This leaves plenty of room in the control interval at load time in which to place these consecutive insertions later.

If several volume record additions are to be made in key ranges that do not currently exist and that will not affect the current CIs, then it is best to allow for a small percentage of CI freespace and a much larger amount of CA freespace. This will allow VSAM to place these new records into the empty CIs located at the end of the control area.

If there will be evenly dispersed insertions throughout the data set, it would probably be best to allocate a modest percentage, say 20%, for CI freespace and little or no CA freespace.

Some applications require insertion of records with keys higher than any that currently exist, as, for example, in the case of an application that requires access to data by **date**. Records with key ranges outside a given CA will never be placed in that CA, even if freespace is available. In this situation records will be added to the back of the file. Little or no CI/CA freespace would be required when initially loading the file. The thing to watch out for in this case would be the occurrence of CA splits that could cause excessive system overhead.

NO RECORD ADDITIONS

If records are never added to a data set once it is loaded, both CI and CA freespace can be set to zero. There is no reason to allocate space if you are certain that no records will ever be added to this data set.

A trick that can be used at times is to partially load a file with a certain key range using a certain CI/CA freespace percentage, then altering through AMS the CI/CA specifications for the next key range; this is continued until the file is completely loaded. The purpose of this would be to optimize the file space along with the desired performance characteristics. Obviously, this would require some study involving the measurement of file key allocations as well as daily and seasonal file usages.

17.7 KSDS REORGANIZATION

Even when the freespace choices for a KSDS have been well thought out, CI and CA splits will occur. When this happens, records are no longer in any physical sequential order. If enough control area freespace has been defined, and only CI splits have occurred, the data is simply moved to another location on the same cylinder; this causes no additional arm movement. When, however, CA splits occur, some of the records in the control area to be split will be moved to another control area outside that cylinder. This situation will cause additional arm movement when record retrieval is sequential. If many CA splits have occurred, processing time may increase considerably. There is a simple solution to this: file reorganization.

A KSDS data set can be **reorganized** by using the Access Method Services commands REPRO, DELETE, and DEFINE. These are the steps to be followed:

REPRO the data set to sequential tape or DASD
DELETE the cluster
DEFINE the cluster once again
REPRO from your sequential back-up to restore

The DELETE and DEFINE are not needed for REUSABLE data sets.

This operation restores the data in physical as well as logical sequence.

TEST YOUR UNDERSTANDING

1. Name the five areas that directly affect VSAM's performance or can affect the operating system's performance.
2. Explain how choosing the right size for a control interval can affect performance.

3. What is one of the problems associated with very large control areas?
4. What are some of the options available when determining buffer space?
5. How can you bring the entire index set into main storage?
6. What advantage can be obtained by placing the index and data components on separate volumes?
7. Explain imbedding and replication.
8. If record additions are always at the end of a KSDS data set, what should your freespace specification be?

appendix A

LISTCAT AND LISTCRA SAMPLES

The following examples are contained on the following pages:


```
IDCAMS  SYSTEM SERVICES                                    TIME  10 35 09        03/23/84      PAGE   1

                 LISTCAT ENTRIES(ESDSTST) ALL CATALOG(USERCAT.VSAM02)

IDCAMS  SYSTEM SERVICES                                    TIME  10 35 09        03/23/84      PAGE   2

                      LISTING FROM CATALOG -- USERCAT.VSAM02

CLUSTER ------- ESDSTST
     HISTORY
       OWNER-IDENT-------(NULL)      CREATION----------84.083
       RELEASE---------------2       EXPIRATION--------00.000
     PROTECTION---------(NULL)
     ASSOCIATIONS
       DATA-----ESDSTST.DATA

   DATA ------ ESDSTST.DATA
     HISTORY
       OWNER-IDENT-------(NULL)      CREATION----------84.083
       RELEASE---------------2       EXPIRATION--------00.000
     PROTECTION---------(NULL)
     ASSOCIATIONS
       CLUSTER--ESDSTST
     ATTRIBUTES
       KEYLEN----------------0       AVGLRECL-------------850    BUFSPACE-----------2048    CISIZE------------1024
       RKP-------------------0       MAXLRECL-------------850    EXCPEXIT----------(NULL)   CI/CA---------------15
       SHROPTNS(2,3)     SPEED       SUBALLOC         NOERASE    NONINDEXED      VSAMDATSET NOWRITECHK     NOIMBED
       NOREPLICAT    UNORDERED       NOREUSE       NONSPANNED
```

Figure A.1 Sample LISTCAT using 'ENTRIES' parameter for ESDS.

```
STATISTICS
  REC-TOTAL--------------13      SPLITS-CI--------------0      EXCPS------------------10
  REC-DELETED-----------0        SPLITS-CA--------------0      EXTENTS-----------------1
  REC-INSERTED----------0        FREESPACE- CI----------0      SYSTEM-TIMESTAMP
  REC-UPDATED-----------0        FREESPACE- CA----------0            X'97156EC9FFD4D080'
  REC-RETRIEVED---------0        FREESPC-BYTES-------2048
ALLOCATION
  SPACE-TYPE---------TRACK
  SPACE-PRI--------------1       USECLASS-PRI-----------0      HI-ALLOC-RBA--------15360
  SPACE-SEC--------------0       USECLASS-SEC-----------0      HI-USED-RBA---------13312
VOLUME
  VOLSER------------VSAM02       PHYREC-SIZE---------1024      HI-ALLOC-RBA--------15360     EXTENT-NUMBER----------1
  DEVTYPE------X'3010200B'       PHYRECS/TRK-----------15      HI-USED-RBA---------13312     EXTENT-TYPE--------X'00'
  VOLFLAG-----------PRIME        TRACKS/CA--------------1
  EXTENTS
  LOW-CCHH-----X'00F5000A'       LOW-RBA----------------0      TRACKS------------------1
  HIGH-CCHH----X'00F5000A'       HIGH-RBA-----------15359

IDCAMS  SYSTEM SERVICES                                        TIME  10 35 09       03/23/84      PAGE   3

                        LISTING FROM CATALOG -- USERCAT.VSAM02

        THE NUMBER OF ENTRIES PROCESSED WAS
                    AIX -------------------0
                    CLUSTER ---------------1
                    DATA ------------------1
                    INDEX -----------------0
                    NONVSAM ---------------0
                    PATH ------------------0
                    SPACE -----------------0
                    USERCATALOG -----------0
                    TOTAL -----------------2

        THE NUMBER OF PROTECTED ENTRIES SUPPRESSED WAS 0

IDC0001I FUNCTION COMPLETED, HIGHEST CONDITION CODE WAS 0
```

Figure A.1 Continued.

```
IDCAMS  SYSTEM SERVICES                                        TIME  10 35 09       03/23/84      PAGE

IDC0002I IDCAMS PROCESSING COMPLETE. MAXIMUM CONDITION CODE WAS 8


IDCAMS  SYSTEM SERVICES                                        TIME  10 36 11       03/23/84      PAGE   2

                        LISTING FROM CATALOG -- USERCAT.VSAM02

CLUSTER ------- APTRANE
   DATA ------- APTRANE.DATA
   INDEX ------ APTRANE.INDEX
CLUSTER ------- APTRNXE
   DATA ------- APTRNXE.DATA
   INDEX ------ APTRNXE.INDEX
CLUSTER ------- COSTMST
   DATA ------- COSTMST.DATA
   INDEX ------ COSTMST.INDEX
CLUSTER ------- DMPSEC
   DATA ------- DMPSEC.DATA
   INDEX ------ DMPSEC.INDEX
CLUSTER ------- ESDSTST
   DATA ------- ESDSTST.DATA
CLUSTER ------- HGVDEP.CLUSTER
   DATA ------- HGVDEP.DATA
   INDEX ------ HGVDEP.INDEX
```

Figure A.2 Sample LISTCAT using 'CATALOG' parameter.

```
CLUSTER ------- MACFILE
   DATA ------- MACFILE.DATA
   INDEX ------ MACFILE.INDEX
CLUSTER ------- MAILDAT
   DATA ------- MAIL.DATA
   INDEX ------ MAIL.INDEX
CLUSTER ------- MANFSTE
   DATA ------- MANFSTE.DATA

IDCAMS  SYSTEM SERVICES                              TIME  10 36 11        03/23/84     PAGE   3
                       LISTING FROM CATALOG -- USERCAT.VSAM02
   INDEX ------ MANFSTE.INDEX
CLUSTER ------- MNDMSTE
   DATA ------- MNDMSTE.DATA
   INDEX ------ MNDMSTE.INDEX
CLUSTER ------- MNDNDXE
   DATA ------- MNDNDXE.DATA
   INDEX ------ MNDNDXE.INDEX
CLUSTER ------- PGNMTBL
   DATA ------- PGNMTBL.DATA
   INDEX ------ PGNMTBL.INDEX
CLUSTER ------- POMVNDR
   DATA ------- POMVNDR.DATA
   INDEX ------ POMVNDR.INDEX
CLUSTER ------- POSMDE
   DATA ------- POSMDE.DATA
   INDEX ------ POSMDE.INDEX
CLUSTER ------- SGTLIBU
   DATA ------- SGTLIBU.DATA
   INDEX ------ SGTLIBU.INDEX
CLUSTER ------- SGTLIB1
   DATA ------- SGTLIB1.DATA
   INDEX ------ SGTLIB1.INDEX
CLUSTER ------- SGTLIB2
   DATA ------- SGTLIB2.DATA
   INDEX ------ SGTLIB2.INDEX
IDCAMS  SYSTEM SERVICES                              TIME  10 36 11        03/23/84     PAGE   4
                       LISTING FROM CATALOG -- USERCAT.VSAM02
CLUSTER ------- TAPELIB
   DATA ------- TAPELIB.DATA
   INDEX ------ TAPELIB.INDEX
CLUSTER ------- TPLIBX1
   DATA ------- TPLIBX1.DATA
   INDEX ------ TPLIBX1.INDEX
CLUSTER ------- USERCAT.VSAM02
   DATA ------- VSAM.CATALOG.BASE.DATA.RECORD
   INDEX ------ VSAM.CATALOG.BASE.INDEX.RECORD
VOLUME -------- VSAM02
```

Figure A.2 Continued.

```
IDCAMS  SYSTEM SERVICES                                       TIME  10 36 11        03/23/84      PAGE   5

                              LISTING FROM CATALOG -- USERCAT.VSAM02

        THE NUMBER OF ENTRIES PROCESSED WAS
                  AIX -------------------0
                  CLUSTER --------------20
                  DATA -----------------20
                  INDEX ----------------19
                  NONVSAM ---------------0
                  PATH ------------------0
                  SPACE -----------------1
                  USERCATALOG -----------0
                  TOTAL ----------------60

        THE NUMBER OF PROTECTED ENTRIES SUPPRESSED WAS 0

IDC0001I FUNCTION COMPLETED, HIGHEST CONDITION CODE WAS 0
```

Figure A.2 Continued.

```
IDCAMS  SYSTEM SERVICES                                       TIME  10 36 11        03/23/84      PAGE   6

 LISTCAT VOLUME CATALOG(USERCAT.VSAM02)

IDCAMS  SYSTEM SERVICES                                       TIME  10 36 11        03/23/84      PAGE   7

                              LISTING FROM CATALOG -- USERCAT.VSAM02

CLUSTER ------- APTRANE
     HISTORY
       OWNER-IDENT-------(NULL)      CREATION----------84.080
       RELEASE----------------2      EXPIRATION--------00.000

   DATA ------- APTRANE.DATA
     HISTORY
       OWNER-IDENT-------(NULL)      CREATION----------84.080
       RELEASE----------------2      EXPIRATION--------00.000
     VOLUMES
       VOLSER------------VSAM02      DEVTYPE------X'3010200B'

   INDEX ------ APTRANE.INDEX
     HISTORY
       OWNER-IDENT-------(NULL)      CREATION----------84.080
       RELEASE----------------2      EXPIRATION--------00.000
     VOLUMES
       VOLSER------------VSAM02      DEVTYPE------X'3010200B'

CLUSTER ------- APTRNXE
     HISTORY
       OWNER-IDENT-------(NULL)      CREATION----------84.080
       RELEASE----------------2      EXPIRATION--------00.000

   DATA ------- APTRNXE.DATA
     HISTORY
       OWNER-IDENT-------(NULL)      CREATION----------84.080
       RELEASE----------------2      EXPIRATION--------00.000
     VOLUMES
       VOLSER------------VSAM02      DEVTYPE------X'3010200B'

   INDEX ------ APTRNXE.INDEX
     HISTORY
       OWNER-IDENT-------(NULL)      CREATION----------84.080
       RELEASE----------------2      EXPIRATION--------00.000
     VOLUMES
       VOLSER------------VSAM02      DEVTYPE------X'3010200B'

CLUSTER ------- COSTMST
     HISTORY
       OWNER-IDENT-------(NULL)      CREATION----------84.080
       RELEASE----------------2      EXPIRATION--------00.000

   DATA ------- COSTMST.DATA
     HISTORY
       OWNER-IDENT-------(NULL)      CREATION----------84.080
       RELEASE----------------2      EXPIRATION--------00.000
     VOLUMES
       VOLSER------------VSAM02      DEVTYPE------X'3010200B'
```

Figure A.3 Sample LISTCAT using 'VOLUME' parameter.

```
IDCAMS  SYSTEM SERVICES                                          TIME  10 36 11        03/23/84      PAGE   8

                              LISTING FROM CATALOG -- USERCAT.VSAM02

  INDEX ------ COSTMST.INDEX
    HISTORY
      OWNER-IDENT-------(NULL)      CREATION----------84.080
      RELEASE---------------2       EXPIRATION--------00.000
    VOLUMES
      VOLSER------------VSAM02      DEVTYPE------X'3010200B'

CLUSTER ------- DMPSEC
    HISTORY
      OWNER-IDENT-------(NULL)      CREATION----------84.080
      RELEASE---------------2       EXPIRATION--------99.365

  DATA ------- DMPSEC.DATA
    HISTORY
      OWNER-IDENT-------(NULL)      CREATION----------84.080
      RELEASE---------------2       EXPIRATION--------99.365
    VOLUMES
      VOLSER------------VSAM02      DEVTYPE------X'3010200B'

  INDEX ------ DMPSEC.INDEX
    HISTORY
      OWNER-IDENT-------(NULL)      CREATION----------84.080
      RELEASE---------------2       EXPIRATION--------99.365
    VOLUMES
      VOLSER------------VSAM02      DEVTYPE------X'3010200B'

CLUSTER ------- ESDSTST
    HISTORY
      OWNER-IDENT-------(NULL)      CREATION----------84.083
      RELEASE---------------2       EXPIRATION--------00.000

  DATA ------- ESDSTST.DATA
    HISTORY
      OWNER-IDENT-------(NULL)      CREATION----------84.083
      RELEASE---------------2       EXPIRATION--------00.000
    VOLUMES
      VOLSER------------VSAM02      DEVTYPE------X'3010200B'

CLUSTER ------- HGVDEP.CLUSTER
    HISTORY
      OWNER-IDENT-------(NULL)      CREATION----------84.080
      RELEASE---------------2       EXPIRATION--------00.000

  DATA ------- HGVDEP.DATA
    HISTORY
      OWNER-IDENT-------(NULL)      CREATION----------84.080
      RELEASE---------------2       EXPIRATION--------00.000
    VOLUMES
      VOLSER------------VSAM02      DEVTYPE------X'3010200B'

IDCAMS  SYSTEM SERVICES                                          TIME  10 36 11        03/23/84      PAGE   9

                              LISTING FROM CATALOG -- USERCAT.VSAM02

  INDEX ------ HGVDEP.INDEX
    HISTORY
      OWNER-IDENT-------(NULL)      CREATION----------84.080
      RELEASE---------------2       EXPIRATION--------00.000
    VOLUMES
      VOLSER------------VSAM02      DEVTYPE------X'3010200B'

CLUSTER ------- MACFILE
    HISTORY
      OWNER-IDENT-------(NULL)      CREATION----------84.080
      RELEASE---------------2       EXPIRATION--------00.000

  DATA ------- MACFILE.DATA
    HISTORY
      OWNER-IDENT-------(NULL)      CREATION----------84.080
      RELEASE---------------2       EXPIRATION--------00.000
    VOLUMES
      VOLSER------------VSAM02      DEVTYPE------X'3010200B'

  INDEX ------ MACFILE.INDEX
    HISTORY
      OWNER-IDENT-------(NULL)      CREATION----------84.080
      RELEASE---------------2       EXPIRATION--------00.000
    VOLUMES
      VOLSER------------VSAM02      DEVTYPE------X'3010200B'

CLUSTER ------- MAILDAT
    HISTORY
      OWNER-IDENT-------(NULL)      CREATION----------84.080
      RELEASE---------------2       EXPIRATION--------99.365

  DATA ------- MAIL.DATA
    HISTORY
      OWNER-IDENT-------(NULL)      CREATION----------84.080
      RELEASE---------------2       EXPIRATION--------99.365
```

Figure A.3 Continued.

```
      VOLUMES
        VOLSER------------VSAM02        DEVTYPE------X'3010200B'

    INDEX ------ MAIL.INDEX
      HISTORY
        OWNER-IDENT-------(NULL)        CREATION----------84.080
        RELEASE----------------2        EXPIRATION--------99.365
      VOLUMES
        VOLSER------------VSAM02        DEVTYPE------X'3010200B'

CLUSTER ------- MANFSTE
      HISTORY
        OWNER-IDENT-------(NULL)        CREATION----------84.080
        RELEASE----------------2        EXPIRATION--------00.000
```

```
IDCAMS  SYSTEM SERVICES                                         TIME  10 36 11        03/23/84     PAGE  10

                              LISTING FROM CATALOG -- USERCAT.VSAM02

    DATA ------- MANFSTE.DATA
      HISTORY
        OWNER-IDENT-------(NULL)        CREATION----------84.080
        RELEASE----------------2        EXPIRATION--------00.000
      VOLUMES
        VOLSER------------VSAM02        DEVTYPE------X'3010200B'

    INDEX ------ MANFSTE.INDEX
      HISTORY
        OWNER-IDENT-------(NULL)        CREATION----------84.080
        RELEASE----------------2        EXPIRATION--------00.000
      VOLUMES
        VOLSER------------VSAM02        DEVTYPE------X'3010200B'

CLUSTER ------- MNDMSTE
      HISTORY
        OWNER-IDENT-------(NULL)        CREATION----------84.080
        RELEASE----------------2        EXPIRATION--------00.000

    DATA ------- MNDMSTE.DATA
      HISTORY
        OWNER-IDENT-------(NULL)        CREATION----------84.080
        RELEASE----------------2        EXPIRATION--------00.000
      VOLUMES
        VOLSER------------VSAM02        DEVTYPE------X'3010200B'

    INDEX ------ MNDMSTE.INDEX
      HISTORY
        OWNER-IDENT-------(NULL)        CREATION----------84.080
        RELEASE----------------2        EXPIRATION--------00.000
      VOLUMES
        VOLSER------------VSAM02        DEVTYPE------X'3010200B'

CLUSTER ------- MNDNDXE
      HISTORY
        OWNER-IDENT-------(NULL)        CREATION----------84.080
        RELEASE----------------2        EXPIRATION--------00.000

    DATA ------- MNDNDXE.DATA
      HISTORY
        OWNER-IDENT-------(NULL)        CREATION----------84.080
        RELEASE----------------2        EXPIRATION--------00.000
      VOLUMES
        VOLSER------------VSAM02        DEVTYPE------X'3010200B'

    INDEX ------ MNDNDXE.INDEX
      HISTORY
        OWNER-IDENT-------(NULL)        CREATION----------84.080
        RELEASE----------------2        EXPIRATION--------00.000
      VOLUMES
```

```
IDCAMS  SYSTEM SERVICES                                         TIME  10 36 11        03/23/84     PAGE  11

                              LISTING FROM CATALOG -- USERCAT.VSAM02

        VOLSER------------VSAM02        DEVTYPE------X'3010200B'

CLUSTER ------- PGNMTBL
      HISTORY
        OWNER-IDENT-------(NULL)        CREATION----------84.080
        RELEASE----------------2        EXPIRATION--------00.000

    DATA ------- PGNMTBL.DATA
      HISTORY
        OWNER-IDENT-------(NULL)        CREATION----------84.080
        RELEASE----------------2        EXPIRATION--------00.000
      VOLUMES
        VOLSER------------VSAM02        DEVTYPE------X'3010200B'

    INDEX ------ PGNMTBL.INDEX
      HISTORY
        OWNER-IDENT-------(NULL)        CREATION----------84.080
        RELEASE----------------2        EXPIRATION--------00.000
```

Figure A.3 Continued.

```
    VOLUMES
      VOLSER------------VSAM02      DEVTYPE------X'3010200B'

CLUSTER ------- POMVNDR
    HISTORY
      OWNER-IDENT-------(NULL)      CREATION----------84.080
      RELEASE----------------2      EXPIRATION--------00.000

  DATA ------- POMVNDR.DATA
    HISTORY
      OWNER-IDENT-------(NULL)      CREATION----------84.080
      RELEASE----------------2      EXPIRATION--------00.000
    VOLUMES
      VOLSER------------VSAM02      DEVTYPE------X'3010200B'

  INDEX ------ POMVNDR.INDEX
    HISTORY
      OWNER-IDENT-------(NULL)      CREATION----------84.080
      RELEASE----------------2      EXPIRATION--------00.000
    VOLUMES
      VOLSER------------VSAM02      DEVTYPE------X'3010200B'

CLUSTER ------- POSMDE
    HISTORY
      OWNER-IDENT-------(NULL)      CREATION----------84.080
      RELEASE----------------2      EXPIRATION--------00.000

  DATA ------- POSMDE.DATA
    HISTORY
      OWNER-IDENT-------(NULL)      CREATION----------84.080
      RELEASE----------------2      EXPIRATION--------00.000
    VOLUMES

IDCAMS  SYSTEM SERVICES                                        TIME  10 36 11        03/23/84     PAGE  12

                             LISTING FROM CATALOG -- USERCAT.VSAM02

      VOLSER------------VSAM02      DEVTYPE------X'3010200B'

  INDEX ------ POSMDE.INDEX
    HISTORY
      OWNER-IDENT-------(NULL)      CREATION----------84.080
      RELEASE----------------2      EXPIRATION--------00.000
    VOLUMES
      VOLSER------------VSAM02      DEVTYPE------X'3010200B'

CLUSTER ------- SGTLIBU
    HISTORY
      OWNER-IDENT-------(NULL)      CREATION----------84.080
      RELEASE----------------2      EXPIRATION--------00.000

  DATA ------- SGTLIBU.DATA
    HISTORY
      OWNER-IDENT-------(NULL)      CREATION----------84.080
      RELEASE----------------2      EXPIRATION--------00.000
    VOLUMES
      VOLSER------------VSAM02      DEVTYPE------X'3010200B'

  INDEX ------ SGTLIBU.INDEX
    HISTORY
      OWNER-IDENT-------(NULL)      CREATION----------84.080
      RELEASE----------------2      EXPIRATION--------00.000
    VOLUMES
      VOLSER------------VSAM02      DEVTYPE------X'3010200B'

CLUSTER ------- SGTLIB1
    HISTORY
      OWNER-IDENT-------(NULL)      CREATION----------84.080
      RELEASE----------------2      EXPIRATION--------00.000

  DATA ------- SGTLIB1.DATA
    HISTORY
      OWNER-IDENT-------(NULL)      CREATION----------84.080
      RELEASE----------------2      EXPIRATION--------00.000
    VOLUMES
      VOLSER------------VSAM02      DEVTYPE------X'3010200B'

  INDEX ------ SGTLIB1.INDEX
    HISTORY
      OWNER-IDENT-------(NULL)      CREATION----------84.080
      RELEASE----------------2      EXPIRATION--------00.000
    VOLUMES
      VOLSER------------VSAM02      DEVTYPE------X'3010200B'

CLUSTER ------- SGTLIB2
    HISTORY
      OWNER-IDENT-------(NULL)      CREATION----------84.080
```

Figure A.3 Continued.

```
                         LISTING FROM CATALOG -- USERCAT.VSAM02
      RELEASE----------------2          EXPIRATION--------00.000

    DATA ------- SGTLIB2.DATA
      HISTORY
        OWNER-IDENT-------(NULL)        CREATION----------84.080
        RELEASE----------------2        EXPIRATION--------00.000
      VOLUMES
        VOLSER------------VSAM02        DEVTYPE------X'3010200B'

    INDEX ------ SGTLIB2.INDEX
      HISTORY
        OWNER-IDENT-------(NULL)        CREATION----------84.080
        RELEASE----------------2        EXPIRATION--------00.000
      VOLUMES
        VOLSER------------VSAM02        DEVTYPE------X'3010200B'

CLUSTER ------- TAPELIB
      HISTORY
        OWNER-IDENT-------(NULL)        CREATION----------84.083
        RELEASE----------------2        EXPIRATION--------00.000

    DATA ------- TAPELIB.DATA
      HISTORY
        OWNER-IDENT-------(NULL)        CREATION----------84.083
        RELEASE----------------2        EXPIRATION--------00.000
      VOLUMES
        VOLSER------------VSAM02        DEVTYPE------X'3010200B'

    INDEX ------ TAPELIB.INDEX
      HISTORY
        OWNER-IDENT-------(NULL)        CREATION----------84.083
        RELEASE----------------2        EXPIRATION--------00.000
      VOLUMES
        VOLSER------------VSAM02        DEVTYPE------X'3010200B'

CLUSTER ------- TPLIBX1
      HISTORY
        OWNER-IDENT-------(NULL)        CREATION----------84.083
        RELEASE----------------2        EXPIRATION--------00.000

    DATA ------- TPLIBX1.DATA
      HISTORY
        OWNER-IDENT-------(NULL)        CREATION----------84.083
        RELEASE----------------2        EXPIRATION--------00.000
      VOLUMES
        VOLSER------------VSAM02        DEVTYPE------X'3010200B'

    INDEX ------ TPLIBX1.INDEX
      HISTORY
        OWNER-IDENT-------(NULL)        CREATION----------84.083
```



```
                         LISTING FROM CATALOG -- USERCAT.VSAM02
        RELEASE----------------2        EXPIRATION--------00.000
      VOLUMES
        VOLSER------------VSAM02        DEVTYPE------X'3010200B'

CLUSTER ------- USERCAT.VSAM02
      HISTORY
        OWNER-IDENT-------(NULL)        CREATION----------83.264
        RELEASE----------------2        EXPIRATION--------00.000

    DATA ------- VSAM.CATALOG.BASE.DATA.RECORD
      HISTORY
        OWNER-IDENT-------(NULL)        CREATION----------83.264
        RELEASE----------------2        EXPIRATION--------00.000
      VOLUMES
        VOLSER------------VSAM02        DEVTYPE------X'3010200B'

    INDEX ------ VSAM.CATALOG.BASE.INDEX.RECORD
      HISTORY
        OWNER-IDENT-------(NULL)        CREATION----------83.264
        RELEASE----------------2        EXPIRATION--------00.000
      VOLUMES
        VOLSER------------VSAM02        DEVTYPE------X'3010200B'

VOLUME -------- VSAM02
      HISTORY
        RELEASE----------------2
      VOLUMES
        VOLSER------------VSAM02        DEVTYPE------X'3010200B'
```

Figure A.3 Continued.

```
IDCAMS  SYSTEM SERVICES                                   TIME  10 36 11        03/23/84      PAGE  15

                         LISTING FROM CATALOG -- USERCAT.VSAM02

      THE NUMBER OF ENTRIES PROCESSED WAS
             AIX -------------------0
             CLUSTER --------------20
             DATA -----------------20
             INDEX ----------------19
             NONVSAM ---------------0
             PATH ------------------0
             SPACE -----------------1
             USERCATALOG -----------0
             TOTAL ----------------60

      THE NUMBER OF PROTECTED ENTRIES SUPPRESSED WAS 0

IDC0001I FUNCTION COMPLETED, HIGHEST CONDITION CODE WAS 0
```

Figure A.3 Continued.

```
IDCAMS  SYSTEM SERVICES                                   TIME  10 36 11        03/23/84      PAGE  16

 LISTCAT SPACE ALL CATALOG(USERCAT.VSAM02)

IDCAMS  SYSTEM SERVICES                              TIME  10 36 11        03/23/84      PAGE  17

                        LISTING FROM CATALOG -- USERCAT.VSAM02

VOLUME -------- VSAM02
   HISTORY
     RELEASE---------------2
   CHARACTERISTICS
     BYTES/TRK-------------0     DEVTYPE---------........   MAX-PHYREC-SZ----------0    DATASETS-ON-VOL-------38
     TRKS/CYL--------------0     VOLUME-TIMESTAMP           MAX-EXT/ALLOC----------5    DATASPCS-ON-VOL--------2
     CYLS/VOL--------------0          X'96E893ACDEADA080'
   DATASPACE
     DATASETS--------------1     FORMAT-1-LABEL             ATTRIBUTES
     EXTENTS---------------1     CCHHR------X'022A000003'   SUBALLOC
     SEC-ALLOC-------------0     TIMESTAMP                  EXPLICIT
     TYPE--------------TRACK          X'962E7AFB747C4080'   USERCAT
     CLASS-----------------0
     EXTENT-DESCRIPTOR
     TRACKS-TOTAL---------30     BEG-CCHH-----X'00FA0000'   SPACE-MAP-----------1E
     TRACKS-USED----------30
     DATASET-DIRECTORY
       DSN----USERCAT.VSAM02                                ATTRIBUTES--------(NULL)    EXTENTS---------------3
   DATASPACE
     DATASETS-------------37     FORMAT-1-LABEL             ATTRIBUTES
     EXTENTS---------------2     CCHHR------X'022A000004'   SUBALLOC
     SEC-ALLOC-------------0     TIMESTAMP                  EXPLICIT
     TYPE--------------TRACK          X'96E893ACDEADA080'
     CLASS-----------------0
     EXTENT-DESCRIPTOR
     TRACKS-TOTAL--------7499    BEG-CCHH-----X'00000001'   SPACE-MAP-----------FD1CC0135A1E
     TRACKS-USED---------7450
     TRACKS-TOTAL--------9090    BEG-CCHH-----X'00FB0000'   SPACE-MAP-----------FD097EFD1A04
     TRACKS-USED---------2430
     DATASET-DIRECTORY
       DSN----APTRANE.DATA                                  ATTRIBUTES--------(NULL)    EXTENTS---------------1
       DSN----APTRANE.INDEX                                 ATTRIBUTES--------(NULL)    EXTENTS---------------1
       DSN----APTRNXE.DATA                                  ATTRIBUTES--------(NULL)    EXTENTS---------------1
       DSN----APTRNXE.INDEX                                 ATTRIBUTES--------(NULL)    EXTENTS---------------1
       DSN----COSTMST.DATA                                  ATTRIBUTES--------(NULL)    EXTENTS---------------1
       DSN----COSTMST.INDEX                                 ATTRIBUTES--------(NULL)    EXTENTS---------------1
       DSN----DMPSEC.DATA                                   ATTRIBUTES--------(NULL)    EXTENTS---------------1
       DSN----DMPSEC.INDEX                                  ATTRIBUTES--------(NULL)    EXTENTS---------------1
       DSN----HGVDEP.DATA                                   ATTRIBUTES--------(NULL)    EXTENTS---------------1
       DSN----HGVDEP.INDEX                                  ATTRIBUTES--------(NULL)    EXTENTS---------------1
       DSN----MAIL.DATA                                     ATTRIBUTES--------(NULL)    EXTENTS---------------1
       DSN----MAIL.INDEX                                    ATTRIBUTES--------(NULL)    EXTENTS---------------1
       DSN----MANFSTE.DATA                                  ATTRIBUTES--------(NULL)    EXTENTS---------------1
       DSN----MANFSTE.INDEX                                 ATTRIBUTES--------(NULL)    EXTENTS---------------1
       DSN----MNDMSTE.DATA                                  ATTRIBUTES--------(NULL)    EXTENTS---------------1
       DSN----MNDMSTE.INDEX                                 ATTRIBUTES--------(NULL)    EXTENTS---------------1
       DSN----MNDNDXE.DATA                                  ATTRIBUTES--------(NULL)    EXTENTS---------------1
       DSN----MNDNDXE.INDEX                                 ATTRIBUTES--------(NULL)    EXTENTS---------------1
       DSN----TAPELIB.DATA                                  ATTRIBUTES--------(NULL)    EXTENTS---------------1
       DSN----TAPELIB.INDEX                                 ATTRIBUTES--------(NULL)    EXTENTS---------------1

 IDCAMS  SYSTEM SERVICES                             TIME  10 36 11        03/23/84      PAGE  18

                         LISTING FROM CATALOG -- USERCAT.VSAM02

       DSN----POSMDE.DATA                                   ATTRIBUTES--------(NULL)    EXTENTS---------------1
       DSN----POSMDE.INDEX                                  ATTRIBUTES--------(NULL)    EXTENTS---------------1
       DSN----SGTLIBU.DATA                                  ATTRIBUTES--------(NULL)    EXTENTS---------------1
       DSN----SGTLIBU.INDEX                                 ATTRIBUTES--------(NULL)    EXTENTS---------------1
```

Figure A.4 Sample LISTCAT using 'SPACE' parameter.

```
DSN----SGTLIB1.DATA                                       ATTRIBUTES--------(NULL)    EXTENTS---------------1
DSN----SGTLIB1.INDEX                                      ATTRIBUTES--------(NULL)    EXTENTS---------------1
DSN----TPLIBX1.DATA                                       ATTRIBUTES--------(NULL)    EXTENTS---------------1
DSN----TPLIBX1.INDEX                                      ATTRIBUTES--------(NULL)    EXTENTS---------------1
DSN----PGNMTBL.DATA                                       ATTRIBUTES--------(NULL)    EXTENTS---------------1
DSN----PGNMTBL.INDEX                                      ATTRIBUTES--------(NULL)    EXTENTS---------------1
DSN----POMVNDR.DATA                                       ATTRIBUTES--------(NULL)    EXTENTS---------------1
DSN----POMVNDR.INDEX                                      ATTRIBUTES--------(NULL)    EXTENTS---------------1
DSN----MACFILE.DATA                                       ATTRIBUTES--------(NULL)    EXTENTS---------------1
DSN----MACFILE.INDEX                                      ATTRIBUTES--------(NULL)    EXTENTS---------------1
DSN----SGTLIB2.DATA                                       ATTRIBUTES--------(NULL)    EXTENTS---------------1
DSN----SGTLIB2.INDEX                                      ATTRIBUTES--------(NULL)    EXTENTS---------------1
DSN----ESDSTST.DATA                                       ATTRIBUTES--------(NULL)    EXTENTS---------------1

IDCAMS  SYSTEM SERVICES                                          TIME  10 36 11        03/23/84     PAGE  19

                              LISTING FROM CATALOG -- USERCAT.VSAM02

       THE NUMBER OF ENTRIES PROCESSED WAS
                  AIX -------------------0
                  CLUSTER ---------------0
                  DATA ------------------0
                  INDEX -----------------0
                  NONVSAM ---------------0
                  PATH ------------------0
                  SPACE -----------------1
                  USERCATALOG -----------0
                  TOTAL -----------------1

       THE NUMBER OF PROTECTED ENTRIES SUPPRESSED WAS 0

IDC0001I FUNCTION COMPLETED, HIGHEST CONDITION CODE WAS 0
```

Figure A.4 Continued.

```
IDCAMS  SYSTEM SERVICES                                          TIME  10 36 11        03/23/84     PAGE  20

 LISTCAT ALLOCATION CATALOG(USERCAT.VSAM02)

IDCAMS  SYSTEM SERVICES                                      TIME  10 36 11        03/23/84     PAGE  21

                              LISTING FROM CATALOG -- USERCAT.VSAM02

CLUSTER ------- APTRANE
     HISTORY
       OWNER-IDENT-------(NULL)       CREATION----------84.080
       RELEASE----------------2       EXPIRATION--------00.000

   DATA ------- APTRANE.DATA
     HISTORY
       OWNER-IDENT-------(NULL)       CREATION----------84.080
       RELEASE----------------2       EXPIRATION--------00.000
     ALLOCATION
       SPACE-TYPE------CYLINDER
       SPACE-PRI-------------25       USECLASS-PRI-----------0       HI-ALLOC-RBA----13440000
       SPACE-SEC--------------2       USECLASS-SEC-----------0       HI-USED-RBA------6451200
     VOLUME
       VOLSER------------VSAM02       PHYREC-SIZE---------3584       HI-ALLOC-RBA----13440000     EXTENT-NUMBER----------1
       DEVTYPE------X'3010200B'       PHYRECS/TRK------------5       HI-USED-RBA------6451200     EXTENT-TYPE--------X'00'
       VOLFLAG------------PRIME       TRACKS/CA-------------30
       EXTENTS
       LOW-CCHH-----X'00010000'       LOW-RBA----------------0       TRACKS---------------750
       HIGH-CCHH----X'0019001D'       HIGH-RBA--------13439999

   INDEX ------ APTRANE.INDEX
     HISTORY
       OWNER-IDENT-------(NULL)       CREATION----------84.080
       RELEASE----------------2       EXPIRATION--------00.000
     ALLOCATION
       SPACE-TYPE---------TRACK
       SPACE-PRI-------------26       USECLASS-PRI-----------0       HI-ALLOC-RBA-------66560
       SPACE-SEC--------------3       USECLASS-SEC-----------0       HI-USED-RBA--------33280
     VOLUME
       VOLSER------------VSAM02       PHYREC-SIZE---------2560       HI-ALLOC-RBA-------66560     EXTENT-NUMBER----------1
       DEVTYPE------X'3010200B'       PHYRECS/TRK------------7       HI-USED-RBA--------33280     EXTENT-TYPE--------X'00'
       VOLFLAG------------PRIME       TRACKS/CA--------------1
       EXTENTS
       LOW-CCHH-----X'00000001'       LOW-RBA----------------0       TRACKS----------------26
       HIGH-CCHH----X'0000001A'       HIGH-RBA-----------66559

CLUSTER ------- APTRNXE
     HISTORY
       OWNER-IDENT-------(NULL)       CREATION----------84.080
       RELEASE----------------2       EXPIRATION--------00.000

   DATA ------- APTRNXE.DATA
     HISTORY
       OWNER-IDENT-------(NULL)       CREATION----------84.080
       RELEASE----------------2       EXPIRATION--------00.000
```

Figure A.5 Sample LISTCAT using 'ALLOCATION' parameter.

```
    ALLOCATION
      SPACE-TYPE------CYLINDER
      SPACE-PRI--------------4      USECLASS-PRI-----------0      HI-ALLOC-RBA-----2150400
      SPACE-SEC--------------2      USECLASS-SEC-----------C      HI-USED-RBA------1612800

IDCAMS  SYSTEM SERVICES                                      TIME  10 36 11         03/23/84      PAGE  22

                          LISTING FROM CATALOG -- USERCAT.VSAM02

    VOLUME
      VOLSER------------VSAM02      PHYREC-SIZE---------3584      HI-ALLOC-RBA-----2150400      EXTENT-NUMBER----------1
      DEVTYPE------X'3010200B'      PHYRECS/TRK------------5      HI-USED-RBA------1612800      EXTENT-TYPE--------X'00'
      VOLFLAG------------PRIME      TRACKS/CA-------------30
      EXTENTS
      LOW-CCHH-----X'001A0000'      LOW-RBA----------------0      TRACKS---------------120
      HIGH-CCHH----X'001D001D'      HIGH-RBA---------2150399

  INDEX ------ APTRNXE.INDEX
    HISTORY
      OWNER-IDENT-------(NULL)      CREATION----------84.080
      RELEASE----------------2      EXPIRATION--------00.000
    ALLOCATION
      SPACE-TYPE---------TRACK
      SPACE-PRI--------------1      USECLASS-PRI-----------0      HI-ALLOC-RBA-------17920
      SPACE-SEC--------------1      USECLASS-SEC-----------0      HI-USED-RBA--------10240
    VOLUME
      VOLSER------------VSAM02      PHYREC-SIZE---------2560      HI-ALLOC-RBA-------17920      EXTENT-NUMBER----------1
      DEVTYPE------X'3010200B'      PHYRECS/TRK------------7      HI-USED-RBA--------10240      EXTENT-TYPE--------X'00'
      VOLFLAG------------PRIME      TRACKS/CA--------------1
      EXTENTS
      LOW-CCHH-----X'0000001B'      LOW-RBA----------------0      TRACKS-----------------1
      HIGH-CCHH----X'00000C1B'      HIGH-RBA-----------17919

CLUSTER ------- COSTMST
    HISTORY
      OWNER-IDENT-------(NULL)      CREATION----------84.080
      RELEASE----------------2      EXPIRATION--------00.000

  DATA ------- COSTMST.DATA
    HISTORY
      OWNER-IDENT-------(NULL)      CREATION----------84.080
      RELEASE----------------2      EXPIRATION--------00.000
    ALLOCATION
      SPACE-TYPE------CYLINDER
      SPACE-PRI-------------75      USECLASS-PRI-----------0      HI-ALLOC-RBA---36864000
      SPACE-SEC--------------2      USECLASS-SEC-----------0      HI-USED-RBA----27525120
    VOLUME
      VOLSER------------VSAM02      PHYREC-SIZE---------2048      HI-ALLOC-RBA---36864000       EXTENT-NUMBER----------1
      DEVTYPE------X'3010200B'      PHYRECS/TRK------------8      HI-USED-RBA----27525120       EXTENT-TYPE--------X'00'
      VOLFLAG------------PRIME      TRACKS/CA-------------30
      EXTENTS
      LOW-CCHH-----X'001E0000'      LOW-RBA----------------0      TRACKS--------------2250
      HIGH-CCHH----X'0068001D'      HIGH-RBA--------36863999

  INDEX ------ COSTMST.INDEX
    HISTORY
      OWNER-IDENT-------(NULL)      CREATION----------84.080
      RELEASE----------------2      EXPIRATION--------00.000
    ALLOCATION

IDCAMS  SYSTEM SERVICES                                      TIME  10 36 11         03/23/84      PAGE  23

                          LISTING FROM CATALOG -- USERCAT.VSAM02

      SPACE-TYPE---------TRACK
      SPACE-PRI-------------16      USECLASS-PRI-----------0      HI-ALLOC-RBA------286720
      SPACE-SEC--------------1      USECLASS-SEC-----------0      HI-USED-RBA-------204288
    VOLUME
      VOLSER------------VSAM02      PHYREC-SIZE---------3584      HI-ALLOC-RBA------286720      EXTENT-NUMBER----------1
      DEVTYPE------X'3010200B'      PHYRECS/TRK------------5      HI-USED-RBA-------204288      EXTENT-TYPE--------X'00'
      VOLFLAG------------PRIME      TRACKS/CA--------------1
      EXTENTS
      LOW-CCHH-----X'00690000'      LOW-RBA----------------0      TRACKS----------------16
      HIGH-CCHH----X'0069000F'      HIGH-RBA----------286719

CLUSTER ------- DMPSEC
    HISTORY
      OWNER-IDENT-------(NULL)      CREATION----------84.080
      RELEASE----------------2      EXPIRATION--------99.365

  DATA ------- DMPSEC.DATA
    HISTORY
      OWNER-IDENT-------(NULL)      CREATION----------84.080
      RELEASE----------------2      EXPIRATION--------99.365
    ALLOCATION
      SPACE-TYPE------CYLINDER
      SPACE-PRI--------------2      USECLASS-PRI-----------0      HI-ALLOC-RBA------983040
      SPACE-SEC--------------1      USECLASS-SEC-----------0      HI-USED-RBA-------491520
    VOLUME
      VOLSER------------VSAM02      PHYREC-SIZE---------2048      HI-ALLOC-RBA------983040      EXTENT-NUMBER----------1
      DEVTYPE------X'3010200B'      PHYRECS/TRK------------8      HI-USED-RBA-------491520      EXTENT-TYPE--------X'00'
      VOLFLAG------------PRIME      TRACKS/CA-------------30
      EXTENTS
      LOW-CCHH-----X'006A0000'      LOW-RBA----------------0      TRACKS----------------60
      HIGH-CCHH----X'006B001D'      HIGH-RBA----------983039
```

Figure A.5 Continued.

```
  INDEX ------ DMPSEC.INDEX
    HISTORY
      OWNER-IDENT-------(NULL)      CREATION----------84.080
      RELEASE----------------2      EXPIRATION--------99.365
    ALLOCATION
      SPACE-TYPE---------TRACK
      SPACE-PRI--------------1      USECLASS-PRI-----------0      HI-ALLOC-RBA-------17920
      SPACE-SEC--------------1      USECLASS-SEC-----------0      HI-USED-RBA---------3584
    VOLUME
      VOLSER------------VSAM02      PHYREC-SIZE---------3584      HI-ALLOC-RBA-------17920      EXTENT-NUMBER----------1
      DEVTYPE------X'3010200B'      PHYRECS/TRK------------5      HI-USED-RBA---------3584      EXTENT-TYPE--------X'00'
      VOLFLAG------------PRIME      TRACKS/CA--------------1
      EXTENTS
      LOW-CCHH-----X'0000001C'      LOW-RBA----------------0      TRACKS-----------------1
      HIGH-CCHH----X'0000001C'      HIGH-RBA-----------17919

CLUSTER ------- ESDSTST
    HISTORY

IDCAMS  SYSTEM SERVICES                                           TIME  10 36 11        03/23/84      PAGE  24

                                  LISTING FROM CATALOG -- USERCAT.VSAM02

      OWNER-IDENT-------(NULL)      CREATION----------84.083
      RELEASE----------------2      EXPIRATION--------00.000

  DATA ------- ESDSTST.DATA
    HISTORY
      OWNER-IDENT-------(NULL)      CREATION----------84.083
      RELEASE----------------2      EXPIRATION--------00.000
    ALLOCATION
      SPACE-TYPE---------TRACK
      SPACE-PRI--------------1      USECLASS-PRI-----------0      HI-ALLOC-RBA-------15360
      SPACE-SEC--------------0      USECLASS-SEC-----------0      HI-USED-RBA--------13312
    VOLUME
      VOLSER------------VSAM02      PHYREC-SIZE---------1024      HI-ALLOC-RBA-------15360      EXTENT-NUMBER----------1
      DEVTYPE------X'3010200B'      PHYRECS/TRK-----------15      HI-USED-RBA--------13312      EXTENT-TYPE--------X'00'
      VOLFLAG------------PRIME      TRACKS/CA--------------1
      EXTENTS
      LOW-CCHH-----X'00F5000A'      LOW-RBA----------------0      TRACKS-----------------1
      HIGH-CCHH----X'00F5000A'      HIGH-RBA-----------15359

CLUSTER ------- HGVDEP.CLUSTER
    HISTORY
      OWNER-IDENT-------(NULL)      CREATION----------84.080
      RELEASE----------------2      EXPIRATION--------00.000

  DATA ------- HGVDEP.DATA
    HISTORY
      OWNER-IDENT-------(NULL)      CREATION----------84.080
      RELEASE----------------2      EXPIRATION--------00.000
    ALLOCATION
      SPACE-TYPE------CYLINDER
      SPACE-PRI--------------5      USECLASS-PRI-----------0      HI-ALLOC-RBA-----2457600
      SPACE-SEC--------------1      USECLASS-SEC-----------0      HI-USED-RBA-------491520
    VOLUME
      VOLSER------------VSAM02      PHYREC-SIZE---------4096      HI-ALLOC-RBA-----2457600      EXTENT-NUMBER----------1
      DEVTYPE------X'3010200B'      PHYRECS/TRK------------4      HI-USED-RBA-------491520      EXTENT-TYPE--------X'00'
      VOLFLAG------------PRIME      TRACKS/CA-------------30
      EXTENTS
      LOW-CCHH-----X'006C0000'      LOW-RBA----------------0      TRACKS---------------150
      HIGH-CCHH----X'0070001D'      HIGH-RBA---------2457599

  INDEX ------ HGVDEP.INDEX
    HISTORY
      OWNER-IDENT-------(NULL)      CREATION----------84.080
      RELEASE----------------2      EXPIRATION--------00.000
    ALLOCATION
      SPACE-TYPE---------TRACK
      SPACE-PRI--------------1      USECLASS-PRI-----------0      HI-ALLOC-RBA-------16384
      SPACE-SEC--------------1      USECLASS-SEC-----------0      HI-USED-RBA---------2048
    VOLUME
      VOLSER------------VSAM02      PHYREC-SIZE---------2048      HI-ALLOC-RBA-------16384      EXTENT-NUMBER----------1

IDCAMS  SYSTEM SERVICES                                           TIME  10 36 11        03/23/84      PAGE  25

                                  LISTING FROM CATALOG -- USERCAT.VSAM02

      DEVTYPE------X'3010200B'      PHYRECS/TRK------------8      HI-USED-RBA---------2048      EXTENT-TYPE--------X'00'
      VOLFLAG------------PRIME      TRACKS/CA--------------1
      EXTENTS
      LOW-CCHH-----X'0000001D'      LOW-RBA----------------0      TRACKS-----------------1
      HIGH-CCHH----X'0000001D'      HIGH-RBA-----------16383

CLUSTER ------- MACFILE
    HISTORY
      OWNER-IDENT-------(NULL)      CREATION----------84.080
      RELEASE----------------2      EXPIRATION--------00.000

  DATA ------- MACFILE.DATA
    HISTORY
      OWNER-IDENT-------(NULL)      CREATION----------84.080
      RELEASE----------------2      EXPIRATION--------00.000
    ALLOCATION
      SPACE-TYPE------CYLINDER
      SPACE-PRI--------------2      USECLASS-PRI-----------0      HI-ALLOC-RBA------983040
      SPACE-SEC--------------1      USECLASS-SEC-----------0      HI-USED-RBA-------491520
    VOLUME
      VOLSER------------VSAM02      PHYREC-SIZE---------4096      HI-ALLOC-RBA------983040      EXTENT-NUMBER----------1
      DEVTYPE------X'3010200B'      PHYRECS/TRK------------4      HI-USED-RBA-------491520      EXTENT-TYPE--------X'00'
```

Figure A.5 Continued.

```
      VOLFLAG-----------PRIME       TRACKS/CA-------------30
      EXTENTS
      LOW-CCHH----X'01140000'       LOW-RBA----------------0     TRACKS---------------60
      HIGH-CCHH---X'0115001D'       HIGH-RBA----------983039

   INDEX ------ MACFILE.INDEX
     HISTORY
      OWNER-IDENT-------(NULL)      CREATION----------84.080
      RELEASE---------------2       EXPIRATION--------00.000
     ALLOCATION
      SPACE-TYPE---------TRACK
      SPACE-PRI--------------1      USECLASS-PRI-----------0     HI-ALLOC-RBA-------16384
      SPACE-SEC--------------1      USECLASS-SEC-----------0     HI-USED-RBA---------2048
     VOLUME
      VOLSER-----------VSAM02       PHYREC-SIZE---------2048     HI-ALLOC-RBA-------16384     EXTENT-NUMBER----------1
      DEVTYPE------X'3010200B'      PHYRECS/TRK------------8     HI-USED-RBA---------2048     EXTENT-TYPE--------X'00'
      VOLFLAG-----------PRIME       TRACKS/CA--------------1
      EXTENTS
      LOW-CCHH----X'0069001D'       LOW-RBA----------------0     TRACKS----------------1
      HIGH-CCHH---X'0069001D'       HIGH-RBA-----------16383

CLUSTER ------- MAILDAT
     HISTORY
      OWNER-IDENT-------(NULL)      CREATION----------84.080
      RELEASE---------------2       EXPIRATION--------99.365

   DATA ------- MAIL.DATA
     HISTORY

IDCAMS  SYSTEM SERVICES                                          TIME  10 36 11        03/23/84     PAGE  26

                              LISTING FROM CATALOG -- USERCAT.VSAM02

      OWNER-IDENT-------(NULL)      CREATION----------84.080
      RELEASE---------------2       EXPIRATION--------99.365
     ALLOCATION
      SPACE-TYPE------CYLINDER
      SPACE-PRI--------------3      USECLASS-PRI-----------0     HI-ALLOC-RBA-----1474560
      SPACE-SEC--------------1      USECLASS-SEC-----------0     HI-USED-RBA-------491520
     VOLUME
      VOLSER-----------VSAM02       PHYREC-SIZE---------4096     HI-ALLOC-RBA-----1474560     EXTENT-NUMBER----------1
      DEVTYPE------X'3010200B'      PHYRECS/TRK------------4     HI-USED-RBA-------491520     EXTENT-TYPE--------X'00'
      VOLFLAG-----------PRIME       TRACKS/CA-------------30
      EXTENTS
      LOW-CCHH----X'00710000'       LOW-RBA----------------0     TRACKS---------------90
      HIGH-CCHH---X'0073001D'       HIGH-RBA---------1474559

   INDEX ------ MAIL.INDEX
     HISTORY
      OWNER-IDENT-------(NULL)      CREATION----------84.080
      RELEASE---------------2       EXPIRATION--------99.365
     ALLOCATION
      SPACE-TYPE---------TRACK
      SPACE-PRI--------------1      USECLASS-PRI-----------0     HI-ALLOC-RBA-------16384
      SPACE-SEC--------------1      USECLASS-SEC-----------0     HI-USED-RBA---------2048
     VOLUME
      VOLSER-----------VSAM02       PHYREC-SIZE---------2048     HI-ALLOC-RBA-------16384     EXTENT-NUMBER----------1
      DEVTYPE------X'3010200B'      PHYRECS/TRK------------8     HI-USED-RBA---------2048     EXTENT-TYPE--------X'00'
      VOLFLAG-----------PRIME       TRACKS/CA--------------1
      EXTENTS
      LOW-CCHH----X'0069001D'       LOW-RBA----------------0     TRACKS----------------1
      HIGH-CCHH---X'0069001D'       HIGH-RBA-----------16383

CLUSTER ------- MANFSTE
     HISTORY
      OWNER-IDENT-------(NULL)      CREATION----------84.080
      RELEASE---------------2       EXPIRATION--------00.000

   DATA ------- MANFSTE.DATA
     HISTORY
      OWNER-IDENT-------(NULL)      CREATION----------84.080
      RELEASE---------------2       EXPIRATION--------00.000
     ALLOCATION
      SPACE-TYPE------CYLINDER
      SPACE-PRI-------------15      USECLASS-PRI-----------0     HI-ALLOC-RBA-----7372800
      SPACE-SEC--------------1      USECLASS-SEC-----------0     HI-USED-RBA------2457600
     VOLUME
      VOLSER-----------VSAM02       PHYREC-SIZE---------4096     HI-ALLOC-RBA-----7372800     EXTENT-NUMBER----------1
      DEVTYPE------X'3010200B'      PHYRECS/TRK------------4     HI-USED-RBA------2457600     EXTENT-TYPE--------X'00'
      VOLFLAG-----------PRIME       TRACKS/CA-------------30
      EXTENTS
      LOW-CCHH----X'00740000'       LOW-RBA----------------0     TRACKS--------------450
      HIGH-CCHH---X'0082001D'       HIGH-RBA---------7372799

IDCAMS  SYSTEM SERVICES                                          TIME  10 36 11        03/23/84     PAGE  27

                              LISTING FROM CATALOG -- USERCAT.VSAM02

   INDEX ------ MANFSTE.INDEX
     HISTORY
      OWNER-IDENT-------(NULL)      CREATION----------84.080
      RELEASE---------------2       EXPIRATION--------00.000
     ALLOCATION
      SPACE-TYPE---------TRACK
      SPACE-PRI--------------2      USECLASS-PRI-----------0     HI-ALLOC-RBA-------32768
      SPACE-SEC--------------1      USECLASS-SEC-----------0     HI-USED-RBA--------12288
```

Figure A.5 Continued.

```
        VOLUME
          VOLSER------------VSAM02     PHYREC-SIZE---------2048     HI-ALLOC-RBA-------32768     EXTENT-NUMBER----------1
          DEVTYPE------X'3010200B'     PHYRECS/TRK------------8     HI-USED-RBA--------12288     EXTENT-TYPE--------X'00'
          VOLFLAG------------PRIME     TRACKS/CA--------------1
          EXTENTS
          LOW-CCHH-----X'00690011'     LOW-RBA----------------0     TRACKS-----------------2
          HIGH-CCHH----X'00690012'     HIGH-RBA-----------32767

    CLUSTER ------- MNDMSTE
        HISTORY
          OWNER-IDENT-------(NULL)     CREATION----------84.080
          RELEASE----------------2     EXPIRATION--------00.000

      DATA ------- MNDMSTE.DATA
        HISTORY
          OWNER-IDENT-------(NULL)     CREATION----------84.080
          RELEASE----------------2     EXPIRATION--------00.000
        ALLOCATION
          SPACE-TYPE------CYLINDER
          SPACE-PRI------------100     USECLASS-PRI-----------0     HI-ALLOC-RBA----47513600
          SPACE-SEC--------------2     USECLASS-SEC-----------0     HI-USED-RBA-----25182208
        VOLUME
          VOLSER------------VSAM02     PHYREC-SIZE---------4096     HI-ALLOC-RBA----47513600     EXTENT-NUMBER----------1
          DEVTYPE------X'3010200B'     PHYRECS/TRK------------4     HI-USED-RBA-----25182208     EXTENT-TYPE--------X'00'
          VOLFLAG------------PRIME     TRACKS/CA-------------30
          EXTENTS
          LOW-CCHH-----X'00830000'     LOW-RBA----------------0     TRACKS--------------3000
          HIGH-CCHH----X'00E6001D'     HIGH-RBA--------47513599

      INDEX ------ MNDMSTE.INDEX
        HISTORY
          OWNER-IDENT-------(NULL)     CREATION----------84.080
          RELEASE----------------2     EXPIRATION--------00.000
        ALLOCATION
          SPACE-TYPE---------TRACK
          SPACE-PRI--------------1     USECLASS-PRI-----------0     HI-ALLOC-RBA------322560
          SPACE-SEC--------------1     USECLASS-SEC-----------0     HI-USED-RBA-------178176
        VOLUME
          VOLSER------------VSAM02     PHYREC-SIZE---------3072     HI-ALLOC-RBA-------15360     EXTENT-NUMBER----------1
          DEVTYPE------X'3010200B'     PHYRECS/TRK------------5     HI-USED-RBA---------3072     EXTENT-TYPE--------X'00'
          VOLFLAG------------PRIME     TRACKS/CA--------------1
          EXTENTS
```

```
    IDCAMS  SYSTEM SERVICES                                              TIME  10 36 11        03/23/84     PAGE  28

                                    LISTING FROM CATALOG -- USERCAT.VSAM02

          LOW-CCHH-----X'00690013'     LOW-RBA----------------0     TRACKS-----------------1
          HIGH-CCHH----X'00690013'     HIGH-RBA-----------15359
        VOLUME
          VOLSER------------VSAM02     PHYREC-SIZE---------3072     HI-ALLOC-RBA------322560     EXTENT-NUMBER----------1
          DEVTYPE------X'3010200B'     PHYRECS/TRK------------5     HI-USED-RBA-------178176     EXTENT-TYPE--------X'80'
          VOLFLAG------------PRIME     TRACKS/CA-------------30
          EXTENTS
          LOW-CCHH-----X'00830000'     LOW-RBA------------15360     TRACKS--------------3000
          HIGH-CCHH----X'00E6001D'     HIGH-RBA----------322559

    CLUSTER ------- MNDNDXE
        HISTORY
          OWNER-IDENT-------(NULL)     CREATION----------84.080
          RELEASE----------------2     EXPIRATION--------00.000

      DATA ------- MNDNDXE.DATA
        HISTORY
          OWNER-IDENT-------(NULL)     CREATION----------84.080
          RELEASE----------------2     EXPIRATION--------00.000
        ALLOCATION
          SPACE-TYPE------CYLINDER
          SPACE-PRI--------------5     USECLASS-PRI-----------0     HI-ALLOC-RBA-----2688000
          SPACE-SEC--------------1     USECLASS-SEC-----------0     HI-USED-RBA------1075200
        VOLUME
          VOLSER------------VSAM02     PHYREC-SIZE---------2560     HI-ALLOC-RBA-----2688000     EXTENT-NUMBER----------1
          DEVTYPE------X'3010200B'     PHYRECS/TRK------------7     HI-USED-RBA------1075200     EXTENT-TYPE--------X'00'
          VOLFLAG------------PRIME     TRACKS/CA-------------30
          EXTENTS
          LOW-CCHH-----X'00E70000'     LOW-RBA----------------0     TRACKS---------------150
          HIGH-CCHH----X'00EB001D'     HIGH-RBA---------2687999

      INDEX ------ MNDNDXE.INDEX
        HISTORY
          OWNER-IDENT-------(NULL)     CREATION----------84.080
          RELEASE----------------2     EXPIRATION--------00.000
        ALLOCATION
          SPACE-TYPE---------TRACK
          SPACE-PRI--------------2     USECLASS-PRI-----------0     HI-ALLOC-RBA-------30720
          SPACE-SEC--------------1     USECLASS-SEC-----------0     HI-USED-RBA---------9216
        VOLUME
          VOLSER------------VSAM02     PHYREC-SIZE---------3072     HI-ALLOC-RBA-------30720     EXTENT-NUMBER----------1
          DEVTYPE------X'3010200B'     PHYRECS/TRK------------5     HI-USED-RBA---------9216     EXTENT-TYPE--------X'00'
          VOLFLAG------------PRIME     TRACKS/CA--------------1
          EXTENTS
          LOW-CCHH-----X'00690014'     LOW-RBA----------------0     TRACKS-----------------2
          HIGH-CCHH----X'00690015'     HIGH-RBA-----------30719

    CLUSTER ------- PGNMTBL
        HISTORY
          OWNER-IDENT-------(NULL)     CREATION----------84.080
```

Figure A.5 Continued.

```
                                    LISTING FROM CATALOG -- USERCAT.VSAM02

          RELEASE----------------2          EXPIRATION--------00.000

      DATA ------- PGNMTBL.DATA
        HISTORY
          OWNER-IDENT-------(NULL)          CREATION----------84.080
          RELEASE----------------2          EXPIRATION--------00.000
        ALLOCATION
          SPACE-TYPE------CYLINDER
          SPACE-PRI--------------1          USECLASS-PRI-----------0          HI-ALLOC-RBA------491520
          SPACE-SEC--------------1          USECLASS-SEC-----------0          HI-USED-RBA-------491520
        VOLUME
          VOLSER------------VSAM02          PHYREC-SIZE---------2048          HI-ALLOC-RBA------491520          EXTENT-NUMBER----------1
          DEVTYPE------X'3010200B'          PHYRECS/TRK------------8          HI-USED-RBA-------491520          EXTENT-TYPE--------X'00'
          VOLFLAG------------PRIME          TRACKS/CA-------------30
          EXTENTS
          LOW-CCHH-----X'00F80000'          LOW-RBA----------------0          TRACKS----------------30
          HIGH-CCHH----X'00F8001D'          HIGH-RBA-----------491519

      INDEX ------ PGNMTBL.INDEX
        HISTORY
          OWNER-IDENT-------(NULL)          CREATION----------84.080
          RELEASE----------------2          EXPIRATION--------00.000
        ALLOCATION
          SPACE-TYPE---------TRACK
          SPACE-PRI--------------1          USECLASS-PRI-----------0          HI-ALLOC-RBA-------15360
          SPACE-SEC--------------1          USECLASS-SEC-----------0          HI-USED-RBA---------3072
        VOLUME
          VOLSER------------VSAM02          PHYREC-SIZE---------3072          HI-ALLOC-RBA-------15360          EXTENT-NUMBER----------1
          DEVTYPE------X'3010200B'          PHYRECS/TRK------------5          HI-USED-RBA---------3072          EXTENT-TYPE--------X'00'
          VOLFLAG------------PRIME          TRACKS/CA--------------1
          EXTENTS
          LOW-CCHH-----X'0069001C'          LOW-RBA----------------0          TRACKS-----------------1
          HIGH-CCHH----X'0069001C'          HIGH-RBA-----------15359

    CLUSTER ------- POMVNDR
        HISTORY
          OWNER-IDENT-------(NULL)          CREATION----------84.080
          RELEASE----------------2          EXPIRATION--------00.000

      DATA ------- POMVNDR.DATA
        HISTORY
          OWNER-IDENT-------(NULL)          CREATION----------84.080
          RELEASE----------------2          EXPIRATION--------00.000
        ALLOCATION
          SPACE-TYPE------CYLINDER
          SPACE-PRI-------------30          USECLASS-PRI-----------0          HI-ALLOC-RBA----14745600
          SPACE-SEC--------------1          USECLASS-SEC-----------0          HI-USED-RBA-----11304960
        VOLUME
          VOLSER------------VSAM02          PHYREC-SIZE---------4096          HI-ALLOC-RBA----14745600          EXTENT-NUMBER----------1
          DEVTYPE------X'3010200B'          PHYRECS/TRK------------4          HI-USED-RBA-----11304960          EXTENT-TYPE--------X'00'
```



```
                                    LISTING FROM CATALOG -- USERCAT.VSAM02

          VOLFLAG------------PRIME          TRACKS/CA-------------30
          EXTENTS
          LOW-CCHH-----X'01160000'          LOW-RBA----------------0          TRACKS---------------900
          HIGH-CCHH----X'0133001D'          HIGH-RBA--------14745599

      INDEX ------ POMVNDR.INDEX
        HISTORY
          OWNER-IDENT-------(NULL)          CREATION----------84.080
          RELEASE----------------2          EXPIRATION--------00.000
        ALLOCATION
          SPACE-TYPE---------TRACK
          SPACE-PRI--------------4          USECLASS-PRI-----------0          HI-ALLOC-RBA-------65536
          SPACE-SEC--------------1          USECLASS-SEC-----------0          HI-USED-RBA--------49152
        VOLUME
          VOLSER------------VSAM02          PHYREC-SIZE---------2048          HI-ALLOC-RBA-------65536          EXTENT-NUMBER----------1
          DEVTYPE------X'3010200B'          PHYRECS/TRK------------8          HI-USED-RBA--------49152          EXTENT-TYPE--------X'00'
          VOLFLAG------------PRIME          TRACKS/CA--------------1
          EXTENTS
          LOW-CCHH-----X'00F50004'          LOW-RBA----------------0          TRACKS-----------------4
          HIGH-CCHH----X'00F50007'          HIGH-RBA-----------65535

    CLUSTER ------- POSMDE
        HISTORY
          OWNER-IDENT-------(NULL)          CREATION----------84.080
          RELEASE----------------2          EXPIRATION--------00.000

      DATA ------- POSMDE.DATA
        HISTORY
          OWNER-IDENT-------(NULL)          CREATION----------84.080
          RELEASE----------------2          EXPIRATION--------00.000
        ALLOCATION
          SPACE-TYPE------CYLINDER
          SPACE-PRI--------------8          USECLASS-PRI-----------0          HI-ALLOC-RBA-----3932160
          SPACE-SEC--------------1          USECLASS-SEC-----------0          HI-USED-RBA------1474560
        VOLUME
          VOLSER------------VSAM02          PHYREC-SIZE---------4096          HI-ALLOC-RBA-----3932160          EXTENT-NUMBER----------1
          DEVTYPE------X'3010200B'          PHYRECS/TRK------------4          HI-USED-RBA------1474560          EXTENT-TYPE--------X'00'
          VOLFLAG------------PRIME          TRACKS/CA-------------30
          EXTENTS
          LOW-CCHH-----X'00ED0000'          LOW-RBA----------------0          TRACKS---------------240
          HIGH-CCHH----X'00F4001D'          HIGH-RBA---------3932159
```

Figure A.5 Continued.

```
      INDEX ------ POSMOE.INDEX
        HISTORY
          OWNER-IDENT-------(NULL)       CREATION----------84.080
          RELEASE----------------2       EXPIRATION--------00.000
        ALLOCATION
          SPACE-TYPE---------TRACK
          SPACE-PRI--------------2       USECLASS-PRI-----------0     HI-ALLOC-RBA-------32768
          SPACE-SEC--------------1       USECLASS-SEC-----------0     HI-USED-RBA---------8192

IDCAMS  SYSTEM SERVICES                                                TIME  10 36 11        03/23/84      PAGE  31

                                   LISTING FROM CATALOG -- USERCAT.VSAM02

        VOLUME
          VOLSER------------VSAM02       PHYREC-SIZE---------2048     HI-ALLOC-RBA-------32768     EXTENT-NUMBER----------1
          DEVTYPE------X'3010200B'       PHYRECS/TRK------------8     HI-USED-RBA---------8192     EXTENT-TYPE--------X'00'
          VOLFLAG------------PRIME       TRACKS/CA--------------1
          EXTENTS
          LOW-CCHH----X'00690017'        LOW-RBA----------------0     TRACKS-----------------2
          HIGH-CCHH---X'00690018'        HIGH-RBA-----------32767

CLUSTER ------- SGTLIBU
        HISTORY
          OWNER-IDENT-------(NULL)       CREATION----------84.080
          RELEASE----------------2       EXPIRATION--------00.000

      DATA ------- SGTLIBU.DATA
        HISTORY
          OWNER-IDENT-------(NULL)       CREATION----------84.080
          RELEASE----------------2       EXPIRATION--------00.000
        ALLOCATION
          SPACE-TYPE------CYLINDER
          SPACE-PRI-------------10       USECLASS-PRI-----------0     HI-ALLOC-RBA-----4915200
          SPACE-SEC--------------1       USECLASS-SEC-----------0     HI-USED-RBA------2949120
        VOLUME
          VOLSER------------VSAM02       PHYREC-SIZE---------8192     HI-ALLOC-RBA-----4915200     EXTENT-NUMBER----------1
          DEVTYPE------X'3010200B'       PHYRECS/TRK------------2     HI-USED-RBA------2949120     EXTENT-TYPE--------X'00'
          VOLFLAG------------PRIME       TRACKS/CA-------------30
          EXTENTS
          LOW-CCHH----X'00FB0000'        LOW-RBA----------------0     TRACKS---------------300
          HIGH-CCHH---X'0104001D'        HIGH-RBA---------4915199

      INDEX ------ SGTLIBU.INDEX
        HISTORY
          OWNER-IDENT-------(NULL)       CREATION----------84.080
          RELEASE----------------2       EXPIRATION--------00.000
        ALLOCATION
          SPACE-TYPE---------TRACK
          SPACE-PRI--------------2       USECLASS-PRI-----------0     HI-ALLOC-RBA-------32768
          SPACE-SEC--------------1       USECLASS-SEC-----------0     HI-USED-RBA--------14336
        VOLUME
          VOLSER------------VSAM02       PHYREC-SIZE---------2048     HI-ALLOC-RBA-------32768     EXTENT-NUMBER----------1
          DEVTYPE------X'3010200B'       PHYRECS/TRK------------8     HI-USED-RBA--------14336     EXTENT-TYPE--------X'00'
          VOLFLAG------------PRIME       TRACKS/CA--------------1
          EXTENTS
          LOW-CCHH----X'00690019'        LOW-RBA----------------0     TRACKS-----------------2
          HIGH-CCHH---X'0069001A'        HIGH-RBA-----------32767

CLUSTER ------- SGTLIB1
        HISTORY
          OWNER-IDENT-------(NULL)       CREATION----------84.080
          RELEASE----------------2       EXPIRATION--------00.000

IDCAMS  SYSTEM SERVICES                                                TIME  10 36 11        03/23/84      PAGE  32

                                   LISTING FROM CATALOG -- USERCAT.VSAM02

      DATA ------- SGTLIB1.DATA
        HISTORY
          OWNER-IDENT-------(NULL)       CREATION----------84.080
          RELEASE----------------2       EXPIRATION--------00.000
        ALLOCATION
          SPACE-TYPE------CYLINDER
          SPACE-PRI-------------24       USECLASS-PRI-----------0     HI-ALLOC-RBA----11796480
          SPACE-SEC--------------1       USECLASS-SEC-----------0     HI-USED-RBA------5406720
        VOLUME
          VOLSER------------VSAM02       PHYREC-SIZE---------8192     HI-ALLOC-RBA----11796480     EXTENT-NUMBER----------1
          DEVTYPE------X'3010200B'       PHYRECS/TRK------------2     HI-USED-RBA------5406720     EXTENT-TYPE--------X'00'
          VOLFLAG------------PRIME       TRACKS/CA-------------30
          EXTENTS
          LOW-CCHH----X'01340000'        LOW-RBA----------------0     TRACKS---------------720
          HIGH-CCHH---X'014B001D'        HIGH-RBA--------11796479

      INDEX ------ SGTLIB1.INDEX
        HISTORY
          OWNER-IDENT-------(NULL)       CREATION----------84.080
          RELEASE----------------2       EXPIRATION--------00.000
        ALLOCATION
          SPACE-TYPE---------TRACK
          SPACE-PRI--------------4       USECLASS-PRI-----------0     HI-ALLOC-RBA-------65536
          SPACE-SEC--------------1       USECLASS-SEC-----------0     HI-USED-RBA--------24576
        VOLUME
          VOLSER------------VSAM02       PHYREC-SIZE---------2048     HI-ALLOC-RBA-------65536     EXTENT-NUMBER----------1
          DEVTYPE------X'3010200B'       PHYRECS/TRK------------8     HI-USED-RBA--------24576     EXTENT-TYPE--------X'00'
          VOLFLAG------------PRIME       TRACKS/CA--------------1
          EXTENTS
          LOW-CCHH----X'00F50000'        LOW-RBA----------------0     TRACKS-----------------4
          HIGH-CCHH---X'00F50003'        HIGH-RBA-----------65535
```

Figure A.5 Continued.

```
CLUSTER ------- SGTLIB2
     HISTORY
       OWNER-IDENT-------(NULL)      CREATION----------84.080
       RELEASE----------------2      EXPIRATION--------00.000

   DATA ------- SGTLIB2.DATA
     HISTORY
       OWNER-IDENT-------(NULL)      CREATION----------84.080
       RELEASE----------------2      EXPIRATION--------00.000
     ALLOCATION
       SPACE-TYPE------CYLINDER
       SPACE-PRI-------------15      USECLASS-PRI-----------0      HI-ALLOC-RBA-----7372800
       SPACE-SEC--------------1      USECLASS-SEC-----------0      HI-USED-RBA------3440640
     VOLUME
       VOLSER------------VSAM02      PHYREC-SIZE---------8192      HI-ALLOC-RBA-----7372800     EXTENT-NUMBER----------1
       DEVTYPE------X'3010200B'      PHYRECS/TRK------------2      HI-USED-RBA------3440640     EXTENT-TYPE--------X'00'
       VOLFLAG------------PRIME      TRACKS/CA-------------30
       EXTENTS

IDCAMS  SYSTEM SERVICES                                            TIME  10 36 11        03/23/84      PAGE  33

                                   LISTING FROM CATALOG -- USERCAT.VSAM02

       LOW-CCHH----X'01050000'       LOW-RBA----------------0      TRACKS---------------450
       HIGH-CCHH----X'0113001D'      HIGH-RBA---------7372799

   INDEX ------ SGTLIB2.INDEX
     HISTORY
       OWNER-IDENT-------(NULL)      CREATION----------84.080
       RELEASE----------------2      EXPIRATION--------00.000
     ALLOCATION
       SPACE-TYPE---------TRACK
       SPACE-PRI--------------2      USECLASS-PRI-----------0      HI-ALLOC-RBA-------32768
       SPACE-SEC--------------1      USECLASS-SEC-----------0      HI-USED-RBA--------16384
     VOLUME
       VOLSER------------VSAM02      PHYREC-SIZE---------2048      HI-ALLOC-RBA-------32768     EXTENT-NUMBER----------1
       DEVTYPE------X'3010200B'      PHYRECS/TRK------------8      HI-USED-RBA--------16384     EXTENT-TYPE--------X'00'
       VOLFLAG------------PRIME      TRACKS/CA--------------1
       EXTENTS
       LOW-CCHH----X'00F5000B'       LOW-RBA----------------0      TRACKS-----------------2
       HIGH-CCHH----X'00F5000C'      HIGH-RBA-----------32767

CLUSTER ------- TAPELIB
     HISTORY
       OWNER-IDENT-------(NULL)      CREATION----------84.083
       RELEASE----------------2      EXPIRATION--------00.000

   DATA ------- TAPELIB.DATA
     HISTORY
       OWNER-IDENT-------(NULL)      CREATION----------84.083
       RELEASE----------------2      EXPIRATION--------00.000
     ALLOCATION
       SPACE-TYPE------CYLINDER
       SPACE-PRI--------------2      USECLASS-PRI-----------0      HI-ALLOC-RBA------983040
       SPACE-SEC--------------1      USECLASS-SEC-----------0      HI-USED-RBA-------983040
     VOLUME
       VOLSER------------VSAM02      PHYREC-SIZE---------4096      HI-ALLOC-RBA------983040     EXTENT-NUMBER----------1
       DEVTYPE------X'3010200B'      PHYRECS/TRK------------4      HI-USED-RBA-------983040     EXTENT-TYPE--------X'00'
       VOLFLAG------------PRIME      TRACKS/CA-------------30
       EXTENTS
       LOW-CCHH----X'00F60000'       LOW-RBA----------------0      TRACKS----------------60
       HIGH-CCHH----X'00F7001D'      HIGH-RBA----------983039

   INDEX ------ TAPELIB.INDEX
     HISTORY
       OWNER-IDENT-------(NULL)      CREATION----------84.083
       RELEASE----------------2      EXPIRATION--------00.000
     ALLOCATION
       SPACE-TYPE---------TRACK
       SPACE-PRI--------------1      USECLASS-PRI-----------0      HI-ALLOC-RBA-------16384
       SPACE-SEC--------------1      USECLASS-SEC-----------0      HI-USED-RBA---------6144
     VOLUME
       VOLSER------------VSAM02      PHYREC-SIZE---------2048      HI-ALLOC-RBA-------16384     EXTENT-NUMBER----------1

IDCAMS  SYSTEM SERVICES                                            TIME  10 36 11        03/23/84      PAGE  34

                                   LISTING FROM CATALOG -- USERCAT.VSAM02

       DEVTYPE------X'3010200B'      PHYRECS/TRK------------8      HI-USED-RBA---------6144     EXTENT-TYPE--------X'00'
       VOLFLAG------------PRIME      TRACKS/CA--------------1
       EXTENTS
       LOW-CCHH----X'00690015'       LOW-RBA----------------0      TRACKS-----------------1
       HIGH-CCHH----X'00690016'      HIGH-RBA-----------16383

CLUSTER ------- TPLIBX1
     HISTORY
       OWNER-IDENT-------(NULL)      CREATION----------84.083
       RELEASE----------------2      EXPIRATION--------00.000

   DATA ------- TPLIBX1.DATA
     HISTORY
       OWNER-IDENT-------(NULL)      CREATION----------84.083
       RELEASE----------------2      EXPIRATION--------00.000
```

Figure A.5 Continued.

```
      ALLOCATION
        SPACE-TYPE------CYLINDER
        SPACE-PRI--------------1      USECLASS-PRI-----------0      HI-ALLOC-RBA------491520
        SPACE-SEC--------------1      USECLASS-SEC-----------0      HI-USED-RBA-------491520
      VOLUME
        VOLSER------------VSAM02      PHYREC-SIZE---------4096      HI-ALLOC-RBA------491520      EXTENT-NUMBER----------1
        DEVTYPE------X'3010200B'      PHYRECS/TRK------------4      HI-USED-RBA-------491520      EXTENT-TYPE--------X'00'
        VOLFLAG-------------PRIME     TRACKS/CA-------------30
        EXTENTS
        LOW-CCHH-----X'00EC0000'      LOW-RBA----------------0      TRACKS----------------30
        HIGH-CCHH----X'00EC001D'      HIGH-RBA----------491519

    INDEX ------ TPLIBX1.INDEX
      HISTORY
        OWNER-IDENT-------(NULL)      CREATION----------84.083
        RELEASE----------------2      EXPIRATION--------00.000
      ALLOCATION
        SPACE-TYPE---------TRACK
        SPACE-PRI--------------1      USECLASS-PRI-----------0      HI-ALLOC-RBA-------16384
        SPACE-SEC--------------1      USECLASS-SEC-----------0      HI-USED-RBA---------2048
      VOLUME
        VOLSER------------VSAM02      PHYREC-SIZE---------2048      HI-ALLOC-RBA-------16384      EXTENT-NUMBER----------1
        DEVTYPE------X'3010200B'      PHYRECS/TRK------------8      HI-USED-RBA---------2048      EXTENT-TYPE--------X'00'
        VOLFLAG------------PRIME      TRACKS/CA--------------1
        EXTENTS
        LOW-CCHH-----X'0069001B'      LOW-RBA----------------0      TRACKS-----------------1
        HIGH-CCHH----X'0069001B'      HIGH-RBA-----------16383

CLUSTER ------- USERCAT.VSAM02
      HISTORY
        OWNER-IDENT-------(NULL)      CREATION----------83.264
        RELEASE----------------2      EXPIRATION--------00.000

    DATA ------- VSAM.CATALOG.BASE.DATA.RECORD
      HISTORY

IDCAMS  SYSTEM SERVICES                                                TIME  10 36 11        03/23/84     PAGE  35

                                  LISTING FROM CATALOG -- USERCAT.VSAM02

        OWNER-IDENT-------(NULL)      CREATION----------83.264
        RELEASE----------------2      EXPIRATION--------00.000
      ALLOCATION
        SPACE-TYPE---------TRACK
        SPACE-PRI-------------27      USECLASS-PRI-----------0      HI-ALLOC-RBA------248832
        SPACE-SEC--------------3      USECLASS-SEC-----------0      HI-USED-RBA-------248832
      VOLUME
        VOLSER------------VSAM02      PHYREC-SIZE----------512      HI-ALLOC-RBA------221184      EXTENT-NUMBER----------1
        DEVTYPE------X'3010200B'      PHYRECS/TRK-----------27      HI-USED-RBA-------221184      EXTENT-TYPE--------X'00'
        VOLFLAG------------PRIME      TRACKS/CA--------------3
        LOW-KEY---------------00
        HIGH-KEY--------------3F
        HI-KEY-RBA--------218112
        EXTENTS
        LOW-CCHH-----X'00FA0000'      LOW-RBA----------------0      TRACKS----------------24
        HIGH-CCHH----X'00FA0017'      HIGH-RBA----------221183
      VOLUME
        VOLSER------------VSAM02      PHYREC-SIZE----------512      HI-ALLOC-RBA------248832      EXTENT-NUMBER----------1
        DEVTYPE------X'3010200B'      PHYRECS/TRK-----------27      HI-USED-RBA-------248832      EXTENT-TYPE--------X'00'
        VOLFLAG------------PRIME      TRACKS/CA--------------3
        LOW-KEY---------------40
        HIGH-KEY--------------FF
        HI-KEY-RBA--------222208
        EXTENTS
        LOW-CCHH-----X'00FA001B'      LOW-RBA-----------221184      TRACKS-----------------3
        HIGH-CCHH----X'00FA001D'      HIGH-RBA----------248831

    INDEX ------ VSAM.CATALOG.BASE.INDEX.RECORD
      HISTORY
        OWNER-IDENT-------(NULL)      CREATION----------83.264
        RELEASE----------------2      EXPIRATION--------00.000
      ALLOCATION
        SPACE-TYPE---------TRACK
        SPACE-PRI--------------3      USECLASS-PRI-----------0      HI-ALLOC-RBA-------46080
        SPACE-SEC--------------3      USECLASS-SEC-----------0      HI-USED-RBA--------46080
      VOLUME
        VOLSER------------VSAM02      PHYREC-SIZE----------512      HI-ALLOC-RBA-------41472      EXTENT-NUMBER----------1
        DEVTYPE------X'3010200B'      PHYRECS/TRK-----------27      HI-USED-RBA----------512      EXTENT-TYPE--------X'00'
        VOLFLAG------------PRIME      TRACKS/CA--------------1
        EXTENTS
        LOW-CCHH-----X'00FA0018'      LOW-RBA----------------0      TRACKS-----------------3
        HIGH-CCHH----X'00FA001A'      HIGH-RBA-----------41471
      VOLUME
        VOLSER------------VSAM02      PHYREC-SIZE----------512      HI-ALLOC-RBA-------45568      EXTENT-NUMBER----------1
        DEVTYPE------X'3010200B'      PHYRECS/TRK-----------27      HI-USED-RBA--------45568      EXTENT-TYPE--------X'80'
        VOLFLAG------------PRIME      TRACKS/CA--------------3
        LOW-KEY---------------00
        HIGH-KEY--------------3F
        EXTENTS
        LOW-CCHH-----X'00FA0000'      LOW-RBA------------41472      TRACKS----------------24

IDCAMS  SYSTEM SERVICES                                                TIME  10 36 11        03/23/84     PAGE  36

                                  LISTING FROM CATALOG -- USERCAT.VSAM02

        HIGH-CCHH----X'00FA0017'      HIGH-RBA-----------45567
      VOLUME
        VOLSER------------VSAM02      PHYREC-SIZE----------512      HI-ALLOC-RBA-------46080      EXTENT-NUMBER----------1
        DEVTYPE------X'3010200B'      PHYRECS/TRK-----------27      HI-USED-RBA--------46080      EXTENT-TYPE--------X'80'
        VOLFLAG------------PRIME      TRACKS/CA--------------3
```

Figure A.5 Continued.

```
    LOW-KEY--------------40
    HIGH-KEY-------------FF
    EXTENTS
    LOW-CCHH----X'00FA001B'     LOW-RBA------------45568     TRACKS-----------------3
    HIGH-CCHH----X'00FA001D'    HIGH-RBA-----------46079

IDCAMS  SYSTEM SERVICES                                       TIME  10 36 11        03/23/84      PAGE  37

                         LISTING FROM CATALOG -- USERCAT.VSAM02

        THE NUMBER OF ENTRIES PROCESSED WAS
                   AIX --------------------0
                   CLUSTER --------------20
                   DATA -----------------20
                   INDEX ----------------19
                   NONVSAM ---------------0
                   PATH ------------------0
                   SPACE -----------------0
                   USERCATALOG -----------0
                   TOTAL ----------------59

        THE NUMBER OF PROTECTED ENTRIES SUPPRESSED WAS 0

IDC0001I FUNCTION COMPLETED, HIGHEST CONDITION CODE WAS 0
```

Figure A.5 Continued.

```
IDCAMS  SYSTEM SERVICES                                       TIME  10 36 11        03/23/84      PAGE  38

 LISTCAT ENTRIES(POSMDE) ALL CATALOG(USERCAT.VSAM02)

IDCAMS  SYSTEM SERVICES                                   TIME  10 36 11        03/23/84      PAGE  39

                        LISTING FROM CATALOG -- USERCAT.VSAM02

CLUSTER ------- POSMDE
     HISTORY
       OWNER-IDENT-------(NULL)     CREATION----------84.080
       RELEASE---------------2      EXPIRATION--------00.000
     PROTECTION---------(NULL)
     ASSOCIATIONS
       DATA-----POSMDE.DATA
       INDEX----POSMDE.INDEX

   DATA ------- POSMDE.DATA
     HISTORY
       OWNER-IDENT-------(NULL)     CREATION----------84.080
       RELEASE---------------2      EXPIRATION--------00.000
     PROTECTION---------(NULL)
     ASSOCIATIONS
       CLUSTER--POSMDE
     ATTRIBUTES
       KEYLEN---------------19      AVGLRECL-------------100     BUFSPACE-----------20480     CISIZE--------------4096
       RKP-------------------0      MAXLRECL-------------100     EXCPEXIT-----------(NULL)    CI/CA----------------120
       SHROPTNS(2,3)     SPEED      SUBALLOC         NOERASE     INDEXED         NOWRITECHK   NOIMBED       NOREPLICAT
       UNORDERED         REUSE      NONSPANNED
     STATISTICS
       REC-TOTAL-----------9507     SPLITS-CI-------------29     EXCPS--------------1955
       REC-DELETED---------1420     SPLITS-CA--------------0     EXTENTS---------------1
       REC-INSERTED---------695     FREESPACE- CI---------15     SYSTEM-TIMESTAMP
       REC-UPDATED---------9086     FREESPACE- CA---------10          X'971484AD7B040080'
       REC-RETRIEVED------13886     FREESPC-BYTES----2457600
     ALLOCATION
       SPACE-TYPE------CYLINDER
       SPACE-PRI-------------8      USECLASS-PRI-----------0     HI-ALLOC-RBA-----3932160
       SPACE-SEC-------------1      USECLASS-SEC-----------0     HI-USED-RBA------1474560
     VOLUME
       VOLSER------------VSAM02     PHYREC-SIZE---------4096     HI-ALLOC-RBA-----3932160     EXTENT-NUMBER----------1
       DEVTYPE------X'3010200B'     PHYRECS/TRK------------4     HI-USED-RBA------1474560     EXTENT-TYPE--------X'00'
       VOLFLAG-------------PRIME    TRACKS/CA-------------30
       EXTENTS
       LOW-CCHH-----X'00ED0000'     LOW-RBA----------------0     TRACKS---------------240
       HIGH-CCHH----X'00F4001D'     HIGH-RBA---------3932159

   INDEX ------ POSMDE.INDEX
     HISTORY
       OWNER-IDENT-------(NULL)     CREATION----------84.080
       RELEASE---------------2      EXPIRATION--------00.000
     PROTECTION---------(NULL)
     ASSOCIATIONS
       CLUSTER--POSMDE
     ATTRIBUTES
       KEYLEN---------------19      AVGLRECL---------------0     BUFSPACE---------------0     CISIZE--------------2048
       RKP-------------------0      MAXLRECL------------2041     EXCPEXIT-----------(NULL)    CI/CA------------------8
       SHROPTNS(2,3)  RECOVERY      SUBALLOC         NOERASE     NOWRITECHK         NOIMBED   NOREPLICAT       UNORDERED
```

Figure A.6 Sample LISTCAT using 'ENTRIES' parameter for KSDS.

```
IDCAMS  SYSTEM SERVICES                                                    TIME  10 36 11         03/23/84      PAGE  40

                                  LISTING FROM CATALOG -- USERCAT.VSAM02

      REUSE
    STATISTICS
      REC-TOTAL--------------4       SPLITS-CI--------------0         EXCPS----------------1483        INDEX
      REC-DELETED------------0       SPLITS-CA--------------0         EXTENTS------------------1       LEVELS-------------------2
      REC-INSERTED-----------0       FREESPACE- CI----------0         SYSTEM-TIMESTAMP                 ENTRIES/SECT------------10
      REC-UPDATED------------0       FREESPACE- CA----------0              X'971434ADB4A60080'         SEQ-SET-RBA--------------0
      REC-RETRIEVED----------0       FREESPC-BYTES------24576                                          HI-LEVEL-RBA----------4096
    ALLOCATION
      SPACE-TYPE---------TRACK
      SPACE-PRI--------------2       USECLASS-PRI-----------0         HI-ALLOC-RBA--------32768
      SPACE-SEC--------------1       USECLASS-SEC-----------0         HI-USED-RBA----------8192
    VOLUME
      VOLSER------------VSAM02       PHYREC-SIZE---------2048         HI-ALLOC-RBA--------32768        EXTENT-NUMBER------------1
      DEVTYPE------X'3010200B'       PHYRECS/TRK------------8         HI-USED-RBA----------8192        EXTENT-TYPE---------X'00'
      VOLFLAG------------PRIME       TRACKS/CA--------------1
      EXTENTS
      LOW-CCHH-----X'00690C17'       LOW-RBA----------------0         TRACKS-------------------2
      HIGH-CCHH----X'00690C18'       HIGH-RBA-----------32767

IDCAMS  SYSTEM SERVICES                                                    TIME  10 36 11         03/23/84      PAGE  41

                                  LISTING FROM CATALOG -- USERCAT.VSAM02

          THE NUMBER OF ENTRIES PROCESSED WAS
                      AIX -------------------0
                      CLUSTER ---------------1
                      DATA ------------------1
                      INDEX -----------------1
                      NONVSAM ---------------0
                      PATH ------------------0
                      SPACE -----------------0
                      USERCATALOG -----------0
                      TOTAL -----------------3

          THE NUMBER OF PROTECTED ENTRIES SUPPRESSED WAS 0

IDC0001I FUNCTION COMPLETED, HIGHEST CONDITION CODE WAS 0
```

Figure A.6 Continued.

```
IDCAMS  SYSTEM SERVICES                                                    TIME  11 23 04         03/08/84      PAGE   1

 LISTCRA INFILE(DD)                    -
         COMPARE                       -
         CATALOG(VSAMCAT.DIST01/    CATDD) -
         MASTERPW(MOT)

IDCAMS  SYSTEM SERVICES                                                    TIME  11 23 04         03/08/84      PAGE   2

                         LISTING OF CATALOG RECOVERY AREA FOR VOLUME -- DIST01 -- VSAM ENTRIES

    CATVOLRCD  -  03/07/84    16 33 57
    CRAVOLRCD  -  03/07/84    16 33 57
    F4DSCBVSAM -  03/07/84    16 33 57
    F4DSCBDUMP -  03/07/84    16 33 57

CLUS - VSDIST01.DSMP31KW

* MISCOMPARES - CATALOG ENTRY HAS DIFFERENT NAME

  DATA - VSDIST01.DSMP31KW.DATA
    DATA VOL -
      DIST01

* MISCOMPARES - CATALOG ENTRY HAS DIFFERENT NAME

  INDX - VSDIST01.DCG02007.INDEX
    INDX VOL -
      DIST01
      DIST01

CLUS - VSDIST01.DSMP31KW

  DATA - VSDIST01.DSMP31KW.DATA
    DATA VOL -
      DIST01

* MISCOMPARES - CATALOG ENTRY HAS DIFFERENT NAME

  INDX - VSDIST01.DCG02007.INDEX
    INDX VOL -
      DIST01
      DIST01
```

Figure A.7 Sample LISTCRA using 'COMPARE' parameter.

```
IDCAMS  SYSTEM SERVICES                                              TIME  11 23 04        03/08/84      PAGE   3
                         LISTING OF CATALOG RECOVERY AREA FOR VOLUME -- DIST01 -- UNSORTED ENTRIES

NUMBER OF ENTRIES PROCESSED
 NONV -     1
 CLUS -    93
 DATA -    93
 INDX -    58
 VOL  -     1
 SUM  -   246

IDC0665I NUMBER OF ENTRIES THAT MISCOMPARED IN THIS CRA - 2

IDC0877I NUMBER OF RECORDS THAT MISCOMPARED IN THIS CRA - 3

IDC0001I FUNCTION COMPLETED, HIGHEST CONDITION CODE WAS 4

IDCAMS  SYSTEM SERVICES                                              TIME  11 23 04        03/08/84      PAGE   4


IDC0002I IDCAMS PROCESSING COMPLETE. MAXIMUM CONDITION CODE WAS 4
```

Figure A.7 Continued.

```
IDCAMS  SYSTEM SERVICES                                              TIME  10 19 27        03/08/84      PAGE   1

 LISTCRA INFILE(DD)

IDCAMS  SYSTEM SERVICES                                              TIME  10 19 27        03/08/84      PAGE   2
                         LISTING OF CATALOG RECOVERY AREA FOR VOLUME -- DIST01 -- VSAM ENTRIES

VOL  - DIST01
    CRAVOLRCD  -  03/07/84   16 33 57
    F4DSCBVSAM -  03/07/84   16 33 57
    F4DSCBDUMP -  03/07/84   16 33 57

CLUS - VSDIST01.CARDFILE

  DATA - VSDIST01.CARDFILE.DATA
    DATA VOL -
      DIST01

CLUS - VSDIST01.CUSTADT

  DATA - VSDIST01.CUSTADT.DATA
    DATA VOL -
      DIST01

CLUS - VSDIST01.DIAP1006

  DATA - VSDIST01.DIAP1006.DATA
    DATA VOL -
      DIST01

  INDX - VSDIST01.DIAP1006.INDEX
    INDX VOL -
      DIST01

CLUS - VSDIST01.DIAT1006

  DATA - VSDIST01.DIAT1006.DATA
    DATA VOL -
      DIST01

  INDX - VSDIST01.DIAT1006.INDEX
    INDX VOL -
      DIST01

CLUS - VSDIST01.DIA01006

  DATA - VSDIST01.DIA01006.DATA
    DATA VOL -
      DIST01

  INDX - VSDIST01.DIA01006.INDEX
    INDX VOL -
      DIST01

CLUS - VSDIST01.DIA02P13
```

Figure A.8 Sample LISTCRA using 'NOCOMPARE' parameter.

```
IDCAMS  SYSTEM SERVICES                                              TIME  10 19 27        03/08/84      PAGE   3
                               LISTING OF CATALOG RECOVERY AREA FOR VOLUME -- DISTO1 -- VSAM ENTRIES
  DATA - VSDISTO1.DIAO2P13.DATA
    DATA VOL -
      DISTO1

  INDX - VSDISTO1.DIAO2P13.INDEX
    INDX VOL -
      DISTO1
      DISTO1

CLUS - VSDISTO1.DIAO2013

  DATA - VSDISTO1.DIAO2013.DATA
    DATA VOL -
      DISTO1

  INDX - VSDISTO1.DIAO2013.INDEX
    INDX VOL -
      DISTO1
      DISTO1

CLUS - VSDISTO1.DIA10P10

  DATA - VSDISTO1.DIA10P10.DATA
    DATA VOL -
      DISTO1

  INDX - VSDISTO1.DIA10P10.INDEX
    INDX VOL -
      DISTO1
      DISTO1

CLUS - VSDISTO1.DIA10010

  DATA - VSDISTO1.DIA10010.DATA
    DATA VOL -
      DISTO1

  INDX - VSDISTO1.DIA10010.INDEX
    INDX VOL -
      DISTO1
      DISTO1

CLUS - VSDISTO1.DIHAPF.CHI

  DATA - VSDISTO1.DIHAPF.CHI.DATA
    DATA VOL -
      DISTO1

CLUS - VSDISTO1.DIHAPF.CLF

IDCAMS  SYSTEM SERVICES                                              TIME  10 19 27        03/08/84      PAGE   4
                               LISTING OF CATALOG RECOVERY AREA FOR VOLUME -- DISTO1 -- VSAM ENTRIES
  DATA - VSDISTO1.DIHAPF.CLF.DATA
    DATA VOL -
      DISTO1

CLUS - VSDISTO1.DIHAPF.SNF

  DATA - VSDISTO1.DIHAPF.SNF.DATA
    DATA VOL -
      DISTO1

CLUS - VSDISTO1.DIHHCNTL.CHI

  DATA - VSDISTO1.DIHHCNTL.CHI.DATA
    DATA VOL -
      DISTO1

  INDX - VSDISTO1.DIHHCNTL.CHI.INDEX
    INDX VOL -
      DISTO1
      DISTO1

CLUS - VSDISTO1.DIHHCNTL.CLF

  DATA - VSDISTO1.DIHHCNTL.CLF.DATA
    DATA VOL -
      DISTO1

  INDX - VSDISTO1.DIHHCNTL.CLF.INDEX
    INDX VOL -
      DISTO1
      DISTO1

CLUS - VSDISTO1.DIHHCNTL.SNF

  DATA - VSDISTO1.DIHHCNTL.SNF.DATA
    DATA VOL -
      DISTO1
```

Figure A.8 Continued.

```
  INDX - VSDIST01.DIHHCNTL.SNF.INDEX
    INDX VOL -
      DIST01
      DIST01

CLUS - VSDIST01.DIHMISCF.CHI

  DATA - VSDIST01.DIHMISCF.CHI.DATA
    DATA VOL -
      DIST01

IDCAMS  SYSTEM SERVICES                                      TIME  10 19 27        03/08/84      PAGE    5
                        LISTING OF CATALOG RECOVERY AREA FOR VOLUME -- DIST01 -- VSAM ENTRIES

  INDX - VSDIST01.DIHMISCF.CHI.INDEX
    INDX VOL -
      DIST01
      DIST01

CLUS - VSDIST01.DIHMISCF.CLF

  DATA - VSDIST01.DIHMISCF.CLF.DATA
    DATA VOL -
      DIST01

  INDX - VSDIST01.DIHMISCF.CLF.INDEX
    INDX VOL -
      DIST01
      DIST01

CLUS - VSDIST01.DIHMISCF.SNF

  DATA - VSDIST01.DIHMISCF.SNF.DATA
    DATA VOL -
      DIST01

  INDX - VSDIST01.DIHMISCF.SNF.INDEX
    INDX VOL -
      DIST01
      DIST01

CLUS - VSDIST01.DIHP0100

  DATA - VSDIST01.DIHP0100.DATA
    DATA VOL -
      DIST01

CLUS - VSDIST01.DIHP0200

  DATA - VSDIST01.DIHP0200.DATA
    DATA VOL -
      DIST01

CLUS - VSDIST01.DIHP0300

  DATA - VSDIST01.DIHP0300.DATA
    DATA VOL -
      DIST01

CLUS - VSDIST01.DIHP0400

  DATA - VSDIST01.DIHP0400.DATA
    DATA VOL -

IDCAMS  SYSTEM SERVICES                                      TIME  10 19 27        03/08/84      PAGE    6
                        LISTING OF CATALOG RECOVERY AREA FOR VOLUME -- DIST01 -- VSAM ENTRIES

      DIST01

CLUS - VSDIST01.DIHP0500

  DATA - VSDIST01.DIHP0500.DATA
    DATA VOL -
      DIST01

CLUS - VSDIST01.DIHP0600

  DATA - VSDIST01.DIHP0600.DATA
    DATA VOL -
      DIST01

  INDX - VSDIST01.DIHP0600.INDEX
    INDX VOL -
      DIST01

CLUS - VSDIST01.DIHP0700

  DATA - VSDIST01.DIHP0700.DATA
    DATA VOL -
      DIST01

CLUS - VSDIST01.DIHP0800
```

Figure A.8 Continued.

```
    DATA - VSDIST01.DIHP0800.DATA
      DATA VOL -
        DIST01

  CLUS - VSDIST01.DIH08100

    DATA - VSDIST01.DIH08100.DATA
      DATA VOL -
        DIST01

  CLUS - VSDIST01.DIH00100

    DATA - VSDIST01.DIH00100.DATA
      DATA VOL -
        DIST01

  CLUS - VSDIST01.DIH00200

    DATA - VSDIST01.DIH00200.DATA
      DATA VOL -
        DIST01

  CLUS - VSDIST01.DIH00300


IDCAMS  SYSTEM SERVICES                                          TIME  10 19 27        03/08/84      PAGE   7
                        LISTING OF CATALOG RECOVERY AREA FOR VOLUME -- DIST01 -- VSAM ENTRIES

    DATA - VSDIST01.DIH00300.DATA
      DATA VOL -
        DIST01

  CLUS - VSDIST01.DIH00400

    DATA - VSDIST01.DIH00400.DATA
      DATA VOL -
        DIST01

  CLUS - VSDIST01.DIH00500

    DATA - VSDIST01.DIH00500.DATA
      DATA VOL -
        DIST01

  CLUS - VSDIST01.DIH00600

    DATA - VSDIST01.DIH00600.DATA
      DATA VOL -
        DIST01

    INDX - VSDIST01.DIH00600.INDEX
      INDX VOL -
        DIST01

  CLUS - VSDIST01.DIH00700

    DATA - VSDIST01.DIH00700.DATA
      DATA VOL -
        DIST01

  CLUS - VSDIST01.DIH00800

    DATA - VSDIST01.DIH00800.DATA
      DATA VOL -
        DIST01

  CLUS - VSDIST01.DIH00900

    DATA - VSDIST01.DIH00900.DATA
      DATA VOL -
        DIST01

    INDX - VSDIST01.DIH00900.INDEX
      INDX VOL -
        DIST01
        DIST01


IDCAMS  SYSTEM SERVICES                                          TIME  10 19 27        03/08/84      PAGE   8
                        LISTING OF CATALOG RECOVERY AREA FOR VOLUME -- DIST01 -- VSAM ENTRIES

  CLUS - VSDIST01.DIH00950

    DATA - VSDIST01.DIH00950.DATA
      DATA VOL -
        DIST01

  CLUS - VSDIST01.DIH01000

    DATA - VSDIST01.DIH01000.DATA
      DATA VOL -
        DIST01
```

Figure A.8 Continued.

```
  INDX - VSDIST01.DIH01000.INDEX
    INDX VOL -
      DIST01
      DIST01

CLUS - VSDIST01.DIH01050

  DATA - VSDIST01.DIH01050.DATA
    DATA VOL -
      DIST01

CLUS - VSDIST01.DIH01060

  DATA - VSDIST01.DIH01060.DATA
    DATA VOL -
      DIST01

CLUS - VSDIST01.DIS00100

  DATA - VSDIST01.DIS00100.DATA
    DATA VOL -
      DIST01

  INDX - VSDIST01.DIS00100.INDEX
    INDX VOL -
      DIST01
      DIST01

CLUS - VSDIST01.DIT03005.INTFROM

  DATA - VSDIST01.DIT03005.INTFROM.DATA
    DATA VOL -
      DIST01

  INDX - VSDIST01.DIT03005.INTFROM.INDEX
    INDX VOL -
      DIST01

IDCAMS  SYSTEM SERVICES                                    TIME  10 19 27        03/08/84      PAGE   9

                      LISTING OF CATALOG RECOVERY AREA FOR VOLUME -- DIST01 -- VSAM ENTRIES

      DIST01

CLUS - VSDIST01.DIV02P08

  DATA - VSDIST01.DIV02P08.DATA
    DATA VOL -
      DIST01

  INDX - VSDIST01.DIV02P08.INDEX
    INDX VOL -
      DIST01
      DIST01

CLUS - VSDIST01.DIV02008

  DATA - VSDIST01.DIV02008.DATA
    DATA VOL -
      DIST01

  INDX - VSDIST01.DIV02008.INDEX
    INDX VOL -
      DIST01
      DIST01

CLUS - VSDIST01.DPEP1001

  DATA - VSDIST01.DPEP1001.DATA
    DATA VOL -
      DIST01

  INDX - VSDIST01.DPEP1001.INDEX
    INDX VOL -
      DIST01

CLUS - VSDIST01.DPE01001

  DATA - VSDIST01.DPE01001.DATA
    DATA VOL -
      DIST01

  INDX - VSDIST01.DPE01001.INDEX
    INDX VOL -
      DIST01

CLUS - VSDIST01.DPE14P01

  DATA - VSDIST01.DPE14P01.DATA
    DATA VOL -
      DIST01
```

Figure A.8 Continued.

```
IDCAMS  SYSTEM SERVICES                                              TIME  10 19 27        03/08/84      PAGE  10
                         LISTING OF CATALOG RECOVERY AREA FOR VOLUME -- DIST01 -- VSAM ENTRIES
CLUS - VSDIST01.DPE14001

  DATA - VSDIST01.DPE14001.DATA
    DATA VOL -
      DIST01

CLUS - VSDIST01.DPP5P009

  DATA - VSDIST01.DPP5P009.DATA
    DATA VOL -
      DIST01

  INDX - VSDIST01.DPP5P009.INDEX
    INDX VOL -
      DIST01
      DIST01

CLUS - VSDIST01.DPP5P109

  DATA - VSDIST01.DPP5P109.DATA
    DATA VOL -
      DIST01

  INDX - VSDIST01.DPP5P109.INDEX
    INDX VOL -
      DIST01
      DIST01

CLUS - VSDIST01.DPP50009

  DATA - VSDIST01.DPP50009.DATA
    DATA VOL -
      DIST01

  INDX - VSDIST01.DPP50009.INDEX
    INDX VOL -
      DIST01
      DIST01

CLUS - VSDIST01.DPP50109

  DATA - VSDIST01.DPP50109.DATA
    DATA VOL -
      DIST01

  INDX - VSDIST01.DPP50109.INDEX
    INDX VOL -
      DIST01
      DIST01

IDCAMS  SYSTEM SERVICES                                              TIME  10 19 27        03/08/84      PAGE  11
                         LISTING OF CATALOG RECOVERY AREA FOR VOLUME -- DIST01 -- VSAM ENTRIES
CLUS - VSDIST01.DSMP31KW

  DATA - VSDIST01.DSMP31KW.DATA
    DATA VOL -
      DIST01

  INDX - VSDIST01.DSMP31KW.INDEX
    INDX VOL -
      DIST01
      DIST01

CLUS - VSDIST01.DSMP31KW

  DATA - VSDIST01.DSMP31KW.DATA
    DATA VOL -
      DIST01

  INDX - VSDIST01.DCG02007.INDEX
    INDX VOL -
      DIST01
      DIST01

CLUS - VSDIST01.DSMP31KW

  DATA - VSDIST01.DSMP31KW.DATA
    DATA VOL -
      DIST01

  INDX - VSDIST01.DCG02007.INDEX
    INDX VOL -
      DIST01
      DIST01

CLUS - VSDIST01.DSMP31TM

  DATA - VSDIST01.DSMP31TM.DATA
    DATA VOL -
      DIST01
```

Figure A.8 Continued.

```
    INDX - VSDIST01.DSMP31TM.INDEX
      INDX VOL -
        DIST01
        DIST01

  CLUS - VSDIST01.DSMP31TU

    DATA - VSDIST01.DSMP31TU.DATA
      DATA VOL -
        DIST01

IDCAMS  SYSTEM SERVICES                                    TIME  10 19 27        03/08/84      PAGE  12

                      LISTING OF CATALOG RECOVERY AREA FOR VOLUME -- DIST01 -- VSAM ENTRIES

  CLUS - VSDIST01.DSM031TM

    DATA - VSDIST01.DSM031TM.DATA
      DATA VOL -
        DIST01

    INDX - VSDIST01.DSM031TM.INDEX
      INDX VOL -
        DIST01
        DIST01

  CLUS - VSDIST01.DSM031TU

    DATA - VSDIST01.DSM031TU.DATA
      DATA VOL -
        DIST01

  CLUS - VSDIST01.DSM15P01

    DATA - VSDIST01.DSM15P01.DATA
      DATA VOL -
        DIST01

  CLUS - VSDIST01.DSM15001

    DATA - VSDIST01.DSM15001.DATA
      DATA VOL -
        DIST01

  CLUS - VSDIST01.DSM2P002

    DATA - VSDIST01.DSM2P002.DATA
      DATA VOL -
        DIST01

  CLUS - VSDIST01.DSM20002

    DATA - VSDIST01.DSM20002.DATA
      DATA VOL -
        DIST01

  CLUS - VSDIST01.DSM30001

    DATA - VSDIST01.DSM30001.DATA
      DATA VOL -
        DIST01

    INDX - VSDIST01.DSM30001.INDEX
      INDX VOL -

IDCAMS  SYSTEM SERVICES                                    TIME  10 19 27        03/08/84      PAGE  13

                      LISTING OF CATALOG RECOVERY AREA FOR VOLUME -- DIST01 -- VSAM ENTRIES

        DIST01
        DIST01

  CLUS - VSDIST01.DSM82P01

    DATA - VSDIST01.DSM82P01.DATA
      DATA VOL -
        DIST01

    INDX - VSDIST01.DSM82P01.INDEX
      INDX VOL -
        DIST01
        DIST01

  CLUS - VSDIST01.DSM82001

    DATA - VSDIST01.DSM82001.DATA
      DATA VOL -
        DIST01

    INDX - VSDIST01.DSM82001.INDEX
      INDX VOL -
        DIST01
        DIST01
```

Figure A.8 Continued.

```
CLUS - VSDIST01.DST01P04

  DATA - VSDIST01.DST01P04.DATA
    DATA VOL -
      DIST01

  INDX - VSDIST01.DST01P04.INDEX
    INDX VOL -
      DIST01
      DIST01

CLUS - VSDIST01.DST01004

  DATA - VSDIST01.DST01004.DATA
    DATA VOL -
      DIST01

  INDX - VSDIST01.DST01004.INDEX
    INDX VOL -
      DIST01
      DIST01

CLUS - VSDIST01.DUT01007

IDCAMS  SYSTEM SERVICES                                        TIME  10 19 27        03/08/84      PAGE  14
                        LISTING OF CATALOG RECOVERY AREA FOR VOLUME -- DIST01 -- VSAM ENTRIES

  DATA - VSDIST01.DUT01007.DATA
    DATA VOL -
      DIST01

  INDX - VSDIST01.DUT01007.INDEX
    INDX VOL -
      DIST01
      DIST01

CLUS - VSDIST01.DUT02007

  DATA - VSDIST01.DUT02007.DATA
    DATA VOL -
      DIST01

  INDX - VSDIST01.DUT02007.INDEX
    INDX VOL -
      DIST01
      DIST01

CLUS - VSDIST01.DUT03007

  DATA - VSDIST01.DUT03007.DATA
    DATA VOL -
      DIST01

  INDX - VSDIST01.DUT03007.INDEX
    INDX VOL -
      DIST01
      DIST01

CLUS - VSDIST01.HCONTROL

  DATA - VSDIST01.HCONTROL.DATA
    DATA VOL -
      DIST01

  INDX - VSDIST01.HCONTROL.INDEX
    INDX VOL -
      DIST01
      DIST01

CLUS - VSDIST01.HOWADV

  DATA - VSDIST01.HOWADV.DATA
    DATA VOL -
      DIST01

CLUS - VSDIST01.HOWADV.BKUP

IDCAMS  SYSTEM SERVICES                                        TIME  10 19 27        03/08/84      PAGE  15
                        LISTING OF CATALOG RECOVERY AREA FOR VOLUME -- DIST01 -- VSAM ENTRIES

  DATA - VSDIST01.HOWADV.BKUP.DATA
    DATA VOL -
      DIST01

CLUS - VSDIST01.HOWBKP

  DATA - VSDIST01.HOWBKP.DATA
    DATA VOL -
      DIST01

CLUS - VSDIST01.HOWCUST
```

Figure A.8 Continued.

```
  DATA - VSDIST01.HOWCUST.DATA
    DATA VOL -
      DIST01

  INDX - VSDIST01.HOWCUST.INDEX
    INDX VOL -
      DIST01
      DIST01

CLUS - VSDIST01.HOWLOTS

  DATA - VSDIST01.HOWLOTS.DATA
    DATA VOL -
      DIST01

  INDX - VSDIST01.HOWLOTS.INDEX
    INDX VOL -
      DIST01
      DIST01

CLUS - VSDIST01.HOWPROD

  DATA - VSDIST01.HOWPROD.DATA
    DATA VOL -
      DIST01

  INDX - VSDIST01.HOWPROD.INDEX
    INDX VOL -
      DIST01
      DIST01

CLUS - VSDIST01.MISCFIL

  DATA - VSDIST01.MISCFIL.DATA
    DATA VOL -
      DIST01


IDCAMS  SYSTEM SERVICES                                              TIME  10 19 27        03/08/84      PAGE  16

                        LISTING OF CATALOG RECOVERY AREA FOR VOLUME -- DIST01 -- VSAM ENTRIES

  INDX - VSDIST01.MISCFIL.INDEX
    INDX VOL -
      DIST01
      DIST01

CLUS - VSDIST01.OII7P4US

  DATA - VSDIST01.OII7P4US.DATA
    DATA VOL -
      DIST01

  INDX - VSDIST01.OII7P4US.INDEX
    INDX VOL -
      DIST01
      DIST01

CLUS - VSDIST01.OII704US

  DATA - VSDIST01.OII704US.DATA
    DATA VOL -
      DISTC1

  INDX - VSDIST01.OII704US.INDEX
    INDX VOL -
      DIST01
      DIST01

CLUS - VSDIST01.OPT7P0US

  DATA - VSDIST01.OPT7P0US.DATA
    DATA VOL -
      DIST01

  INDX - VSDIST01.OPT7P0US.INDEX
    INDX VOL -
      DIST01
      DIST01

CLUS - VSDIST01.OPT7P1US

  DATA - VSDIST01.OPT7P1US.DATA
    DATA VOL -
      DIST01

  INDX - VSDIST01.OPT7P1US.INDEX
    INDX VOL -
      DIST01
      DIST01
```

Figure A.8 Continued.

```
IDCAMS  SYSTEM SERVICES                                    TIME  10 19 27         03/08/84      PAGE  17
                         LISTING OF CATALOG RECOVERY AREA FOR VOLUME -- DIST01 -- VSAM ENTRIES
CLUS - VSDIST01.OPT7P2US

  DATA - VSDIST01.OPT7P2US.DATA
    DATA VOL -
      DIST01

  INDX - VSDIST01.OPT7P2US.INDEX
    INDX VOL -
      DIST01
      DIST01

CLUS - VSDIST01.OPT7P3US

  DATA - VSDIST01.OPT7P3US.DATA
    DATA VOL -
      DIST01

  INDX - VSDIST01.OPT7P3US.INDEX
    INDX VOL -
      DIST01
      DIST01

CLUS - VSDIST01.OPT7P4US

  DATA - VSDIST01.OPT7P4US.DATA
    DATA VOL -
      DIST01

  INDX - VSDIST01.OPT7P4US.INDEX
    INDX VOL -
      DIST01
      DIST01

CLUS - VSDIST01.OPT700US

  DATA - VSDIST01.OPT700US.DATA
    DATA VOL -
      DIST01

  INDX - VSDIST01.OPT700US.INDEX
    INDX VOL -
      DIST01
      DIST01

CLUS - VSDIST01.OPT701US

  DATA - VSDIST01.OPT701US.DATA
    DATA VOL -
      DIST01


IDCAMS  SYSTEM SERVICES                                    TIME  10 19 27         03/08/84      PAGE  18
                         LISTING OF CATALOG RECOVERY AREA FOR VOLUME -- DIST01 -- VSAM ENTRIES
  INDX - VSDIST01.OPT701US.INDEX
    INDX VOL -
      DIST01
      DIST01

CLUS - VSDIST01.OPT702US

  DATA - VSDIST01.OPT702US.DATA
    DATA VOL -
      DIST01

  INDX - VSDIST01.OPT702US.INDEX
    INDX VOL -
      DIST01
      DIST01

CLUS - VSDIST01.OPT703US

  DATA - VSDIST01.OPT703US.DATA
    DATA VOL -
      DIST01

  INDX - VSDIST01.OPT703US.INDEX
    INDX VOL -
      DIST01
      DIST01

CLUS - VSDIST01.OPT704US

  DATA - VSDIST01.OPT704US.DATA
    DATA VOL -
      DIST01

  INDX - VSDIST01.OPT704US.INDEX
    INDX VOL -
      DIST01
      DIST01
```

Figure A.8 Continued.

```
CLUS - VSDIST01.PRODADT

  DATA - VSDIST01.PRODADT.DATA
    DATA VOL -
      DIST01

CLUS - VSDIST01.TEST.UFOCOB

  DATA - VSDIST01.TEST.UFOCOB.DATA
    DATA VOL -
      DIST01


IDCAMS  SYSTEM SERVICES                                              TIME  10 19 27        03/08/84      PAGE  19

                         LISTING OF CATALOG RECOVERY AREA FOR VOLUME -- DIST01 -- VSAM ENTRIES

  INDX - VSDIST01.TEST.UFOCOB.INDEX
    INDX VOL -
      DIST01
      DIST01


IDCAMS  SYSTEM SERVICES                                              TIME  10 19 27        03/08/84      PAGE  20

                         LISTING OF CATALOG RECOVERY AREA FOR VOLUME -- DIST01 -- OTHER ENTRIES

NONV - TAPE.D.DIST01
  DATA VOL -
    011091


IDCAMS  SYSTEM SERVICES                                              TIME  10 19 27        03/08/84      PAGE  21

                         LISTING OF CATALOG RECOVERY AREA FOR VOLUME -- DIST01 -- UNSORTED ENTRIES

DATA - VSDIST01.DSMP31KW.DATA
  DATA VOL -
    DIST01

NUMBER OF ENTRIES PROCESSED
 NONV -     1
 CLUS -    93
 DATA -    94
 INDX -    58
 VOL  -     1
 SUM  -   247

IDC0001I FUNCTION COMPLETED, HIGHEST CONDITION CODE WAS 0


IDCAMS  SYSTEM SERVICES                                              TIME  10 19 27        03/08/84      PAGE  22


IDC0002I IDCAMS PROCESSING COMPLETE. MAXIMUM CONDITION CODE WAS 0
```

Figure A.8 Continued.

```
IDCAMS  SYSTEM SERVICES                                              TIME: 13:25:39        06/07/84      PAGE   1

          DEFINE  CLUSTER                                   -
                  (                                         -
                    NAME(TVNBOB.OBS.CUST.CLUSTER)           -
                    CYLINDERS(2,1)                          -
                    FREESPACE(25 25)                        -
                    INDEXED                                 -
                    KEYS(013 000)                           -
                    NOIMBED                                 -
                    OWNER(OBS)                              -
                    RECORDSIZE(300 300)                     -
                    REPLICATE                               -
                    NOREUSE                                 -
                    SHR(2 3)                                -
                    SPEED                                   -
                    VOLUMES(VSAM03)                         -
                    WCK                                     -
                  )                                         -
                  DATA                                      -
                  (                                         -
                    NAME(TVNBOB.OBS.CUST.DATA)              -
                    CISZ(4096)                              -
                  )                                         -
                  INDEX                                     -
                  (                                         -
                    NAME(TVNBOB.OBS.CUST.INDEX)             -
                    CISZ(512)                               -
                  )
IDC0508I DATA ALLOCATION STATUS FOR VOLUME VSAM03 IS 0
IDC0509I INDEX ALLOCATION STATUS FOR VOLUME VSAM03 IS 0
IDC0001I FUNCTION COMPLETED, HIGHEST CONDITION CODE WAS 0


IDC0002I IDCAMS PROCESSING COMPLETE. MAXIMUM CONDITION CODE WAS 0
```

Figure A.9 Definition of Base Clusters.

```
IDCAMS  SYSTEM SERVICES                                          TIME: 16:28:11        05/18/84      PAGE    1

          REPRO    INFILE(STFILE)                                     -
                   OUTDATASET(TVNBOB.OBS.CUST.CLUSTER)
IDC0005I NUMBER OF RECORDS PROCESSED WAS 461
IDC0001I FUNCTION COMPLETED, HIGHEST CONDITION CODE WAS 0

IDC0002I IDCAMS PROCESSING COMPLETE. MAXIMUM CONDITION CODE WAS 0
```

Figure A.10 Execution of REPRO to load Base Cluster.

```
IDCAMS  SYSTEM SERVICES                                          TIME: 13:26:17        06/07/84      PAGE    1

          DEFINE   AIX                                                -
                   (                                                  -
                     NAME(TVNBOB.OBS.CUST.AIX)                        -
                     CYLINDERS(1,1)                                   -
                     RELATE(TVNBOB.OBS.CUST.CLUSTER)                  -
                     KEYS(08 05)                                      -
                     NCNUNICUEKEY                                     -
                     CWNER(OBS)                                       -
                     SHR(2 3)                                         -
                     SPEED                                            -
                     UPGRADE                                          -
                     VCLUMES(VSAM03)                                  -
                    )
IDC0508I CATA ALLCCATICN STATUS FCR VCLUME VSAM03 IS 0
IDC0509I INDEX ALLOCATICN STATUS FCR VCLUME VSAM03 IS 0
IDC0512I NAME GENERATED-(D) TVNBUB.T74A0748.VDD84159.T9774E48
IDC0512I NAME GENERATED-(I) TVNBOB.T74A0C1E.VID84159.T9774E48
IDC0001I FUNCTION CCMPLETED, HIGHEST CCNDITICN CODE WAS 0

IDC0002I ICCAMS PROCESSING COMPLETE. MAXIMUM CCNDITION CCDE WAS 0
```

Figure A.11 Definition of an Alternate Index.

```
IDCAMS  SYSTEM SERVICES                                          TIME: 13:31:09        06/07/84      PAGE    1

          BLDINDEX  INDATASET(TVNBOB.OBS.CUST.CLUSTER)                -
                    OUTDATASET(TVNBOB.OBS.CUST.AIX)
IDC0652I TVNBOB.OBS.CUST.AIX SUCCESSFULLY BUILT
IDC0001I FUNCTION COMPLETED, HIGHEST CONDITION CODE WAS 0

IDC0002I IDCAMS PROCESSING COMPLETE. MAXIMUM CONDITION CODE WAS 0
```

Figure A.12 Execution of BLDINDEX.

```
IDCAMS  SYSTEM SERVICES                                          TIME: 14:38:14        06/08/84      PAGE    1

          DEFINE   PATH                                               -
                   (                                                  -
                     NAME(TVNBOB.OBS.CUST.PATH)                       -
                     PATHENTRY(TVNBOB.OBS.CUST.AIX)                   -
                     UPDATE                                           -
                   )
IDC0001I FUNCTION COMPLETED, HIGHEST CONDITION CODE WAS 0

IDC0002I IDCAMS PROCESSING COMPLETE. MAXIMUM CONDITION CODE WAS 0
```

Figure A.13 Definition of a PATH.

```
IDCAMS  SYSTEM SERVICES                                             TIME: 14:41:27        06/08/84     PAGE    1

          LISTCAT ENTRIES(TVNBOB.CBS.CUST.CLUSTER)  -
                  ALL

CLUSTER ------- TVNBOB.CBS.CUST.CLUSTER
     IN-CAT --- SYS1.ICFUCAT.VSAM03
     HISTORY
       OWNER-IDENT----------OBS      CREATION----------84.159
       RELEASE-----------------2     EXPIRATION--------00.000
     PROTECTION-PSWD-----(NULL)      RACF----------------(NC)
     ASSOCIATIONS
       DATA-----TVNBOB.CBS.CUST.DATA
       INDEX----TVNBOB.OBS.CUST.INDEX
       AIX------TVNBOB.CBS.CUST.AIX

   DATA ------- TVNBOB.CBS.CUST.DATA
     IN-CAT --- SYS1.ICFUCAT.VSAM03
     HISTORY
       OWNER-IDENT-------(NULL)      CREATION----------84.159
       RELEASE-----------------2     EXPIRATION--------00.000
     PROTECTION-PSWD-----(NULL)      RACF----------------(NC)
     ASSOCIATIONS
       CLUSTER--TVNBOB.CBS.CUST.CLUSTER
     ATTRIBUTES
       KEYLEN-----------------13     AVGLRECL-------------300     BUFSPACE-----------10240     CISIZE--------------4096
       RKP---------------------0     MAXLRECL-------------300     EXCPEXIT-----------(NULL)    CI/CA----------------150
       SHROPTNS(2,3)      SPEED      UNIQUE           NOERASE     INDEXED         WRITECHECK   NOIMBED       NOREPLICAT
       UNORDERED        NOREUSE      NONSPANNED
     STATISTICS
       REC-TOTAL--------------48     SPLITS-CI---------------0    EXCPS------------------21
       REC-DELETED-------------0     SPLITS-CA---------------0    EXTENTS-----------------1
       REC-INSERTED------------0     FREESPACE-%CI----------25    SYSTEM-TIMESTAMP:
       REC-UPDATED-------------0     FREESPACE-%CA----------25         X'9774E4CA4F8FD610'
       REC-RETRIEVED-----------0     FREESPC-BYTES----1208320
     ALLOCATION
       SPACE-TYPE------CYLINDER      HI-ALLOC-RBA-----1228800
       SPACE-PRI---------------2     HI-USED-RBA-------614400
       SPACE-SEC---------------1
     VOLUME
       VOLSER------------VSAM03      PHYREC-SIZE---------4096     HI-ALLOC-RBA-----1228800     EXTENT-NUMBER----------1
       DEVTYPE------X'3010200E'      PHYRECS/TRK-----------10     HI-USED-RBA-------614400     EXTENT-TYPE--------X'00'
       VOLFLAG------------PRIME      TRACKS/CA-------------15
       EXTENTS:
       LOW-CCHH-----X'01700000'      LOW-RBA-----------------0    TRACKS-----------------30
       HIGH-CCHH----X'0171000E'      HIGH-RBA---------1228799

   INDEX ------ TVNBOB.CBS.CUST.INDEX
     IN-CAT --- SYS1.ICFUCAT.VSAM03
     HISTORY
       OWNER-IDENT-------(NULL)      CREATION----------84.159
       RELEASE-----------------2     EXPIRATION--------00.000


IDCAMS  SYSTEM SERVICES                                             TIME: 14:41:27        06/08/84     PAGE    2

     PROTECTION-PSWD-----(NULL)      RACF----------------(NC)
     ASSOCIATIONS
       CLUSTER--TVNBOB.OBS.CUST.CLUSTER
     ATTRIBUTES
       KEYLEN-----------------13     AVGLRECL----------------0    BUFSPACE----------------0    CISIZE--------------2048
       RKP---------------------0     MAXLRECL-------------2041    EXCPEXIT-----------(NULL)    CI/CA-----------------18
       SHROPTNS(2,3)   RECOVERY      UNIQUE           NOERASE     WRITECHECK         NOIMBED   REPLICATE      UNORDERED
       NOREUSE
     STATISTICS
       REC-TOTAL---------------1     SPLITS-CI---------------0    EXCPS-------------------4    INDEX:
       REC-DELETED-------------0     SPLITS-CA---------------0    EXTENTS-----------------1    LEVELS-----------------1
       REC-INSERTED------------0     FREESPACE-%CI-----------0    SYSTEM-TIMESTAMP:            ENTRIES/SECT----------12
       REC-UPDATED-------------0     FREESPACE-%CA-----------0         X'9774E4CA4F8FD61C'     SEQ-SET-RBA------------0
       REC-RETRIEVED-----------0     FREESPC-BYTES--------4096                                 HI-LEVEL-RBA-----------0
     ALLOCATION
       SPACE-TYPE---------TRACK      HI-ALLOC-RBA--------6144
       SPACE-PRI---------------3     HI-USED-RBA---------2048
       SPACE-SEC---------------2
     VOLUME
       VOLSER------------VSAM03      PHYREC-SIZE---------2048     HI-ALLOC-RBA--------6144     EXTENT-NUMBER----------1
       DEVTYPE------X'3010200E'      PHYRECS/TRK-----------18     HI-USED-RBA---------2048     EXTENT-TYPE--------X'00'
       VOLFLAG------------PRIME      TRACKS/CA--------------1
       EXTENTS:
       LOW-CCHH-----X'009C0000'      LOW-RBA-----------------0    TRACKS------------------3
       HIGH-CCHH----X'009C0002'      HIGH-RBA------------6143


IDCAMS  SYSTEM SERVICES                                             TIME: 14:41:27        06/08/84     PAGE    3

         THE NUMBER OF ENTRIES PROCESSED WAS:
                    AIX -----------------0
                    ALIAS ---------------0
                    CLUSTER -------------1
                    DATA ----------------1
                    GDG -----------------0
                    INDEX ---------------1
                    NONVSAM -------------0
                    PAGESPACE -----------0
                    PATH ----------------0
                    SPACE ---------------0
                    USERCATALOG ---------0
                    TOTAL ---------------3

         THE NUMBER OF PROTECTED ENTRIES SUPPRESSED WAS 0

IDC0001I FUNCTION COMPLETED, HIGHEST CONDITION CODE WAS 0

          LISTCAT ENTRIES(TVNBOB.CBS.CUST.AIX)      -
                  ALL

AIX ----------- TVNBOB.CBS.CUST.AIX
     IN-CAT --- SYS1.ICFUCAT.VSAM03
     HISTORY
       OWNER-IDENT----------OBS      CREATION----------84.159
       RELEASE-----------------2     EXPIRATION--------00.000
     PROTECTION-PSWD-----(NULL)      RACF----------------(NC)
     ASSOCIATIONS
       DATA-----TVNBOB.T74A0748.VD084159.T9774E4B
       INDEX----TVNBOB.T74A0C1E.VI084159.T9774E4B
       CLUSTER--TVNBOB.OBS.CUST.CLUSTER
       PATH-----TVNBOB.CBS.CUST.PATH
     ATTRIBUTES
       UPGRADE

   DATA ------- TVNBOB.T74A0748.VD084159.T9774E4B
     IN-CAT --- SYS1.ICFUCAT.VSAM03
     HISTORY
       OWNER-IDENT-------(NULL)      CREATION----------84.159
       RELEASE-----------------2     EXPIRATION--------00.000
     PROTECTION-PSWD-----(NULL)      RACF----------------(NC)
     ASSOCIATIONS
       AIX------TVNBOB.OBS.CUST.AIX
     ATTRIBUTES
       KEYLEN------------------8     AVGLRECL------------4086     BUFSPACE-----------10240     CISIZE--------------4096
       RKP---------------------5     MAXLRECL-----------32600     EXCPEXIT-----------(NULL)    CI/CA----------------150
       AXRKP-------------------5
       SHROPTNS(2,3)      SPEED      UNIQUE           NOERASE     INDEXED        NOWRITECHK    NOIMBED       NOREPLICAT
       UNORDERED        NOREUSE      SPANNED        NONUNIQKEY
     STATISTICS
```

Figure A.14 LISTCAT of Base Cluster, AIX, and PATH.

```
IDCAMS  SYSTEM SERVICES                                                 TIME: 14:41:27        06/08/84      PAGE   4
       REC-TOTAL--------------0       SPLITS-CI---------------0       EXCPS------------------0
       REC-DELETED------------0       SPLITS-CA---------------0       EXTENTS----------------1
       REC-INSERTED-----------0       FREESPACE-%CI-----------0       SYSTEM-TIMESTAMP:
       REC-UPDATED------------0       FREESPACE-%CA-----------0            X'0000000000000000'
       REC-RETRIEVED----------0       FREESPC-BYTES-----614400
     ALLOCATION
       SPACE-TYPE------CYLINDER       HI-ALLOC-RBA------614400
       SPACE-PRI--------------1       HI-USED-RBA-------------0
       SPACE-SEC--------------1
     VOLUME
       VOLSER------------VSAM03       PHYREC-SIZE----------4096       HI-ALLOC-RBA------614400       EXTENT-NUMBER----------1
       DEVTYPE------X'3010200E'       PHYRECS/TRK------------10       HI-USED-RBA-------------0       EXTENT-TYPE--------X'40'
       VOLFLAG-------------PRIME      TRACKS/CA--------------15
       EXTENTS:
       LOW-CCHH-----X'01720000'       LOW-RBA-----------------0       TRACKS----------------15
       HIGH-CCHH----X'0172000E'       HIGH-RBA-----------614399

   INDEX ------ TVNBOB.T74A0C1E.VID84159.T9774E4B
     IN-CAT --- SYS1.ICFUCAT.VSAM03
     HISTORY
       OWNER-IDENT-------(NULL)       CREATION-----------84.159
       RELEASE----------------2       EXPIRATION---------00.000
     PROTECTION-PSWD-----(NULL)       RACF----------------(NO)
     ASSOCIATIONS
       AIX------TVNBOB.OBS.CUST.AIX
     ATTRIBUTES
       KEYLEN-----------------8       AVGLRECL----------------0       BUFSPACE---------------0       CISIZE--------------2048
       RKP--------------------5       MAXLRECL-------------2041       EXCPEXIT----------(NULL)       CI/CA-----------------18
       SHROPTNS(2,3)   RECOVERY       UNIQUE            NOERASE       NOWRITECHK        NOIMBED       NOREPLICAT     UNORDERED
       NOREUSE
     STATISTICS
       REC-TOTAL--------------0       SPLITS-CI---------------0       EXCPS------------------0       INDEX:
       REC-DELETED------------0       SPLITS-CA---------------0       EXTENTS----------------1       LEVELS-----------------0
       REC-INSERTED-----------0       FREESPACE-%CI-----------0       SYSTEM-TIMESTAMP:              ENTRIES/SECT----------12
       REC-UPDATED------------0       FREESPACE-%CA-----------0            X'0000000000000000'       SEQ-SET-RBA------------0
       REC-RETRIEVED----------0       FREESPC-BYTES------36864                                       HI-LEVEL-RBA-----------0
     ALLOCATION
       SPACE-TYPE---------TRACK       HI-ALLOC-RBA-------36864
       SPACE-PRI--------------1       HI-USED-RBA-------------0
       SPACE-SEC--------------1
     VOLUME
       VOLSER------------VSAM03       PHYREC-SIZE----------2048       HI-ALLOC-RBA-------36864       EXTENT-NUMBER----------1
       DEVTYPE------X'3010200E'       PHYRECS/TRK------------18       HI-USED-RBA-------------0       EXTENT-TYPE--------X'40'
       VOLFLAG-------------PRIME      TRACKS/CA---------------1
       EXTENTS:
       LOW-CCHH-----X'0000000E'       LOW-RBA-----------------0       TRACKS-----------------1
       HIGH-CCHH----X'0000000E'       HIGH-RBA------------36863

   PATH ------- TVNBOB.OBS.CUST.PATH
     IN-CAT --- SYS1.ICFUCAT.VSAM03
     HISTORY


IDCAMS  SYSTEM SERVICES                                                 TIME: 14:41:27        06/08/84      PAGE   5
       OWNER-IDENT-------(NULL)       CREATION-----------84.160
       RELEASE----------------2       EXPIRATION---------00.000
     PROTECTION-PSWD-----(NULL)       RACF----------------(NO)
     ASSOCIATIONS
       AIX------TVNBOB.OBS.CUST.AIX
       DATA-----TVNBOB.T74A0748.VD084159.T9774E4B
       INDEX----TVNBOB.T74A0C1E.VID84159.T9774E4B
       DATA-----TVNBOB.OBS.CUST.DATA
       INDEX----TVNBOB.OBS.CUST.INDEX
     ATTRIBUTES
       UPDATE


IDCAMS  SYSTEM SERVICES                                                 TIME: 14:41:27        06/08/84      PAGE   6
         THE NUMBER OF ENTRIES PROCESSED WAS:
                    AIX -----------------1
                    ALIAS ---------------0
                    CLUSTER -------------0
                    DATA ----------------1
                    GDG -----------------0
                    INDEX ---------------1
                    NONVSAM -------------0
                    PAGESPACE -----------0
                    PATH ----------------1
                    SPACE ---------------0
                    USERCATALOG ---------0
                    TOTAL ---------------4

         THE NUMBER OF PROTECTED ENTRIES SUPPRESSED WAS 0

IDC0001I FUNCTION COMPLETED, HIGHEST CONDITION CODE WAS 0

           LISTCAT ENTRIES(TVNBOB.OBS.CUST.PATH)      -
                   ALL

PATH ---------- TVNBOB.OBS.CUST.PATH
     IN-CAT --- SYS1.ICFUCAT.VSAM03
     HISTORY
       OWNER-IDENT-------(NULL)       CREATION-----------84.160
       RELEASE----------------2       EXPIRATION---------00.000
     PROTECTION-PSWD-----(NULL)       RACF----------------(NO)
     ASSOCIATIONS
       AIX------TVNBOB.OBS.CUST.AIX
       DATA-----TVNBOB.T74A0748.VD084159.T9774E4B
       INDEX----TVNBOB.T74A0C1E.VID84159.T9774E4B
       DATA-----TVNBOB.OBS.CUST.DATA
       INDEX----TVNBOB.OBS.CUST.INDEX
     ATTRIBUTES
       UPDATE
```

Figure A.14 Continued.

```
IDCAMS  SYSTEM SERVICES                                   TIME: 14:41:27        06/08/84      PAGE   7
        THE NUMBER OF ENTRIES PROCESSED WAS:
                     AIX -----------------0
                     ALIAS ---------------0
                     CLUSTER -------------0
                     DATA ----------------0
                     GDG -----------------0
                     INDEX ---------------0
                     NONVSAM -------------0
                     PAGESPACE -----------0
                     PATH ----------------1
                     SPACE ---------------0
                     USERCATALOG ---------0
                     TOTAL ---------------1

        THE NUMBER OF PROTECTED ENTRIES SUPPRESSED WAS 0
IDC0001I FUNCTION COMPLETED, HIGHEST CONDITION CODE WAS 0


IDC0002I IDCAMS PROCESSING COMPLETE. MAXIMUM CONDITION CODE WAS 0
```

Figure A.14 Continued.

```
IDCAMS  SYSTEM SERVICES                                   TIME: 13:40:00        06/07/84      PAGE   1

          DELETE    TVNBOB.OBS.CUST.PATH            -
                    PATH                            -
                    PURGE
IDC0550I ENTRY (R) TVNBOB.OBS.CUST.PATH DELETED
IDC0001I FUNCTION COMPLETED, HIGHEST CONDITION CODE WAS 0


IDC0002I IDCAMS PROCESSING COMPLETE. MAXIMUM CONDITION CODE WAS 0
```

Figure A.15 Deletion of PATH.

```
IDCAMS  SYSTEM SERVICES                                   TIME: 13:41:22        06/07/84      PAGE   1

          DELETE    TVNBOB.OBS.CUST.AIX             -
                    AIX                             -
                    PURGE
IDC0550I ENTRY (D) TVNBOB.TD5A6FAE.VDD84159.T9774DF9 DELETED
IDC0550I ENTRY (I) TVNBOB.TD5A73A4.VID84159.T9774DF9 DELETED
IDC0550I ENTRY (G) TVNBOB.OBS.CUST.AIX DELETED
IDC0001I FUNCTION COMPLETED, HIGHEST CONDITION CODE WAS 0


IDC0002I IDCAMS PROCESSING COMPLETE. MAXIMUM CONDITION CODE WAS 0
```

Figure A.16 Deletion of AIX.

```
IDCAMS  SYSTEM SERVICES                                   TIME: 13:46:58        06/07/84      PAGE   1

          DELETE    TVNBOB.OBS.CUST.CLUSTER         -
                    CLUSTER                         -
                    PURGE
IDC0550I ENTRY (D) TVNBOB.OBS.CUST.DATA DELETED
IDC0550I ENTRY (I) TVNBOB.OBS.CUST.INDEX DELETED
IDC0550I ENTRY (C) TVNBOB.OBS.CUST.CLUSTER DELETED
IDC0001I FUNCTION COMPLETED, HIGHEST CONDITION CODE WAS 0


IDC0002I IDCAMS PROCESSING COMPLETE. MAXIMUM CONDITION CODE WAS 0
```

Figure A.17 Deletion of Clusters.

appendix B

FORMAT OF CONTROL INTERVALS

THE FORMAT OF THE CIDF

The **CIDF** (Control Interval Definition Field), is a four-byte field that resides in the rightmost four positions of a control interval, the purpose of which is to keep track of space usage within the CI.

The format of the CI is as follows:

Position	Purpose
Bytes 0–1	This value represents the displacement from the beginning of the control interval to the beginning of the unused space in the CI. If a control interval contains no data, the value in this field is zero. The value in this field is represented in binary.
Bytes 2–3	Contains the length of the unused usable space within the control interval. The high-order bit of this field also serves a purpose. When a CI split is in progress, the

high-order bit is turned on. It is turned off when the split is completed. If VSAM encounters a control interval that has this bit on when no split is in progress, VSAM can use this information to weed out any duplicate records that might have been duplicated during the shifting operation that takes place during a CI split. This can only happen if there was some kind of failure while a control interval split was in progress.

A CIDF containing all binary zeros (low-value) indicates a software end-of-file.

FORMAT OF THE RDF FIELD

The **RDF** field provides information about the **records** stored in a control interval. The information contained in the RDF can vary slightly, depending on the type of data set (KSDS, RRDS, or ESDS). The **general** format of the RDF is as follows:

Position	Purpose
Byte 0	Contains **control information** (described in the following).
Bytes 1–2	Contains the length of the data record it corresponds to when bit 4 of byte 0 is 0. When bit 4 of byte 0 is 1 **and** bits 2 and 3 of byte 0 are 0, this field contains the number of consecutive records of the same length. This means that an RDF is not required for each logical record contained within the CI.
Control information— Byte 0 For all types of VSAM data sets:	
Bits 0	Unused.
Bit 1	Indicates whether the RDF is **paired**, that is, whether two of them are used to contain information. Bit 1 = 1 if yes, 0 if no.
Bits 2–3	Indicates whether this CI contains a spanned record segment. Bits 2–3 = '00' if no, '01'

	if this is the first segment, '10' if this is the last segment, or '11' if this is an intermediate segment.
Bit 4	If = 0, specifies that the value in bytes 1–2 specify the length, segment, or slot, If = 1, the value in bytes 2–3 represent the number of consecutive records with the same length.
Bit 5	For RRDS only, specifies whether the corresponding slot contains (=0) or does not contain (=1) a data record.
Bits 6–7	Unused.

INDEX

Boldface numbers refer to principle information.